62

TURNER, Barry
Suez 1956

This item should be returned on or before the last date
stamped above. If not in demand it may be renewed for a
further period by personal application, by telephone, or in
writing. The author, title, above number and date due back
should be quoted.   LS/3

SUEZ
1956

Also by Barry Turner

. . . And the Policeman Smiled

When Daddy Came Home

Equality For Some

A Place in the Country

Countdown to Victory

AS EDITOR

The Writers' Handbook

The Statesman's Yearbook

SUEZ 1956

BARRY TURNER

HODDER &
STOUGHTON

First published in Great Britain in 2006 by Hodder & Stoughton
A division of Hodder Headline

A Hodder & Stoughton book

I

A CIP catalogue record for this title is available from the British Library

ISBN 0 340 83768 3

Typeset in Monotype Plantin Light by
Rowland Phototypesetting Ltd,
Bury St Edmunds, Suffolk

Maps by Raymond Turvey

Printed and bound by
Mackays of Chatham Ltd,
Chatham, Kent

Hodder Headline's policy is to use papers that are natural,
renewable and recyclable products and made from wood
grown in sustainable forests. The logging and manufacturing
processes are expected to conform to the environmental
regulations of the country of origin.

Hodder & Stoughton Ltd
A division of Hodder Headline
338 Euston Road
London NW1 3BH

CONTENTS

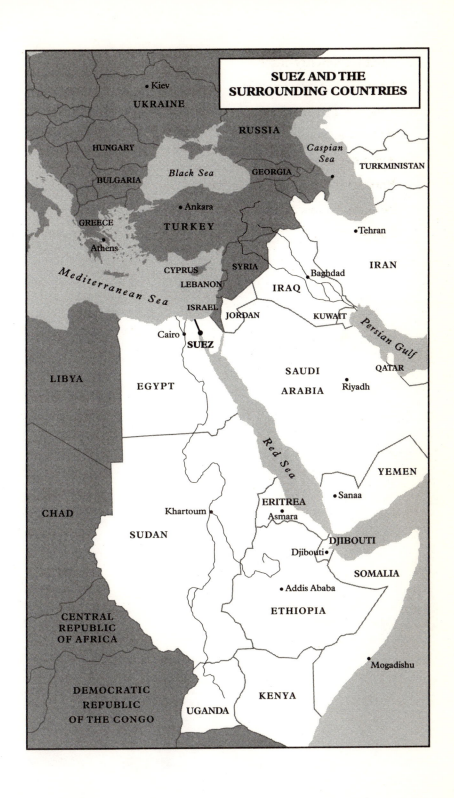

SUEZ AND THE
SURROUNDING COUNTRIES

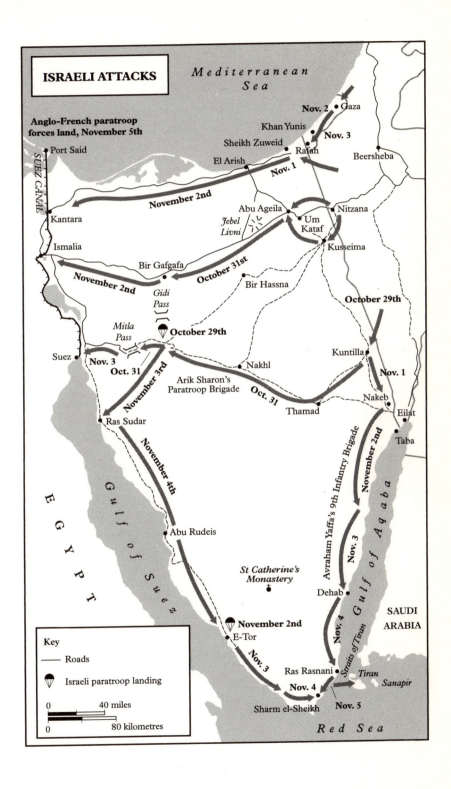

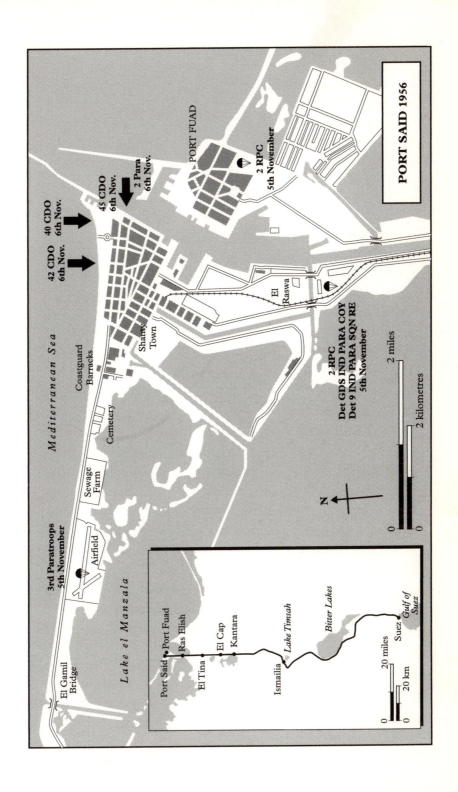

PORT SAID 1956

Mediterranean Sea

PORT FUAD

2 RPC
5th November

45 CDO
6th Nov.

2 Para
6th Nov.

40 CDO
6th Nov.

42 CDO
6th Nov.

Coastguard
Barracks

Cemetery

Shanty
Town

El
Raswa

Sewage
Farm

2 RPC
Det GDS IND PARA COY
Det 9 IND PARA SQN RE
5th November

3rd Paratroops
5th November

Airfield

El Gamil
Bridge

Lake el Manzala

N

0   2 miles

0   2 kilometres

Port Said
Port Fuad
Ras Elish
El Tina
El Cap
Kantara

Ismailia
Lake Timsah

Bitter Lakes

Suez
Gulf of
Suez

0   20 miles

0   20 km

The Suez Canal is 101 miles long (excluding 7 miles of approach channels to the harbours), connecting the Mediterranean with the Red Sea. Its minimum width is 197 ft. at a depth of 33 ft., and its depth permits the passage of vessels up to 34 ft. draught. It was opened for navigation on 17 November, 1869. The concession to the Suez Canal Company expires on 17 Nov., 1968. By the convention of Constantinople of 29 Oct., 1888, the canal is open to vessels of all nations and is free from blockade.

The Statesman's Yearbook, 1955

The Suez Canal, a work attempted centuries ago by ancient Egyptians, by Persians and Greeks and Romans and Arabs; advocated by some of the greatest minds of history; and finally executed under the genius of Ferdinand de Lesseps, has not been altogether a blessing. While serving the needs of mankind, promoting civilization and progress and bringing closer the East to the West, it has also been the cause of discord, of international rivalries, of economic imperialism and of war.

Charles W. Hallberg, *The Suez Canal.*
Its History and Diplomatic Importance,
Columbia University Press, 1931

I

Sunrise, 6 November 1956. On the placid blue waters of the Mediterranean, 130 British and French warships with aircraft carriers and heavy cruisers, accompanied by scores of destroyers and frigates – the largest amphibious fighting force since the end of the Second World War – stretched along the Egyptian coastline. For Donald Edgar, a reporter with the *Daily Express* and one of only two journalists invited to witness the invasion at first hand, it was a scene so spectacular as never to be forgotten.

> It was a bright morning with a blue sky and our ship was in the centre of a great array of warships and transports which covered a great arc of sea from Port Fuad to the left of the Suez Canal to Port Said in the centre and Gamil airfield on the right. Our ship was nearly stationary about three miles off shore, distant enough to reduce the scene to the size of a coloured picture postcard and the warships to toys on the Round Pond in Kensington Gardens. It was only with an effort of will I could grasp that it was all for real, not a sequence from a film. It was really happening.[1]

The anticipation had seemed interminable. The event that had sparked the action, the declaration by Gamal Abdel Nasser, head of Egypt's ruling council, that the Suez Canal was to come under exclusive Egyptian control, had taken place three months and ten days earlier. It is hard now to imagine the consternation caused by a simple act of nationalisation. But the Suez Canal was not like any other waterway. Built by the French and long administered by an Anglo-French company, the canal was seen as Europe's lifeline, the route by which Middle East oil was delivered to energy-hungry economies. Egypt was not to be trusted; Nasser was not to be trusted. The 'act of piracy', as the headline writers called it, had to be avenged. This was the moment.

While those on deck watched and waited below, troops in full battle gear were climbing into their landing craft. When they broke their routine to listen to muffled explosions coming from no one knew where, a loudspeaker voice calmed fears with an announcement that RAF jets were bombing the beaches. Soon after, the close-support destroyers opened up with broadsides.

> To the left of the Canal entrance a great cloud of black smoke from burning oil tanks was drifting over Port Said forming a sinister cloud. Along the sea-front puffs of white smoke were rising from shell-fire and red flames were taking hold on the right where the shanty town lay . . . To the extreme left, off Port Fuad, the French sector, lay a great battleship, the *Jean Bart*, and from time to time it fired a heavy shell from its great guns which made the air tremble a little where I stood.[2]

At 4.15 the troop carriers opened their bow doors and the ramps were lowered. Second Lieutenant Peter Mayo, a conscript officer with the Royal Marines, was in one of the first landing craft to hit the water.

> Almost immediately some shore battery fired two rounds which landed in the sea about 100 yards to our right, but that was all. There was a tremendous barrage going on, and the noise was something with the shells passing close overhead and bursting all along the beach. We were about a mile out. There was a huge pall of smoke and dust through which at times we could see the outline of the first buildings on the beach. Luckily two or three prominent church towers were quite visible to give us direction. A stirring sight was the RAF jets which came screaming down in a steep dive to sweep through the dust cloud, dropping bombs first and then zooming out the other end to turn and make a second run firing rockets and cannon, whose tracers could be seen jabbing viciously along the beach. Soon many of the

beach huts were blazing. At one moment there was a huge explosion and fire ball some way inland which was a large petroleum installation going up. It was to go on burning for three days.[3]

Still the passive observer, Donald Edgar was telling himself how lucky he was,

> . . . standing on the bridge watching the most impressive military operation the British had put on for many a year, with parachutists, marine commandos, tanks, aircraft and a naval bombardment. What is more I was looking at it all in safety. In the cussed way of the English I think this last factor was beginning to have its effect on me. I was beginning to feel sorry for the people of Port Said who were on the receiving end.
>
> I remembered only too well what it felt like. In 1940 in France it was the Germans who had the tanks, the aircraft and the overwhelming force and I was at the receiving end, taking shelter in ditches and cellars. However, I fought these feelings back. A few miles away British troops were fighting their way through a city, perhaps against heavy opposition, suffering casualties.[4]

Edgar was stretching the imagination in mentioning the parachutists. The drop had taken place twenty-four hours earlier after the French and British bombers had virtually wiped out the Egyptian air force before it could even get into the air. More than two hundred aircraft had run relays over the twelve main Egyptian airfields, attacking the hangars and installations every fifteen minutes over eleven and a half hours with rockets, cannon and multiple machine guns. 'If the Egyptian airforce was ever a serious military factor,' reported Hanson Baldwin of the *New York Times*, 'its remnants were certainly of little importance by sundown.'[5]

Even so, the paratroopers, whose objective was to secure essential communication points, did not have an easy time of it. It was the job of the Deuxième Régiment de Parachutistes Coloniaux to capture the canal bridges south of Port Said which opened the road to Suez. The dropping zone was a narrow strip of land between Lake Manzoleh and the canal. The risk was landing in water and being dragged down by heavy equipment. There was only one way to minimise the hazard and that was to orchestrate the drop at an altitude low enough to avoid drift. The trouble was, if it was too low there would be no time for a canopy to open. The decision was taken. The drop would be from 450 feet, 100 feet down from the accepted safety level.

> With even the weakest A-A fire, it had the appearance of Operation Suicide. The pilots took their maps scored with red lines. They must not deviate one yard from the marked lines; they must not hasten nor delay the drop by a second.
>
> At 7.32 the aircraft were over the dropping-zone. 'Water, water, everywhere,' murmured a paratrooper. They dropped the equipment containers. The Egyptian A-A massed about the bridge opened up furiously. The containers, dangling below the parachutes, burst open as the shells struck them. They dropped smoke-bombs. Soon the bridge was lost in a cloud of smoke. The aircraft turned back for the second run. This time the double-doors at the rear of the fuselage opened and the men jumped, two by two, one couple every second.
>
> Miraculously nobody fell in the water. But the smoke-screen began to fade. Egyptian cannon, machine-guns and mortars opened up on the swinging silhouettes and on those on the ground, struggling from their harness.[6]

One bridge was blown up before the French could get to it but a second bridge, which carried the main road and railway, was captured intact. They went on to take Port Fuad.

A perilous drop by the 3rd Battalion The Parachute Regiment also met with success. El Gamil airfield was no more than 800 yards wide and consisted of a pair of runways and a makeshift control tower. It was bordered on one side by the sea and on the other by Lake Manzala. Like their French colleagues, the paras risked a watery grave.

> Although the lack of good intelligence about the strength and dispositions of the Egyptians had resulted in the briefers

exaggerating their numbers, it still surprised the men of 3 Para to see red tracer arching towards them as they floated earthwards. Fortunately for them, it is an even more frightening experience to see a cloud of several hundred parachutists descending upon one than it is to be shot at in the air when the adrenalin is flowing freely. Apart from that, men hanging from parachutes lack freedom of action, while those on the ground can make themselves scarce and unless they are of exceptional staunchness this is what generally occurs. It says much for the Egyptian soldiers that they fought for as long as they did, but within thirty minutes of landing 3 Para had cleared the airfield, which they found had been held by about a company of infantry defending a couple of concrete pill-boxes and a number of trenches dug along the beach and the airfield perimeter.[7]

Four hours after being taken, the airfield was once again ready for use. The link-up between the paras and those troops ferried in by helicopter or landing craft took place the following day.

Port Said beach line was ablaze from end to end, and a massive pall of smoke dragged away to the east, bringing to mind newsreel pictures of the evacuation of Dunkirk. It billowed from a point behind the town to form an oily and ominous backdrop to the whole electrifying panorama. The sky around us seemed full of shrieking jets and clattering helicopters; the sea dotted with naval vessels of every description.[8]

The area around Port Said was not the only scene of action. Egypt was at war on two fronts. On 29 October a crack parachute force of Israelis had dropped at the Mitla Pass in the Sinai Desert, just 40 miles east of Suez. As the sixteen Dakotas flew above the Kuntilla border crossing, the paratroopers could see below clouds of smoke and dust thrown up by the tanks and trucks of the Israeli land force racing towards the Egyptian bases that guarded the road to Mitla.

As his plane approached the drop site, battalion commander Raful Eitan stood by the door, first in line.

I had a feeling of great excitement, despite having jumped many times before. This jump was part of a wide-ranging military operation and was far from the Israeli border. When I got the go-ahead I jumped and drifted slowly down toward the Mitla crossroads. It was five o'clock in the afternoon and the sun was beginning to set. There was a stillness interrupted only by the sounds of our planes and isolated gunfire.

After freeing ourselves from our parachutes, we quickly re-grouped and unloaded our weapons. We spread out and assumed positions in the staging area. The sun had already set as we began to set up roadblocks, lay mines and dig in. The task of fortifying our positions was made easy by the bunkers and communication trenches that were still standing from the days of the Turks. After positioning two units at the Parker monument to the west, we completed our day's work by marking the area the French planes would need to drop our supplies.

Not long after digging in, the Israelis had their first encounter with Egyptian forces.

They were travelling past us, unaware of our presence, when we took them by surprise. We captured several of their vehicles and were lucky to find a generous supply of drinking water as well. After the French completed their drop, we were confident that we were well supplied.

Late that night I prepared to sleep. Sleeping the night before a battle is always difficult because there is great tension and excitement. Yet, I dug myself a foxhole, upholstered it with card-board, cushioned it with parachutes and went to sleep.

At dawn I awoke and examined the area. Our troops were engaging in minor clashes with Egyptian forces that were passing through the Mitla Pass as they fled our advancing troops.[9]

Those troops were led by a maverick commando officer and a future Israeli prime minister – Ariel Sharon. Advancing over 90 miles in four days, it was this Israeli incursion into Egypt that gave apparent legitimacy to the Anglo-French action.

As bombs fell on Port Said, the French and British forces offshore braced themselves for the invasion. Their declared objective, received with incredulity by the rest of the world and not least by the United States, was to restore peace in the Middle East. In fact, as everybody knew, the aim was to take back control of the Suez Canal and to overthrow a demonised enemy, President Nasser.

So it was that Lieutenant Peter Mayo, whom we met earlier as his landing craft nudged the beach at Port Said, experienced his first action.

> I drove straight up the land through the beach huts and in a couple of minutes we were disembarking behind the wall in front of the first of our three houses. These turned out to be still in the last stages of construction, the tallest being seven or eight stories high. 1 and 2 sections took cover in some rubble, covering the mosque to the left, while 5 section cleared the first house. There was no one inside and my section moved straight on into the third house and cleared it, sections leap-frogging upwards till we reached the roof where there was a balcony. Almost immediately several Wogs (as all Egyptians are generally known, though there seemed to be the understanding that 'Wog' meant an armed wog, all the others being termed 'civvies') appeared running down the street immediately in front of us. They had rifles but no uniform, and must have been Home Guard. Whatever they were, Soggers shot four of them with his bren-gun. I didn't actually see it happen, but when I looked at the figures sprawled on the pavement in widening pools of their own blood I wasn't as affected as I thought I should be, but viewed them in a detached and objective sort of way.[10]

The horror of it wasn't brought home to Mayo until a few minutes later when another Egyptian suddenly appeared and started running up the street.

> People said he had a pistol in his hand, but I didn't see whether he had or not; but he hadn't taken more than a dozen crouching

steps before five or six shots tore into him, and as he fell he half twisted to look up where the fire came from with a look of furious surprise on his face. He fell out of sight under a bush. I felt slightly sick. We weren't supposed to be shooting at civilians, but it was very difficult to tell, as most of the people we met were civilians with rifles. There were very few uniforms to be seen. We spent an hour or so up there, shooting at what were mostly fleeting targets. The incredible thing was the way civilians, women and children, wandered around apparently unconcerned only a few hundred yards away.[11]

The next ten minutes were said by Peter Mayo to be the most unpleasant of his life. Riding in Assault Landing Craft (LCAs), each with two Bren guns mounted in front, A Troop moved forward into the built-up area.

Things happened too quickly at the time for me to become really consciously frightened. It is only on looking back at it that one realises quite how dicey it was, and really how very lucky we were not to have more casualties. We started off down the street with high houses on both sides, and almost immediately we were fired on. A lot of windows held snipers, and all the side streets too. From then till we got out the other end there was a continual boil of fire. We kept shooting all the time, half the time not at anyone in particular, because moving as we were it was difficult to catch more than a fleeting glimpse of the Wogs. However it must have done something to discourage them, and their aim must have been pretty poor. There was the continual crack of bullets passing by, but luckily it is difficult to tell just how close they are – lucky that is for our peace of mind.

Then suddenly in the middle of a lot of firing from some house on our right I felt a sharp sting on my right arm, just where it was bent at the elbow next to my side. The bullet slightly tore my smock and left a small, red blister on my arm without even breaking the skin. It must then have passed an inch or so in front of my body. There was no time to think of this, for at the same moment Thistleton and a Sergeant of the Tanks in command of the landing craft who were standing with me on the platform at the front, all three of us actually touching each other, both turned to me with a look of shock and surprise on their faces.

Thistleton, the bren-gunner, said he had been hit. The Tank sergeant made a sort of inarticulate noise and pointed to his chest which was already soaked in blood. I shoved Thistleton in the bottom of the craft where someone started helping him. He was quite conscious and behaving terribly well, trying to refuse morphia, and insisting he drink only from his own water-bottle. He had a shot through his left shoulder, another in his chest which didn't seem to have come out, and a third in his thigh. The sergeant had been hit by what we afterwards discovered from a hole in the landing craft to be a 50 calibre round in the right chest. I opened his shirt, put on a field dressing and gave him morphia. I thought he was dead then, or else he died in the next minute or so. I don't think he felt very much. My hands were covered with his blood, and I shall never forget the sweet, hot smell of it. It required an effort of will to stand up again from the comparative safety of kneeling down to deal with him, and the cowardly sense of relief it brought. The whole thing had been a bit of a shock.[12]

This was the reality of war. Mayo was not alone in wondering how it had come to this. What 'eruption of the irrational', as one diplomat put it, had caused two leading European powers to pitch their combined military weight against Egypt? The showdown was a brief affair. After a mere week of fighting, world pressure led by the United States forced a ceasefire. But though it was one of the shortest wars in modern history, for drama on and off the battlefield the Suez crisis has few equals. And the consequences are with us to this day.

2

In enforced retirement on the island of St Helena, Napoleon Bonaparte reflected that Egypt was the world's most important country. It was no delusion. Touching two seas, the Mediterranean to the north and the Red Sea to the south-east, Egypt was the natural trade junction of three continents – Europe, Asia and Africa. Moreover, it was here that Britain, the greatest threat to French ambitions for world leadership, was most vulnerable. With possession of Egypt came control of the Suez land route, Britain's shortest line of communication with the East. The prize was India, 'the only basis for Britain's grandeur in Europe',[1] said Napoleon. It was a bold strategy made yet more audacious by Napoleon's intention to fulfil a recurring dream of French power politics, that of slicing through the Suez isthmus with a canal to be navigated exclusively by French merchant vessels and warships.

Napoleon had had his own reasons for striking east. While victories in Italy secured his reputation as a decisive and imaginative commander, he was not without rivals. At a time when Europe, with the exception of Britain and Portugal, had reconciled itself to French hegemony, there were too many generals chasing too little destructive employment. Napoleon had needed to assert himself. What better than to gratify his political mentors by humbling Britain without the cost and risks of cross-Channel invasion – an option still in prospect but with an ever lower rating.

The alternative was not without its problems. For one thing little was known about Egypt except that a once proud nation, cut off from advanced civilisations for hundreds of years, had been reduced to subservience by a collection of vicious tyrants known as the Mamelukes. What had been originally a boy slave race (*mameluke* is a male white slave) from what is now Turkmeni-stan had become a military caste and finally a ruling class. In principle, if rarely in practice, the Mamelukes owed allegiance to the Sultan of Turkey, which raised the intriguing question of how it would be possible for France to occupy Egypt without making an enemy of the Ottoman Empire. Napoleon's answer to that was to invade in a spirit of friendship, claiming that what was being done was in the best interests of Turkey, a not entirely specious claim since a weak and corrupt dynasty in Constantinople could not alone hope to assert authority over the Mamelukes. In any case, if France did not act, Egypt might fall to Russia or Austria or Britain. Much diplomatic effort went into persuading the sultan that France was by far the best of a choice of evils.

On 12 April 1798, Napoleon was given his orders. He was to seize Malta and Egypt, dislodge the English from their bases in the East and pierce the isthmus of Suez while maintaining good relations with the sultan. He had ten weeks to assemble and fit out the expedition, and all this to be accomplished in utmost secrecy. The British were led to believe that if the French were preparing anything it was an invasion of Ireland or Portugal.

The departure from Toulon on 19 May made quite a sight for the local citizenry. Thirteen ships of the line with frigates, brigs, avisos and transports of every description carried 17,000 troops, as many sailors and marines, over a thousand pieces of field artillery, 100,000 rounds of ammunition, 567 vehicles and 700 horses. Also accompanying Napoleon was a virtual academy of scientists, artists and technicians. It was they who were to have the lasting influence on Egypt. En route the fleet was joined by three lesser convoys, from Genoa, Ajaccio and Civita Vecchia, bringing the total number of men to about 55,000 and the number of ships to almost four hundred. On the open sea, the armada covered up to 4 square miles.[2]

Once the news spread that the French squadron was under sail – destination still unknown, even by many of those who had signed up for the adventure – the reaction in London was to send Admiral Horatio Nelson in pursuit. His difficulty was in finding his quarry. The two fleets got close off Malta on 22 June but it happened at night when Nelson unwittingly overtook the enemy, leaving the French vessels far behind in his ever more desperate search for his objective. Having reasoned accurately that Alexandria might be the port Napoleon was heading for, Nelson turned up to find an empty harbour and almost immediately set off again, this time for Crete. Later the same day, a French frigate, sent ahead by Napoleon, anchored at Alexandria. Neither side was aware of the flukes that were keeping them apart.

It was to be over a month before Nelson struck lucky. After Crete, his next best hope was Sicily. Another disappointment. He had, as he wrote, 'gone round of near six hundred leagues' with nothing to show for his efforts. Then, having heard word in Greece that the French had made for Egypt, Nelson returned to Alexandria. A few miles east of the port, at Abukir Bay, perseverance brought its reward – the sight of the entire French squadron at anchor. Nelson, who was in a state of nervous exhaustion, relaxed for the first time in weeks. He ordered dinner to be served and the French fleet to be attacked, in that order. But by that time, Napoleon was in Cairo.

The French invasion force had not had an easy time. Ill trained and ill equipped for a desert campaign, missing even basic kit like water bottles, three divisions had marched on Alexandria. After five weeks at sea, a night landing over rocks and reefs and with little to eat, the men were exhausted before they started. Dragging themselves along, however, losing stragglers to marauding Bedouins who raped the men (much admired for their white, smooth skins) and beat the women,[3] the French columns, with Napoleon at their head, came at last within sight of the outer fortifications of Alexandria. Such was their reputation for hard fighting, wretched though they were, that opposition was slight. By midday, the city was in French hands.

Cairo was a tougher proposition since Mameluke forces were certain to gather strength to defend the capital. But Napoleon's luck and tactical superiority held out. The battle of the Pyramids, fought on 21 July 1798, turned into a massacre. 'The combat', wrote a chronicler, 'lasted more than two hours – but two hours of indescribable terror. The populace was cowed and stupefied by the infernal noise of the incessant thunderous firing . . . The people sobbed, struck their own faces, and screamed, "Woe to us! Now we are slaves of the French."'[4]

While it might be doubted that the citizens of Cairo were so distressed at the humiliation of the Mamelukes, eyewitnesses agree that the city was in panic. When order of a sort had been restored, Napoleon reported his first impressions of Egypt to Paris. 'It would be difficult to find a richer land and a more wretched, ignorant and brutish people.'[5]

In little more than a week, Napoleon's mood of triumphalism was dented by news from Abukir, where Nelson won his peerage, a life pension and undying fame by destroying the French fleet. Though this was a hefty blow to French pride, Napoleon escaped direct blame for the battle of the Nile (named more for easy public recognition than for geographical accuracy). More disturbing to him was news that fighting had resumed in Italy, that Turkey had declared war on France and that Britain was again putting together a coalition of powers hostile to France. It was Nelson's real triumph to prove that France was not invincible. By way of balancing the achievement, Napoleon, or Sultan Kabir, the Great Sultan, as the Egyptians came to know him, worked hard to reconcile the native political and religious leaders to his cause, that of bringing civilisation and prosperity to the people and profitable trade to France. In this, the academics and scientists he had brought with him had a vital role to play, not least in helping him further the grandest of engineering projects – the creation of a water link between the Mediterranean and the Red Sea.

The first objective was to identify the ruins of a canal built in the days of the pharaohs.

He [Napoleon] went to the port of Suez . . . and advancing north, discovered and pointed out to those who accompanied him, the vestiges of the canal constructed by the ancient kings in the design of joining the Nile to the Red Sea. He followed its lines for a long time and a few days later, again drawing near to the lands made fertile by its waters, he recognised the opposite extremity of the canal, to the east of ancient Bubastis. He ordered all necessary measures to prepare the execution of the great work he meditated. The annals of men offer no more heroic scene than that which took place at the Gates of Asia. The Liberator of Egypt himself had come to decide a famous question, which belonged at once to history to politics, to the exact sciences and to the civil arts. He stamped a new route on the commerce of the East.[6]

Napoleon was to be disappointed. The engineer, J. M. Le Père, who was charged with making a survey of the Suez isthmus, concluded that the level of the Red Sea was 30 feet higher than that of the Mediterranean, a calculation not disproved until 1847. As an alternative, he recommended an indirect route from the Nile to the Red Sea which he estimated would cost between 25 and 30 million francs, a figure that put the project out of economic reach.

And that, for a half-century, was as far as it went. The Egyptian adventure soon lost its appeal for Napoleon. Military setbacks culminating in a disastrous attempt to take Syria, where his troops were decimated by Turkish and British forces, were accompanied by yawns of apathy in Paris, where attention was focused on continental affairs. Napoleon was in the wrong place at the wrong time. Still little more than thirty years old, he had ambitions that could only be fulfilled by returning to France. He left just in time. Starved of supplies and fresh troops, in 1801 the French army surrendered Egypt to the British, who in turn restored it to Ottoman rule. The rationale in London was that once the French were off the scene there was no good reason for British troops to remain in the country. Maritime and commercial interests put greater emphasis on forging trade agreements with local rulers along the Persian Gulf and the Gulf of Oman; treaties that were eventually to formalise British control, which lasted into the second half of the twentieth century.

Napoleon never forgot Egypt. On St Helena, he meditated on the rich opportunities he had missed.

What could be made of that beautiful country [Egypt] in fifty years of prosperity and good government? One's imagination delights in the enchanting vistas. A thousand irrigation sluices would tame and distribute the overflow of the Nile over every part of the territory. The eight to ten billion cubic yards of water now lost every year to the sea would be channelled to the lower parts of the desert ... all the way to the oases and even farther west ... Numerous immigrants from deepest Africa, from Arabia, from Syria, from Greece, from France, from Italy, from Poland, from Germany, would quadruple the population. Trade with India would again flow through its ancient route ... France, being mistress of Egypt, would also gain mastery over Hindustan.[7]

Fanciful stuff. But then, the Suez Canal was no less fanciful. In the absence of Napoleon's vaunting ambition it might never have been built.

After the departure of the French and British, the power vacuum in Egypt was filled by a young Albanian officer of a mercenary army sent by the sultan to re-establish the authority of the Ottoman Empire. Confirmed as viceroy by the sultan in 1807, Muhammad Ali, a ruthless and energetic moderniser who eliminated his rivals in a mass assassination, founded a dynasty that was to last for 145 years, ending with the sorry reign of King Farouk and the revolution that brought Gamal Abdel Nasser to power.

French culture had made an indelible mark on Egypt. In seeking to raise the commercial and political standing of his country, it was only natural that Muhammad Ali should look to French skills. Dams were built, derelict land irrigated, cotton and sugar introduced as staple crops. European traders took advantage of the improved overland route between Alexandria and Suez. With an efficient army to guarantee order and security, Egypt was suddenly a rising power in the Middle East, a development that gave concern to its Ottoman masters, who saw a potential rival for loyalty across the entire region.

Having had their problems with Napoleon, the British too were made nervous by the rising ambitions of the Egyptian potentate. As set out by Viscount Palmerston, Britain's Foreign Secretary, government policy was for the Ottoman monolith to be protected as a bulwark against Russian expansion. But as Muhammad Ali extended his reach into Syria and Arabia, there came the real possibility that Russia would intervene. When the Turkish navy defected to Muhammad Ali in 1839, the threat to Constantinople called for action. While British and Turkish forces drove the Egyptians back to their own border, Palmerston proved himself the master of diplomacy by forging a deal with Austria, Russia and Prussia (the 1841 Treaty of London) to confirm Egypt as part of the Ottoman Empire and to limit her armed forces. With his dreams of Egyptian independence propelled into the distant future, Muhammad Ali died a frustrated man, though with French help he was able to hold on to the hereditary rights of his dynasty and to enforce a generous interpretation of the powers of viceroy.

Britain was now prepared, once again, to stand back from Egyptian affairs. It mattered not to Palmerston or his successors what went on in Cairo as long as there was no risk of another power – France was the obvious candidate – becoming dominant. Meanwhile, even without a canal, Egypt was beginning to take on the critical role in world communications envisaged by Napoleon. While British troopships and merchantmen still favoured the Cape route to India, the monthly service to Bombay via Alexandria, opened in 1842 by the P&O Navigation Company, soon gained popularity, particularly for the transit of mail. Claiming, with justification, to be the fastest and most comfortable means of traversing a quarter of the globe, it carried P&O passengers through the Mediterranean to Alexandria, then overland to Suez and on to Bombay across the Red Sea and the Arabian Sea. The route was protected by a British base on Aden, a volcanic peninsular annexed in 1839 as a coaling station. The drawback of the overland section of the journey – 200 or so miles in four-horse vans – was largely overcome in 1858 with the completion of the Cairo–Suez railway, an enterprise that stunted the appeal of a waterway.

But Napoleon's grand plan would not go away. In the early 1830s, it was taken up by a young engineer and French vice-consul, Ferdinand de Lesseps, who, trading on his father's diplomatic service in Cairo and himself steeped in the romance of Arabia, had built up a powerful network of connections leading all the way to Muhammad Ali. The canal project appealed to the viceroy but his endorsement came too late in his reign, and when he died in 1849 his son Ibrahim and his xenophobic successor, Muhammad Ali's grandson Abbas, put a brake on de Lesseps's ambitions.

Fortunately for de Lesseps, Abbas did not last long. Having reversed most of his grandfather's policies and seen off the foreign, mostly French, mentors, he was struck down by an assassin. Such was his lack of appeal, it was said at his death that the Egyptians endured with fortitude an accompanying heat wave in the belief that it was the opening of hell's gates for the reception of their former ruler. Now it was the turn of Said Pasha, a boyhood friend of de Lesseps, to occupy the viceregal throne. Weighing in at nearly 20 stone, Said lived up to the popular image of the fat man as a bon vivant. He was:

> One of those hearty colossi, good livers, big jokers, great eaters, and magnificent drinkers. His hand was of a size to box the ears of elephants; his face wide, of high colour, and with a full beard, showed geniality, sincerity, courage, and cynicism . . . He jovially decapitated misbehaving sheiks and made a jolly bonfire of eighty million piastres of village tax arrears. He entertained visiting Sovereigns with funny French stories, and made his pashas, with lighted candles in their hands, wade with him through loose gunpowder to test their nerves . . . He covered his parade-ground with iron plates to keep the dust off his Paris clothes. Life with Said was never dull. 'Give him two hundred!' he would shout,

without explaining whether he meant *kurbash*, the whip, or *bak-sheesh*, cash. He was as popular as a gross joke, and some of his reforms, such as the abolition of slavery (1856), of corporal punishment (1863), and of conscription, were much appreciated jests.[8]

Invited to accompany the viceroy on a ten-day excursion into the Western Desert, de Lesseps found the moment to appeal to Said's nationalist sentiment. Skirting details, he argued for the Canal des Deux Mers as a 'title to glory' and a 'passport to riches'.

> Mohammed-Said listened with interest to my exposition. I begged him, if he had any doubts, to tell me them; and he did offer several intelligent objections to which I replied in a manner calculated to satisfy him. Then at last he said to me, 'I am persuaded. I accept your plan. For the rest of the journey we will concern ourselves with means for its execution.'[9]

Granted the franchise to cut through the isthmus of Suez and buoyed up by his conviction of the rightness of his cause, de Lesseps set about attracting the finance for a private company that would build and manage the canal.

The challenge turned out to be more formidable than he had ever anticipated. Certain in his own mind that the canal would be 'sure of the support of all enlightened persons in all countries', it came as a shock to him to find that the political establishment in Britain was unanimously opposed to a scheme that could only enhance French influence in the Middle East. The views of the Foreign Office were set out so plainly as to rule out any possibility of misunderstanding.

> For both commercial and military purposes we are nearer to India than any European nation except Spain and Portugal, which are nothing. When the canal is open, all the coasts of the Mediterranean and the Black Sea will be nearer India than we are. The first proposer of the canal was Bonaparte, for the purpose of injuring England. At present India is unattackable. It will no longer be so when Bombay is only 4,600 miles from Marseilles;

and although we shall be able to send troops through the canal, our present position of perfect safety is far better than the amplest means of defence.[10]

Even more of a surprise was the less than enthusiastic response from Paris. De Lesseps could be forgiven for misreading the signs. France had lately rediscovered her enthusiasm for Bonapartist rule. In 1852, the nephew of the first emperor was proclaimed Napoleon III with near-absolute power to restore the glory days of his illustrious predecessor. Surely, the Suez Canal was ideally suited to a strategy for advancing French prestige? De Lesseps had no trouble in attracting the emperor's attention. His empress, the glamorous and cosmopolitan Eugénie, was a cousin of de Lesseps. Moreover, she shared her husband's enthusiasm for the trappings of modern life, notably speedier and more comfortable travel, as attested by a succession of decrees extending French road and railway networks. The building of the Suez Canal would seem to have been a logical follow-on to the domestic modernisation programme.

Unfortunately for de Lesseps, he failed to take account of the centrepiece of French foreign policy, which was to keep Britain onside. The relationship between the two countries was uneasy at the best of times, but when de Lesseps began lobbying for diplomatic and financial support for his canal, France and Britain were united in their concern over Russia's predatory incursions into the Ottoman Empire. This was to lead to the war in the Crimea – a fair disaster all round – but meanwhile Napoleon had no intention of sowing discord across the Channel.

De Lesseps suffered another setback in his efforts to seduce the money men. Short-term profits were hard to identify. With steam power still in its infancy, most sea cargo was carried by sail, which was better adapted to the longer Cape route than to the narrows of the Red Sea, where the going was slow and arduous. There was a third obstacle that de Lesseps had to surmount. While Said remained a convinced *canaliste*, he was subject to pressures that were hard to resist. It was not simply that Britain was obstructive and France, at best, neutral. He also had to take account of the views of the sultan, whose approval was unlikely to be forthcoming while he was indebted to Britain for holding on to his throne. There must have been times when Said seriously thought of jilting de Lesseps. It would have gained him credit in London and Constantinople, the two capitals where he most needed friends.

The Frenchman was not deterred. It was to his advantage that he was neither an engineer nor a banker. As a result he faced problems with an infectious enthusiasm untarnished by expertise. Slowly, mercantile interests in France, but more significantly in Britain, were persuaded that the Suez venture was not as hare-brained as they had first been led to assume. From Paris, de Lesseps put the final touches to the flotation of his Suez Canal Company, guaranteeing a concession of ninety-nine years with just 15 per cent of the profits going to the Egyptian government. The official announcement came on 5 October 1858. Of the 400,000 shares on offer, 222,000 were taken up before the books were closed while another sizeable block was credited to Said Pasha's accounts. This caused a certain amount of confusion since it was not at all clear that the viceroy had the resources to pay for his shares, which meant that de Lesseps had to begin fulfilling his part of the deal – the actual digging of the canal – with less than half the capital he needed to cover essential costs.

On the plus side, Said's enthusiasm was fully restored. He was prepared to brush aside the feeble protests of his sultan, but more, much more, he was ready to provide de Lesseps with conscripted fellahin (peasant) labour to do the hard manual work. Loud voices were raised against de Lesseps's resort to what was commonly described as slavery. His response was a master stroke of public relations. While making no attempt to deny that his discipline could be heavy handed, he claimed to be no worse than other employers of mass labour, and went to pains to show that in many respects he was a lot better. His agreement with Said promised that workers would be paid a third more than they would normally expect and that in addition to their pay they would be entitled to food, accommodation, medical and other welfare services. How much of this translated into reality was open to question, but de Lesseps could, with some justice, ask innocently where in Europe better conditions were on offer.

Digging started on 25 April 1859. The first of the 100 million cubic feet of sand and rock that would eventually be shifted, was turned by the zealot who had made it all possible. As the news spread of work actually in progress, there was praise in France from many small investors, who were relieved to hear that their hard-earned money was being used to some purpose. At more exalted levels there was no comment. The Emperor Napoleon was preoccupied with his war with Austria and the liberation of Italy from Hapsburg rule, events that were to lead to the acquisition of Savoy and Nice and a boost to his reputation as a worthy successor to his uncle. In Britain, however, political opinion was unreservedly hostile. Diplomatic coercion in Cairo and Constantinople brought work on the canal virtually to a standstill. De Lesseps fought back, but even a promise of freedom of navigation on the canal with ships of all nations to pay the same tolls did nothing to mitigate fears in London that a French plot was under way to frustrate Britain's imperial destiny.

Now prime minister, leading his second government, Palmerston was determined that the canal would not be built. Carried along by his Francophobia, British opponents of de Lesseps revived the myth that if, by some miracle, the canal was completed before the money ran out, a supposed variance in the levels of the Red Sea and the Mediterranean would cause a watery disaster akin to pulling the plug on a very large basin. When this and other scare stories were shown to be unfounded, Palmerston kept up the pressure on the Turkish sultan to refuse permission for the work to proceed. The sultan did as he was asked, but by now Napoleon was more openly sympathetic to de Lesseps. Moreover, not just France but other maritime nations could see how the Suez Canal might benefit their fortunes.

In 1863, Said died and was succeeded by his nephew, the thirty-three-year-old Ismail Pasha, who was taken with the idea of having his name associated with what was already coming to be regarded as one of the greatest engineering achievements of the century. But Ismail was not in awe of de Lesseps and his French connections. A nationalist in so far as he resented being pushed about in a European power game, he demanded a revision of the canal concession that would limit the company's territorial rights. Matters were brought to a head when de Lesseps and Ismail agreed to submit their differences to a Commission of Arbitration headed by Napoleon III. The choice of arbitrators naturally irritated Britain but after the sultan gave his approval there was no going back.

The judgement required the company to surrender its claim to land adjoining the canal and to subsidiary waterways. In deference to European liberal sensitivities, there was to be no further resort to conscripted labour. It was not all bad news for the company. Much of the pain was taken away by compensation of 130 million francs to be partly covered by interest on shares held by Ismail. Such was the viceroy's lack of grasp of elementary finance that he did not see the risk in this of sacrificing yet more bargaining power to his creditors. Even the withdrawal of forced labour turned out to be less damaging than first feared after a newly patented chain bucket dredger proved to be hugely effective. By December 1868, when 70 per cent of the canal was ready for traffic, Britain had abandoned her Palmerstonian defiance, taking comfort instead in the argument that 'a hole in the sand is an excellent place for sinking capital'. The truth, as recognised by other European nations, was that Britain was alone on a fragile limb, though, as it happened, not without the ability to scramble back to a stronger bough.

The opening of the Suez Canal in November 1869 was the defining moment in the reign of Ismail Pasha. Even for a ruler whose extravagance had become legendary (in the accounts of one of Ismail's daughters figured a bill from a Paris dressmaker for black velvet costing £10,000),[11] the celebrations were on a scale that surpassed all expectations. With a new title to celebrate – a shower of lavish presents had persuaded the sultan to acclaim him Khedive of Egypt – Ismail drew up a guest list that ran to 6,000 distinguished visitors, all expenses paid. Thousands more turned up uninvited. At the head of the European contingent was the Empress Eugénie, the emperor having decided to stay at home rather than upset Britain by seeming to make political capital out of the event. Other European heads of state were disinclined to offend the sultan, who, despite the pleas of Eugénie, who stopped off at Constantinople in the hope of putting her beauty and charm to good diplomatic purpose, made clear that he had no intention of being upstaged by Ismail.

This was a great disappointment to the khedive, whose transparent purpose in staging 'the greatest drama ever witnessed or enacted in Egypt'[12] was to persuade the European nations that power was shifting inexorably from Constantinople to Cairo. But while Ismail was a dedicated Western moderniser who enthused over new roads, railways, street lighting and telegraph offices, not to mention a world-renowned canal, he was still a long way short of the sultan in the international pecking order. The Ottoman Empire had certainly fallen a long way since the great days of the sixteenth century, when Saleen the Grim had overrun Syria and Egypt, and of his successor Suleiman the Magnificent, who had led his armies into Europe as far as the walls of Vienna, but strategic considerations gave the sultan his edge. After Eugénie it was the second rank of European royalty that attended the Suez Canal opening. The exception was the Hapsburg emperor, Francis Joseph, who was there only to make sure that no Prussian upstart prince was allowed to take precedence over Austrian majesty. A grateful Canal Company gave his name to a quay at Port Said. Wisely, he stayed close to Empress Eugénie as she presided over what was essentially a triumph of French enterprise.

> Everywhere Her Majesty had the place of honour. She was the one centre of attraction. The *Entente Cordiale* was not even dreamt of in those days, when the offices, the railroads, the steam-boat services in Egypt were all filled with Frenchmen; French was the language of the cosmopolitan society of Cairo.

The Khedive, the Princes, the Ministers and the courtiers of the vice-regal palaces, all, as a rule, spoke French.[13]

The celebrations got under way on 16 November when the imperial yacht *Aigle* steamed into Port Said.

Over eighty vessels, many of them warships, had assembled to welcome the Empress. They were dressed overall, with rails and yards manned, and as *Aigle* entered harbour, each fired a salute, through which the cheering of the multitude broke in waves which brought people near to tears. As *Aigle* dropped anchor Eugénie exclaimed, 'Never in my life have I seen anything so beautiful!' The weather was superb, the shores gay with thousands of pennants fluttering above the heads of the dense crowd of many nations, many shades. In the foreground was the paintshop perfection of the royal yachts in an unofficial contest for the smartest ship. Beyond them were the newest of passenger ships, each chosen by some delegation or group for this particular honour.[14]

The following day the international flotilla anchored halfway along the canal on Lake Timsah, where Ismail's hospitality defied superlatives.

The entire town had been garlanded with fresh green-stuff, to symbolise the fertile land won back from the desert. A palace had been built for the occasion, in the halls of which Ismail that evening received between four and five thousand of the *elite*, while the lower orders also enjoyed themselves at his expense. The desert Arabs increased the commotion by bringing in with them their own shrill orchestras. Though up all night – after a long night in Port Said, and what must have seemed one of the longest days in her life – the Empress was out at eight o'clock next morning. She rode to the famous Seuil of El Guisr on horseback, but for the return journey insisted upon mounting a camel – which must have been something of an achievement sartorially as well as in terms of equitation. It is hardly likely that Eugénie had ever been on a camel before. The authorities who

watched over her evidently considered it a somewhat undignified procedure, and so she was followed all the way home by a
carriage drawn by eight white dromedaries.[15]

For Britain, 'the greatest enterprise achieved in Egypt since
the days of the Pharaohs'[16] was a humiliation disguised by a
national sulk. The Union Jack was noticeably absent from the
decorations at Port Said and a P&O paddle steamer brought up
the rear of the inaugural procession of vessels. The English guests
were correspondingly grudging, though at home more could be
read into P&O's decision to reduce its first-class passenger fare
to Bombay. A sharp fall in freight rates on the Cape-to-India
route followed in late November. The *Saturday Review* unkindly
pointed out that while the Empress Eugénie was opening the Suez
Canal, the best that Britain could offer Queen Victoria was the
opportunity to cut the tape across the new Holborn Viaduct,[17] an
undeniable improvement to London's snarled traffic system but
hardly to be compared to an international waterway of such costly
magnificence.

The achievement was not complete. Though three new ports
had been created at Port Said, Port Ibrahim and Ismailia,[18] no
harbour had been built on Lake Timsah. Because the canal's
bottom width of 72 feet was only half that laid down in 1856
as the absolute minimum, the channel was equivalent to a one-
way railway and required passing stations. The total costs were
£18,144,000, or 108 per cent over the 1856 estimate.

The completion of the Suez Canal did nothing to help Ismail
extricate himself from his money problems. As he pushed ahead
with this programme of modernisation, he sank farther into debt
and into increasingly acrimonious exchanges with his international creditors. He could expect no help from Turkey. The
'sick man of Europe' was also in dire financial straits. The obvious
solution, to appeal for help to France, was made less obvious by
the Franco-Prussian war of 1870, which brought about the end
of the Second Empire and the exile of Napoleon III to a London
suburb. Having seen the Empress Eugénie at Suez, at the height

of her majesty, it was a sadness for one old Egyptian hand when he next spotted her 'arriving in a one-horse fly at the Charing Cross Station in London on her way to Chislehurst, and struggling in vain to force her way to the platform through a dense crowd of holiday folk, amongst whom she passed unknown and unnoticed'.[19]

Burdened by heavy reparations and governed by a new wave of politicians who were unmoved by imperial sentiment, France cold-shouldered Ismail, who, in desperation, put up for sale his only disposable asset of any worth, a 44 per cent holding in the Suez Canal. He found a ready purchaser in Benjamin Disraeli, the British prime minister, who, in the days of his opposition to the venture, had said of it that it was 'a most futile attempt and totally impossible to be carried out'. Older and wiser, Disraeli now made haste to raise the modest £4 million asked for the shares. Instead of going to Parliament, where he was sure to encounter opposition to a suspect overseas entanglement, he made for the House of Rothschild, a banker with an unfailing eye for a safe bet, in this case 2 per cent commission on a three-month loan secured by the British government.

Disraeli was subsequently to make great play of his coup, claiming to have 'out-generaled' the French government to take control of the Suez Canal. In fact, the minority interest he had acquired, having been mortgaged by Ismail in 1871, did not even have voting rights until 1895. On the other hand, with four-fifths of canal traffic carried under the British flag, there was clearly an advantage in denying France exclusive control of the company.

Britain's bargaining strength was further enhanced after she sided with Turkey when the Russians invaded Ottoman-controlled Bulgaria, ostensibly in defence of the persecuted Christian minority. As a reward for sending warships to the Dardanelles, a grateful sultan handed over the Mediterranean island of Cyprus. Disraeli may not have been able to assert British dominance over the Suez Canal but with the largest fleet in the world and naval bases at each end of the canal, in Cyprus and Aden, it was undeniable that Britain had the upper hand. Moreover, the Suez shares turned out to be a highly profitable investment. When they came out of pawn in 1895, the annual dividend was put at £690,000. In the year before the Great War they were valued at over £40 million.

The share purchase led to a dramatic shift in conservative opinion. Having first dismissed the canal as impractical, then as a financial disaster in the making (how familiar is this pattern to those who follow European Union negotiations?), it now saw the Suez Canal as essential to British interests. With all the enthusiasm of the convert, the British press praised the canal as '. . . the most valuable of all the public works of Egypt' and 'a glorious enterprise by which the world will profit when the pyramids have crumbled into the sands of the desert'. In the euphoria of the moment there seemed little doubt that 'we shall come to possess the whole property and build arsenals on the canal, whence we can supply India in any time of need'. It followed that 'Egypt is as necessary to England as Alsace and Lorraine to Germany' . . . holding 'Turkey and Egypt in the hollow of our hands, the Mediterranean is an English lake, and the Suez Canal is only another name for the Thames and the Mersey'.[20]

The downside, as Disraeli's critics had predicted, was that involvement in Egypt could not stop at participation in the management of the Suez Canal. Despite the £4 million from Rothschild, Ismail was still in deep money trouble, made worse by the impending collapse of Turkish finances. The easy way out for Britain and France would simply have been to sacrifice the creditors and to let Egypt go bust – national bankruptcy was already an established pattern in South America – but Egypt's position across what was now one of the world's great trade routes put her in a different category. So it was that a year after Britain had bought into the Suez Canal Company, an Anglo-French Commission was set up to take charge of Egypt's budget and, by barely disguised implication, to institute a new regime. Ismail made a last-ditch effort to hold on to his country and his job, but with the sultan siding with the Europeans, Ismail accepted the inevitable and abdicated in favour of his eldest son, Prince Tewfik.

Egypt's debts were consolidated with repayments fixed at 7 per cent, absorbing up to two-thirds of the state's revenues.

Events now followed what was soon to become a familiar pattern. Native resentment at the growing number of European administrators whose work on the finer points of financial management went unappreciated created a power gap between Tewfik as their protector and the rising star of nationalist regeneration, a peasant who had made his way up the army ranks to the rank of colonel. But Ahmed Arabi was more religious leader than soldier. His appeal was to the fellahin, who looked to the imminent (as they hoped) triumph of Islam over the infidel. Recognising a popular movement that had to be accommodated, Tewfik tried to neutralise Arabi by making him war minister and by accepting a quasi-parliament in which the official language was Arabic. In support of Tewfik, French and British fleets put on a display of strength off Alexandria, but the effect was the reverse of that intended. Riots in Alexandria, leading to the death of fifty Europeans, prompted fears in London and Paris that the canal was threatened. Pressure built up for an Anglo-French expedition to restore European authority.

The fall of an interventionist government in Paris, however, left the problem with Britain. After much heart-searching, for now a Liberal government under Gladstone was instinctively opposed to imperialist gambles, the importance of the Suez Canal as the route to India was taken as justification for an expeditionary force. On the morning of 13 September 1882, troops led by Sir Garnet Wolseley routed nationalist forces at Tel-el-Kebir. Thanks to liberal opinion in Britain, the death sentence passed on Arabi was commuted to exile.

Interestingly, at no time during the crisis was any attempt made by the dissidents to block the canal or to disrupt the free passage of cargoes and passengers. Moreover, no shipping company felt the need for armed protection and no plans were made for diverting vessels. Was intervention thus strictly necessary? The question remained unanswered, though it was surely surprising that the politicians who were most strongly in favour of action did not bother to consult the people who were directly responsible for traffic on the canal. It was a failing that was to recur in similar circumstances seventy-four years later – but with rather more tragic consequences.

If, from this point, Britain played the dominant role in Egypt, French interest in what went on in the country remained strong. It was not simply that the Suez Canal Company was seen as a predominantly French enterprise – it remained headquartered in Paris – or even that Egypt was imbued with the French language and culture. What really concerned the politicians in Paris was the possible run-on effect of events in Egypt on France's neighbouring colonial possessions in North Africa. Algeria, never the easiest place to govern, had been under French control since the 1850s, while Tunisia was declared a French protectorate just a year before Britain invaded and occupied Egypt. With French imperial aspirations now directed towards Morocco, the last thing needed was nationalist troubles in Egypt spreading over into a movement for pan-Arabism. Here again we see the start of a political axiom that was to influence diplomatic thinking for most of the following century and to have its baneful impact on the crisis of 1956.

Unlike France, Britain was not at first set on extending its imperial reach. The plan was to get out of Egypt as speedily as the troops had gone in. Gladstone himself, who had opposed intervention but had been outmanoeuvred by his colleagues, was determined that Egypt should be left to the Egyptians. But such sentiments were conditional on Egypt being capable of looking after herself. How long would that be possible?

Returning to Cairo after several years' absence, Edward Dicey called off in Paris to visit a diplomat friend. 'To a question of his, as to the intentions of the British Government, I replied that they considered our military occupation as simply *provisoire*. His answer was "*J'admets bien que c'est provisoire, mais c'est un provisoire qui durera éternellement*".'[21] It was an opinion that found favour with the man now chosen to direct Egyptian affairs. A former army officer from a famous banking family, Sir Evelyn

Baring, later Lord Cromer, had a track record in Egypt as the British representative on the Anglo-French Dual Control Commission. Though technically responsive to the wishes of the khedive, with powers limited to 'inspection and admin', in practice the first British regent and controller-general had almost unfettered authority. And he meant to keep it.

'All history', he wrote, 'is there to prove that once a civilised Power lays its hands on a weak State in a barbarous or semi-civilised condition, it rarely relaxes its grip.'[22]

Cromer's voice was to be dominant in Egypt for the next twenty-four years.

3

Almost immediately Cromer's tenure was made to look longer-term than Gladstone had ever intended by events in the anarchic border state of Sudan. In the complex way of the Ottoman Empire, the Sudan came within the province of Egypt's khedive. In the time of Ismail Pasha, the Sudan had been governed on his behalf by an evangelical British army officer, Charles George Gordon, who had made peace of a sort between the tribes and abolished the slave trade. After his retirement in 1881, the internecine warfare, for which the country is still notorious, was renewed this time by Mohammed Ahmed, a religious fanatic who proclaimed himself the Mahdi, saviour, a descendant of the Prophet Muhammad, who had come among his people to guide all Muslims in the true faith, which was certainly not that of the infidel-led Egyptians. With military gifts to match his charismatic leadership, the Mahdi's dervishes routed a 10,000-strong British-led Egyptian force, thereby taking control of most of the country. With Egypt now at risk, action was called for, but who was to take it was a matter of lengthy dispute. Gordon was the obvious man for the job, but his histrionic personality was anathema to the studiously precise Cromer, who thought him 'about as much fit for the work in hand as I am to be Pope'. Still, he had to recognise that no one else was likely to do the job.

In February 1884, Gordon was welcomed back to Khartoum. When his peace feelers failed to connect he began evacuating Egyptian civilians while calling for reinforcements to defend the city. Prevarication in London allowed the Mahdi's forces to gather in strength cross the Nile at Omdurman. By mid-March, Khartoum was under siege. Repeated attacks were beaten off while the British government agonised over sending a relief force. It was not until August that General Wolseley, the victor at Tel-el-Kabir, mounted a rescue operation. It took over two months for the troops to be assembled and another month for them to fight their way through to Khartoum.

It was all too late. By then, the Mahdi had launched an over-whelming assault on the city, ending a siege that had lasted forty-five weeks. Gordon was immortalised in *General Gordon's Last Stand*, a highly romanticised painting showing the commander at the head of a flight of steps, calmly waiting his fate as the dervishes gather around him, their spears poised for the kill. The Mahdi died soon afterwards, probably from typhus, but was succeeded by an equally ferocious warrior, known as the Khalifa, who kept the Sudan in a state of anarchy for the next decade.

With an ever present danger on the Egyptian border there was no longer any talk of Cromer's early departure from Cairo. But while the other European powers accepted that Britain should have control in Egypt, assurances were needed that the Suez Canal would remain an international waterway. France wanted the canal to be declared a neutral thoroughfare to prevent the passage of warships. Britain could not agree to this. To close the canal to Britain in wartime was to put India at risk. A counter-proposal suggested limitations on the time that warships could remain on the canal and a ban on troops disembarking along the route. This seemed at least to offer a basis for negotiation, but France, backed by Russia and Germany, demanded an inter-national commission to enforce an agreement. Again, Britain felt she was being made a hostage to other countries' fortunes.

A complicating factor was the attitude of Turkey, whose leader-ship was never easy to fathom. A large part of the problem was the latest sultan, Abdul Hamid II, whose achievement was to give a whole new meaning to royal eccentricity. An austere and God-fearing character who was sympathetic to modernisation in so far as it bolstered his own power, he so feared for his life that on the rare occasions he appeared in public he had one of his infant sons ride beside him in the imperial carriage as a psychological deterrent to assassins. Otherwise, he was at home in his fortress palace high above the Bosporus, where he was occupied carving elaborate wood scrollwork, playing the piano – Offenbach was his favourite composer – and reading the adventures of Sherlock Holmes.

Despite this less than favourable context for serious diplomacy, the effort was made by Lord Salisbury's Tory government to come to an understanding on Britain's role in Egypt. In 1885, Britain was given responsibility for reorganizing the Egyptian army and for putting in order the national administration. The following year, it was agreed that the British garrison should withdraw after three years but with the right of re-entry 'if there are reasons to fear an invasion from without, or if order and security in the interior were disturbed'. A blanket condition that gave so much favour to Britain was opposed by France and Russia, but while they succeeded in frightening off Turkey from ratifying the convention, they recognised by default the British occupation of Egypt. Safe in this knowledge, Salisbury was ready to be more accommodating on an international accord for the protection of the canal, even accepting a watered-down French proposal for a supervisory commission. This paved the way to a settlement, signed at Constantinople on 19 October 1888 by representatives of Britain, France, Germany, Austria, Hungary, Italy, Russia, Spain, Turkey and the Netherlands.

Guaranteeing 'at all times and for all Powers, the free use of the Suez Maritime Canal', the Convention declared the waterway to be 'open in time of war as well as in time of peace, to all vessels, whether merchantmen or warships'. There was more in the small print forbidding fortifications or the stationing of troops or warships within fighting distance of the canal.

It was a bold attempt to set the law above purely national interests, but as with other similar agreements it was to founder on the reality of war. Twenty-six years later, Suez was part of the European conflict that brought an end to the Ottoman Empire and Turkish sovereignty over Egypt. After 1918, lip-service continued to be paid to the 1888 Convention, but nobody could believe that freedom of navigation on the canal was dependent on anything but power politics.

Meanwhile, the British administration led by Cromer was free to do whatever was necessary to transform Egypt into a modern state. He brought a banker's mentality to his task. He knew how to balance the books and took appropriate measures to stimulate the economy, including irrigation schemes to increase the area of cultivated land and expand the production of cotton – the best in the world. But though an outstanding administrator, Cromer was none too sensitive to Arab pride. Adopting an air 'of rather distant, lofty superiority to all but a very few of the people he felt comfortable with',[1] he was contemptuous of a 'nondescript country' where, in his view, the citizens were incapable of the meanest responsibilities. A policy of 'British heads and Egyptian hands' was instituted, whereby 'it soon became the established notion that any young Englishman with a university degree could do a job better than any Egyptian however experienced'.[2]

It is unlikely that Cromer in all his grandeur would have taken it as a compliment but he was a great publicist. In his speeches and writing he never wasted an opportunity to proclaim the British duty to civilise the world in general and Egypt in particular. The tone was that of a condescending patronage of lesser mortals, an assumption of superiority that is now hideously embarrassing. The mass of Egyptians, said Cromer, were 'sunk in the deepest ignorance'. As for the aristocracy, their 'incapacity for government has been clearly demonstrated' and their return to power would bring 'corruption, misgovernment and oppression'.[3]

Cromer was in tune with the times. Towards the end of the century, notwithstanding problems in South Africa where British forces were about to receive a mauling from the Dutch settlers, imperial sentiment was on the rise with a strong body of opinion holding that by doing good abroad Britain could do well for herself at home. The fusion of self-interest with missionary zeal made for a powerful manifesto. Of the literary patriots who took up the cause the best known was J. E. Seeley, a history don who turned a series of lectures on the virtues of empire unity into a bestseller that remained in print for over thirty years. In *The Expansion of England*, Seeley held out the prospect that 'England may prove able to do what the United States does so easily, that is to bind together in a federal union countries very remote from each other'.[4]

This was the start of a campaign to abandon the traditional policy of free trade in favour of a system of imperial preference. Where Egypt, technically part of the Ottoman Empire, fitted in to all this was never adequately explained. But the Suez Canal was central to the grand scheme for imperial economic union. And when the debate turned to the higher purpose of Britain's role in the world, Egypt was counted among the fortunate beneficiaries. In Egypt, as in other countries across the globe, 'Britain is laying the foundations of states unborn, civilizations undreamed till now, as Rome in the days of Tacitus was laying the foundations of states and civilizations unknown'.[5] This was J. A. Cramb, another history professor who in his day was as well known as any modern television pundit. Cramb's *bête noire* was Germany, which he saw as the greatest threat to Britain's imperial destiny. Above all, Germany had to be kept out of Egypt, 'which, next to India, is the most sacred region in this earth'.[6]

The romance of an ancient civilisation, rich in archaeological finds, was taken up by Rudyard Kipling, who 'conjured up a vision of a world of warmth and light and colour ... in the mystery of the Orient, the splendour of the gorgeous East and the magic of the Arabian Nights'.[7] To Kipling, Port Said was more than a bunkering station for the canal. It was the mid-way meeting point for colonials journeying to and from India, a terminus like Charing Cross station, where it was said that if you waited long enough you met everyone you ever knew in life.

Bound in the wheel of Empire, one by one,
The chain-gangs of the East from sire to son,
The Exiles' line takes out the exiles' line
And ships them homeward when their work is done.[8]

Those who knew Suez at first hand could have told the poet that he was short on facts. By the 1880s the Suez Canal was a 'stinking ditch', a breeding ground for disease, while Port Said was 'a den of thieves and assassins'.[9] In the days before night traffic through the canal, racketeers and brothel keepers flourished on the trade of voyagers whose ships had to pass the night in port. But Kipling's flights of romance made the greater impact on popular opinion.

Leaving the sentimental side to the poets, Cromer stressed the economic benefits of British rule in Egypt, including improvements in irrigation that led to a near-doubling of cotton production between 1885 and 1900. The gain for Britain was the supply of high-quality raw material for the Lancashire mills. But it was the canal itself which offered the best return. Every increase in trade between the two hemispheres raised the stakes for British control over 'the most important piece of water in the world outside of our own home waters'.[10] Thus traffic multiplied with every advance in international trade from the final victory of steam over sail to the invention of refrigeration, which allowed for frozen meat to be carried from Australia and New Zealand to markets halfway across the world. By 1893, the canal shares held by Britain had appreciated in value to close on £18 million, a government estimate that inspired *The Times* to credit Disraeli with 'one of the most brilliant strokes of finance ever accomplished either by financier or statesman'.[11] In its praise for Cromer, *The Times* was hardly less euphoric, its editor, Moberley Bell, going so far as to seek Cromer's advice on a correspondent for Egypt who would 'make discreet use of information not available to the general public'.[12]

Cromer's closest ally in the campaign to persuade opinion in Britain that Egypt was to all intents and purposes part of its imperial system was Alfred Milner, a former journalist who was recruited by Cromer to serve as his director general of accounts. In 1891, Milner published *England in Egypt*, a book in praise of the British talent for exercising fair and just government over the 'motley mass' of Egyptians. Not surprisingly his views did not go down too well with the natives, but political circles in London were favourably impressed. In 1885 Lord Salisbury returned to power, this time at the head of a determinedly pro-empire Tory administration. His trust in Cromer was made clear when, in response to a telegram asking for instructions, he responded with a laconic 'Do as you like'.[13] As Colonial Secretary, Joseph Chamberlain took the same line, having declared on returning from a visit to Egypt that Britain had 'no right to abandon the duty which has been cast upon us'.[14]

The objective of advancing Egypt to self-rule seemed to recede with every official pronouncement. Instead, the imperial grip tightened. Having rebuilt and retrained the Egyptian army, General Sir Herbert Kitchener was ordered to reconquer the Sudan. It was all done in the name of the khedive, but while, to use Salisbury's words, the twenty-two-year-old 'Abbas Hilmi was keen to plant the Egyptian foot further up the Nile',[15] he was well aware that he was acting on behalf of his British overlords. Against a background chorus of ministerial squabbling over the costs of the operation, Kitchener planned meticulously for the advance. Though the dervishes were without modern arms, under the Khalifa's leadership their fighting spirit demanded respect.

In March 1896, Kitchener's Anglo-Egyptian force congregated on the banks of the Nile, where there were steamers to carry them as far as Wadi Halfa. From there, and taking no chances, Kitchener built a railway to take his supply line to within 200 miles of Khartoum. Having accumulated three months of supplies, he advanced towards the dervishes' camp at Omdurman, near Khartoum. At 5.30 on the morning of 2 September 1898 his 25,000-strong army stood to arms behind stone barricades. Twenty minutes later, the first line of dervishes were spotted as the Khalifa signalled a mass frontal attack. Kitchener waited until his adversaries, the fuzzy-wuzzies, as they were known to the British forces, were within 2,000 yards before opening fire with artillery, Maxim machine guns and Lee-Metfords, the army's first repeating rifles. When the dervishes fell back the battlefield was strewn with the dead and dying.

The fighting was not quite over. But the battle of Omdurman, in which the Anglo-Egyptian forces suffered fewer than five hundred casualties, was decisive. Among the dervishes, the dead alone were some 11,000. Two days later the British and Egyptian flags were raised over Khartoum and a funeral service was held on the steps where General Gordon was thought to have perished. The Sudan was never fully conquered. As recent events have shown, internecine warfare has continued to frustrate civilised government. But the slaughter of the dervishes extended British influence to the upper Nile and thus to the northern edge of central Africa, where the European nations were carving out their colonial patches. So it was that the Suez Canal made another gain in commercial and strategic value.

Kitchener rounded off his triumph by journeying upriver to confront a French force that had raised the tricolour at Fashoda, in the southern wilds of the Sudan. The dispute was handled in gentlemanly spirit with Kitchener insisting that he was acting on behalf of the khedive, whose territory had been violated by the French. It was not until after the French government had reluctantly decided to give way that the Union Jack was run up alongside the Turco-Egyptian Star and Crescent. As a further acknowledgement of French sensitivity, Fashoda disappeared from the map, the settlement being renamed Kodok. Thereafter, Britain was given a virtually free hand in Egypt and Sudan, a French concession formally recognised by the *entente cordiale*, which, in return, left France unchallenged by Britain in Morocco.

Victory at Omdurman seemed to confirm the jingoists' claim that when the natives were restless a tough response would soon restore normality. Possibly for this reason, Cromer ignored the discordant notes that were reported back to him by his officials. It was not hard to find reasons for popular discontent. To start with the most obvious, a healthy economy, for which Cromer was much praised at home, had done little to ease the lot of the fellahin, who struggled to raise large families while paying off debts at exorbitant rates of interest. There was resentment too at the ever growing number of Europeans employed at inflated salaries at state expense in jobs that could quite easily have been filled by Egyptians.

Even those Egyptians who had done well under the Cromer regime found it hard to reconcile themselves to a government that was so clearly alien. Partly it was a matter of religion. Nine-tenths of the population were followers of Islam, whose allegiance, in so far as it lay anywhere outside Egypt, was to the sultan, the Protector of the Faithful. But social distinction played the bigger part in creating disaffection. Having no great opinion of Egyptian capabilities, Cromer was sufficiently aware, or maybe just sufficiently polite, not to broadcast his views in circumstances that would give offence. Those lower in the European pecking order were less inhibited in voicing prejudices as established truths. The typical Egyptian was seen as oily, idle and corrupt. It was an image hardened by the time-honoured custom of baksheesh, mitigating against the performance of any task, however simple, without the appropriate backhander. The Egyptians saw it as fair game; anyway, complaints of financial chicanery came ill from unwelcome guests who carried exploitation to the level of purloining over 70 per cent of the revenues from the Suez Canal.

In the 1890s nationalism grew apace. Khedive Abbas Hilmi, a relatively sophisticated product of the royal line who spoke excellent Turkish, French, German and English, made no secret of his resentment of the British occupation. It was a French-educated lawyer, however, Mustafa Kamel, who caught the popular mood by founding a National Party dedicated to the libertarian and egalitarian ideals of the French Revolution. Localised disturbances – a riot in Alexandria, an attempt to blow up the arsenal at Khartoum, demonstrations supporting Turkish sovereignty – culminated in the Denshawai incident, an event that was as powerful a stimulant to nationalism in Egypt as the 1916 Dublin uprising in Ireland or the Amritsar massacre in India.

The trouble started when a shooting party of English officers killed some birds reared by Denshawai locals. An unfortunate accident, it was later claimed; a deliberate provocation, argued Mustafa Kamel. In a subsequent encounter in the same village, on 13 June 1906, a gun went off, wounding at least one resident, whose neighbours retaliated with a shower of stones. An officer who was sent off to get help was struck on the head and died that same evening from a combination of concussion and sunstroke. It was time for another firm smack of government, decided Cromer. A special tribunal presided over by the minister of justice was set up to try the miscreants. Cromer was en route home for his annual leave when the sentences were handed down – four to hang publicly, eight to be flogged, two to endure penal servitude for life and ten to five terms of imprisonment ranging from one to fifteen years.

In the biggest mistake of his career, Cromer chose to back his deputy, who had confirmed the sentences. His defenders argued that he had no choice, but this was to ignore the obvious let-outs. The khedive, had he been asked, would almost certainly have granted a pardon or recommended less savage punishments. As it was he was furious at having been deliberately bypassed. Cromer could have justified intervention without seeming to retreat before nationalist pressure. It was he, after all, who had approved the abolition of public execution some years earlier and who had led the way in putting an end to the use of the kourbash or heavy whip, the one-time instrument of persuasion common to tax-gatherers and overseers of forced labour. But the law, such as it was, took its course. The reaction in Egypt was to transform nationalism into a mass movement.

In London, Cromer's old enemy, the Tory anti-imperialist Wilfred Blunt, who had long campaigned for Egypt to be handed back to the Egyptians, took up his pen. In a diatribe translated into Arabic and published in two Cairo newspapers in October, he attacked all things British in the Egyptian administration. But it was Bernard Shaw, already famous for his anti-establishment stance, who did most to quicken the liberal conscience. In his play *John Bull's Other Island*, a parody of Anglo-Irish relations, he devoted a preface to the Denshawai Horror, in which he challenged his readers to:

Try to imagine the feelings of an English village if a party of Chinese officers suddenly appeared and began shooting the ducks, the geese, the hens and the turkeys and carried them off, asserting that they were wild birds as everybody in China knew, and that the pretended indignation of the farmers was a cloak for hatred of the Chinese, and perhaps for a plot to overthrow the religion of Confucius and establish the Church of England in its place.[16]

In the play itself Shaw derided the British character in business and politics, embodying a world where action overrode the emotions and intellect.

After Cromer retired – soon after but not as a result of the Denshawai incident – the heavy hand of British administration in Egypt was relaxed somewhat. There was greater freedom of debate and more opportunities for educated Egyptians to join the civil service. Those imprisoned as a result of the Denshawai trial were released. The concessions came too late to pacify the nationalists, who vented their frustration on Boutros Ghali, the first true-born Egyptian ever to be appointed prime minister, but who also had the less enviable distinction of being the presiding judge at the Denshawai trial. What ended his career, however, was Suez. Having negotiated better terms for his country, Boutros was vilified by the nationalists for agreeing to a forty-year extension to the company's territorial concession. A single bullet fired by a Muslim fanatic killed Boutros and the Suez agreement.

The assassination brought the inevitable response from London. What was needed in Cairo, it was said in clubland, was a strong man who the Egyptians would respect. Kitchener of Khartoum was admirably fitted to the task – a single-minded, none too imaginative autocrat capable of staring down the mob. It was Cromer all over again, but with the difference that Kitchener had more sympathy for the Egyptian underclass. For his land reforms he was hailed as the 'Friend of the Fallah', a rallying cry that served him well on his regal tours of the countryside. Where

Kitchener failed, as Cromer had failed before him, was in not giving the Egyptians the chance to run their own affairs. Another influx of Englishmen to fill administrative jobs nurtured resentment, as did their smug, patronising manners and their total inability to realise when they were giving offence.

It did not help that Cairo was seen as a soft posting, one in which a government official of no great distinction might while away his days in genteel pursuits until seniority earned him a decent pension. Lord David Cecil, who was Kitchener's financial adviser, parodied Colonial Service recruitment with an invented but not untypical letter of application.

> Dear Sir – I am fifty years of age, and have never had a profession. It was suggested to me by a friend who lives near me, and whom I see almost every day, that the only cure for the weak health from which I have been suffering for some years would be to go abroad for a long period. He suggested some hot climate would suit me best. I thought of Egypt. Could you give me a post under Government with light duties and a moderate salary? I write a good hand and am a great admirer of Mr Balfour, whose governess's second cousin married a connection of my wife's. Awaiting a favourable reply, – Believe me, Yours. *PS* – I should add that I am slightly deaf.[17]

In another popular travelogue, *With Kitchener in Cairo*, the journalist Sydney Moseley explained why the Englishman was disliked. 'The Land of Paradox', he found, 'has become the City of British Snobs. Officialism is there in its element. Petty tyranny, narrow-mindedness, tactlessness, and bumptiousness germinate and thrive.' Though contemptuous of the half-Turkish upperclass Egyptian, he thought the friendship of the 'growing Egyptian' well worth cultivating, but appreciated the barrier imposed by his servile manner. 'The cringing and abjectness of the native have transformed many responsible Britons in Egypt from masters tolerant towards their inferiors into the kind of tyrant who recalls Egypt's darkest hour.'[18]

Cairo was not to everybody's taste. When Harry Boyle, a

devoted Arabist and one of Cromer's closest aides, first arrived, Cairo was, in his own words, 'still an Oriental town'.

> There was, of course, a considerable European quarter and European houses dotted about, but these were of very little account compared with what they have been for a good many years past. Where now stand 'Maisons de Rapport', seven and eight stories high, were then large wooden mansions belonging to the Egyptian or Turkish dignitaries, surrounded by extensive gardens thick with palm trees and flowers. All the streets were lined with acacia trees and dimly lighted at night by occasional oil lamps ... The native quarters were practically as they had been in the time of the Mamelukes; large tracts within the city were waste land littered with every sort of filth and refuse, and the nightly haunt of prowling thieves and prostitutes. The whole city was teeming with dogs.[19]

Nonetheless, in the European quarter life was elegant and congenial.

> A typical Cairo sun shone over the bevy of stylishly dressed ladies at the Winter Flower Show at the Ghezireh on Saturday, and one's fancy was perhaps as much taken with their smart summer toilettes as with the dazzling display of roses, though these were undeniably beautiful. The magnificent palms and decorative plants from Prince Hussein's gardens transformed the central hall into a fit setting for the gorgeous blooms exhibited, among which a charming collection shown by the Countess of Cromer gained a well-merited prize.[20]

4

With the close of the first decade of the new century, European political thinking was preoccupied with the rise of Germany and the threat of continental war brought on by territorial rivalry. Little attention was given to Egypt and even less to Turkey. Weak and tottering though it was, the Ottoman Empire was assumed to be so dependent on Anglo-French diplomacy to keep it going that the sultan would never dare do anything to compromise his friends in Paris and London. But the oldest allies are not necessarily the most reliable. What passed notice in the Quai d'Orsay and in Whitehall was the assiduous efforts made by Germany to gain favour in Constantinople. As early as 1889 the Kaiser had paid a state visit to the sultan, the first and only Christian monarch to do so, and he came again with even grander ceremony in 1898, the year of Omdurman. Tokens of friendship included the latest German weaponry, along with instructors to modernise the army. Egypt as a factor in Britain's vulnerability, the concept fostered by Napoleon, was discussed openly by German strategists.

Relations with Turkey were made more problematic after 1909, when a revolutionary movement known as the Young Turks forced the abdication of Abdul Hamid in favour of his brother Reshad (Mehmed V), who was content for the country to be handed over to the 'unstable rule of ambitious and insecure army officers'.[1] Threatened by a resurgence of Turkish nationalism, the Balkan states formerly under Ottoman rule fought to maintain their independence and to eliminate Turkey's role in Europe. The loss of Christian dependencies was accepted with relative equanimity but religious and cultural affiliations with the Arab provinces put the Middle East in a different category. The Young

Turks had visions of a unified Islamic state centred on Istanbul. Germany offered encouragement.

Even so, with rather more attention from Britian a declaration of Turkish neutrality might well have been secured. But as war came closer, British impatience gave an edge to diplomatic requests, making them sound more like demands. The general failure in communication tipped over into crisis when Britain purloined two battleships being built for the Turkish navy on Tyneside. This was on 31 July 1914, four days before Britain responded to the violation of Belgian neutrality by declaring war on Germany. On 2 August, Turkey signed a secret treaty with Germany while proclaiming her intention of avoiding hostilities. The pretence lasted until early November, when Turkey formally joined the war.

The British response was to declare Egypt a British protectorate, a wonderfully ambiguous term implying that a request had been made rather than an order given. The lie was quickly put to any suggestion that Egyptian wishes had been taken into account when Abbas Hilmi, whose Turkish sympathies were well known and who happened to be on a European tour when the war started, was told to extend his travels indefinitely. He was replaced by his uncle, Prince Hussein Kamel, who, in a calculated snub to his former sovereign, was proclaimed Sultan of Egypt. But his power was illusory. Martial law was declared and the citizenry dragooned into supporting the British war effort. Government was in the hands of the senior British military officer and of the consul-general, now known as the high commissioner, who assumed absolute control over foreign affairs.

The first objective – at this stage, the only objective – was the protection of the Suez Canal as an exclusive preserve of Britain and her allies. Though it was in direct contravention of the 1888 Convention, which pledged freedom of navigation, there can be no doubt that Germany had ambitions to occupy the Canal Zone for its own purposes. In January 1915, after the British had been forced out of Gallipoli, a German-led expedition of some twenty thousand Turkish troops crossed the Sinai Desert, intending to launch an attack across the canal on pontoons and rafts. The main blow was struck on the night of 2/3 February, between Tussum and Serapeum, while a secondary attack was launched in the direction of the Ismailia ferry post. The fighting, which began in a heavy sandstorm, continued until the late after-noon. Only three of the craft succeeded in crossing to the west bank.[2]

With a loss of 1,300 men, the Turks retreated across the desert. This disaster for the Axis powers was compounded by the failure of the Egyptians to rise up in support of their Islamic brothers. But given the strength of the British forces in Egypt – 70,000 by February 1915 – such a noble act of self-sacrifice was a lot to ask. That the Egyptian nationalists were capable of action when conditions were favourable was to be proved all too conspicuously four years later.

Egypt saw little action for the rest of the war, though she did play a critical role in the Allied war effort – as a source of recruits and a military depot, with Cairo as a leave and convalescent centre. This third activity came into prominence after 1916, when the war in the east took on a fresh urgency. Up to then, fighting strength had been concentrated on the Western Front. To keep Turkey busy, in the Arabian desert, generous subsidies were paid to tribal leaders to persuade them to compromise their allegiance to the sultan.

Abd-al-Aziz ibn Saud, who controlled most of eastern Arabia (now part of Saudi Arabia), agreed to stay out of the war and let the British handle his foreign relations. A more ambitious arrangement was reached with the Hashemite leader, Hussein ibn Ali, Sharif of Mecca, and as such custodian of the holy places, who was encouraged to believe that once free from Ottoman rule, he and his family could carve out territories to call their own. On this understanding, Hussein proclaimed open rebellion, staging guerrilla attacks on Turkish forces led by his son Faisal. Much of their success was owed to the inspired leadership of Faisal's chief of-staff, Captain T. E. Lawrence, soon to be better known as Lawrence of Arabia, whose devotion to the Arab cause was imbued with a romanticism that was at odds with military convention.

Paradoxically, it was a commanding officer reputed to be of a distinctly traditional mindset who recognised Lawrence's genius. In fact, General Sir Edmund Allenby was blessed with great imagination but managed to keep it hidden under a veneer of rule-book orthodoxy. Transferred from the Western Front, where the two sides were log-jammed in their trenches, Allenby was under orders to break the impasse by gingering up the war in the east. Lawrence would help him in his mission, of that he was certain. The maverick was paid a respect by Allenby that other senior officers found hard to credit. Why, the man did not even wear the king's uniform, preferring to doll himself up in Arab costume.

As Faisal, with Lawrence by his side, attacked Turkish supply lines, Allenby led a rejuvenated army to capture Jerusalem, four centuries almost to the year after the Turks had gained possession. Allenby's appreciation of Arab sensitivities was made plain when he rejected a ceremonial entry to the city on a white charger. Instead, he came on foot and left on foot and throughout the solemnities no Allied flag was flown.[3] He went on to break through German and Turkish lines to take Damascus. What is now Syria and Palestine were in Allied hands.

The moment had come to live up to promises, however vague, of Arab self-government. There was encouragement from the USA, where President Wilson elaborated his Fourteen Points specifying that the non-Turkish nations in the Ottoman Empire should be given 'an absolute unmolested opportunity of development'. America's decisive role in the defeat of Germany ensured that the American concept of self-determination, precluding any form of colonial dominance, was a premier theme at the Versailles Peace Conference. For Wilson it was all quite simple and straightforward. 'On the one hand', he said,

> stand the peoples of the world – not only the peoples actually engaged, but many others who suffer under mastery, but cannot

act; peoples of many races and in every part of the world ...
Opposed to them, masters of many armies, stand an isolated,
friendless group of governments who speak no common purpose
but only selfish ambitions of their own which can profit but
themselves ...; governments clothed with the strange trappings
and the primitive authority of an age that is altogether alien and
hostile to our own.

'There can be', he concluded, 'but one issue. The settlement must
be final. There can be no compromise. No halfway decision would
be tolerable. No halfway decision is conceivable.'

But transposing the American ideal to a European, let alone
an Arab, setting was beset by complications. For one thing, there
was no tradition of democracy in the Arab provinces or, indeed,
anywhere loyal to Islam, which taught unqualified obedience to a
single political and religious authority. Self-government in the
Wilsonian sense was simply not a practical proposition. If power
was to be handed over it had to go to Arab leaders who, by title
or military powers, were able to command broad allegiance. How
they treated their subjects was unlikely to be determined by
articles of the American constitution. France and Britain were
not worried by this because they were not in the least anti-colonial.
For them, imperial possessions were an endorsement of their
status as world powers. Their ideal was to have strong local rulers
with whom they could cooperate to serve mutual interests. Notwithstanding promises made to Hussein, the European victors
had no intention of giving up on the Middle East, where, in
addition to the importance attached to the Suez Canal, there was
now the prospect of tapping into substantial oil reserves. The
USA already had a flourishing oil industry. France and Britain
had no wish to be left behind.

Just how hard it would be for President Wilson to play the role
of empire-breaker was revealed when the Bolshevik revolutionaries who had taken power in Russia published the Sykes–Picot–
Sazanov Agreement. This secret deal for a three-way carve-up of
the Ottoman Empire diluted the pledges made to Arab leaders

and ran counter to the interpretation of nationality enshrined in Wilson's Fourteen Points. The Sykes–Picot Agreement (Sazanov was airbrushed out after the fall of the Tsarist regime) was later used by Arab nationalists to prove the iniquities of the imperialists. But this was to overstate the argument. While the agreement was indeed secret in so far as it was not proclaimed across the Middle East, it is now clear that Hussein had a fair knowledge of what was planned. Not wishing, however, to be portrayed as a traitor who was ready to conspire with Christian states against the sultan, the protector of Islam, he protested innocence and shock when the terms of the agreement were made known.[4] Then again, the Sykes–Picot Agreement was not entirely selfishly motivated. The prospect of chaos in the wake of the break-up of the Ottoman Empire was real. While American delegates to the Paris Peace Conference insisted that there were, in the East, 'nations in the modern and Western sense of the term', this was not altogether clear to those on the ground who saw only aspiring Arab rulers scrabbling for position.

In the end, America accepted, and the newly founded League of Nations approved, a compromise whereby France and Britain acquired 'mandates' over former Ottoman territories, a diplomatic catch-all which satisfied the anti-empire lobby while freeing the mandatory powers to exercise as much or as little authority as suited their purposes. France was to be responsible for Lebanon and Syria; Britain for Palestine, the area to the east of it known as Transjordan, later Jordan, and a new territory, later Iraq, consisting of the old provinces of Basra, Baghdad and Mosul. Prince Feisal, with Lawrence in support, argued the case for an independent Syria with himself as ruler. When the French proved obstinate and Britain, after some prevarication, weighed in on the side of a European ally, a way was found to compensate the aspiring monarch by offering him the kingdom of Iraq. Feisal's brother, Abdullah, became ruler of Jordan. However neat and tidy this looked on paper, it was a ramshackle arrangement marked by artificial boundaries that paid little attention to political, tribal or ideological rivalries.

The biggest muddle of all was reserved for Palestine, selected by Britain as a setting for a Jewish homeland. It was in early November 1917 that British Foreign Secretary Arthur Balfour put his signature to a letter to Lord Rothschild assuring him of his government's 'sympathy with Jewish Zionist aspirations' to the extent of supporting the 'establishment in Palestine of a national home for the Jewish people', and promising 'best endeavours to facilitate the achievement of this object'. The only proviso was that 'nothing shall be done which may prejudice the civil and religious rights of existing non-Jewish communities in Palestine, or the rights and political status enjoyed by Jews in any other country'.

This brave or mad attempt to reconcile the irreconcilable was intended to persuade the Zionist lobby in the USA to put pressure on Washington to enter the war. In this it may well have succeeded, but it was soon clear that any short-term gains came at a heavy cost. Some 3,500 years had passed since Moses had led the Jews to Palestine, the Promised Land. Had they stayed their right of occupancy would have been incontrovertible. But the failed revolution against the Romans in AD 70 had led to the dispersal of the Jews across the known world, integrating more or less successfully but like any minority finding that times could be hard whenever the powers were on the lookout for scapegoats. Virulent anti-Semitism in Europe towards the end of the nineteenth century gave birth to the Zionist movement dedicated to 'establishing for the Jewish people a publicly and legally assured home in Palestine'. Hence, the Balfour Declaration. The rider promising to safeguard the rights of non-Jewish communities was not, however, well received by those it was intended to reassure. It seemed to the Arabs that Europe was pushing on to them a problem of its own making, a feeling that was to intensify when the next wave of anti-Semitism carried thousands of refugees from Nazi Germany. From the first days of the British mandate, Palestine was marred by violence. Nearly a century later, little has changed.

There was violence too in Egypt, where President Wilson's

pledge of self-determination, not to mention the creation of the League of Nations, the very existence of which seemed to endorse the Fourteen Points, raised nationalist expectations to a fever pitch. With the ending of the war and the dismantling of the Ottoman Empire, what reason could there be for denying independence to Egypt, a clearly identifiable nation with its own distinct culture and traditions? Two days after the armistice of 11 November 1918, three leading Egyptian nationalists called on the high commissioner, Sir Reginald Wingate. Their request was to be allowed to go to London to discuss the ending of the protectorate proclaimed four years earlier. Wingate was inclined to take his visitors seriously. Moreover, their spokesman was well known to the British authorities and, indeed, had worked alongside them under Cromer. Saad Zaghloul, a former lawyer, now in his late fifties, had served as minister of education and minister of justice. He was seen as a liberal who was sympathetic to constitutional reform. But he was also a powerful demagogue capable of rousing the mob in the crusade for Egyptian rights. It was therefore unwise to offend Zaghloul. Yet this was precisely what the government in London proceeded to do. Zaghloul was told that 'no useful purpose would be served' by his coming to London, while in the House of Commons Arthur Balfour assured members that 'British supremacy [in Egypt] will be maintained'. Nobody needed reminding that it was the Suez Canal, the imperial lifeline, not Egypt itself, which prompted such dogmatism.

Zaghloul made an attempt to allay British fears with an assurance that an independent Egypt would be 'ready to accept any measure which the Powers may regard as useful for safeguarding the neutrality of the Suez Canal'.[5] It was not enough. Ostracised in official circles, Zaghloul made a direct appeal to the Paris Peace Conference, where Arab leaders who had fought with Allenby were presenting their case for autonomy. Egypt was to be denied this privilege. In response to what was deemed an insolent challenge to British authority, Zaghloul and three of his colleagues were arrested and deported to Malta. This was the signal for popular unrest to break into open rebellion. It started on 10 March 1919, the day after the arrests, with student demonstrations in Cairo. Street lights were shattered, tramcars overturned, shops stoned and pillaged, and the offices of Anglophile newspapers ransacked. The violence spread quickly across the country. Egyptian army detachments hit back, killing over fifty rioters, but not before the rebels succeeded in blocking the approaches to Cairo, leaving European enclaves unprotected. In the worst atrocity, three unarmed officers and five men on the night train from Luxor were brutally murdered, their bodies mutilated and hung up for display.

In the absence of inspired commanders on the ground, the formidable Allenby, soon to be Field Marshal Viscount Allenby, was dispatched to Cairo to restore order. His arrival was greeted enthusiastically by European residents, who expected him to mete out retribution. But Allenby was now more the diplomat than the soldier, and his inclination, born of a conviction that he could win converts to a British sense of fair play, was to offer concessions. Ignoring accusations that he had surrendered to the forces of disorder, Allenby released Zaghloul from exile. Back in Cairo, the nationalist leader put himself at the head of a campaign for full independence. As a reminder of his first approach to the high commissioner, he called his movement the Wafd (people's delegation) and promptly announced that he was off to Paris to join other Arab leaders in their appeal for self-rule. The feeble reaction from London was characteristic of politicians in need of a respite. Responsibility was handed over to a commission of inquiry led by the colonial secretary, Alfred Milner (Lord Milner), Cromer's former associate and devoted admirer. The Egyptians, not unreasonably, saw this as a delaying tactic with the result that the commission was given a rough ride.

We had not been many days, or even hours, in Cairo before we had ample evidence of active and organised antagonism. Telegrams poured in announcing the intention of the senders to go on strike as a protest against our presence . . . The Egyptian vernacular press, with rare exceptions, exhausted the repertory of vituperation and innuendo, proclaiming that any recognition of the Mission would be interpreted as an acceptance of the existing situation and that any Egyptian who had dealings with its members would be guilty of treason to his country.[6]

Returning to London in March 1920, Milner recommended a treaty of alliance that would recognise Egyptian independence while allowing Britain to maintain a military force to protect the canal. However:

> Great Britain's strategic interest in Egypt is not limited to secur-
> ing a free passage through the Suez Canal. 'The defense of her
> Imperial communications' involves much more than that. For
> Egypt is becoming more and more a 'nodal point' in the complex
> of these communications by land and air as well as by sea.[7]

For this reason Britain wanted some sort of control over Egypt's foreign affairs, which in turn suggested a continuing involvement in her administration; a protectorate by another name. The two sides were not quite back where they had started. Opening direct negotiations with Zaghloul, Milner downgraded Britain's minimum requirements to the right to safeguard her strategic interests and imperial communications while retaining responsibility for protecting the privileges of foreigners in Egypt. It seemed that Zaghloul was prepared to go along with this but in referring a decision to his supporters at home he made it known that, in his view, nothing less than full independence was acceptable.

With continuing unrest and frequent attacks on Europeans, Allenby felt compelled to crack down. Zaghloul was again deported, this time to the Seychelles. He was later transferred to Gibraltar, where he remained until his release in April 1923. But Allenby knew that disposing of the chief agitator did not solve the larger problem. He was convinced that nothing short of a declaration of independence would prevent a bloody revolution. As for the canal, Britain could afford to give way to most of the nationalist demands without loss of influence simply by

maintaining a military base at Suez while relying on naval superiority to protect the approaches.

What, in retrospect, was a perfectly sensible proposal did not
go down well with the imperialists, whose spokesman, the young
and ambitious Winston Churchill, led a press campaign against
Allenby. 'The Bull' was not deterred. Faced with a collapse of
government in Cairo and continuing obstruction at Westminster,
Allenby returned to face his critics. Ever the realist, he came to
recognise that a British withdrawal to the Canal Zone was not a
winnable proposition – though it was still the simplest and the
safest option. Nonetheless, he held to the view that Egypt had to
be given her freedom, albeit with favoured-nation guarantees for
Britain that were close to those recommended by Milner. Allenby
was put under heavy pressure to tone down his demands. He
remained resolute. After five frustrating weeks battling with an
intransigent foreign secretary (Lord Curzon) and a distinctly
unhelpful colonial secretary (Winston Churchill), the prime minister was brought into the affair as the final arbiter.

> Lloyd George began by firing off a great many questions at
> Allenby, no doubt to put himself in authority from the start. This
> did not please Allenby, who eventually said (there were three
> others present): 'Well, it is no good disputing any longer. I have
> told you what I think is necessary . . . I have waited five weeks
> for a decision, and I can't wait any longer. I shall tell Lady
> Allenby to come home.' On this Lloyd George, never one to
> resist a turn of phrase, said: 'You have waited five weeks, Lord
> Allenby; wait five more minutes.' He thereupon capitulated and
> agreed to Allenby's proposals, with only a few minor amend-
> ments. With the Government in danger, Lloyd George was not
> the man to mistake the lesser of two evils. The interview was at
> an end.[8]

In the subsequent House of Commons debate, ministerial blushes
were spared by the inference that Allenby had accepted the government's liberal proposals for Egypt instead of the other way round.

What became known as the 1922 Declaration gave Egypt

independence of a sort. While the protectorate was to be ended
and constitutional government created, certain critical matters
were 'absolutely reserved to the discretion of His Majesty's
Government until such time as it may be possible . . . to conclude
agreements'. Under this heading came the 'security of the communications of the British Empire in Egypt . . . the defence of
Egypt against all foreign aggression or interference . . .' and control over the Sudan. This was quite a portfolio of retained powers,
but though Zaghloul held back from a formal endorsement, he
had no choice but to accept the broad terms of the settlement.
To ease the transition, there were titles to be handed out. Sultan
Ahmed Fuad Pasha was styled King of Egypt while Zaghloul was
elected prime minister under a new constitution that made great
play of democratic principles while reserving effective power to
the traditional ruling class.

Could it have worked? The compromise depended on mutual
goodwill, of which there was a short supply. Zaghloul and King
Fuad wanted more for their independence but were at odds on
how to achieve it; the British were intent on giving less. As with
so much else in the Middle East, a crisis was preceded by mindless
violence. It came on 19 November 1924 around 1.30 p.m. The
governor general of the Sudan and head of the Egyptian army,
Sir Lee Stack, was shot and seriously wounded while his car was
stuck in a Cairo traffic jam. His chauffeur, who was also wounded,
drove him to the nearby residency where Allenby was lunching
with an official guest. Stack was carried into the drawing room,
where Allenby sat with him until the doctors arrived. Nothing
could be done. Stack died the next day in the Anglo-American
Hospital.

Mourning a close friend and upbraided by the Europeans in
Cairo for being too soft on the Egyptians, Allenby could have
been forgiven his sense of betrayal. But in overreacting the way
he did, he wrecked any remaining chance of a lasting settlement
under the 1922 Declaration and ended his own career as a soldier-
statesman. Without waiting for approval from London, Allenby
slapped an injunction on the Egyptian government demanding

an apology, payment of a fine of £500,000 and a withdrawal from the Sudan of all Egyptian troops. It was too much for an ailing Zaghloul, who shortly resigned, giving way to a government willing to comply with British demands. For Allenby it was a short-lived triumph. Out of sorts with his masters in London, he resigned in June 1925. His successor was Lord Lloyd, a fervent Arabist but an imperialist of the old school, who, even if he had been of more liberal persuasion, could not have coped with the conflicting demands of his job.

As far as Lloyd could understand his mission his priorities were 'a) to protect British and foreign interests at all costs and, b) not to interfere in the internal affairs of Egypt'. He concluded, not unreasonably, that 'each one contradicts the other.'[9] As he wrote to a friend, 'Our present position is impossible. We cannot carry on much longer as we are. We have magnitude without position, power without authority; responsibility without control.' He took comfort from the presence of the military, 'which is in fact our sole remaining, effective argument'.[10]

The option of withdrawing British forces altogether was given barely a passing thought.

> The position of Egypt is of such importance that without its control England can hardly expect to maintain her hold on India. Moreover, 'Egypt is the center from which British imperialism can dominate the Sudan, Hedjaz and Arabia, Palestine and Mesopotamia, and from which, too, it can exercise an effective surveillance over the operation of French and Italian imperialism in northern and eastern Africa, to say nothing of the French Syrian Mandate'.[11]

A more pragmatic view was put by Sir Frederick Maurice, a retired general who became professor of military studies at London University.

> The canal is commonly called in the British press 'the vital artery of the British Empire'. That, like most catch phrases, is an exaggeration. The British Empire existed long before the Suez Canal

was constructed and, if the canal were to disappear today the British Empire would not therefore collapse ... It would be a matter of vital importance to Great Britain if in time of war a hostile fleet could come through the Suez Canal and the Red Sea to attack her communications across the Indian Ocean, but that would be prevented more certainly by a British fleet based upon Malta and the British possessions of Perim and Aden at the southern exit of the Red Sea than by a garrison in Egypt. If in war with a Mediterranean naval power the canal were to be closed to both belligerents, either by sabotage or by some other means, the loss to Great Britain would not be great, for with the modern large and fast steamers, troops could be sent to the East by the Cape route more rapidly than they could have been sent by the canal route when de Lesseps had completed his great work. Further, in the event of war against a Mediterranean naval power, the submarine for the employment of which the indented coasts of that Sea are admirably adapted, would almost certainly make traffic between Port Said and Gibraltar so precarious that it would have to be abandoned. For this reason we had during the latter part of the War to rely more and more upon the Cape route.[12]

Maurice concluded that Britain could, without risk, limit her involvement in Egypt to 'a small garrison to protect the canal against sabotage'. A proposal on these lines would almost certainly have been acceptable to the Egyptian nationalists. But British politicians and military alike could not bring themselves to believe that anything but a strong presence would ensure good behaviour. In truth, there was little on the Egyptian scene to inspire confidence.

Monarch and ministers, forever in conflict, were liable to invoke the evil British whenever it could help them score over their rivals. Self-interest took precedence over national interest. 'When in power they [the politicians] looked upon the state and its administrative apparatus as a bowl of soup from which to sup themselves, and to feed followers and clients.'[13]

By the time the search for a compromise was resumed there was an added complication. British nervousness at the prospect of leaving Egypt to its own devices had been heightened by the rise of the fascist powers and their undisguised greed for territory. The immediate threat was from Italy, where Mussolini was thumping the imperial drum. His conquest of Abyssinia (now Ethiopia), the only non-colonial, independent state in Africa, was warning enough of his ambitions. But he was also known to have set his sights on Egypt, reasoning that the Suez Canal was Italy's best exit from the Mediterranean and thus a vital link with the rest of the world. In 1935 the military presence in the Italian colony of Libya was increased substantially and work started on a trans-Libyan coast road that was to bring Egypt within easy fighting distance. These developments gave a sense of urgency to the Anglo-Egyptian negotiations, both sides recognising that they might have a problem in common. The only serious obstacle was King Fuad, who was more at home in Italy than in Britain, but with his death in April 1936, the way was clear for serious talks.

On the Egyptian side negotiations were led by Nahas Pasha, prime minister and popular leader of the Wafd. A sturdily built man who made no secret of his peasant origins, he had a disfiguring cast in one eye so that, according to one diplomatic observer, 'when he looked at you with his good eye the other kept rolling wildly in its socket, apparently searching the farthest corner of the room and failing to find what it sought there'.[14] If this were not disconcerting enough, he was given to unpredictable bursts of wild rhetoric, suggesting to his listeners that he might be having some sort of fit.

By August, however, the business had been done. The occupation was to end. British troops, no longer the oppressor but the forces of an allied power, reduced to a strength of 10,000, would withdraw to the Canal Zone. Other more modest concessions allowed Egyptians unrestricted entry into the Sudan and renounced British protection of foreign privileges in Egypt, thus ending certain tax and legal exemptions that had infuriated the nationalists. Subsequent negotiations with the Suez Canal

Company allowed for the canal tariff to be fixed in Egyptian money and for Egypt to share in the company's profits.

The Anglo-Egyptian Treaty was signed in London. Representing Britain was a young politician who had joined the cabinet as minister responsible for League of Nations affairs. In December 1936, at just thirty-seven, Anthony Eden, noted for his matinée-idol looks and feline charm, had advanced to be foreign secretary. Putting his signature to the treaty, Eden would have been less than human if he had not seen it as the first of many diplomatic triumphs. What he could not have guessed was that the document contained within it more than a hint of the finale of his political career. The agreed period for the entitlement of the British military to remain in Egypt was to end in 1956.

5

Greeted as a once-and-for-all settlement, the Anglo-Egyptian Treaty inspired extravagant praise and mutual congratulations. Nahas Pasha, who returned to Cairo to a hero's welcome, described the agreement as 'a sincere understanding achieved in a spirit of peace', while Anthony Eden, who had impressed his visitors with his knowledge of Islamic history and his ability to speak Arabic, was portrayed on an Egyptian postage stamp, a unique distinction for an Englishman. But it was not long before disenchantment set in. Much of the problem had to do with appearances. After nearly fifty years of exercising power at all levels of Egyptian life, the British community could see no good reason to change its ways. Though demoted from high commissioner to ambassador, Sir Miles Lampson (later Lord Killearn), 'an old-fashioned, straightforward, robustly patriotic imperialist'[1] who was unable to suffer lesser mortals gladly, contrived to act as if he were heir to Lord Cromer. Evelyn Shuckburgh, who was shortly to join the embassy in Cairo in his first diplomatic posting, felt that the tone was all wrong. 'We make a treaty, give them independence, leaving the same man in the same building, one of the grandest in Cairo, and the same flag flying, and the same big motor car with outriders and whistles blowing, as before. I think that was a grave mistake and was bound to have an effect on the young Egyptian officers . . . we should have been more imaginative.'[2] Lampson's lead was followed by wealthy expatriates whose enjoyment of the good life in exclusive clubs and restaurants depended on a large but unacknowledged class of subservient gofers.

In terms of respect, even common courtesy, the higher reaches of native society fared little better. The Egyptian military, though with an honourable record, was treated as a joke; promotion was said to depend on the size of an officer's stomach. It didn't help that the British army was still much in evidence. Work on new barracks in the Canal Zone, which the Egyptians had agreed to build, proceeded slowly. In the ever lengthening interval before construction was completed, British soldiers continued to parade down the main thoroughfares of Cairo and Alexandria just as in the old days. To the casual observer, nothing had changed. That said, it was a recurring irony of British–Egyptian relations that when Britain did try to make amends the results were counter-productive. It was a British initiative which opened the Military Academy in Cairo to those other than the offspring of the land-owning aristocracy. One of the first young talents to take advantage of this opportunity was the son of a postal clerk, Gamal Abdel Nasser, who might otherwise have followed in his father's career. Instead, at his second attempt, he was accepted into the officer elite. Mixing with others of humble background, he emerged as their natural leader, a dedicated exponent of Egyptian nationalism, spiced by anti-British rhetoric. For Nasser, and others of his generation, military education was a means to an end of imperialism, monarchy and feudalism, an objective that was as much a threat to the Egyptian ruling class as it was to the occupying forces.

It might all have been quite different had there emerged an Egyptian leader strong enough to challenge British supremacy over the conventions of a static society. A royal was the likeliest candidate, but after the death of King Faid, more an intriguer than a visionary, the throne was occupied by his twenty-year-old son, Farouk. Not without ability, Farouk was schooled in a tra-dition familiar to royal families across the world, that whatever he did not wish to do himself, someone would be on hand to do it for him. Having mastered Arabic and English, he was sent to London, with a contingent of personal tutors, to round off his education at the Royal Military Academy at Woolwich. Sadly, he had been misinformed as to the entrance requirements. Faced with the examination papers, he waited for an aide to appear to fill in the answers. Had it not been for the call to return to Cairo to take up his inheritance, it would have been necessary to find a face-saving device, although doubtless it would have been no harder for an Egyptian prince to circumvent the rules than, say, the dim son of a British family with social connections.

It was not long after Farouk came of age in July 1937 that he began to assert his authority over the Wafd politicians, whom he suspected, with some justification, of intriguing against him. Nahas was dismissed and elections were called in which anti-Wafdist factions prevailed, allowing Farouk to divide and rule. He was less successful in bringing the British ambassador to heel. Sir Miles Lampson, who was 6 feet 5 inches tall and weighed 18 stone, overawed the young king, treating him as a petulant child who needed the occasional diplomatic smack to keep him in line. This served British interests well enough until the outbreak of war with Germany and Italy. Under the 1936 treaty, Britain had every right to send in an occupying force to protect Egypt and the canal from the threat of an Italian invasion across the Libyan border. But this was quite different from assuming, as Britain under the Churchill administration was inclined to do, that Egypt owed gratitude for its salvation. The reality was an underlying sympathy for the Axis powers.

Gaining in confidence and acquiring a hearty detestation of Lampson, Farouk surrounded himself with Italian advisers who fed him the anti-Semitic theme that promised a solution to the Palestinian problem. Then again, it was fondly imagined that a defeat for Britain, seen as well nigh inevitable after the reverses of 1940/41, would at last bring freedom from foreign interference. Unlikely though it may seem that the Italian and Germany military should have been cast in such a benign light, it only needed the argument to be turned round by the nationalists to see that any enemy of Britain should be rewarded with friendship. British forces did little to win hearts. Servicemen fresh to the country were quick to adopt the expatriate perception of the typical Egyptian as a 'wily oriental', or more familiarly a 'bloody wog'.

A favourite story of the time gives the flavour of misplaced British humour.

> King Farouk had been involved in a collision between his car and a British Army vehicle. At the Court of Inquiry the British Officer in charge called the lorry driver to give his evidence, which began as follows: 'Sir, I was driving at 16.30 hours on the road in the direction of the Canal Zone when I saw a big sports car approaching with two wogs . . .'
>
> 'Stop, close the court! Sergeant, take that man away; teach him how to give his evidence in a proper manner.'
>
> When the inquiry reassembled the driver was recalled to give his evidence, having spent a full ten minutes under the earnest tuition of his sergeant who endeavoured to instil in the man the correct phraseology to be used. He began again: 'Sir, I was driving at 16.30 hours on the road in the direction of the Canal Zone when I saw a big sports car approaching. This car was driven by His Majesty King Farouk of Egypt and another wog . . .'[3]

It was a significant though largely unnoticed sign of the times that Farouk was never so popular as when he was being insulted by British troops. For his part, the king was not averse to putting out feelers towards Italian and German emissaries, though he was not prepared to go as far as some of his young army officers, who made direct contact with Axis headquarters in Libya. One of these was El-Sadat, destined one day to succeed Abdel Nasser as president of the Egyptian republic. Warned that he and his co-conspirators were under surveillance, Sadat adopted a lower profile and was later interned, regretting 'that if ill luck had not so dogged our enterprise, we might have struck a blow at the British, joined forces with the Axis, and changed the course of events'.[4]

The gathering of Axis strength on the Egyptian border, and further intelligence of anti-British plotting in Cairo, led to a decision that, whatever its short-term gain, reduced the Anglo-Egyptian relationship to its nadir. Events elsewhere in the Middle

East further encouraged the use of strong-arm tactics to bring Egypt into line. In Iraq, independent since 1932, German sympathisers had mounted a coup. It failed, but not without a heavy response from British forces. Persia (now Iran) was also a dubious ally. For over thirty years it had been a shared sphere of interest between Britain and Russia. So it was that after the Soviet Union joined the Allies it was deemed wise for Anglo-Russian troops to carve out areas of control. But Egypt was different. A country that had so recently had its sovereignty acknowledged by solemn treaty might reasonably have expected Britain to observe the diplomatic niceties.

Not a bit of it. King Farouk was delivered an ultimatum; appoint a prime minister chosen by Britain or be forced to abdicate. Since the favoured nominee was the Wafdist leader, Nahas Pasha, whom Farouk had earlier dismissed, the king was faced with a double humiliation. A feeble effort at resistance consisted of a resolution signed by a cross-section of notables protesting that Lampson, the force behind the ultimatum, had 'violated the treaty of friendship' at a time when, ironically, 'Great Britain in war is defending the democracy and liberty of nations'. Lampson was unmoved. When the deadline passed, the ambassador, with General Stone, the commander of British troops in Egypt, called for the embassy Rolls and drove to the palace followed by a convoy of tanks, armoured cars and military trucks. According to Stone,

> The Ambassador and myself were admitted and conducted upstairs to the waiting room from which, after a few minutes, we were taken along the corridor to the King's study where we found him with his Court Chamberlain Hassanein Pasha. We were invited to sit down with him at the table. After a few preliminary words the Ambassador read out his prepared statement.[5]

With 'full emphasis and increasing anger' Lampson made clear his conviction that 'Your Majesty has been influenced by advisers who are not only unfaithful to the alliance with Great Britain but are actually working against it ... Your Majesty has moreover wantonly and unnecessarily provoked a crisis making it clear that Your Majesty is no longer fit to occupy the throne.'[6]

Farouk was then handed a paper to sign, surrendering his throne. According to Stone:

> The King took it all in a calm and dignified manner but was obviously a bit shaken on reading the abdication form. It looked for a moment as if he intended to sign it, but Hassanein came round behind him and they had a short consultation which I could not hear. The King then said he agreed to summon Nahas to be Prime Minister and select his own Cabinet and the Ambassador had won his point.[7]

The story was later much embroidered. Lampson claimed that the king asked 'with none of his previous bravado if I would give him one more chance and . . . even even thanked me personally for having always tried to help him'.[8] Farouk counter-claimed that he had had armed guards standing behind a curtain ready to defend their king if he had given the word. Moreover, he was said to have told Lampson that he would come to regret his action and that he agreed to sign only to prevent the streets of Cairo running in blood.

Whatever the variations on the record, the king chose capitulation as the better part of valour. Lampson returned to his embassy confessing that he 'could not have more enjoyed' the events of the evening. 'It was sorely tempting to have insisted on King Farouk's abdication which I could have extracted.'[9] Nahas, summoned to the palace the next day, formed a government that remained loyal to Britain for the rest of the war, even when German forces were so close to Cairo that Lampson was prompted to order the burning of secret papers.

What would have happened if Farouk had proved a tougher proposition? Lampson was not without experienced advisers. Oliver Lyttelton (later Viscount Chandos), minister of state in Cairo since June 1941, was technically senior to Lampson since it was his job to coordinate the work of British ambassadors in the Middle East. Also on hand was Walter Monckton, lawyer and politician, who had recently been named director general of British propaganda and information services. Monckton was destined to play a not insignificant part in the 1956 Suez crisis. As minister of defence he was to oppose military action but nonetheless stay in his job for fear that a resignation would be seen as a betrayal of a government under pressure. Perhaps he used the same reasoning in his relations with Lampson. While Lyttelton urged caution, Monckton was content to follow Lampson's imperious lead. It is almost certain that had Farouk showed any spirit, the ambassador would have packed him off into exile. Various options had already been discussed. There was talk of accommodating the deposed monarch on board a warship until the politicians had decided what to do with him. Lampson favoured sending him to Ceylon. An alternative was retirement in Khartoum. The word from London was that Lampson was to be given a free hand.

As leader of a country that few imagined could withstand the German onslaught, Churchill could be forgiven for not worrying overmuch about the feelings of those unsympathetic to the British cause. Likewise Anthony Eden, who, after a brief period out of office in protest against his party's vain attempts to oppose the European dictators, was back as foreign secretary, this time in the wartime coalition. He cabled Lampson, 'I congratulate you warmly. Result justifies your firmness and our confidence.'[10] But even in extremity, Eden might just have thought twice about flouting the spirit of an agreement that he had brought about a mere five years earlier. By hardening anti-British sentiment, not to mention the political ambitions of Abdel Nasser and other young officers, who were more pro-nationalist than they were anti-monarchist, Eden would, before long, regret his oversight. Or maybe not. The unshakeable belief on the British side was that once again prompt action had saved Egypt from its own imbecilities. As Dr Johnson observed, 'He that overvalues himself will undervalue others, and he that undervalues others will oppress them.' When, later on, Nasser voiced his resentment of British pretensions, he was denigrated for his ingratitude.

Meanwhile, there was a war to be won. With Britain pushed out of Europe by Germany and out of Singapore and the Far East by Japan, it was strategically and politically vital that she should hold her position in the Middle East. The battle of the titans, when the forces of Montgomery and Rommel met at El Alamein, proved to the world that Germany could be beaten. But more than that, the British achievement was to assume huge significance at home as the only major victory of the Hitler war that owed nothing to America. In the collective political mind it seemed to confirm Britain as the dominant power in the Middle East.

Churchill certainly believed this to be so, which is why, towards the end of the war, after the Big Three conference at Yalta, presided over by Stalin, Churchill was much exercised to find that his old friend President Roosevelt was planning to stop off on the way home to hold meetings with the King of Saudi Arabia. It did not need a clairvoyant to predict that top of the agenda would be American participation in the exploitation of oil.

Hopes of a major find somewhere in the Middle East had been sustained for well over half a century. The discovery of surface traces of oil in Egypt in the 1880s had led to exploratory drilling but without success. Elsewhere in the region the maladministration of the Ottoman Empire deterred serious investment, though Persia and Iraq were known to be likely prospects. Even after petrol-driven vehicles went into mass production, the Middle East remained a minor participant in the oil industry, producing a mere 1 per cent of the world's output in 1920. When the post-war mandates approved by the League of Nations came into effect, however, geologists descended on Persia and Iraq. Their findings were so impressive as to start a race for concessions. Britain forged ahead in Persia, where the Anglo-Iranian Oil Company became the country's dominant economic force and the world's fourth-largest oil producer.

It was a different story in Iraq. Despite Britain's best efforts to corner the market, American and French interests were powerful enough to gain a substantial share of the monopoly known as the

Iraq Petroleum Company. American and French oil interests also gained a foothold in the Gulf sheikhdoms of Kuwait, Bahrain, Qatar, Oman and Abu Dhabi (the latter now part of the United Arab Emirates), where Britain had acted as overlord and protector for more than a century.

Then there was Saudi Arabia, a country carved out by Abd-al-Aziz Ibn Saud, who had stayed clear of the Great War, but who subsequently had annihilated his rivals by a combination of guile and brute force to make his family dominant over a desert region stretching from the Red Sea to the Persian Gulf. Saudi Arabia was independent, the only country in the Middle East apart from Yemen to claim that distinction. But Ibn Saud was also in need of money to develop his country and to secure his succession. In the closing stages of the Second World War neither Britain nor France was in any position to give Ibn Saud what he most needed. But America was in another league, and Ibn Saud was well aware that he could hold the attention of the power brokers in Washington.

The American connection with Saudi Arabia had started in 1933 when the Standard Oil Company had gained permission to explore for oil. It was not long before Standard chanced on a major find. So colossal were the estimated reserves that three other American oil companies were encouraged to join a consortium dubbed Aramco. By now the American military was taking an interest. If the experience of modern warfare proved anything it was the dependence of fighting machines on a plentiful supply of oil. In September 1943 the American joint chiefs of staff were urging that 'everything possible be done to give the US access to Saudi Arabian oil', emphasising that 'in the unhappy event of another war in Europe, possession or access to Near Eastern oil supplies were essential to any successful campaign by the Americans'.[11] When one of America's leading geologists concluded that 'the centre of world oil production is shifting from the Caribbean to the Middle East',[12] Roosevelt needed no further encouragement to put on a post-Yalta reception for King Saud on board his battle cruiser *Quincy*, as it lay at anchor in the Great Bitter Lake, near Cairo.

It was, noted Roosevelt's chief of staff, 'like something transported by magic from the Middle Ages': Ibn Saud and his forty-
two-strong retinue, all dressed in white, made a grand spectacle.
Flanked by ten sabre-armed guards chosen from the leading tribes
of Saudi Arabia, he was accompanied by the Royal Fortune-teller,
the Royal Food-taster, the Chief Server of the Ceremonial Coffee
and the Royal Purse-bearers.'[13]

If oil had been the only subject of conversation the meeting
could have been counted a great success. Raising no objection to
Saud's autocratic rule, Roosevelt promised a vast public works
programme and other measures to help raise living standards just
so long as the oil contrived to flow westwards. But the president
struck a log jam when he raised the issue of Palestine.

What was soon to become the Jewish homeland was already a
world trouble spot with political violence part of the social fabric.
With the advent of Nazism, immigrant numbers had soared to a
point where, in 1939, Jews accounted for one third of the Palestine
population. Hovering between sympathy for Jewish refugees and
an appreciation of Arab fears that they would soon be outnumbered in their own country, Britain as the mandatory power
settled for acting as referee, hoping that the contenders would
eventually settle their differences. It was an impossible dream.
When Jews and Arabs were not fighting each other they took it
out on the British. A proposal to divide the country was rejected
by both sides, the Arabs because they could see no reason to
surrender territory, the Jews because they expected more. In 1939
the British government fixed at 75,000 the number of Jewish
immigrants who could enter Palestine in the next five years. With
the outbreak of war Jews escaped from Europe any way they
could and headed for Palestine with no right to land in ships that
were so unseaworthy there was no certainty they would get there.
The inevitable tragedies heightened tensions between Arabs and
Jews and between both and the ineffectual peacemakers.

Aware of a growing Zionist lobby in America, Roosevelt was
keen to do something without getting too closely involved with
what he most fervently hoped would remain a British affair.

Hence, in his meeting with King Saud, Roosevelt took the opportunity to press for more Jews to be allowed into Palestine.

> He was greatly shocked when Ibn Saud, without a smile, said 'No.' Ibn Saud emphasised the fact that the Jews in Palestine were successful in making the countryside bloom only because American and British capital had been poured in in millions of dollars and said if those same millions had been given to the Arabs they could have done quite as well. He also said that there was a Palestine army of Jews all armed to the teeth and he remarked that they did not seem to be fighting the Germans but were aiming at the Arabs. He stated plainly that the Arabs would not permit a further extension beyond the commitment already made for future Jewish settlement in Palestine.[14]

With a politician's capacity for ignoring what he does not wish to hear, Roosevelt soon returned to the theme, voicing the hope that Arabs and Jews would somehow get along together.

> Ibn Saud politely but firmly gave the President a lesson in the history of Palestine from the Arab point of view. The King, with great dignity and courtesy and with a smile, said that if Jews from outside Palestine continued to be imported with their foreign financial backing and their higher standards of living, they would make trouble for the Arab inhabitants. When this happened, as a good Arab and a True Believer, he would have to take the Arab side against the Jews, and he intended to do so.[15]

And there the matter rested. The deal on oil was done, but Roosevelt, like successive American presidents, had no firm policy for solving the most critical problem threatening peace in the Middle East.

Before setting off for home, Roosevelt also met King Farouk. This was more of a courtesy call; the president was, after all, parked on Egyptian territory. But it is a measure of his innocence that he seemed not to have realised that Egypt was another postwar crisis in the making. The nationalist movement had taken on a sharper edge with the emergence of the Muslim Brotherhood, which began as a welfare organisation but soon turned to violence as a means of attracting anti-British and anti-monarchist partisans. A clear warning of what was to come was given soon after Roosevelt made his farewells to Farouk. In haste to qualify for a seat in the newly fledged United Nations, Egypt declared war on Germany. It was purely a symbolic act but it cost the prime minister his life. The young assassin was a fascist sympathiser.

It was plain to see that Egypt was in trouble. The days of a stable economy managed by British bankers had long since gone. A burgeoning population up from 11 million in 1905 to over 16 million forty years on had overwhelmed what few services were in place. Ninety per cent of the population suffered from ophthalmia, 85 per cent from hookworm. A few wealthy Egyptians had made themselves even wealthier from the war but over a million were on the starvation line and unemployment was up to 50 per cent. A more fertile breeding ground for revolution would be hard to imagine. But Britain had no intention of giving up on Egypt or the Suez Canal, which had become the chief thoroughfare to Europe for essential oil supplies and thus central to Britain's fortunes in the Middle East and beyond.

France too retained a strong interest in the Middle East. Though pushed out of its two mandatory territories – Syria and Lebanon joined the UN as independent states in 1946 – what happened in Egypt and neighbouring countries was seen to have an impact on Algeria and other French colonies in North Africa. Nationalism had a tendency to spread and multiply. Moreover, France had her own oil interests to protect, while the Suez Canal was still regarded essentially as a French operation.

This remained the British and French position even after the departure from power of the two arch imperialists – General Charles de Gaulle in a huff at the rejection of his plans for a strong presidency capable of overriding party rivalries, Churchill in dark mood having discovered that his status as war hero was not enough to save his party from a devastating defeat at the polls. Their successors, politicians of the centre left, spoke up for the independence of subject peoples but, in practice, turned out to be more concerned with maintaining national prestige, in particular to stand alongside the United States and the Soviet Union in directing world affairs. This obsession with keeping up international appearances required huge military expenditure, devoted in large measure to the trappings of empire, the traditional symbol of great-power status.

As Anthony Eden put it, in one of many observations that should have warned of conflicts to come in the Middle East, the empire 'is our life; without it we should be no more than some millions of people living in an island off the coast of Europe, in which nobody wants to take any particular interest'.[1] Or as a delegate to the 1948 Conservative conference put it more bluntly, 'We are an imperial power or we are nothing.'

This conviction, which led Foreign Office thinking, was faithfully echoed in the Quai d'Orsay. So often was it said that the French overseas territories in Indo-China (Vietnam, Laos and Cambodia) and North Africa (Tunisia, Morocco and Algeria) conferred international authority that the converse was assumed to be equally beyond question – France *'n'est rien sans les colonies'*. And the people cheered. For all the grand talk of spreading democracy and liberty, the British and French bolstered a fragile self-confidence with boasts of superiority to other countries and to other races.

Barely disguised propaganda started in the schools. As French children were taught that the empire was integral to hopes for a better future, so too were British youngsters brought up to glory in the great swaths of the world map coloured red (with Britain at the centre, of course). State occasions from the 14 July celebrations across France to the coronation of Elizabeth II were given an imperial slant. Empire Day was an annual fixture in the British ceremonial calendar. At an Empire Day service held at St Paul's Cathedral in May 1945, the dean spoke of British influence as 'a stabilizing influence in the world' and of the Empire itself as 'the greatest creation of British political genius'.[2] No one was heard to argue the point.

Considered now, such sentiments pose an obvious question. What precisely was so terrible about accepting a lower placing in the international league? Both France and Britain were up to their necks in post-war debt, dependent on American handouts. Both faced the awesome challenge of reconciling economic reconstruction with popular demands for better living standards and advances in social welfare. But a more realistic view of British and French conceits, free of world war sensitivities, had to wait on the younger generation, the product of social reforms and the expansion of education. Meanwhile, the stage was held by those who were used to playing the great game in international politics. They were to remain unchallenged until the Suez crisis, the little war that brought them crashing down.

Nonetheless, we can still wonder. Given an informed choice, would ordinary families in Britain or France have opted for international prestige against the prospect of acquiring more of the basics of civilised living? If they had had the chance to visit the Netherlands, Sweden, Denmark, Norway or Switzerland – countries that were sneered at by the Anglo-French establishment for their lack of influence in world affairs – would they really have turned down decent homes with efficient public services and advanced social security just so that their elected leaders could prance on the world stage telling others how to run their lives? The questions are forever hypothetical because, of course, there was no informed choice.

To be fair, seen from the point of view of those in the front line of diplomacy, there was an understandable desire to show the Americans and the Russians that they could not have it all their own way; more, that the achievements of France and Britain over the centuries of their predominance were not to be scorned. Underlying the arrogant, often pompous rhetoric was a conviction held by many decent politicians that Britain and France were a force for good in a world that was not at its happiest under the aegis of the two superpowers. It was hard for them to give up on what they saw as their solemn responsibilities. It was harder still to accept that, as individuals having clawed their way up to positions of power, they were to be any less effective than their predecessors who had made France and Britain great.

Then again, overseas commitments were strengthened by cultural and social ties. Colonial peoples were a mixed bunch with expatriates or their first-, second- or third-generation descendants living alongside the native populations in varying degrees of edginess. They were not to be lightly abandoned.

Finally, there was the economic imperative. The case was particularly strong for Britain, which relied on the empire for well over half of its two-way trade and income from foreign investment. This was to change, but slowly – too slowly for the good of the British economy. For the first five years after the war, Britain had no trouble in selling abroad whatever she produced, but too often this was to soft, protected markets on a take-it-or-leave-it basis that soon had customers looking elsewhere for higher quality at competitive prices. Even then British industry was more inclined to look back to the good old days than to plan for a dynamic future. Despite appearances, France was rather better at managing its long-term future. Derided for its political instability – twenty governments between 1945 and 1954, high inflation, tax avoidance on a massive scale and wildcat strikes – France provoked assumptions that the civil administration was equally chaotic. In reality, as President Auriol commented, 'though France might frequently change the horses, the carriage continues to move forward'.

While the politicians argued, a planning team led by Jean Monnet, accountable only to the prime minister, got on with the job of 'transforming France into a modern country'. Its achievements included the construction of the Rhône dams, the electrification of the railway system, the re-equipment of the iron and steel industry and the development of natural gas reserves. As a result, France's economic miracle paralleled that of Germany, and both were well ahead of Britain.

Economics aside, the problem for the latter-day imperialists was that chauvinism was a two-way track. However loudly they called for Britain or France to assert their worldwide authority, there was an even louder response from the colonies demanding independence. The British solution was to aim to turn the colonies into self-governing nations within the Commonwealth, a more or less free association of former dependencies, led by Britain, which had the potential for becoming a powerful world lobby. This posed many questions of detail. At precisely what point a colony was ready for independence was a matter of prolonged, often bitter, contention. India's claim, a priority for the new Labour government, was deferred to 1947 by the need to settle terms between Hindus and Muslims. In Kenya, where up to 100,000 Africans but few whites had taken part in the war, the whites were prepared to fight rather than accept universal suffrage, while in the Gold Coast (Ghana) progress towards self-government was set back when the funeral of the Ashanti paramount chief, Nana Sir Ofori Atta, climaxed with a human sacrifice.

Seen from Paris, the imperial future was envisioned in terms of a French Union with an elected assembly in each colonial capital taking care of local affairs while representatives in the National Assembly in Paris devoted themselves to defence and foreign and economic relations. In this way, it was predicted, all French citizens, irrespective of race or place of origin, would enjoy full equality.

Neither of these romantic strategies had application to the mandatory territories of the Middle East or to Egypt, a sovereign power still under occupation. With France jostled out of Syria and Lebanon, Britain was left to patch up agreements that satisfied nationalist aspirations while protecting the right to maintain sufficient forces in the region to deter Soviet incursions. America, experiencing a brief period of post-war isolationism, was happy to keep a distance, the more so because it was useful to have Britain take the flak over Palestine.

In Egypt, grievances against the British multiplied from day to day. While, at first, there were encouraging signals from London that a total evacuation of British troops was in prospect, it soon became clear that the Labour government was as keen to hold on to the Suez base as its Conservative predecessor. Or, maybe, not quite. As the latest incumbent of 10 Downing Street, Clement Attlee was a diminutive but tough prime minister who tried to inject a note of realism into government defence policy, warning of the growing gap between Britain's overseas commitments and the resources available to carry them out. He was backed by his deputy, Herbert Morrison, and by his chancellor, Hugh Dalton, who confessed to being 'worn down' by the imbalance of Britain's external overheads and the exhaustion of American loans.

But the cost-cutters in the cabinet were outflanked by foreign minister Ernest Bevin, in alliance with the military chiefs, who made the most of their post-war prestige to boost defence expenditure. Bevin (Ernie to his friends) was a politician of humble origins who had been schooled in trade union hard bargaining and had served in Churchill's wartime coalition as minister of labour. In his latest role, the blunt, no-nonsense sixty-four-year-old came on like John Bull incarnate, intensely patriotic and passionately anti-communist. Embracing the traditional foreign office interpretation of Britain's world role, he was adopted by the conservative establishment as one of their own. It was significant that Lord Alanbrooke, Churchill's wartime chief of staff and later a dominant voice in the defence committee, should have noted in his diary, 'The more I see of Bevin, the more impressed I am by him and his great qualities.'[3] One of those 'qualities' was agreeing with Alanbrooke that British influence abroad had to be sustained at all costs.

Bevin presided over a collection of worldwide responsibilities greater than at any time in British history. In addition to manning occupation zones in West Germany and Austria, there were troops in Italy, Libya, Malta and Cyprus, not to mention bases in a patchwork of colonial outposts where a military presence was thought to be a necessary mainstay to flying the flag. In the Middle East, Transjordan (formally declared independent in 1946 but still relying on a British subsidy and troops commanded by British officers), Iraq, Iran and the Persian Gulf sheikhdoms were still in Britain's thrall. Some 100,000 servicemen were in Palestine trying, in vain, to break the cycle of terror and counter-terror. In

Egypt, the Suez Canal Zone complex of barbed wire and corrugated iron, 120 miles long by 30 wide, was the largest military base in the world. One ammunition depot alone covered 8 square miles.

Urged on by the military, Bevin became obsessed with the Middle East as the centrepiece of British foreign policy. Though not strictly part of the British Empire, it offered more than all the other imperial territories put together. Bevin needed no persuading that British and European economic recovery depended on the free flow of oil. By 1946 shipments of crude oil through the Suez Canal were more than half the volume of northbound cargo. From 1948, oil dominated the shipping, cargo and revenue of the canal.[4] The chief suppliers were Kuwait, Saudi Arabia and Iran. Thirty per cent of Britain's overseas investments, mostly in oil, were in the Middle East. How to hold on to those assets exercised Bevin's imagination beyond all other issues.

One strand of his thinking was linked to ideas for developing the Commonwealth. The Labour government had grand plans for economic and technical support for the colonies, which would lead to 'a common basis of partnerships'. As a start, the 1945 Colonial Development Act led to a five-year programme of loans and grants totalling £40 million for building roads, schools and hospitals. The fallacy at the heart of this policy was that Britain could afford to do all that it most desired. Critics pointed out the nonsense of handing out money to the colonies for worthy projects while some £250 million earned from exports by those same colonies was held by the Bank of England to bolster sterling reserves.

Ambitious schemes dreamed up by the economic planners were no help. The mass production of groundnuts in East Africa was supposed to promote the regional economy while saving on dollar imports by providing oils and fat for the British market. In practice, the site was ill chosen and the entire project came to a miserable and costly end, just one example of well-intentioned imperialism going badly wrong.

As for the Middle East, there was no desire for a closer relationship with Britain, economic or otherwise. Nationalist criticism focused on the niggardly returns on oil (the Anglo-Iranian Oil

Company, while advertising its claim to be a model employer, purloined 75 per cent of oil revenues) and on restrictions on the use of sterling balances. Egypt alone was owed £400 million for its services as a war base but had no chance of laying her hands on more than a small share while the currency remained frozen.

In his clearer moments, Bevin realised that Britain's best chance of holding her economic grip in the Middle East was to loosen up on the military side. In this he was encouraged by Attlee, who continued to urge a military rethink that would 'make the most of our limited resources', even to the extent of abandoning the Middle East and Mediterranean altogether. 'It may be we shall have to consider the British Isles as an easterly extension of a strategic area the centre of which is the American continent rather than as a power looking eastwards through the Mediterranean to India and the East.'

Bevin and the military establishment begged to differ. As 'the last bastion of social democracy' in Europe, argued Bevin, Britain had a responsibility to countries vulnerable to Soviet expansion.

> The Mediterranean is the area through which we bring influence to bear on Southern Europe, the soft underbelly of France, Italy, Yugoslavia, Greece and Turkey. Without our physical presence in the Mediterranean, we should cut little ice with these states which would fall, like Eastern Europe, under the totalitarian yoke ... If we move out of the Mediterranean, Russia will move in, and the Mediterranean countries, from the point of view of commerce and trade, economy and democracy, will be finished.[5]

The chiefs of staff of the three armed services went even farther. In 1946 they had come up with a Commonwealth defence plan which fixed a main base in the Canal Zone as the direct link with India, Australia and the Far East. That India was soon to gain independence in no way influenced their thinking. As part of the Commonwealth, India was entitled to British protection and was thus still central to defence strategy.

Bevin played with the idea of making East Africa, probably Kenya, an alternative to Egypt as a centre for British overseas military operations, but while the chiefs of staff were ready to consider a withdrawal from Cairo and the Nile Delta, the payback was a strengthening of the Canal Zone. Moreover, Palestine as the only territory in the Middle East directly under British rule was 'of growing and vital importance in the defence of the Middle East'. What now must be seen as a policy bordering on lunacy was justified at the time on the assumption that if sufficient man-power were devoted to the task (the chiefs of staff had a weak grasp of economic reality) the Jews and Arabs would be forced to an accommodation.

In fact, holding the balance between Jews and Arabs had already become an impossible task. By the end of the Second World War, Britain was spending more on law and order in Palestine than on domestic health and education combined. And it was a losing battle. The opening of the Nazi concentration camps had resulted in huge pressure, not least from America, to lift restrictions on Jewish immigration, a pressure that Bevin resisted, knowing what a free-for-all would do for a hard-pressed peacekeeping force. For the militant Zionists, this put Bevin on the side of the Devil and made all things British a legitimate target for terrorist attacks.

At midday on 22 July 1946, there was a delivery of milk to the King David Hotel in Jerusalem. The churns, carrying not milk but a mixture of gelignite and TNT, were taken through to the kitchens. At 12.37 they exploded.

Since the King David was the headquarters of the British army in Palestine and of the secretariat of the British Mandatory Administration, as well as the first call for journalists in need of a story, the attack struck at the very core of British authority. The shock was made yet more brutal by the murder of two British sergeants, their booby-trapped bodies left hanging in a eucalyptus grove near Nathanya. The outrage, committed by an organization called Irgun Zvei Leumi, led by Menahem Begin, a future prime minister of Israel, released passionate denunciations that fell on the peaceful majority of Jews, who were simply bewildered by events and nervous of their future.

It was perhaps understandable that the commanding officer in Palestine, General Sir Evelyn Barker, should declare 'all Jewish places of entertainment, cafés, restaurants, shops and private dwellings' out of bounds to British troops, but less clear why he felt compelled to sign off his orders, circulated to all officers, with the assurance that they would be 'punishing the Jews in a way the race dislikes as much as any – by striking at their pockets and showing our contempt for them'.

Committed to a Jewish national home for more than a quarter of a century, Labour ministers had trouble holding their nerve. With outbreaks of violent anti-Semitism in Liverpool, Manchester and in the East End of London, Bevin gave way to pressure to hand over the Palestinian crisis to the United Nations. Not for one moment did he believe that the strategy would work. Rather, he anticipated the UN making a mess of the job, after which Britain would be called back as the essential mediator. The big difference, as he hoped, would be the closer involvement of the Americans, who up to now had been content to criticise from the sidelines. Bevin was right in one sense. The UN blueprint for the future of Palestine was unworkable. The recommendation was for partition with a Jewish state and an Arab state in economic union and Jerusalem as a neutral international city. It left the map of the region looking like a patchwork quilt with three Zionist sectors and three Arab sectors. There was no way it could work.

But Bevin was wrong in thinking that Britain would be given a second chance to implement its own settlement. The alternative, the only one on offer, was for Britain to take on responsibility for enforcing the UN peace plan, a proposal that was bound to bring conflict with the Arab states that had already voiced implacable opposition. Instead, Britain backed away from the Palestinian imbroglio, adopting a 'strictly neutral' stance while the UN moved inexorably towards recognition of an autonomous Jewish state, knowing full well that it would have to fight for its survival.

The Middle East was about to change as dramatically as at any time in its long history. And not necessarily for the better.

7

On 14 May, 1948 the last British high commissioner left Palestine and the mandate formally ended. The Zionists immediately proclaimed an independent Israel. The following day the armies of Egypt, Syria, Transjordan and Iraq launched an attack across the Palestinian frontier, occupying areas that were still essentially Arab but stopping short of a direct assault on Jewish settlements. Though recognised by the USA and the Soviet Union, the infant state stood alone. Vastly outnumbered, it was expected to put up a spirited but hopeless fight. The armchair strategists, however, overlooked weaknesses on the Arab side that proved to be fatal.

Their most effective leader was King Abdulla of Transjordan, where the Arab Legion was led by General Glubb, better known as Glubb Pasha, a capable British commander devoted to the Arab cause. But Abdulla's authority outside his own closed circle was undermined by a thinly disguised ambition to absorb into his own country the Arab part of Palestine. His readiness to do business with the Zionist leaders to achieve his objective put the lie to Arab unity.

Other political rivalries were compounded by military incompetence. While King Farouk was inspired by the cheers of the crowd to believe that the Egyptian army was heading for a great victory, most of his senior officers were inexperienced in all but ceremonial duties. By contrast, the Israeli force, though small in number, had been hardened by fighting Germans or the British or both. Moreover, they knew very well that they had just one chance of survival. They pursued it with ruthless intensity. Well-intentioned UN peacemakers were lost in a maze of intrigue and double dealing. No sooner was a ceasefire signed than it was broken.

When the fighting ended in January 1949, most of what had been Palestine disappeared from the map. A large part of it went to Israel, the rest to Transjordan (now to be called the Hashemite Kingdom of Jordan), except for Gaza, a coastal strip administered by Egypt, home to thousands of Palestinian refugees who had fled across the border or been forced to leave by trigger-happy Jewish settlers. Peace of a sort was established, but while their humiliated armies returned to barracks, the Arab nations insisted that the war was not over, only in abeyance. Thus Israel, by her own not unfair estimation, remained a little country menaced by hostile neighbours dedicated to its destruction. A blood-soaked sequel was in the making.

If the Arab contenders were humbled by the Israeli experience, how much more so was Britain, the once dominant power in the region, now seen to be totally ineffectual when it came to meeting one of the great challenges. In the apportionment of blame, Britain came top of the list for Arabs looking for a scapegoat. Britain, in turn, pointed the finger at America. The role of the USA in the creation of Israel was that of the back-seat driver, long on advice but short on practicalities. As soon as the Labour government took office it was reminded by President Truman of the 'great interest' of Americans in the Palestinian problem and their 'passionate protest' at restrictions on Jewish immigration. A demand for the immediate entry of 100,000 Jews into Palestine was dispatched from the White House with monotonous regularity, a cause of enormous irritation to Ernest Bevin, who believed that Truman had more concern for the Jewish vote than genuine sympathy for the Zionist cause.

This was unfair. Having emerged from early post-war isolationism, America had accepted its role as the only power capable of resisting Soviet expansion. To this end, not only the defence of Europe but also its economic recovery was largely financed by American dollars. But if Britain was to retain credibility as a world power it had to do something for itself. The Middle East, which

Britain claimed as its prime area of influence, seemed as good a place as any for Britain to live up to its macho image. If this were to prove beyond its capacity, and there were those in the British government, starting with the prime minister, who were ready to admit that it was, then America would have to fill the vacuum. This was a step too far for Bevin and his military advisers, who wanted American support only if it came without strings.

It was true that America was failing to think through its long-term engagement in the Middle East. Truman, like his predecessor, seemed to believe that economic self-interest would eventually bring Jews and Arabs together, a naive assumption that fatally underplayed the religious and racial divide. Meanwhile, there was some satisfaction among the anti-colonial establishment in Washington at witnessing Britain's discomfort. Next on the list of intractable problems was Egypt. It would be interesting, it was said over the cocktails, to see what the Brits would make of that.

It was taken for granted in London as in Cairo that a change in Anglo-Egyptian relations was overdue. Even so, the sense of urgency was all on the Egyptian side. While Bevin had in mind a variation on the economic and political partnership he sought with the colonies, a policy that needed time to evolve, the Egyptian government demanded the immediate evacuation of all British troops. With plenty else to occupy him, Bevin was slow to respond – after all, the 1936 treaty still had ten years to run, so what was the hurry? But when he did get round to accepting that the Egyptians had a case to answer, he acknowledged that the withdrawal of British troops from Cairo and other urban centres was the prerequisite for constructive negotiations. This brought Churchill into the fray, the old warrior accusing the government of a humiliating climb-down. Nothing was calculated to anger Bevin more than doubts cast on his patriotism. The two ailing giants (both had heart trouble) traded insults across the floor of the House of Commons, each claiming to be the standard-bearer of a greater Britain.

In truth, there was not much difference between them. While Bevin was keen to reduce the British presence in Egypt it was only on condition of the right of re-entry in an emergency. This in turn was dependent on keeping military installations in the Canal Zone. The Egyptian government wanted none of that. Another complicating factor was the status of the Sudan. Egypt had a long-standing claim to sovereignty over the country which Britain had marked out for independence under British tutelage. The hope was to establish there a military base strong enough to deter Egypt from any intemperate adventures.

The diplomatic blockage was broken in October 1946 when the Egyptian prime minister, Sidqi Pasha, and his foreign minister came to London for direct talks with Bevin. The deal hammered out was more fragile than either side anticipated largely because they underestimated both the strength of anti-British feeling in Egypt and the strength of dissident forces that were building up against Farouk and his ministers. But at the start all seemed to be going well. A draft treaty allowed for a British evacuation of Cairo, Alexandria and the delta by 31 March 1947, and the rest of Egypt, with the exception of the Canal Zone, by 1 September, 1949. A Joint Defence Board was to be set up to discuss 'all events which may threaten the security of the Middle East' and to recommend action for both governments to approve in concert.[1] On the question of the Sudan, Egyptian sovereignty was implicit in the agreement, but in the end it was up to the Sudanese to decide their future.

Determined to have the compromise ratified, Sidqi was less than straightforward with the Egyptian parliament. Approval was gained on the understanding that the Sudan was now Egyptian. When Bevin put him right, Sidqi was forced to resign and the revised treaty was relegated to the file of lost causes. Britain now acted unilaterally under the 1936 treaty. On the unwarranted assumption that a troublesome Egypt could be replaced by a compliant Palestine, British troops began to move out of Alexandria and Cairo. At one farewell party, the guest of honour was an English matriarch who, as a girl, had cheered the arrival of Wolseley's troops.

The final departure from Cairo a few days later was a subdued affair: The last armoured cars slipped out of Kasr-el-Nil barracks at 5 a.m. on March 28, yet a large crowd had gathered to gaze calmly at them through the pre-dawn gloom. As daylight came, Egyptian soldiers were to be seen at every window of the barracks, tirelessly waving their flags to celebrate the re-occupation of this, the most conspicuous symbol of the British raj, once the scene of Arabi's first great triumph, always a magnet for bugs.[2]

The building was soon pulled down to make way for a skyscraper hotel.

Though British occupation of the Canal Zone was set to continue, even there a withdrawal might have been expected had not Palestine turned out to be inhospitable territory for a military base. With Egyptian attention diverted by the Arab–Israeli war, relations with Britain were put on hold. It was only a short respite. The Zionist victory fuelled Egyptian resentment of a corrupt leadership as much as of foreign intervention. Farouk, no longer the handsome boy king, more the overweight profligate who had so deluded himself as to order a new palace to be built at Gaza so that he could preside over a 'Palestine Arab Government', was clearly at risk. An attempt to suppress the radical Muslim Brotherhood led to the assassination of the prime minister. His successor struck back with wholesale arrests and the murder of El Banna, the founder and Supreme Guide of the Brotherhood.

Less easy to pinpoint and thus destroy was the Blessed Movement of Free Officers, a military conspiracy for which Major Gamal Abdel Nasser was the prime mover. Wounded in the recent fighting, Nasser was convinced that defeat had been self-inflicted by a venal and incompetent senior command. Of the same persuasion was Major-General Muhammad Neguib, a respected leader whose war injuries testified to a courage his peers lacked. His outspoken criticisms marked him out as a likely front man for the revolution that the Free Officers were now energetically plotting.

They were encouraged by events in Syria, where a military coup had disposed of the legitimate government, and in Iraq, where a revised treaty with Britain, which Bevin regarded as a model of its kind, signalled an eruption of mob violence that put a stop to any immediate hopes for a constructive partnership between the two countries. In August 1951 the Iranian government spurred on the nationalist frenzy throughout the Middle East, nationalised the Anglo-Iranian Oil Company and expelled the British employees. It was a sign of the times that, on American urging, Britain held back from direct action. By now Bevin's health had given way. His last attempt to hold the ring in the Middle East was to forge the 1950 Tripartite Agreement with America and France to limit the supply of arms to the region, a fanciful notion when the demand for modern weaponry was so strong. Egypt, in particular, saw the agreement as an attempt to frustrate its recovery as a power to be reckoned with and was not comforted by the unreal promise of the three signatory powers to 'immediately take action' should any Arab country or Israel be attacked.

Further aggravation was caused when, after taking over at the foreign office, Herbert Morrison came up with a plan to create a Middle East Command with the USA, Britain, France and Turkey working in friendly collaboration with Egypt to protect her interests, but in reality to watch over the canal and to deter Soviet meddling. There was no chance that Egypt would agree. It was too much like old times. Any attempt at forging an association with the West was the equivalent of a resignation speech for the politicians held responsible.

Hoping to recover his waning credibility, the wily Nahas Pasha, who was serving his fifth term as prime minister, decided to make his own bid for nationalist support by unilaterally abrogating the 1936 Anglo-Egyptian Treaty. For good measure, Farouk was declared King of the Sudan as well as of Egypt and a state of emergency imposed. This was the preliminary to a campaign of systematic harassment of British troops in the Canal Zone. Civilian workers who were pressured into finding a living elsewhere could not be replaced, food supplies had to be flown in and, at night, raiding parties purloined anything that was not screwed to the ground. The army hated the place. It was a posting associated with 'violence, squalid discomfort, bitter desert cold and unvarying ugliness'.[3] Much of the resentment of ordinary British citizens against Egypt at the time of the Suez crisis can be traced to military service in the Canal Zone.

'No other troops in the world', reported the Conservative MP Charles Mott-Radclyffe,

> would show such discipline and restraint, in face of such provo-
> cation, as the British troops in the canal zone . . . Life is extremely
> monotonous. There are few amenities. Accommodation is very
> poor, with no prospect of improvement in view of the uncertain
> future. Some men are doing guard duty every other night; the
> luckier ones every third night. All vehicles have to travel in pairs;
> all senior officers have a jeep escort, and, except in a few places,
> even bathing parties are accompanied by an armed escort . . . To
> sit in a sandbagged post, illuminated at night by arc lamps, with
> a village 100 yards away from which shots are fired every night
> and quite often during the day, without the slightest prospect of
> being able effectively to return the fire, is quite an ordeal for the
> old sweat, let alone for the National Serviceman.

There were also doubts as to the military relevance of the Canal Zone. Kenneth Hunt served as a lieutenant colonel (operations) in Egypt from 1953 to 1956.

> There were about 80,000 troops in Egypt. All we were really
> doing was taking in our own washing. We had about 40,000
> logistics and support troops maintaining the existing Base, and
> the other 40,000 were guarding it and ourselves. We had some
> spare forces, so that when there was trouble in the Dhofar or
> elsewhere in the region, a battalion or so could go there, but
> basically we were doing little but looking after ourselves. We had
> no connection with Egypt. We were confined to the Canal Zone.
> We were acutely aware of the problem there would be if we did

have to go into the Delta proper. The Delta could soak up men – as of course could Cairo, a seething mass of people.[4]

Harassing British soldiers helped to divert the energies of the Muslim Brotherhood and other radical groups that might otherwise have been attacking their own government for its failure to control prices and raise living standards. But for the nationalists, it was not a strategy that had lasting appeal. The ramshackle structure that was the Egyptian government showed every sign of imminent collapse. King Farouk was despised even by the royal parasites who benefited most from his extravagant lifestyle. 'Intelligent enough to be cynical about the political life of the country but lacking the intellectual and moral stamina to be interested in its improvement',[5] Farouk stepped up efforts to remove the bulk of his wealth to a Swiss banking haven. In October 1951, he told his recently anointed queen to prepare for exile.

Farouk was not alone in realising that Egypt was about to explode. Cultivating direct contacts with Nasser and his Free Officers, the CIA in Cairo marked out the would-be leader as an Arab politician with whom Washington could do business. He was clearly intelligent, capable of arguing a case with a self-assurance that demanded attention. Though with a high, piercing voice, he was gifted at handling a crowd. 'On a platform', commented one observer, 'his personality blazes like a naphtha fire.'[6] He spoke passionately of social and economic reform and of stamping out corruption. He had a devoted wife, a happy family and lived modestly. If there was a drawback to Nasser it was that the visionary in him tended to 'identify his own ambition with the will of Providence',[7] which could lead him to overplay his hand.

The moving force in the American relationship was Kermit (Kim) Roosevelt, grandson of President Theodore Roosevelt, a supremely self-assured young operative who had no sympathy with the British way of doing things. In his view, problems in the Middle East arose from the British faith in shaky alliances with old and discredited regimes. Roosevelt determined on a push 'to encourage the emergence of competent leaders, relatively well disposed toward the West ... including, where possible, a conscious, though perhaps covert, effort to cultivate and aid such potential leaders, even when they are not in power'.[8] Nasser was one such.

As early as 1950, the CIA was backing a military programme in the USA for more than fifty young Egyptian army officers, at least six of whom were close associates of Nasser. Two future members of the Revolutionary Command Council were part of the programme, while Ali Sabri, chief of air force intelligence and a supporter of the Free Officers, attended a six-month intelligence course normally reserved for NATO officers. Later, Sabri conceded that 'the attendance of many Egyptian officers at US service schools during the past two years had a very definite influence on the coup d'état in Egypt'.[9]

Though less well informed on the imminent revolution, British intelligence was sufficiently up to speed to recognise that Farouk was at risk. Anticipating growing pressure on the Canal Zone, a plan was devised for taking control of Cairo and other strategic centres, in effect a repeat performance of the 1882 occupation. Along with other more sensible proposals for solving the Egyptian crisis, it was to remain in abeyance while a general election in October 1951 saw the departure of the Labour government and the return of the conservatives under Churchill, with Eden, yet again, as foreign secretary. There was a neat irony here in that the two men who had signed the 1936 Anglo-Egyptian Treaty, Nahas and Eden, were now compelled to try again to resolve their differences. Left to themselves, they might have worked out a settlement. But both were hostages to domestic pressures that frustrated their best intentions. Eden had the more difficult job. Though temperamentally inclined towards compromise, he was up against a leader whose contempt for the Egyptians was matched by his determination that Britain should not be pushed around by a subservient race.

With little encouragement, Churchill would rage against what he saw as Eden's tendency towards appeasement, declaring that 'he never knew before that Munich was situated on the Nile'. Pushed further, he threatened that 'if we have any more of [Egyptian] cheek we will set the Jews on them and drive them into the gutter from which they should never have emerged'. After his tantrum Churchill would warmly recall his visits to Cairo in the days when the Egyptians had understood their place in the scheme of things.[10]

Like the military, Churchill was seemingly unable to understand that Britain no longer had the capacity to play the world power. For him, as for the generals, a strong presence in Egypt and the Middle East was essential, not just for the protection of oil but for strategic bases that could be used to launch air strikes against a Soviet attack. Yet Britain's only long-range bomber, the Lincoln, could not fly above 19,000 feet and was capable of hitting only a very small part of the southern Soviet Union.[11] Even the more limited objective of simply defending the Middle East was more than Britain alone could manage. It might have been different if America had been willing to commit forces to the region, but Washington had already made the decision to focus on Europe rather than the Middle East as a first line of defence. Paradoxically, this was seen in some quarters as a benefit to Britain because it helped to avoid competition with America for influence over Arab states. The stark fact that Britain could do nothing to prevent a Russian takeover without American support was conveniently ignored.

Echoing Churchill's declaration in 1941 that 'the loss of Egypt would be a disaster of the first magnitude to Great Britain', a small but vocal minority in the Conservative Party kept up an imperialist chant. Known as the Suez Group, its two leading lights were Captain Charles Waterhouse, a backbencher who had once held minor ministerial posts with no great distinction, and Julian Amery, son of Leo Amery, a cabinet minister in Churchill's wartime administration. It was the tragedy of the Amerys that Julian's wayward elder brother, John, had wound up in Berlin during the Hitler years when he had been recruited for Nazi radio propaganda directed at British audiences. At the end of the war, and despite clear medical evidence of a personality disorder that had carried him over into insanity, he was found guilty of treason and hanged. With this family background, it is hardly surprising that Julian should have pushed his credentials as a front-line patriot. Having served in Special Operations in the Balkans during the war, he subsequently made great play of his connections with British intelligence, building on what was almost certainly an inflated reputation for knowing a thing or two about subversive movements, particularly in the Middle East. That he was Harold Macmillan's son-in-law helped him to acquire privileged information.

Amery and Waterhouse were made for each other. Both were political blusterers, immune to strategic and economic realities, who were convinced that higher powers were intent on destroying Britain's imperial heritage with dire consequences for the mother country and for the rest of the world. It must have seemed almost providential when the two conspiracy theorists ran into each other in a hotel in Cape Town.

> We had a drink and began talking. He [Waterhouse] had just returned from the Sudan, where he had been very shocked by what he had seen there. He thought that we were about to hand it over to Egypt. I told him that much more dangerous was the threat to the Base in the Canal Zone because, as long as we were there, we could stop any nonsense in the Sudan, but if we went from there, we would have no power in the area any more. He was rather interested by this and we agreed to meet again after dinner, which we did.
>
> When the House met after the summer recess, we found a number of like-minded and rather significant people at what I call the higher end: Ralph Asheton, John Morrison (Vice-Chairman of the 1922 Committee), Christopher Holland-Martin, who was Treasurer of the Party; and then, at the younger end, we had Enoch [Powell], Angus Maude, Fitzroy Maclean and a number of others. It grew slowly as the evidence accumulated of what looked like a readiness to hand the Sudan over to Egypt and to get out of the Zone.[12]

Such a betrayal, as seen by the Suez Group, would spell the end of British influence.

When we pulled out of India and Palestine, we remained to an extraordinary extent a world empire. The fulcrum of power was now exclusively based on the Canal Zone. This was the base of British power in the Middle East, Africa and, to a large extent, the Far East, because to get there we had to go through the Mediterranean and the Canal Zone. Strategically, this was the hub for any continued role for Britain as a world power. If that went, the backbone of the bird would snap, you would have two wings. In my pursuit of getting the thing right, I got a curious message from the Indian General Staff. I had consulted them, and they replied that their Prime Minister would tell us to get out, but that they felt that if we did, we would be written off as a military factor in that part of the world. All through the Arab world, you got tremendous double talk telling us to get out, but in private saying, 'For God's sake, don't dream of it'.[13]

For Amery, standing up to Egypt was 'a chance to rekindle past greatness'. He told Churchill of his conviction that 'the Egyptian business is going to mark a turning point in our affairs. The Middle East and indeed the whole world may realise that we are still alive and have a heart as well as teeth and claws'.[14]

Trying to hold the balance within his own party, Eden adopted the tough and tender approach. He was ready to consider a fresh treaty, he told the Egyptian prime minister, but while negotiations progressed, the old treaty held good. The Egyptian government would be 'responsible for any breach of the peace and any damage to life and property'. The warning went unheeded. Attacks on British persons and property became so frequent as to put pressure on the army to retaliate. With troop numbers up from 35,000 to 64,000, General Sir George Erskine, the British commander in Egypt, certainly had the means to retake the initiative. Without firing another shot it was within his power to cut off that part of the Egyptian army around Cairo by closing the El Firdan swing bridge near Ismailia. Recognising the threat, Egyptian forces had attempted to take the bridge but had been pushed back with the loss of two men. They now kept their distance behind what was known as the Erskine line.

It was not only the bridge which the Egyptians had to worry about. The oil pipeline on which Cairo depended started in Suez. Erskine contemplated starving the city of fuel and power and, indeed, cut supplies to prove his point. But though tempted to go farther, he was persuaded to hold back from a provocation that was tantamount to a declaration of war. Instead, yet more military reinforcements were flown in and civilian labour from Cyprus was recruited to fill the gaps left by the Egyptian workers who had fled the Canal Zone.

What next? Everyone knew that the stand-off could not continue for long. Rather, the question was whether there was time enough for the diplomats to patch up a settlement before tempers gave way. Beset by conflicting advice, Eden prevaricated. His own foreign office was no help. Though more realistic than the military in assessing British prospects in the Middle East, senior officials were torn between the need to accept Egyptian demands and the heartfelt desire not to do anything that might lose prestige. The contradiction was expressed succinctly if unhelpfully by Sir Pierson Dixon, later British ambassador to the United Nations but then a deputy under-secretary of state in the Foreign Office.

> Thinking over our difficulties in Egypt, it seems to me that the essential difficulty arises from the very obvious fact that we lack power. The Egyptians know this, and that accounts for their intransigence.
>
> On a strictly realistic view we ought to recognise that our lack of power must limit what we can do, and should lead us to a policy of surrender or near surrender imposed by necessity.
>
> But the basic and fundamental aim of British policy is to build up our lost power. Once we despair of doing so, we shall never attain this aim. Power, of course, is not to be measured in terms alone of money and troops: a third ingredient is prestige, or in other words what the rest of the world thinks of us.

Here the dilemma arises. We are not physically strong enough to carry out policies needed if we are to retain our position in the world; if we show weakness our position in the world diminishes with repercussions on our world wide position.

The broad conclusion I am driven to is therefore that we ought to make every conceivable effort to avoid a policy of surrender or near surrender. Ideally we should persuade the Americans of the disaster which such a policy would entail for us and for them, and seek their backing, moral, financial and, if possible, military, in carrying out a strong policy in Egypt.[15]

But the drawback to Dixon's analysis was that the USA and Britain were increasingly at odds over global strategy. As seen from the Pentagon, Britain made too much of the importance of the Middle East, especially Egypt. Holding down large numbers of troops in the region could not in the end guarantee the flow of oil or stop a major Soviet offensive which, in any case, was unlikely. The US view was neatly summarised in a Foreign Office minute:

There is no military or political advantage in a continuation of the present state of affairs in Egypt, and there is little prospect that they will change for the better. The Egypt base must therefore be written off, and arrangements made for the defence of the Eastern Mediterranean without it. Meanwhile the British can best serve our common interests by withdrawing from Egypt as gracefully as they can, and thereby make it possible to get the Arab states to co-operate in the defence of the area.

Unless, therefore, there is soon a favourable turn of events in Egypt, this document may prove to be the starting point of an important schism between the foreign policies of the US and ourselves.[16]

One of the three contributors to this analysis went on to emphasise the hopeless position Britain was in.

We have done everything we can to help [the Egyptian government] with face-saving devices but we have never had the slightest response. After all that has gone by, I frankly cannot see that any 'popular' and parliamentary Egyptian Government can now abandon the national aspirations as its ideal, if it is not to be shouted down by its opponents. It may be that the Egyptian public will in time lose interest in the national aspirations as being impracticable, but this would be a historical novelty and must, I think, be discounted.

All this, if correct, points to the fact that the only sort of Government with which we can hope to get an accommodation is a frankly authoritarian government which is strong enough to sit on nationalism, to pack or if necessary do without a Parliament altogether, and control the press. It would have to be both ruthless and efficient. The question is where to find a man with the courage, force of personality and sagacity to run such a Government. King Farouk is clearly not he, although he might be happy enough to back up a suitable candidate. We need another Mustafa Kemal, to secularise and Westernise his country and direct the political energies of the people away from the British towards the reconstruction of their own economy and social structure. Even so Egyptians are not Turks, and men like Mustafa Kemal cannot be ordered *à la carte*![17]

A colleague added, 'The outlook is not encouraging.' But still the military continued to insist that a base in Egypt was vital to protect British interests. 'Our standard of living stems in large measure from our status as a great power and this depends to no small extent on the visible indication of our greatness, which our forces, particularly overseas, provide.'[18] The chiefs of staff urged the seizure of all points of entry and exit in the Canal Zone and the ordering out of Egyptian troops and 'their removal by force, if necessary'.[19]

Meanwhile, clashes between British troops and Egyptian police culminated in January 1952 in Ismailia when the occupants of two police barracks refused to surrender their arms. An attempt to enter the Bureau Sanitaire, formerly part of a hospital, was met by a fusillade of small-arms fire. Force was met with greater force.

A Centurion tank smashed through the outer wall of the barracks, clearing the way for an assault by the Lancashire Fusiliers. The occupants of the other barracks, the Caracol, held out until noon, suffering minor casualties. In all, the Egyptian police lost fifty killed with one hundred wounded while the Fusiliers counted four dead and ten wounded.

Government supporters proclaimed a decisive victory. 'Britain has made a mighty affirmation of its Imperial destiny,' whooped the *Daily Express*. But the strength of Egyptian resistance surprised the British military, who were now less convinced of the Churchillian view that the natives would always submit to the smack of firm government. Indeed, Churchill himself had to accept that the simplest solution was not necessarily the best, though he continued to advocate a tough line while Eden still searched for a way out by negotiation.

Further evidence of just what the British were up against came at the end of January. 'On the morning of the 26th', wrote General Muhammad Neguib, soon to be installed as first president of the Egyptian republic, 'mobs began to gather all over Cairo . . . Before long they were attacking and setting fire to numerous foreign and luxury establishments.'[20]

On what became known as Black Saturday, Egyptian police and army were nowhere to be seen. The royal calendar, which had Farouk attending a banquet to celebrate the birth of his son, continued uninterrupted, and the prime minister was said to be otherwise engaged.

If it was an orgy it was a controlled orgy. It was confined to the centre of the city, and large European residential quarters, such as Zamalek and Gezira, were virtually unaffected. It began about midday, when small gangs – they were said to have been composed of auxiliary police and unemployed 'refugees' from the Zone – under well-briefed leaders, converged on Opera Square and the streets leading off it. The targets were hotels, restaurants, bars, banks, cinemas and luxury shops, either European or Jewish owned or with obvious European associations.

The destruction of property by arson, pillage and looting was the chief aim; the lives were not spared. In Barclay's Bank clerks, who had taken refuge in the underground strong-rooms, died of suffocation. In the Turf Club, which was attacked when members were going in to luncheon, twelve men – they were most of the elderly retired civilians who had spent their lives in Egypt, but a senior Canadian diplomat was among them – were murdered. At Shepheard's Hotel the guests, who included a cabaret star and a reporter from the *New York Times*, sheltered under a palm tree in the exiguous garden while the hotel blazed and crumbled in front of them. Farther along the street the Continental Hotel, which was closed for repairs and redecoration, was similarly assaulted and destroyed. The attacks were vengeful and selective. Another distinguished American journalist, who chanced to arrive by air from Saudi Arabia that morning, was advised by his taxi-driver not to go to Shepheard's, deposited his bag at the Semiramis Hotel and for several hours roamed the streets unmolested, until (it was alleged, for his own protection) he was taken into custody by the police.[21]

If the Egyptian authorities were slow to act so too were British troops, who were within easy reach of Cairo and might have been expected to dash to the rescue of fellow citizens. But though, according to Eden, there was a plan for intervention, the preferred solution of both Eden and Erskine as advised by the ambassador, Sir Ralph Stevenson, was for the Egyptian army to act first, this being the best chance of preventing a wider conflagration. It did so in the late afternoon. By the end of Black Saturday, nine Britons, one Canadian and some fifty Egyptians had died and over four hundred buildings were destroyed. What was the point of it all? Probably none whatsoever, except to give further proof to the British – as if any were needed – that they were not welcome. The risk to Farouk and Nahas of letting mob violence get out of hand was in demonstrating to Nasser and his revolutionary friends the weakness of the regime. But in the short run it was Farouk who gained best advantage. Protesting shock at the outrages against persons and property, he took the opportunity to dispose of Nahas in favour of his old ally, Ali Maher.

The new regime at least gave Eden the opportunity to reopen negotiations. But first he had to come to an accommodation with his allies, 'to persuade the US', as he put it, 'to assume the real burden . . . while retaining for ourselves as much political control, and hence prestige and world influence, as we can'. He put his faith in a Middle East Defence Organisation centred on Egypt, backed by Britain, America, France and Turkey and 'carrying with it the grant of full facilities to allied forces in time of war'.[22] Once this was in place, British forces could be withdrawn from the Canal Zone within a year. Civilian technicians would replace military personnel at the canal base. It was an ingenious face-saving scheme but it was too much for Churchill, who was not prepared for evacuation to precede the arrival of allied forces under a Middle East command. Eden gave way, even though it was widely accepted in the foreign office that too little was being offered to satisfy the Egyptians.

At the moment I can see no hope whatever of our reaching agreement with the Egyptians. We are not at present prepared to make the minimum concessions necessary to secure an agreement, and it seems impossible to make people here realise this fact and to understand the possible results of failure to reach an agreement . . . It does of course remain to be seen how far down the Egyptians are prepared to climb. Ali Maher, and even I suppose the King, must know quite well that if they do not reach an agreement with us, it may mean the deluge so far as they are concerned.

On the other hand, if they do not achieve something which can be dressed up to look like their national aspirations, it may equally be the end of them. On our side, it seems to me that if we push the Egyptians too far we might get an agreement which no Egyptian Government could get ratified; on the other hand if we hold out for our full requirements and do not get an agreement at all, there may be such an explosion in Egypt that we shall be buried in the ruins.[23]

At this point in his career, Eden was living in the real world. It was all very well for Churchill to demand firmness but his foreign secretary knew that there was no escaping a climb-down. 'We shall be bound to get out of the Canal Zone anyway in 1956 in the absence of some new agreement. If we have to leave, this would mean withdrawing not only our troops but also the stores in our base and leaving the base installations behind.' On the other hand, if there was a four-power Middle East command, the Egyptians could be expected to cooperate in the maintenance of the Middle East base. 'We hope that Egypt would agree that British technicians should be retained in it, while Egyptian troops would probably have to take over guard duties. This base would provide the means of sustaining all the forces of ourselves and our Allies in the Middle East in time of war, and it is thus that we should hope to protect the Suez Canal.' But following Churchill's train of thought,

> If we merely seek to hold the Canal Zone by force, we must expect sooner rather than later a revolution in Egypt. This will mean disturbances in the Delta on a far larger scale than on January 26th, with inevitable loss of many British lives and inter-ests. We may be compelled to reoccupy the Delta towns, which will place upon us an administrative commitment which we can-not possibly afford in terms either of men or money. We must expect that all our commercial interests in Egypt will be lost. As for the base, our military authorities already admit, that, under the conditions prevailing during the last five months, it would be useless from an operational point of view if war came, since our entire resources have been devoted to maintaining ourselves, and we have not had enough to spare to maintain the base. Moreover, we should have no troops for the defence of the Middle East, since they would all be required to hold the position in Egypt.

In these circumstances, Eden could see no chance of winning American support. What, then, was left? 'The plain fact is that we are no longer in a position to impose our will upon Egypt, regardless of the cost in men, money, and international goodwill both throughout the Middle East and the rest of the world.'[24]

Eden might have saved his energies. His good sense was outweighed by the intransigence of Churchill, who could rely on the sheep-like connivance of senior colleagues and the slow-witted strategists on the general staff who continued to insist that a base in Egypt was essential in wartime. Though Eden had all the best arguments, he had not the force of personality to win them, a foreshadow of his brief and inglorious premiership culminating in the Suez crisis, when he allowed himself to be swayed by the small but vocal diehard force in his party.

While, in right-wing parlance, Britain held firm, Egypt fell apart. Martial law and heavy-handed censorship conveyed the popular impression of a society that was firmly under control, but in reality trouble for Farouk and his government was never far away. Efforts to identify and neutralise dissidents in the military were counter-productive as Nasser and his Free Officers continued to attract converts. Farouk had left it too late to make his mark as a creditable leader, and he knew it. The recklessness of his actions in the closing weeks of his reign suggest a card-sharp who was bluffing with a weak hand.

As one government followed another in quick succession (Ali Maher lasted only four weeks, his successor but one a mere seventeen days) Farouk turned to the army command to protect his throne. Aware that the Free Officers were ready to act, the generals sent a company of infantry to arrest Nasser and his accomplices. Instead, they joined the revolutionaries and were sent back to arrest the generals. Farouk was at his summer palace in Alexandria when in the early hours of 23 July 1952 armoured cars and tanks rolled up at Cairo airport, the radio station and the telephone exchange. News of unusual troops movements was passed to Farouk. He gave no orders.

At 7 a.m. a proclamation was broadcast in the name of General Neguib announcing that the army, having delivered the country from 'one of its darkest periods of history', would ensure a smooth transition of power, including the preservation of lives and property of 'brother foreigners'. Following up with a tour of the

country, the friendly and approachable Neguib, puffing content-
edly at his pipe, exuded confidence, confirming his reputation as
a leader who would curb the excesses usually associated with
military coups. There were even encouraging words for the
British people. 'Egypt will always value their friendships,' declared
the avuncular Neguib, extending an olive branch all the way to
the hard men of the British Treasury who released £10 million
to support Egypt's fragile economy.

Still in Alexandria, Farouk held on to a fading hope that America
or Britain would come to his aid. But his appeals went unanswered.
Having no faith in the ability of Farouk to hold together a pro-
Western or even a benevolently neutral administration, American
diplomacy had long since homed in on the Free Officers as the
best hope for productive partnership. Likewise, Britain was not
so enamoured with royalty as to believe that Farouk, once he was
seen to be on the losing side, was worth a fight.

Early on the morning of 26 July, tanks surrounded the Ras
al-Tin Palace. After the royal guards had put up a token resistance, access was gained to Farouk, who was presented with an
act of abdication in favour of his infant son, Ahmen Fuad. As
he pondered the document, memories must have stirred of an
encounter, ten years earlier, when a British ambassador had
forced him to surrender his prerogative. Then he had lost a prime
minister; now it was his throne that he was signing away.

That same evening, Farouk with his young queen, Narriman,
sailed for Naples. That he escaped a trial for his life was largely
thanks to Nasser, now interior minister, who argued that a court
hearing would be costly and time consuming, diverting attention
from more pressing matters. 'Let us spare Farouk and send him
into exile. History will sentence him to death.'

The pretence of an Egyptian monarchy was kept up for less
than a year. In that time, the military junta strengthened its political base by breaking up and redistributing the landed estates
so that no holding was more than 200 acres. The measure was
less radical than it first appeared. The wealthy landowners were
brought to heel but few of the fellahin benefited. Moreover, a

small step towards equality did not imply support for democracy. Along with the clear-out of Farouk's entourage, political parties were abolished and their funds confiscated. Power was concentrated on a revolutionary command council of twelve young officers led by Neguib as president and prime minister. The more perceptive observers spotted Nasser as the rising star; he soon consolidated his position by becoming deputy prime minister as well as minister of the interior. In mid-June 1953, Ahmed Fuad II was formally deposed. Farouk and Narriman remained in the public eye with the publication of their much-embroidered memoirs, culminating in Narriman's announcement that Farouk, the ex-monarch, was about to become an ex-husband. She demanded alimony of £5,000 a month.

Farouk's possessions were put up for sale by the army, which staged a news conference to announce what one newspaper described as 'the world's biggest and most expensive accumulation of junk'.

> The reporters toured through the palace and stared at the hoard. In a gaming room a cabinet was full of roulette wheels, dice, and packs of cards with *Esquire*-type girls on the back. On the keyboard hung keys to apartments in Cairo, each clearly labelled with the girl's name. In the vaults six safes contained medals, coins and stamps. On his study desk, beside the nude statuettes, lay boxes of tricks, including pocket radiation counters inscribed 'Measure Nuclear Energy Yourself' and a penknife bristling with all manner of blades. In his bedroom were glamour girl photographs, Kodachrome nudes with pocket viewers, pictures of Narriman and a pile of US comics. There were six telephones and two radios beside the bed. In the dressing-room were one hundred suits, fifty walking sticks, seventy-five pairs of binoculars, a thousand ties, some with the initial F five inches high. Between the first and second floors there was a windowless room, a sort of treasury with boxes of rubies, diamonds, emerald, and platinum brooches.[25]

So ended the dynasty of Muhammad Ali and the world's oldest kingdom.

8

There was a new man in the White House. Lately wartime supreme commander of allied forces in Europe and subsequently head of NATO, Dwight Eisenhower had a chest full of ribbons to show that he could hold his nerve in a crisis. But though an army man through and through, he was not one to reach for his gun in international disputes, at least not until all else had been tried. Having been persuaded by first-hand experience of the 'cruelty, wastefulness and stupidity of war',[1] he started with the assumption that any problem could be solved by rational discussion. Even the confrontation with Soviet or Chinese expansionism 'was a problem to be managed, not an all-consuming crusade against the forces of evil'.[2]

It was this conviction which inspired his vote-winning pledge to fly to Korea to 'bring to an early and honourable end' a war in which 34,000 Americans had died holding the line against communism. It was largely Eisenhower's initiative which brought about a ceasefire in July 1953. But Korea was just one small segment of the cold war. Keen as Americans were to put world affairs aside to concentrate on enjoying a standard of living that Europeans could barely imagine, there was an underlying anxiety that all would be lost if the Soviet Union and China ever suspected that America was weakening in its resolve. Eisenhower knew that the anxiety was excessive, that sabre-rattling by the Marxist powers was more a demonstration of their own insecurity and a defiance of their internal problems than a real threat to the West. But he also acknowledged that keeping up the pressure was the best insurance against the temptation of potential enemies to take dangerous risks.

To settle fears and satisfy aspirations, a twin policy evolved. The first part, a threat of massive retaliation if the Soviets or Chinese mounted a pre-emptive strike, was the brainchild of Eisenhower's secretary of state, John Foster Dulles. A complex and controversial figure in American politics, Dulles was less of a warmonger than his enemies – and allies – made him out to be. His policy of threatened retaliation was based on the not unreasonable assumption that a deterrent – as from March 1954, it was an H-bomb 750 times more powerful than the A-bomb that had destroyed Hiroshima – was only effective in so far as everyone could be made to believe that in certain circumstances America would use it. To achieve this Dulles expressed himself bluntly, almost brutally. There can be no doubt that he set nerves jangling in the Kremlin. The trouble was, he also put the fear of God into his friends, as in January 1956, when he was quoted by *Life* magazine as saying that the 'art of diplomacy is to bring nations to the brink of war'. A further observation that this had happened three times during his tenure as Secretary of State prompted the quip 'three brinks and he's brunk'.

Though from a political family (his uncle had been secretary of state) and a long-standing Republican spokesman for foreign affairs (Eisenhower said of his colleague that he had been in training for his job all his life), Dulles was not a natural communicator. Given to 'moralistic flourishes more appropriate to church councils than to international conferences,'[3] his solemn monotone wearied and irritated his listeners. Another popular wisecrack attached to his name said it all: 'Dull, Duller, Dulles'.

Eisenhower, who was easily bored, acknowledged the drawback to regular meetings with Dulles but had his own way of coping. '. . . the restless rhythm of the pencil tapping his knee . . . the slow glaze across the blue eyes, signalling the end of all mental contact . . . finally, the patient fixing of the eyes on the most distant corner of the ceiling, there to rest till the end of the Dulles dissertation'.[4]

Churchill and Eden were less indulgent. Both underestimated Eisenhower, who, despite his laid-back image, was a man 'of keen political intelligence and penetration, particularly when it came to foreign affairs',[5] and neither of them could stand Dulles. His pomposities were characterised by the prime minister as a compulsion to 'make a speech every day, hold a press conference every other day and preach on Sunday', while Eden described his counterpart as 'the woolliest type of pontificating American'.[6] The criticism must be offset by the tendency of the British leaders, given half a chance, to dominate a conversation. Their dislike of Dulles was as much as anything an aversion to being upstaged by New World politicians, still seen in Europe as apprentices in the art of diplomacy.

For his part, Dulles had an innate distrust of British foreign policy, which he saw as motivated almost entirely by a hopeless and dangerous desire to interfere in matters that were beyond the country's capacity to control. Many American opinion leaders agreed with him. The consensus on both sides of the Atlantic, however, held that Dulles could be difficult and there was surprise that the cautious, pragmatic Eisenhower was able to rub along with a secretary of state who had a talent for making enemies and in his incautious moments seemed to be relishing the onset of a Third World War.

In fact, they made a good team. While superficially there was a contradiction between Eisenhower's pursuit of peace and the hawk-like sentiments emerging from the Pentagon, the two policies worked well in tandem. It was only by deploying atomic weaponry to strongest effect, reasoned the president, that he had any chance of reducing the dependence on conventional forces and thus of cutting a defence budget that had ballooned from $13.1 billion in 1950 to $50.4 billion by 1953.

Parallel thoughts were beginning to take hold in the British defence establishment. Shortly before the upheaval in Egypt that brought the Free Officers to power, the chiefs of staff (COS) accepted, if reluctantly, a measure of economic common sense. Responding to ever more pressing demands from the Treasury to behave less as if the entire earning power of the country was owed to the armed services, a strategy was advanced for shifting the emphasis from a build-up of conventional forces to relying more on American atomic power to check the 'implacable and unlimited aims of Soviet Russia'.

The major cuts were reserved for NATO, with the other European powers accepting, albeit reluctantly, an increased share of defence costs. As for the Middle East, 'we have concluded that, given a settlement in Egypt, it should be possible to reduce the United Kingdom peace-time garrison to about one division and approximately 160 aircraft'.[7] In other words, a 50 per cent cut. The reduced garrison would be spread across Cyprus, Malta and Libya, with air bases in Iraq and Jordan.

In the autumn of 1952, the British joint forces headquarters was moved from Suez to Cyprus. But Egypt was said to remain critical as part of a Middle East Defence Organisation, even if the base there was under Egyptian command. 'The establishment of new treaty relations with Egypt on a basis which will fulfil these requirements should remain a major objective of British policy.'[8] Though clearly reluctant to backtrack on earlier declarations that any reduction in the British presence in the Middle East would be fatal, the COS took comfort in the recent entry of Turkey into NATO and the expectation that the USA could be persuaded to participate in a Middle East Defence Organisation.

It was a vain hope. A fundamental misunderstanding of American policy in the Middle East led Britain to great expectations and even greater disappointments. That America was increasingly active in the region was plain for all to see – starting and, some might say, ending with oil. Aramco was the dominant economic force in Saudi Arabia (where the USA maintained an air base at Dhahran), while Mobil and Exxon were increasingly active in Iraq, and Gulf concentrated on raising production in Kuwait. Washington's preferential treatment for the oil companies guaranteed protection for the higher-cost wells in the States at the same time as huge profits were made from the cheap crude of the Middle East, most of which was refined and sold in western Europe via the Suez Canal. In this way the economic and military needs of the European allies were satisfied with no great inconvenience to the USA. It was a small but significant sign of the times that the Suez Canal Company now had an American director on its board.

The fifty-fifty split on oil revenues agreed by Aramco in Saudi Arabia seemed to be a fair deal – it was certainly fairer than anything on offer from the British oil companies – but there was more to it than a simple commercial arrangement. The four companies that owned Aramco went along with the spirit of generosity only as long as the dues paid to the Saudi Arabian royals were deductible against business taxes in the States. Thus, while King Ibn Saud received some $500 million a year, the American treasury lost the same amount.[9] The point of the exercise was to subsidise the Saudi Arabian regime – and to keep the oil flowing – without giving undue offence to the supporters of Israel.

From Britain's viewpoint, the Saudi deal had the unfortunate effect of encouraging its own client Arab states to demand better terms. But a more serious point at issue was the Saudi tendency to devote a large part of its economic windfall to supporting nationalist movements working against British interests. With the military coup in Egypt, the Free Officers became the latest recipients of Saudi patronage. Frustratingly for Britain, this seemed not to trouble Washington as long as its culpability was kept under the radar of publicity.

Another British grievance was the failure of America to side with Britain on a long-standing border dispute with Saudi Arabia. This centred on Buraimi, a tiny oasis which Britain argued came within the jurisdiction of Abu Dhabi, a sheikhdom under British protection. The value of a dot in the desert was, of course, the prospect of it yielding large quantities of oil. Saudi interest was taken for granted, but what was galling for Britain was the haste with which Aramco caught on to the chance of added profit and, even worse, the enthusiasm of the CIA, with Kim Roosevelt in the lead, to facilitate what looked very much like a joint Saudi–American bid to gain sovereignty over Buraimi, to the extent of sending in troops transported in Aramco trucks. As Evelyn Shuckburgh, in charge of Middle Eastern affairs at the FO, noted petulantly, 'The fact is that the American oil men have gone into

Saudi Arabia with this vast enterprise which utterly submerged the old economy of the country, without assuming any responsibility for the political effects.'[10] The dispute rolled on until 1955 with an attempt at arbitration breaking down amid accusations of Saudi bribery that amounted to buying off everybody who lived within striking distance of the disputed village while handing out new rifles to those who promised to use them against the British.[11]

A more fruitful Anglo-American relationship was born of the crisis in Iran, where a populist leader, Dr Mohammed Mussadiq and his nationalist party, had gained power on an anti-British ticket, pledging to take control of the Anglo-Iranian Oil Company (AIOC). Though at the time Mussadiq was portrayed in the British press as an unprincipled buccaneer, the Iranians had cause for complaint. While it was true that in addition to paying a large labour force above-average wages the AIOC built schools and hospitals and was generally seen as a model employer, there was something odd in a division of oil revenues that gave Iran a mere £24 million in assured royalties, a figure that was just 1 million more than the British tax authorities skimmed off the company's profits. Put another way, Anglo-Iranian had paid just £122 million in royalties on oil worth £1,200 million extracted since 1913.[12]

Mussadiq was a jumble of contradictions. As one who liked to bill himself as a man of the people, he was in fact a wealthy landowner. A democrat who successfully opposed the absolute rule of the Shah, he was not above fixing elections when it looked as if the result would go against him. Western-educated and surrounded by those of like background, he could work himself into a frenzy in his condemnation of foreign intervention. Intelligent and well possessed of political skills, he was also the buffoon of popular Western imagery, who was liable to collapse in tears, overwhelmed by the power of his own oratory. Seventy-one when he became prime minister in 1951, he played the role of the fragile invalid, yet he lived to be eighty-seven.

With such a complex and apparently vulnerable character it is easy to see how his opponents underrated him. Easy too to understand how it came as a shock to the British government when, in short measure, he succeeded in reducing the Shah to little more than a figurehead. But the heaviest blow to British prestige came in May 1951 when Mussadiq carried out his threat to nationalise the Anglo-Iranian Oil Company, reducing at a stroke the British share of Middle East oil production from 53 to 24 per cent[13] and depriving his old enemy of the refinery at Abadan, an offshore island at the head of the Persian Gulf. The largest installation of its kind, it had cost £100 million to build and was Britain's single biggest overseas asset.

At America's urging, the Attlee government rejected armed intervention in favour of a boycott, supported by the American oil companies, which shut off Iranian oil from the world market. The 4,500 British technicians who ran the oilfields and the Abadan refinery left the country in October 1951. Thereafter, the task of making trouble for Mussadiq and, pious hope, of restoring British power was handed over to British intelligence. The chief MI6 operative in Tehran was Christopher Woodhouse, who quickly recognised that nothing much could be done without the help of the Americans and that they were likely to get involved only if they saw the problem as one of containing communism rather than of re-establishing the British oil monopoly.[14]

With Eisenhower's entry into the White House, the anti-communist argument was strengthened by Dulles's conviction – Eden called it an obsession – that Russia was about to cross the border into Iran, involving 'the loss of Middle East oil supplies or the threat of another world war'. What made the Soviet incursion all the more likely, reasoned Dulles, was the welcome sign put up by the powerful TUDEH, or People's Party, which was communist in all but name.

A fervent anti-communist who could overcome his distaste for European colonialism when American interests were at stake, Dulles was helped towards a decision to topple Mussadiq by his brother Allen Dulles, who had moved up from deputy to head of the CIA. He, in turn, was pressed towards intervention by Kim Roosevelt, now head of CIA operations in the Middle East. While Roosevelt had no time for the British in Egypt he was convinced that in Iran the Soviet threat was real and that, if nothing was done, the oil might be made to flow in the wrong direction.

As one who relished covert operations, Churchill was eager to work off his frustration over Egypt by gaining the upper hand in Iran. Eden was more circumspect, and might indeed have called a halt to the plot to overthrow the Mussadiq regime had he not been rushed into hospital for a gall bladder operation. He was home in the last week of July, but soon after was convalescing in the Mediterranean, leaving his ultra-conservative deputy, Lord Salisbury, to defer all too readily to Churchill's commanding presence. Enjoying a resurgence of wartime adrenalin, Churchill was quick to give the go-ahead for what he dubbed, ungraciously, Operation Boot but was known in the USA as Operation Ajax.

The plan was based on dispensing money, lots of it, to highly placed Iranian friends, who recruited a small army of rabble-rousers and street fighters. The bulk of the funding came from the CIA (in April 1953, Allen Dulles made $1 million available) while British intelligence had the list of contacts with the Shah, the military and the clergy, all essential to the success of the coup. When it came to the showdown in July, Mussadiq blustered against the reactionary forces before dramatically collapsing under the strain and being led away to his trial.

The Shah, who, a few days before, had fled the country, returned in triumph to rule under American auspices for the next quarter-century. Mussadiq was sentenced to three years in prison. On his release, he spent the rest of his life under house arrest on his estate in Ahmadabad.

Churchill was delighted, though whether, in the light of subsequent events, he would have stuck by his judgement that it was 'the finest operation since the end of the war' must be doubted. Allen Dulles's biographer was closer to the mark when he wrote that the Iran venture was 'more reminiscent of Viennese operetta'.

The stock characters strain credibility: the outrageous prime minister, dumb like a fox, who prances across the world stage in his pajamas; the brooding 'gloomy prince' who cannot decide who his friends are; the clever spy [Kim Roosevelt] from abroad who hides in a villa out of town as he flips wild cards and jokers like a street shark; assorted middlemen and go-betweens who find ever-shifting middles and betweens; a chorus of Persian urban peasants and sword-bearers who enter and exit on cue.[15]

The final twist to a bizarre tale came when the Shah, in temporary exile, turned up in Rome at the very hotel where Allen Dulles and his wife were also staying. 'Years later, with Operation Ajax celebrated as an example of a CIA covert action that worked, Allen would respond with a knowing twinkle when asked if he had used the hospitality of the Excelsior to persuade the reluctant Shah to reclaim his sway over Iran.'[16]

As it happened, the reimposition of the Shah on his less than enthusiastic subjects proved to be no more than a strategy of delay, putting off the day when they turned to the Ayatollah Khomeini, a far more dangerous threat to Western interests than Mussadiq had ever been. But, at the time, the only debit on the British side was the flat refusal by the Shah to reinstate the AIOC.

Eager to effect an early settlement, Eisenhower moved in as the honest broker, a role untainted by the charge of hypocrisy since the part of American and British intelligence in the over-throw of Mussadiq was still a tight secret. To front up the negoti-ations, Herbert Hoover Jr, son of the former president, an experienced oilman but an Anglophobe, was appointed special adviser to Foster Dulles. The brief from Washington held that the involvement of the American oil companies was a prerequisite of any deal.

The difficulty for Hoover was that the oil companies were not at all sure that they wanted to be involved. With the huge expan-sion of production in Kuwait and other Gulf states where Anglo-Iranian, now renamed British Petroleum, had more than made up the losses from Iran, the world production of crude was in surplus to the order of 1 million barrels a day. In the end the five major American oil companies submitted to Washington's demands on condition that, by agreeing to concerted action, they would be exempt from American anti-trust laws[17] – in the national interest, of course.

The new management was a consortium of eight companies which gave Britain a 40 per cent share. Five American companies were also awarded 40 per cent, with Royal Dutch Shell taking 14 per cent and a French company the remaining 5 per cent. Profits were to be divided equally with Iran, a formula soon followed by other oil-producing states. While the Shah proved to be a tough negotiator, he was outmanoeuvred by the oil companies in one important respect. Free of the restrictions imposed by American anti-trust legislation, they came to an agreement whereby production of Iranian oil was strictly curtailed to protect world prices. As an American oilman observed, 'This was most profitable patriotism.'[18]

Britain was slow to learn the lessons of Iran. While Eisenhower and Dulles were prepared to sponsor, preferably covertly, forces opposed to communism, this did not extend to giving Britain a free hand in Egypt, where Nasser was seen as the up-and-coming Arab leader who might well lead the way to a Middle East settlement with Israel. That such opinion held sway in Washington was largely the result of intelligence fed through from the CIA office in Cairo.

Britain had few links with the Free Officers. The coup that overthrew Farouk had come as a surprise. As Eden admitted, it 'happened so quickly that no one was aware as late as the morning before'. With his exaggerated regard for royalty, Churchill was instinctively hostile to the new regime. His thoughts turned to a counter-coup. What had been done in Tehran could just as easily be achieved in Cairo. Eden was more realistic. What was the point of staging a confrontation in Egypt? With the shift to a nuclear strategy there was no longer an essential need for a peacetime military force in the Canal Zone. 'He thought that it was one of the areas where we were grossly over-extended, in an untenable position. And then, what with nuclear power having changed the whole concept of war, it seemed absurd that we had to keep an enormous garrison out there on the Canal, at this cost to our whole political position in that area. He thought we had to come out.'[19]

But a get-out had to be presented in a way that did not suggest a humiliating retreat. Eden 'was up against people who didn't see any need for us to give anything away anywhere . . . There were "little Empire" people there who even thought we should be extending the area of pink on the African map . . . And they were not negligible influences in the Party or in Parliament'.[20]

Eden was in a delicate position. As Churchill's preferred successor he was unable to depart too far from his mentor's views without putting his political inheritance at risk. Yet Churchill went along with the nonsense that came from the 'little Empire people' and from the COS. 'Our standard of living stems in large measure from our status as a great power and this depends to no small extent on the visible indication of our greatness, which our forces, particularly overseas, provide.'[21]

For the Suez Group, Julian Amery took heart from the barely concealed support of Churchill.

> There was a debate in 1953 in which Eden indicated that he was prepared to consider withdrawing from the Base and Zone. I made a very strong speech on the subject, the first of several, and John Strachey, who was interested in my speech, gave a detailed reply which enabled me, unusually, to catch the Speaker's eye again. I was fairly critical of Anthony, and rather to my surprise, the next morning the telephone rang and it was one of the secretaries at Number 10. I thought I was going to get a rocket, but he said that the Prime Minister had read my speech and thought it was very good. I used to run into him [Churchill] in the Division Lobby, and he would make it quite clear that he was dead against what Anthony was up to.[22]

The message was clear. There could be no unconditional withdrawal from Egypt if British prestige were to be safeguarded and Conservative right-wing opinion pacified. The excuse of Churchill, as an old man in no hurry whatsoever to depart the political scene, for staying on fastened on Eden's failure to come up with an acceptable response to challenges to British command over large parts of the Middle East. Eden's frustration, together with his fragile health, damaged his performance at a time when the range of problems facing him in Europe, the Far East and the Middle East, and the conflicting views of his cabinet colleagues on how to resolve them, called for diplomatic skills of high order.

Looking for a way out of his Middle East dilemma, Eden focused on winning American support for a joint strategy. Sympathetic noises came from Foster Dulles, but it soon became apparent that British and US ideas on the subject were far apart. Britain wanted a Middle East Command that took in bases in allied Iraq and Jordan as well as a continuing British presence in the Canal Zone. Prompted by the CIA station in Cairo, Dulles was sure that the Egyptians would veto any proposal for the stationing of British army units anywhere on Egyptian territory. In any case, his own thoughts on Middle East strategy were edging towards a northern tier of alliances bringing together Turkey, Iraq, Iran and Pakistan. If this were achieved, then the British entanglement in Egypt would be an irrelevance. Eden was moving to a similar conclusion but he was forever coming up against the diehards in his party.

In March 1953, Dulles reluctantly agreed to a Middle East defence package that included a desirable but, in American eyes, not essential British presence in the Canal Zone to ensure that the base could be made quickly operative in the event of war. It was now up to Britain and Egypt to come to terms on a phased evacuation of the bulk of British forces in Egypt. But without direct American involvement the talks hit stalemate as soon as the opening speeches were over. The British delegation wanted continuing control of the base installations; the Egyptians, with Nasser as their chief spokesman, demanded total peacetime control of the base. Negotiations dragged on until May 1953, when the Egyptian government was told that its proposals were unacceptable.

Two opposing developments followed in quick succession. As the British and Egyptians fell to mutual recriminations, Dulles embarked on a tour of North Africa and the Middle East, where he experienced at first hand the strength of anti-British feeling in the region. Once he had reported back to Eisenhower, the conclusion in the White House supported what the CIA had been saying all along, that the British negotiating stance was untenable. The president then wrote to Churchill to tell him so, holding out the prospect that the best that could be hoped for was 'a private undertaking by Egypt that the base would be made available in case of a general war'. Churchill reacted sharply.

> In the hope of reaching agreement with you and your predecessor we went over all this ground before and agreed to make a number of concessions to the Egyptian point of view. Our object in these discussions was not to obtain military or financial aid from the United States, but only their moral support in what we hoped would be a joint approach to the Egyptian dictatorship. However, you decided to defer to Egyptian objections . . . Since then we have been disappointed not to receive more support particularly in Cairo from your Government in spite of the numerous far-reaching concessions which we made in our joint discussions with you . . . We propose to await developments with patience and composure . . . I should have no objection to your advising the Egyptians to resume the talks, provided of course they were not led to believe that you were whittling us down, or prepared to intervene in a matter in which the whole burden, not nineteen-twentieths but repeat the whole burden, falls on us, and about which I thought we were agreed.

Churchill added what he hoped would be an appeal to touch the presidential heart strings.

> If at the present time the United States indicated divergence from us in spite of the measure of agreement we had reached after making so many concessions, we should not think we had been treated fairly by our great Ally, with whom we are working in so many parts of the globe for the causes which we both espouse. If as the result of American encouragement at this juncture or a promise or delivery of arms, Dictator Neguib is emboldened to

1. How *Punch* saw Nasser's Soviet arms deal.

2. Eden meets Nasser for the first and only time. Cairo, February 1955.

3. Anthony Nutting and Abdul Nasser congratulate each other after signing the Anglo-Egyptian Suez agreement, November 1954.

4. President Nasser is cheered by Egyptian crowds after announcing the nationalisation of the Suez Canal Company, 29 July 1956.

5. Israeli troops in a desert attack.

6. After the ceasefire a start is made on clearing the sunken ships blocking the Suez Canal.

7. Royal naval guns at action stations.

8. Royal Marines on the flight deck of HMS *Theseus* await the airlift to Port Said.

9. The Suez landings make headlines.

10. Tank landing craft in action.

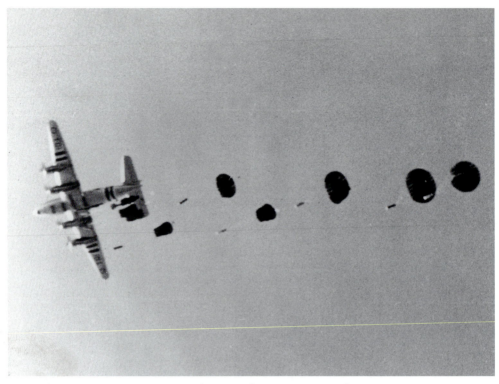

11. British paras drop on Port Said.

12. Paras on the move after seizing Gamal airport.

13. Egyptian army and navy prisoners rounded up during the initial landings at Port Said.

14. A British tank keeps watch over a street in Port Said.

15. Egyptian civilians find their way through the rubble of a bombed street.

translate his threats into action, bloodshed on a scale difficult to measure beforehand might well result, and for this we should feel no responsibility, having acted throughout in a sincere spirit for the defence not of British but of international or inter-Allied interests of a high order.[23]

In the light of developments in Iran, Churchill may have imagined that he was on a winning streak with Eisenhower and could afford to push his luck. Eden would have urged a more constructive response, but the foreign secretary was in hospital and unavailable for consultation. Confrontation with Egypt was now declared government policy. That not much would change in the short run was confirmed in July when Churchill suffered a stroke and Salisbury was left in sole command of foreign policy.

Eisenhower lost patience. The Iranian operation notwithstanding, Dulles was told to work up his own proposals for Middle East defence that would keep Britain on the sidelines. To avoid hard feelings, Britain was assured of support 'in principle', as Salisbury related after a meeting with Dulles in Washington.

Dulles then delivered a tedious lecture about the difference in outlook as between us and them towards countries like Egypt. There was a feeling in the United States that we still considered that the right way to deal with such people was to be completely stern and firm and to deliver a well-placed kick when they made difficulties. They felt that times had changed, etc., etc.

I found this rather hard to bear ... we had already offered enormous concessions to the Egyptians, and if our prolonged negotiations with them were viewed as a whole it would be seen that it was quite unjust to describe our attitude as inflexible ...

I said that the proposals ... on the duration of the agreement and the availability of the base ... represented what the Cabinet considered to be the limit of possible concessions. I recognised, however, that we could not ask the United States Government to stand with us on every word and comma of these formulae. What we did ask was that they should support the fundamental principles which were embodied in the formulae.

> This appeared to modify Dulles's attitude considerably. He said, and repeated, that our proposals had the 'general blessing' of the United States Government . . .[24]

But Dulles was already thinking beyond Egypt to a system of Middle East defence that would focus on the northern tier of states – Turkey, Iraq, Iran and Pakistan; what was soon to become the Baghdad Pact. Meanwhile, Britain had another try at persuading Egypt to accept terms that would satisfy the military while protecting the international status of the Suez Canal. There were three major points at issue – the duration of the agreement, the strength of the British contingent responsible for keeping the canal base in working order and the conditions under which the base could be operated. There was also the question of the status of the British forces. Around four thousand 'technicians' were needed to maintain the base, but while the Egyptians thought in terms of civilian employees the British insisted on military personnel with the right to wear uniforms. In the event, it was this relatively minor issue which brought the negotiations to a grinding halt.

By early September 1953 there was optimism in London that a deal could be struck on a seven-year agreement allowing eighteen months for the withdrawal of troops, and five and a half years with technicians managing the base. The Egyptians countered on points of detail on which compromise was easily within reach, but stuck fast to the principle of removing every symbol of military occupation. No uniforms were to be permitted. The exaggerated regard for the images of power that bedevilled British foreign policy throughout this period brought negotiations close to another breakdown. But whatever Churchill and Salisbury imagined, there could be no return to the old days when London gave the orders. The new regime in Cairo was well aware of its power to exert pressure where it hurt most.

Since the abrogation of the Anglo-Egyptian Treaty in October 1951, a practically continuous campaign had been waged by the Egyptians against British forces in the Canal Zone.

Activity has been directed against our installations, transport and communications. Cable cutting by some of these gangs has continued off and on throughout the period. The more exposed married quarters have suffered constantly from housebreaking and petty thieving. Throughout the whole area our forces have been contained in the Zone, unable to enter the Delta, and deeply committed to guard and internal security duties.[25]

Vehicle hijacking became so commonplace that British troops moved only in convoys and under escort. It was to get worse.

During the first fortnight of August, the Egyptian ban on the sale of goods to British forces was intensified; thefts of WD [War Department] vehicles increased in number; and there have been several incidents in which British soldiers have been shot in unprovoked attacks. The deliberate use of fire-arms by the Egyptians concerned is a new and disturbing development. There is secret evidence that these incidents are being planned by 'Liberation Units' encouraged by the Egyptian Army Intelligence Headquarters.[26]

Cabinet discussions on Egypt were dominated by Churchill and Eden arguing the equivalent of how many angels could dance on the head of a pin. What were to be the accepted working clothes for British technicians? Eden was happy to permit 'overalls or shirts and shorts, with rank distinctions; at other times: plain clothes'. Churchill thought this was going too far.

Within the Base installations and in transit between them British personnel will be entitled to wear the uniform of the Service to which they belong and to carry a weapon for their personal protection. Outside the area of the Base they will wear plain clothes.

Our Delegation might be authorised to inform the Egyptians orally that the British technicians when at work would normally wear overalls or shorts and shirts with rank distinctions. This statement should not, however, be included in the formal agreement itself.[27]

The cabinet sided with the prime minister.

The word in Egyptian diplomatic circles was to relax and to let the British work through their own problems while Nasser confidently expected that further concessions would soon be forthcoming. He was encouraged in his thinking by the more or less open support of the CIA. By now the relationship between Nasser and American intelligence was so close as to persuade the visiting side that the only obstacle to a fruitful relationship between America and Egypt was the British insistence on taking part. It was a neat scenario which called for a large measure of CIA naivety. To push Britain out of Egypt, Nasser was ready to accept help from wherever he could get it. But this was a long way from consenting to America taking over as the dominant force, which was what the CIA had in mind. Nasser was not about to exchange one occupying power for another. For the moment, however, it suited Nasser to humour CIA delusions. Once Britain was out of the way there would be time enough to rethink his strategy. Confident that the CIA, with a quiescent Secretary of State, could only strengthen his bargaining power with the British government, Nasser stuck to his demand for a total withdrawal of British troops from Egyptian soil. The best-laid plans in London for a compromise that would allow Britain to hold a place in the Canal Zone were thus destined for rejection.

The agony of British indecision, of trying in vain to square the circle, was palpable. While the Treasury fretted at the accelerating cost of the canal base, now up to around £500 million a year, the military establishment put the case for spending yet more by stationing troops in Bahrain to defend Britain's oil interests in the Persian Gulf. But did not this suggest that the canal base had outlived its usefulness? If it could not be used to deter Britain's enemies elsewhere in the Middle East, wherein lay its value? The chiefs of staff had a ready answer.

Although the Canal Zone would not be so valuable to us in the future, it was still worthwhile trying for prestige purposes alone to obtain our present objectives in the discussions with the

Egyptians; military as well as political prestige was involved. Although the Base would be almost completely defenceless from the air point of view it should be useful for supporting the smaller forces now envisaged.[28]

The increasingly absurd position in which Britain found itself, spending vast sums on a base it did not really need simply to prove that it could still perform as a leading power in the Middle East, was made yet more ludicrous by Churchill's eagerness to resort to strong-arm tactics to bring the Egyptians into line. As he told Eden:

The exit from all your troubles about Egypt, the Suez Canal, the Sudan, the Southern Sudan and later on in the Middle East will be found in deeds not words, in action not treaties. What security have we got that the Egyptians now breaking your Treaty of 1936 will keep any agreement you will make with them. On the contrary, it is almost certain that increasing bad blood will develop between us over the Sudan; that as our troops in the Canal Zone diminish in strength in carrying out the proposed agreement the Egyptians riots and petty attacks will continue or increase. We shall no longer have available the force to occupy Cairo, etc. All that will happen is that our troops would be tied up half way through their evacuation, and many in our own Party will be able to say 'we told you so', while the others mock.

Churchill now came up with his own ideas for settling the issue.

Find some reason to send 2 battalions of infantry and 3 or 4 squadrons RAF by air to Khartoum. The Governor could perhaps claim that public order required it as protections ... The thing is not to talk about this, but after close, secret, intimate study among a few *to do it*.

Once this sign of strength and action of policy and design has been shown all the Conservative troubles here would be quenched. The negotiations with Egypt would of course be broken off or lapse, but the evacuation would be declared and would begin none the less, and the redeployment of our troops to the extent of an Armoured Division of 4 Brigades in the Middle East and Cyprus could begin and proceed as fast as convenient . . .

The Egyptians should at the same time be told that all fresh additional expense caused by riotous attacks on our troops or rearguards and all damage done to the installations of the obsolescent base would be charged against their Sterling balances . . .

There is no alternative except a prolonged humiliating scuttle before all the world, without advantage goodwill or fidelity from those Egyptian usurpers to whom triumph is being accorded.[29]

Eden responded tactfully, pointing out that the sudden appearance of a military force in the Sudan might suggest that Britain was about to reoccupy the country so recently promised independence. 'On balance, disagreeable as all this undoubtedly is, to go for the Treaty still seems to be the only course. If this is so, I am sure that we can persuade the overwhelming majority of our Party, provided we stand fast and stand together. If the Treaty cannot be obtained then we shall have to fight it out.'[30]

Churchill's frustration in not being able to keep Eden in tow was accentuated by his failure to win unqualified American support for a hard line. Neither Eisenhower nor Dulles could make any sense of the fuss over who wore what at the canal base. When Churchill urged his 'dear friend' at the White House to hold back on economic aid to Egypt, Eisenhower retorted that having 'already made allocations to Israel we have little excuse to avoid moving in the case of the Arab countries'.[31] Military aid amounting to $1 million had stalled; was that not enough? Bureaucratic delays, however, deliberate or otherwise, held up American aid to Egypt until the new year, when Nasser made an unexpected concession. One of the original sticking points on an agreement was the terms on which the canal base could be activated. Britain argued for the widest possible set of circumstances while Egypt was determined to limit the action to meeting an attack on an Arab country. The latest Egyptian offer brought Turkey into the list of countries that would qualify for military backing from the canal base. The result was to throw the British cabinet into total confusion. It was not just the surprise of Nasser making a friendly gesture, though this was directed more at the USA, the likeliest source of economic aid, than at Britain. More to the point was the reaction in Washington if talks with Egypt remained deadlocked for no better reason than a failure to agree on a dress code for technicians.

From his vantage point close to the White House, the British ambassador, Sir Roger Makins, did his best to calm the tattered nerves of his political masters and to reassure them of America's good intentions.

> The mere existence of the United States as the world's greatest power inevitably exercises an influence throughout this area as in other parts of the world. This raises two questions. Are the Americans consciously trying to substitute their influence for ours in the Middle East? And, even if this is not their conscious policy now, is it nevertheless the inevitable conclusion of the present trend of events? I would say that the answer to the first question is 'no', and that the answer to the second will depend largely on our own efforts and in particular on the way in which we adjust ourselves to this new American factor in Middle Eastern politics.

Makins went on to argue that it was not entirely without justification that the USA was suspicious of British policy. There was a feeling 'that we have cast them for a supporting rôle, which is to consist of switching on or off the powerful current of their diplomatic and financial influence at a word from us. Or, to put it differently, they feel that we are asking them to accept limitations on their activity which we do not accept for ourselves'.

Examples included trying to negotiate an agreement about military supplies to Iraq which precluded the USA from playing any part in the equipment and training of the Iraqi armed forces, and training pilots for the Saudi Arabian air force, which the Americans considered to be as much their preserve as the British considered the Iraqi.[32]

Eden now recognised that the only way forward with Egypt was to abandon the idea of keeping troops at the canal base. Essential installations would have to be maintained by civilians who would rely on the Egyptian police for their security. In return for this concession Egypt would be expected to agree a two-year period for the withdrawal of British forces and equipment, a guarantee of free navigation on the Suez Canal and the right of re-entry to the base in case of an attack on Egypt or other Arab states and Turkey.[33] Eden proposed a twenty-year life for the deal as opposed to the seven years originally mooted.

Knowing that Churchill's acceptance of the terms was essential for cabinet approval and that he was likely to shift ground only if Washington approved, Eden urged the US ambassador to bring Eisenhower and Dulles onside. On 22 March, after Churchill had once again pressed for 'positive action', including the dispatch of troops to Khartoum to put pressure on Egypt, the cabinet went along with Eden's plan to the extent of talking to the Americans about maintaining the base with civilian labour.

It was beginning to dawn on ministers and senior military alike that Egypt was no longer central to the defence of the Middle East. With American strategy moving away from the deployment of conventional forces towards atomic weapons as the first line of defence, support grew for the 'Northern Tier' defensive associ-ation of states led by Turkey and Pakistan. As Sir James Bowker, British ambassador to Turkey, put it: 'It is hoped by this means to construct a roof over the vulnerable Middle East region which will help towards the containment of Russia in the cold war and eventually be able to play an effective part if a hot war should break out.'[34]

This effectively sidelined Egypt, suggesting that Britain was wasting its time trying to secure a lasting presence at the canal base. Moreover, as Bowker warned, 'it looks as if any further waiting on events in Egypt may result in our finding ourselves relegated to a secondary role in influencing the course of events'. The realisation that the USA was taking a lead that could leave Britain way behind brought a fresh sense of urgency to finalising a deal with Egypt. The matter in dispute was soon settled, and in Egypt's favour. In July 1954, the two countries finalised an agreement to last for seven years allowing for the canal base to return to a war footing in the event of an attack on Egypt, Turkey and any Arab country that was part of a joint defence treaty. British troops were to leave the base within twenty months, when civilian contractors would take over. An honourable mention for the Suez Canal acknowledged it as 'a waterway economically, commercially and strategically of international importance,' promising 'the determination of both parties to uphold the 1888 Convention guaranteeing the freedom of navigation of the Canal'.

At the signing, Nasser spoke of a 'new era of friendly relations'. He went on, 'We want to get rid of the hatred in our hearts and start building up our relations with Britain on a solid basis of mutual trust and confidence.' Eden responded with a personal message to Nasser:

> I am delighted that full agreement has now been reached between our two Governments. We welcome this important step forward towards a new understanding and friendship between our two countries. We shall do all in our power to make the agreement work in a spirit of co-operation and in the interests of peace. I know that is also the purpose of your Government.

9

The friendly exchanges that sealed the Suez Agreement were not enough to satisfy Eden's critics at home. The Suez Group persuaded twenty-eight members on the government side of the Commons to declare their intention of voting against 'any treaty with Egypt which involved the withdrawal of all fighting troops from the Suez Canal Area'.

When Captain Waterhouse rose to speak it was to prove himself the master of the grand, emotional gesture devoid of intelligence. 'This is not a sell-out,' he roared. 'It is a give-away.' And with characteristic disregard for veracity he plucked out of the air the figure of £500 million as the value of 'stores, plant and buildings . . . we have handed over to the Egyptians'. What would happen, he demanded to know, if this arsenal were used against Palestine? – meaning, presumably, Israel. Eden's response was to show that the question was misdirected. The days of heavy-manpower armies were over. What mattered was military flexibility and mobility. (At this point, in the light of what was to happen later at Suez, the chiefs of staff should have been paying closer attention.) 'What we need', concluded Eden, 'is a working base, not a beleaguered garrison.'

For its part the Labour opposition could not resist taking it out on Churchill for his 'scuttle', the word he had used when a Labour government had backed away from confrontation in Iran. Attlee poked fun by quoting recent Tory speeches that had rejected the very arguments used to seal an agreement that could have been achieved under Labour, and with far less hassle. Churchill glowered. In the debate he spoke up for his Foreign Secretary, saving his anger and frustration for private sessions with Julian Amery.

Having survived its parliamentary drubbing, the government could take some consolation in good news from the Sudan, where, in February 1953, a chance had been taken on resolving the dispute over Egyptian claims to sovereignty. A joint Anglo-Egyptian pledge of independence for Sudan after three years was the signal for each side to lobby for a regime sympathetic to its particular cause. Britain hoped that elections would lead to an anti-Egyptian government; Nasser expected a vote in favour of union with Egypt. As it happened, the new Sudanese government was predominantly pro-Egyptian but nonetheless decided on complete independence, which was finally achieved on 1 January 1956.

With Egypt temporarily off the diplomatic agenda, British attention turned to the wider issue of Middle East defence, with a last-ditch attempt to show that, notwithstanding defence cuts and the retreat from Suez, the country still had a role. The trouble was that every move seemed destined to cause offence in Cairo and to wreck any chance of building on the 'new era of friendly relations' contemplated by Nasser. The most sensitive issue was the proposed Northern Tier defence pact. It was here that Eden's diplomatic antennae began to fail him. In fairness, there were pressures that he found hard to resist. The Americans were keen; so too was the Anglophile prime minister of Iraq, Nuri el-Said, Britain's closest ally in the Middle East. His country's chief oil-producing regions, at Mosul and Kirkuk, were perilously close to the Soviet border. Nuri el-Said needed protection, but he was well aware that Britain alone was no longer capable of giving cover. Eden too could see advantages in an alliance that would accept Britain's leadership while helping to disguise its military weaknesses. Voices were raised urging speed. From Baghdad, the British ambassador, Sir Michael White, warned that while the political climate in Iraq was favourable to an agreement, this could not be expected to last. 'If we allow the pot to come off the boil we may never be able to bring it back again.'[1]

Inevitably, however, what was likely to be well received in Iraq would not go down well in Egypt, where Nasser was now the undisputed leader of the Revolutionary Council. It had been clear for some time that Nasser was winning out in a power struggle with Neguib, the ageing face of revolutionary Egypt. Neguib saw himself as the steadying influence in a governing body of young hotheads. But while he had support in the country, his brand of conservatism was not welcomed by the rising generation. His tendency to hark back to the old days when a strictly limited parliamentary system supported an autocracy set him at odds with Nasser and his friends, who recognised an attempt to put them under political restraint.

The infighting climaxed in April 1954 when Neguib conceded the premiership to Nasser. The consolation of holding on to the presidency did not last long. An assassination attempt on Nasser mounted by the Muslim Brotherhood was linked to Neguib, not in any specific way but with nods and winks, suggestion enough that he should be removed from office and put under house arrest. By the end of 1954 Nasser was unassailable. He was elected President of the Republic in June 1956, the first true Egyptian to rule the country since the time of the pharaohs. He was just thirty-eight.

Eden recognised that Nasser was there to stay, that for the foreseeable future he was the only Egyptian with whom they could do business. Where he went wrong was to underestimate Nasser in the wider scheme of things. It might have helped if he had known more about the cosy relationship between Nasser and the CIA, that while Foster Dulles was pushing Britain towards the Northern Tier as the first line of Middle East defence, the CIA (headed by his brother, it should be remembered) was encouraging Nasser to believe that he would be the centrepiece of any restructuring of regional alliances.

So far was the CIA in control of US policy in Egypt that Miles Copeland, an operative who was described by a colleague as 'almost breathless with impatience,' felt able to deter a new arrival at the CIA station from paying a courtesy call on the American ambassador. 'The old boy has been told this is our show. There's no reason for you to see him.'[2] When Henry Byroade, a stronger-minded ambassador, was sent to Cairo, James Eichelberger, as local CIA chief, and Copeland warned him off being too friendly with his British counterpart. Meanwhile, no attempt was made to dissuade Nasser from voicing his opposition to Middle East defence pacts such as the Northern Tier which cast Egypt as a junior partner. The only alternative that appealed to him was an Arab League with Egypt as the driving force.

Nasser was beginning to see himself as the embodiment of Arab nationalism, a vague concept held in limbo by the mutual rivalry of national leaders. Ironically, since it was by no means generally accepted that Egyptians could even be regarded as Arab, Nasser visualised Cairo as the focus of a new movement of pan-Arabism. Those who wished to discover more of his action programme had only to turn to a little book called *Egypt's Liberation* in which he imagined his country at the centre of 'a community of neighbouring peoples linked by all the material and moral ties possible'.[3] The community took in more than the Arab countries. Looking beyond 'the crossroads of the world, the thoroughfare of its traders and the passageway of its armies', Nasser could see a closer unity with Africa and, more widely again, to 'the domain of our brothers in faith ... building upon the strength of the Islamic tie that binds all Muslims'.[4]

Yet how could it be? What were these 'national and moral ties' that so galvanised Nasser? Jean Lacouture, a French journalist granted several interviews with the Egyptian leader, thought it was all an illusion. 'What did the Muslims of Nigeria, Indonesia, Pakistan, Turkey and Egypt have in common? Nothing. Nasser had more in common with Nehru and the Hindus of India than with Pakistan's Muslims.'[5]

But Nasser's grandiose dreams, taken altogether too seriously by friends and enemies alike, ran parallel with a more realistic vision of Egypt as an independent staging post between East and West. Nasser's leaning towards neutrality was inspired by his bond with Pandit Nehru, India's premier and foreign minister, and President Tito of Yugoslavia, who were seen as the founding members of the club of non-aligned states. From them Nasser learned that to succeed in international politics you did not have to make a hard and fast choice between communism and capitalism. Neutrality was a force every bit as strong and with greater popular appeal.

Nasser's evolving philosophy was noted in Britain but aroused little immediate interest. Immune to Egyptian sensitivities, Eden pressed ahead with plans for a regional defence structure that put Britain, with American backing, at the centre. If this required an Iraqi-led coalition, so be it.

Foremost among the sceptics was Evelyn Shuckburgh, head of Middle Eastern affairs at the Foreign Office.

> There is a difference of emphasis between the US and ourselves in this. They are vigorously pressing forward the Northern tier idea whereas we are not entirely convinced that this is wise having regard to Egyptian objections and the extreme instability of Arab opinion generally . . . No Middle East defence arrangement is likely to have much value unless it enjoys Egyptian support or participation, and we must therefore take account of Egyptian views as to how it should be organized . . . On the other hand, if Nuri does join the Northern tier, it may well be that the Egyptians will change their attitude in order not to be left behind in the queue for Western defence aid. In order words, if the American policy succeeds, it may be a great success but I think it is risky and may well fail. We must avoid being blamed for its failure.[6]

Shuckburgh put up another warning signal. In his view the first priority was a settlement of the Arab–Israeli issue which could not be achieved while both Egypt and Israel felt they were being sidelined. It did not pass notice in Tel Aviv that the Anglo-Egyptian agreement took no note of Israeli concerns. It was 'almost as if', said Prime Minister Moshe Sharett, 'Israel had no place among the countries of the Middle East'. Not only was Israel excluded from those countries that, under armed attack, entitled Britain to reactivate the Suez base, but Britain was also denied this right if Israel herself attacked one of the protected countries. The implication was that Egypt was free to deal with such events as it chose, which hardly accorded with Eden's boast that he was re-establishing friendship with the Arab countries 'without losing the friendship of Israel'.

Claims that Israel was already adequately protected by the 1950 Tripartite Agreement were greeted with a hollow laugh by the Zionist leadership. The agreement looked very well on paper, with the USA, Britain and France promising to come to the aid of Israel or any of the Arab countries should one side be attacked by the other. But even while Eden was telling the House of Commons that he knew 'few if any international instruments which carry as strong a commitment as this one', the jungle law of reprisal in Gaza and on the Jordanian–Israeli border went unchallenged by the tripartite signatories.

As for the Northern Tier, one of the rare points of agreement between Israel and Egypt was that both thought it a thoroughly bad idea. Israel claimed that it was only 'liable to encourage Arab belligerent tendencies, foment aggressive ambitions and undermine the peace and stability of the area'. This was a line that neither America nor Britain was prepared to accept, but the fact remained that some effort had to be made to convince the Arab nation of Israel's right to exist. Eden argued for the Northern Tier as a benefit to Israel, preparing the way for a settlement of all border issues.

An Anglo-American plan codenamed Alpha began to take shape. The idea was to satisfy Egyptian demands for a land link to Jordan and the rest of the Arab world by persuading Israel to surrender the Negev, a wedge of mountains and desert connecting, through the Gulf of Aqaba, to the Red Sea and the Indian Ocean. What in other circumstances might have been described as an endearing innocence characterised these diplomatic fumblings. For one thing, Nasser wanted much more if he were to sell an agreement to the Egyptian people. For another, the Negev was not just any old slice of arid land but an area with Jewish settlers, among them David Ben-Gurion. The first Israeli prime minister and soon to be prime minister again, Ben-Gurion had a vision.

He was firmly convinced that the wilderness of the Negev, empty
of people, would one day become a vital centre of Israel development. The exploitation of potash, phosphates and other minerals
would provide the basis of large industrial plants whose products
would be carried over the desert to Eilat, and this route would
serve as an 'overland Suez Canal'. The bare Negev and the
open Eilat seemed to him to offer the most fruitful development
prospects for Israel.[7]

Even with an offer of economic aid for Israel, help in resettling
Palestinian refugees and a guarantee of frontiers, Alpha was a
non-starter, though negotiations dragged on until March 1956,
when Evelyn Shuckburgh, who had led the way in projecting
Alpha as the only hope for Middle East peace, allowed his frustration to spill out into a paper written for Sir Ivone Kirkpatrick, his
civil service chief at the foreign office.

> The active effort to find a Palestine settlement by negotiation
> between Nasser and Ben-Gurion has been the (hidden) linch-pin
> of our Middle East policy. So long as these efforts had any
> prospect of succeeding we were able to avert our eyes from the
> basic dilemma in which we stood. The collapse of Alpha last
> week has removed the linch-pin. We now have nothing which we
> can offer the Israelis as an alternative to the terrible choice –
> either to attack soon or to be slowly strangled by the unreconciled
> Arab world, which grows stronger every day in wealth, self-
> confidence and Soviet arms. We are left without a Middle East
> policy of any kind.

With no settlement in sight and no prospect of peace:

> The tension and despair of the Israeli position will grow rapidly
> and public opinion in the UK and US will find it impossible not
> to support and arm them, despite the appalling consequences of
> doing so . . . In fact, unless the Israelis commit an aggression, we
> are becoming daily more deeply committed to go to war against
> a Soviet-armed Arab world as soon as they feel strong enough
> or fanatical enough to attack Israel. Every time we refer to the

Tripartite Declaration as an 'obligation' to defend Israel, we get
ourselves more deeply in this position.[8]

Shuckburgh could see only two possible ways forward: either to
impose settlement on Israel that required sacrifices of territory (a
not very practical suggestion) or to seek the overthrow of Nasser
in the hope of finding a more accommodating successor.

Kirkpatrick took the point. A long-time associate of Eden in
his years as foreign secretary, Kirkpatrick was of the tough school
of mandarins. It was to his credit that he had allied himself with
the anti-appeasers in the 1930s, but whatever his other qualities
as a quick and decisive thinker, it is hard to imagine anyone more
unsuitable in charge of the Foreign Office at a period when Britain
needed to adjust to a more modest role in world affairs. Knowing
little of the Middle East, he was nonetheless quick to make sweeping judgements. 'I don't trust those Arabs,' he told Macmillan,
who shot back, 'But you say that about every foreigner that is
mentioned.'[9] Having decided that Nasser was the foremost
troublemaker in the Middle East, Kirkpatrick quickly adopted the
Shuckburgh line that the Egyptian dictator had to go. It was an
objective he pushed with Eden as the cautious foreign secretary
and more successfully with Eden as the less cautious prime
minister.

For the moment, however, the diplomatic initiative passed to
Baghdad, where it was announced that Iraq and Turkey were
about to sign a defence pact. American pressure on Britain to
implement the Northern Tier proposal now intensified, while at a
conference of Arab prime ministers held in Cairo from 22 January
Egyptian opposition was made only too clear, prompting the
British ambassador to report to London that 'the unscrupulous
propaganda in which the controlled Press and Radio and even
Egyptian spokesmen at the conference table indulged, greatly
shocked not only independent observers but also the majority of
the Arab leaders taking part in the Conference'.[10]

In an attempt to dispel Egyptian fears, Eden suppressed his
growing aversion to Nasser long enough to discover what a close

encounter could achieve. In February, as part of a round trip to Bangkok for a meeting of the South-East Asia Treaty Organisation, Eden stopped off at Cairo for an informal two-hour chat with Nasser. According to the foreign secretary's dispatch to Churchill, Nasser was 'forthright and friendly', though 'entirely negative on the question of an ultimate settlement with Israel'. While 'very little progress [was made] on the subject of the Turco-Iraqi pact', Nasser 'made it plain that his interest and sympathy were with the West'.[11]

Eden had indeed made every effort to impress Nasser, showing off his knowledge of Arabic (he had an Oxford first in oriental languages) and presenting his host with a signed copy of the new canal base agreement. (One can imagine his silent response – 'Just what I've always wanted.') But it was more than Eden could manage to treat Nasser as an equal. The sensible opening would have been for Eden to present himself at a venue of Nasser's choosing. He was, after all, the guest. Instead, the Egyptian leader was invited, though it was seen as more of a summons, to the British embassy, still the grandest building in Cairo and the highly visible reminder of the days of British domination. 'What elegance,' Nasser observed ruefully. 'It was made to look as if we were beggars and they were princes.'

According to Woodrow Wyatt, who later interviewed Nasser for UK television, the Egyptian was kept waiting in the embassy drawing room.

> Eden entered and called him Colonel Nasser, which he hated. He walked up and down in front of the seated Nasser and lectured him on British policy in the Middle East and where Egypt fitted into it. He invited no comment or discussion, and when his near-monologue was over looked at his watch: 'I am afraid I must go now. I have to change for dinner. I thought you would like to know what our policy is. It's been very nice meeting you, Colonel Nasser.'
>
> Nasser said to me, 'I know I'm not very important and Egypt is not very important, but I was hurt. The Russians sent me

copies of secret correspondence with Washington. When I asked why, they said it was because Egypt is a very important country. I know it is only flattery, but at least they take the trouble to pretend to treat us as equals.'[12]

The image of a self-effacing Nasser being forced to endure a snobbish put-down was designed to win left-wing sympathy in Britain. But this was to impute too much blame to Eden. A more reliable version of the meeting was recorded by Mohamed H. Heikal, an Egyptian journalist with close links to Nasser. After drinks and social chat about Arab proverbs, the two leaders, advisers in tow, had dinner. The conversation turned to Middle East affairs, with Eden emphasising the unity of interest between Britain and the USA.

> Finally, before the party broke up, Eden said he would like to get clear in his mind the conclusions he thought they had reached: 'First, you appreciate the importance of the defence of the Middle East. Second, you have no objection to what Nuri [Iraq] is proposing to do provided he keeps it to himself.' [i.e. not involve other Arab countries in a defence pact.] Nasser said yes to both. For all his sophistication and expertise Eden had throughout given the impression of being on the defensive. He was dealing with an entirely new breed of Arab leaders – revolutionaries who owed nothing to his country or government, single-minded in their aims and confident in their ability to implement them. It was obviously going to be quite an undertaking for Eden and his colleagues to take the measure of these new men.[13]

Back in London, and presumably forgetting his conversation with Nasser, Eden brushed aside objections to an early decision on Middle East defence. On 15 March, in the absence of an alternative plan – one that might have avoided the implied exclusivity of a regional grouping – cabinet approval was given to Britain joining the Turco-Iraqi Pact. By extension of existing treaties, Pakistan and Iran were soon drawn in to what now became known as the Baghdad Pact. With every justification historians have been hard on the Baghdad Pact. The motivation was all wrong. 'The pact was to be the basis, allegedly, for uniting the Middle East states against the Soviet menace. In reality it was an attempt to fix another layer of prestige and credibility to Britain's declining economic and military power.'[14]

The reaction in Cairo was predictably hostile. Choosing to see the pact as a conspiracy against Egypt, Nasser launched his own defence group incorporating Syria and Saudi Arabia with a joint Arab army under Egyptian command. The real strength of the alliance was almost entirely illusory, but appearances were all. The British ambassador in Cairo, Sir Ralph Stevenson, hastened to assure Nasser that the Baghdad Pact was not anti-Egyptian and that furthermore no attempt would be made to recruit other Arab states. Fortunately for Stevenson he retired before he had to eat his words. Later in the year it fell to Sir Gerald Templer, Chief of the Imperial General Staff, to try to nudge Jordan into the Baghdad Pact.

Best known for a much-lauded success of British post-war colonial policy, Templer had won a decisive victory against communist insurgents in Malaya. He was a gifted, if short-tempered, field commander who was woefully ill-suited to a diplomatic mission, least of all one that depended on knowing the subtleties of Middle East politics. 'Shouting and banging the table'[15] to make his point that it was about time for Jordan to come off the fence, he delivered what he imagined was his *coup de grâce* with a broad hint that further prevarication would lead to a cut-off in the supply of arms.

News of the Templer meeting soon reached Nasser, who naturally assumed a double-cross. So too did Humphrey Trevelyan, the latest British ambassador in Cairo, who, like his predecessor, had been told to reassure Nasser that there were no plans to widen the scope of the pact.[16] When the truth came out, Trevelyan's protests to London were ignored. A stepping up of Egyptian propaganda in Jordan, backed by strategically placed pockets of Saudi money, brought predictable results – riots in the streets and the fall of the government. Nasser now took the lead in offering to supplant Britain as Jordan's paymaster, the last thing that Eden wanted.

It was not only in relations with Egypt that the Baghdad Pact caused discord. Israel too was made increasingly nervous by the parcelling up of the Middle East into rival blocs that put the Jewish state at the centre of any conflagration. Hopes of a peace deal with Egypt had all but disappeared. Expectations had been raised when the combative Ben-Gurion had retired to his kibbutz to be succeeded by Moshe Sharett, a former career diplomat who was prepared to believe the best of his Arab neighbours. But in February 1955, Sharett was undermined by the failure of a plan by the Israeli secret service to force the British to stay in Egypt, and thus restrain Nasser, by creating the impression of political anarchy. Known as the Lavon affair after Pinhas Lavon, the maverick minister of defence who acted without reference to Sharett, a plot to fire-bomb public buildings went horribly wrong when, mistiming an ignition, a saboteur set fire to himself and was promptly arrested. More arrests followed, and on 25 July, there were reports in the Arab press of the rounding up of an Israeli espionage network responsible for arson attacks throughout Egypt. The subsequent trial led to two death sentences and six long prison sentences.

The embarrassment in Israel was acute. So too was the feeling that none of this would have happened if Ben-Gurion had remained at his post. Ever louder calls for his return persuaded Sharett to reshuffle his government. With the departure of Lavon, the way was clear for Ben-Gurion to take over as defence minister. But there was no letting up in the pressure on Sharett. A week after Ben-Gurion was restored to office, the Israeli army carried out a massive raid on Egyptian headquarters in Gaza. A reprisal for fedayeen attacks, the result was yet more violence along the border. Sharett's appeal for moderation and restraint went unheard. Elections in July showed increased support for Ben-Gurion's tough line. Three months later he was back as prime minister.

Immediately there was talk of Israel anticipating Egyptian

aggression by mounting a preventive war. The arms race between Egypt and Israel took on a renewed intensity, with both sides ready to pay top prices for modern weapons. The defence arrangements initiated by Britain for the Middle East were looking increasingly irrelevant.

Battered and bowed by those it was said to protect, the Baghdad Pact was further weakened by a less than enthusiastic endorsement by one of its chief promoters. After the deal was done, the USA did some nimble backtracking. By refusing to store nuclear weapons in bases not under American control, the deterrent effect of the pact on Soviet aggression was all but lost. In a surprise attack Moscow would have been able to direct two nuclear strikes before a Western response could be mounted. But the US military's proprietorial attitude towards the nuclear deterrent was secondary to the belated realisation that the pact found no favour in Israel and was strenuously opposed by the Zionist lobby in Congress.

If anything further were needed to prove that the Baghdad Pact was misconceived, it came a few years later with the acknowledgement that it was based on a misreading of Soviet ability to shape affairs in the Middle East.

> [It] is strange to think now that we were very, very impressed with the threat of Soviet incursion into the Middle East, as there had been a Soviet incursion into Eastern Europe. We were building up defences against them everywhere else, and there was a huge, great gap in this area, as it seemed to us. And therefore what we must do was try and build up a defence system . . . against Russian incursion in that area. Now you can see that was a false fear, because Russian incursion into the Middle East was not stopped by any defensive system. It was stopped by the nature of Middle East opinion, Arab nationalism and so on, which was not clearly seen by us then.[17]

The error was compounded by underestimating the strength of Arab nationalism.

We had not really seen even the nationalism, the perfectly straight nationalism. Some of us saw it. I'm not saying we were brighter, but certainly in the Foreign Office we could see that nationalist opinion had got to be satisfied with any arrangement we made. But we didn't really see it. We didn't really understand that it was a humiliation to Nasser to be asked to join a defence treaty with us and the Iraqis. We wholly failed to see the revival of Muslim extremism.[18]

While the politicians and diplomats busied themselves with making a difficult situation in the Middle East even knottier, British troops sweated out their last days alongside the Suez Canal. Their final departure took place earlier than scheduled, on 13 June 1956, five days ahead of the deadline.

It was a friendly and informal parting. Dressed in his workaday khaki drill, Brigadier John Lacey said a smiling good-bye to his three companions and stepped into a launch off the quay of the former Navy House, Port Said. Thus departed the last commander of British Troops in Egypt, watched only by a chubby little Egyptian colonel of police and by two Englishmen, the consul and a shipping agent. The launch chugged out to a ship moored in the mouth of the Suez Canal, the chartered tank landing ship, *Evan Gibb,* inelegant but strangely imposing in the fleeting orange glow radiated by the sun as it climbed the roof line of Port Fuad. Preceded by an army table, on which Britain's last foothold in Egypt had been signed away, the Brigadier climbed aboard to join the seventy-eight officers and men already embarked, the remnant of an army that had been in occupation for seventy-four years. There were neither cheers nor jeers as their ship steamed into the Mediterranean. The inhabitants of Port Said yawned, stretched or went on sleeping, unaware that the day that dawned was the one for which they had clamoured so long.

Not until 8 a.m. did the ascent of the green and white flag of Egypt up the staff of Navy House bring the joyous message home to the people. The town was in an uproar of delight. The

British had gone, and to hasten them on their way the Egyptian press thundered their valedictory insults. 'Egypt has ended her suffering,' rejoiced Cairo's oldest paper, *Al Ahram*. Others preferred to dwell more on the discomfiture of the erstwhile tormentors with such offerings as, 'With their tails between their legs, the cur dogs slink away'.[19]

For the first time since 525 BC no flag or banner flew in Egypt displaying the authority of a foreign overlord.

It is unlikely that this singular fact registered with Anthony Eden. Into his third month as prime minister of Britain, he had too many other matters to worry about.

IO

Churchill had surrendered the premiership on 5 April 1955. To say that he was dragged kicking and screaming from the Cabinet Room is not a wild exaggeration. Up to the last, he was looking for an excuse, however lame, to stay on. After years of grooming Eden for the succession, Churchill now made known his view that his Foreign Secretary of ten years was not up to the big job. His long-standing private secretary, John Colville, noted 'a cold hatred of Eden who, [Churchill] repeatedly said, had done more to thwart him and prevent him pursuing the policy he thought right than anybody else'.[1] Not least in relation to Egypt, he might have added.

But whoever had been in place to take over, Churchill would have found reasons to object. He was finished; he knew it and he did not like it one little bit, as Evelyn Shuckburgh, then Eden's private secretary, discovered in a chat with Jane Portal, who managed the day-to-day diary for Churchill.

> She now admits that the old boy, whom she loves dearly, is getting senile and failing more and more each day. She says he is open to constant influence and is easily stirred up by his entourage. On Egypt and the Sudan it is Christopher Soames who is egging him on. Life is a misery to him; he half kills himself with work, cannot take in the papers he is given to read and can hardly get up the stairs to bed. Yet he thinks he has a mission on three subjects – Russia, Egypt and the atomic bomb. It is impossible for him to resign, because he can no longer write, dreads solitude and oblivion, fears rest. But he will soon die.[2]

As early as April 1954 Shuckburgh was noting Churchill's tendency to meander. A session at Chequers ended with the prime minister in characteristic depression. '"We have thrown away our glorious Empire." And so the old boy toddled off, looking like a granny of about a hundred.'[3]

'I have sent for you', Churchill told Sir William Hayter, Britain's ambassador to Moscow, 'in order to make your acquaintance.' But it was the third outing for Sir William and the third occasion on which Churchill had said the same thing.[4]

In the end it was the collective Tory fear of giving Labour the advantage in the forthcoming general election ('In my view,' Rab Butler told Churchill, 'another Labour Government would be a disaster from which the country might never recover') which elbowed the old warrior into retirement. So long assumed to be next in line, Eden easily saw off Butler, the only likely rival. At noon on 6 April 1955, Anthony Eden went to Buckingham Palace to receive royal approval for his appointment as prime minister.

Shrewdly investing his political inheritance, Eden called an early election, which the Tories won with an increased majority, up from nineteen seats to sixty-one, while garnering their biggest share of the popular vote since 1935. For once, what was happening abroad had a greater impact on voters' intentions than events at home. A war-weary public responded warmly to a ubiquitous poster portrait of the handsome Eden over the slogan 'Working for Peace'. And so he was. Just how effective his peacemaking efforts would turn out to be was open to question, but for the moment superficial appearances showed Eden in a glowing light. There was more. A feeling across the country that 'Anthony deserved his turn' was strengthened by a voter-friendly budget and the failure of the Labour opposition to capitalise on the weaknesses of a national economy that was low on productivity and high on foreign debt.

It was not long after the election before doubts set in. An opportunity to put his own stamp on government was lost when Eden simply rearranged the old ministerial faces in a different order. At the top the biggest change was the promotion of Harold Macmillan from defence to the foreign office. Macmillan was clearly a politician on the rise. His greatest success to date had been as housing minister, when he had overseen the building of a record number of new homes. A genial, avuncular image disguised a toughness that allowed Macmillan to back Eden just as long as it took to secure the succession. Macmillan was to play a critical and, for Eden, an ill-fated role in the Suez crisis. So too was Selwyn Lloyd, who was plucked from the junior ministerial ranks to succeed Macmillan at defence. Lloyd's weakness of character and intellect, which were to emerge all too obviously as the Eden government unravelled, coexisted with an uncritical devotion to the prime minister, a trait that in good times could be praised as loyalty and in bad as a fatal shortage of moral fibre. Lloyd could at least claim the distinction of an ordinary background, 'a middle class lawyer from Liverpool', as Macmillan sniffily referred to him.[5] Of the rest of the eighteen-strong cabinet, nine were Etonians and sixteen had been to Oxford or Cambridge. Those, like Eden, who had served in the Great War, six in all, were given to tiresome monologues on Britain's glory days.

A government of middle-aged and elderly gents who spent much of their time exchanging snobbisms was so close to the Churchillian model as to invite a comparison between the two leaders that was invariably hostile to Eden. How could it be otherwise when he was up against the 'greatest living Englishman'? The anti-Eden movement was promoted by Randolph Churchill, the errant son, a drunken maverick who had mastered the art of popular journalism. In private and not so private gatherings he referred to 'Jerk Eden'. Beyond a mild rebuke for slanging off 'my friend', Churchill senior made no attempt to rein in his offspring, who snatched at every opportunity to cast Eden in a poor light. He had been at the job for some time. In the mid-1930s, when Eden, already in government, was widely tipped for high office, he came in for a dose of vitriol from Churchill, who saw him as a political climber, adept merely at aping the discredited elders of the Tory Party. 'The Anthony Edens will win every time, as the old gang will always encourage mediocrity rather than brilliance. Real ability will always be suppressed. Hence the only chance is to be a rebel and to seek to master the old men, not to serve them.'[6]

It hardly needs adding that the rebel Randolph most admired was his own father. A quarter of a century on, to hold Eden in an unfavourable light as against the elder Churchill had less justification. To bemoan Eden's delicate health was to ignore Churchill's succession of heart attacks, which reduced him to gibbering incompetence. As for Eden's lack of experience in domestic affairs (he had never held a home ministry) and weak grasp of economics, these were certainly defects in a prime minister, but while Churchill could claim wider ministerial exposure, his mismanagement of the economy – allowing inflation to take hold for the sake of peace with the unions – did not suggest a leader who understood financial matters.

Inside the government, the more telling criticism of Eden was of his acute sensitivity, his aversion to open discussion even in cabinet, his petulance in always wanting his own way and his violent tantrums when he failed to get it. Eden's biographers tend to blame his temper on his father, a notoriously eccentric aristocrat whose well-documented outbursts reveal a wayward character. But the stories about him suggest a sense of fun that was entirely absent in his son. It is hard not to warm to a baronet who hurls his set-fair barometer out into the pouring rain with the injunction 'There, see for yourself, you bloody fool', or who delivers to his butler a:

List of Grievances for Mr House's Consideration

Cold Soup.
Fish not done.
Mutton tough.
Cabbage cold.
Wild duck tough, cold and high.

Floor covered with bread and butter.

No toothpicks.

Dirty dishes.

No ice to the butter.

Small soda instead of large.

Small spoon instead of large for gravy.

> *Sic transit Gloria mundi.*
> House to the rescue.
> Amen.[7]

Anthony Eden was not possessed of such wit. His petulance was of a more malicious nature, causing hurt even when, as was his custom, he later offered profuse apologies.

The instability that came with an ungovernable temper was accentuated by his thin-skinned reaction to any suggestion that he was failing to match his illustrious predecessor. This led him against his nature and, in what Evelyn Shuckburgh called 'a sort of perverted way,'[8] to model himself on Churchill, at the same time putting himself alongside the Tory far-right wing, who professed Churchill to be their hero and who were adept at banging the patriotic drum.

The shift in Eden's political stance was to show most obviously in Britain's relations with Egypt and the Middle East. Whereas, as foreign secretary, Eden had pursued a policy of compromise and accommodation, often in direct opposition to Churchill, now that he was in 10 Downing Street a harder line was adopted. Churchill had been tough; so too had Eden to be tough.

The change was gradual but, early on, sufficiently perceptible to encourage the Tory diehards to hope for more while worrying the left of the party, not to mention a swath of younger, radical voters who were not obsessed by the Hitler war, that Eden and his colleagues were out of touch with opinion beyond the claustrophobic precincts of Westminster.

This judgement was seemingly endorsed at the end of 1955

when the forty-nine-year-old Hugh Gaitskell was elected leader of the Labour Party, taking over from the visibly ageing Clement Attlee. Though from the same private school and upper-middle-class background, Eden and Gaitskell were opposites in almost every regard. Eden saw himself as the pragmatic realist, sophisticated but never, like Gaitskell, the lofty intellectual and social engineer who knew what was best for you though you may not have known it yourself. Allowing for some truth in this caricature, Gaitskell gave a shot of energy to the Labour Party and to a younger generation of politicians, who were eager for social reforms undreamt of by Eden's greybeards.

Labour's rebirth prompted Eden to reassess his own front-bench team. With economic troubles in the forefront of electoral concerns, it was time for a change at the treasury, where, as chancellor, Rab Butler was into his fifth year. With the recent death of his wife, the languid Butler was more than usually withdrawn, an image of complacency where firm command was needed. The obvious candidate to take on the nation's finances was Harold Macmillan, the only senior Tory with an unassailable record of getting things done. But Macmillan was fresh into the job of foreign secretary. It seemed perverse to move him after just nine months in office. Eden concluded otherwise. He may indeed have persuaded himself that Macmillan was best equipped to hold the purse strings, but this was not necessarily the determining factor.

In his short time at the FO, Macmillan had made his mark, not least in forging a relationship with the mercurial John Foster Dulles, an achievement well beyond Eden's powers. If this was a source of irritation for the prime minister, how much more so was Macmillan's determination to go his own way on the international circuit without bothering to refer to Eden for directions. This did not stop Eden from meddling when the mood took him, but he must have known that his advice was not welcome. Moving Macmillan to the treasury, a department that did little to excite Eden, must have appealed as a way of restoring his command of foreign affairs – so long, of course, that a sufficiently compliant replacement for Macmillan could be found. As it happened, waiting in the wings was the ideal candidate, one who was only too ready to speak with his master's voice. The prize went to Selwyn Lloyd, Eden's 'office boy', as Labour dubbed him.

By his own testimony Lloyd was ill suited to the international scene. He told the story of how, in 1951, Churchill had put him into the Foreign Office as a junior minister.

> All my activity had been dealing with the finance bill, fighting the budgets as secretary of the Conservative finance committee and I expected to go to the treasury. Then I got a message that I was to go down to Chartwell to see Mr Churchill. When I got there, he said: 'We haven't seen much of one another, but I hear well of you and I want you to be minister of state at the Foreign Office.' I really could have been knocked over with the proverbial feather, because it had never entered my head. So I said: 'But, sir, I think there must be some mistake. I've never been to a foreign country except in war. I don't speak any foreign language. I don't like foreigners.' (That was a view which I later changed.) 'I've never spoken in a foreign affairs debate, I've never even listened to one.' He said: 'Young man, those all seem to me to be positive advantages.' And he told me to go off to the Foreign Office, where Mr Eden was waiting for me. A friend had lent me a car with a driver, and we went up to London and I said: 'Take me to the foreign office.' He said: 'Where is it, sir?' and I suddenly realised I didn't know. So we had to stop in Whitehall and ask a policeman![9]

It made for a good after-dinner joke but the cynic might wonder why, after Lloyd had ticked off his disqualifications, he did not turn down Churchill's offer. But this would be to miss the point of Lloyd's self-deprecating humour, which he used to try to deflect criticism. 'Dear old Selwyn. He knows his limitations but he's a decent chap for all that.' The effect, as Lloyd was well aware, was for his colleagues to underrate him. Just as it was not in his nature to reject any opportunity for advancement, so it was against his instinct to say or do anything that was not to his own advantage.

As a civil servant and one of four private secretaries, Donald Logan tried hard to understand Lloyd.

> He enjoyed very much the access that he had to prominent people and social life. He enjoyed lively and intelligent conversation. But he had no time whatever for ordinary small talk. People in the Foreign Office would be called in to see him for the first time, and they would be surprised that Selwyn would receive them without much sign of appreciation, and might even appear grumpy. Within a few minutes, they'd be out of the room, wondering what on earth was wrong with the man, or what they had done wrong. They would not have got that impression from Eden and Macmillan. However, being with him [Lloyd] day in and day out as a Private Secretary, you quickly realised that the piece of paper that official had offered Lloyd, and which he had put aside with a cursory reading, had remained very much in his mind, and a day or so later he would ask you to dig it out. The initial reaction was a sort of defensive shield, because he did not have the ease or smoothness to relate in the customary way to people in the Service. Very often he would resort to a sort of banter or joke to try and lighten the atmosphere, but a joke in which the stranger could not easily join. Being closely associated with him in all sorts of ways, personal and professional, you could see that this was a shield, and that he was a different man.[10]

Other diplomatic and political associates were less understanding; political opponents were particularly harsh. His parliamentary initiation as foreign secretary was rough. Richard Crossman observed him from the opposition benches. 'This poor little fellow was rattled and harassed, like a man in the water who had just got his head above the surface but is swallowing a gulp every now and then.'[11]

It was a line soon to be taken up by Lloyd's severest press critics. Writing in *The Spectator* under the pseudonym Taper, Bernard Levin referred to Lloyd as 'Hoylake UDC', a less than flattering reference to his early experience as a local councillor, the only political job, suggested Levin, that matched his talent.

William Hayter, one of the most senior of British ambassadors, found it impossible to take Lloyd seriously.

> It was clear that he'd been put into the Foreign Office as a kind of Minister of State. If I came on leave at that time, it was Eden who I used to go and see. I'd pay a formal call on Selwyn, but it was Eden I would talk to. It was clear that he had no personal initiative and was entirely under Eden's thumb . . . [who] . . . had complete control, as far as I could see. He had almost forgotten that he wasn't Foreign Secretary. On the whole, the Foreign Office is an obedient department. It does what the Foreign Secretary wants it to do, and it was clear at this time that the Foreign Secretary was the Prime Minister.[12]

Macmillan could barely disguise his disappointment at losing out to Lloyd. He felt at home in the foreign office, where he imagined himself making a real contribution to international accord. The consolation was the almost certain knowledge that he was now second in line to Eden, ready to take over should events create room at the top.

Eden's reshuffle raises a tantalising hypothetical question. If Macmillan had remained as foreign secretary would there have been a Suez crisis? His biographer, Alistair Horne, thinks not,[13] on the assumption that Macmillan would have been more aware of the importance of winning over opinion in Washington. Even so, when it had come to a showdown between Saudi Arabia and Britain's client Gulf sheikhdoms over the supposedly oil-rich Buraimi Oasis, he had sent in troops from Abu Dhabi and Muscat commanded by British officers, having 'thought it wiser not to consult the United States or even the old Commonwealth territories about our decision'.[14] The irritation in Washington was ignored by Macmillan. Then again, Macmillan's voice was one of the loudest, if not the loudest, in urging Eden to be tough with Nasser on the assumption that the Americans would eventually join in. What might have made the difference was Macmillan's powerful instinct for survival. Also, he was less in awe of the Churchillian legend.

With his lapdog at the foreign office, Eden felt free to indulge his passion for trying to solve worldwide problems without having to worry too much about ministerial sensitivities or boring details. One of his first moves was to send Robin Turton, one of Lloyd's parliamentary under-secretaries, on a tour of the Middle East. 'This is a great opportunity [for you] to find some solution to our many problems.'[15] In the event Turton came back not so much with answers but with an added load of problems that Eden had not even begun to consider. In Israel he picked up on rumours that Egypt was about to take delivery of large quantities of Soviet arms. Another Arab–Israeli war seemed to be imminent. Moving on to Cairo, Turton was given the charm treatment, with Nasser assuring him that he had no desire for war with Israel, that he was in secret negotiations to avoid such a calamity. A rumoured arms deal with Russia was sidestepped with an appeal to Britain to help push ahead Nasser's ambition to revolutionise Egypt's economy and to release the country from its poverty trap. The means for achieving this was to trap the flood waters of the Nile behind the Aswan High Dam.

Not since the days of the pharaohs had the Egyptians under-taken an engineering enterprise as ambitious as the Aswan Dam. More impressive than the Pyramids and much more useful, the new structure would be 250 feet high at the centre and 3 miles wide. The lake formed by the dam would be 300 miles long. Its purpose was to reclaim 1,300,000 acres of desert and to raise the agricultural potential of another 700,000 acres, as well as provide hydroelectric power for new industries.

The idea had been around for some time. A smaller dam had been built at the end of the nineteenth century, and in Farouk's time plans for a High Dam had been drawn up. As with so many other grand schemes that attracted the monarch's interest, the will to act was weaker than good intentions. Until, that is, Nasser came along. Via his CIA friends, he lobbied successfully for the money to pay for a new survey. When this showed positive results the serious business of raising the necessary $1.3 billion investment got under way. A mix of grants and loans from the

USA, Britain and the World Bank was agreed in principle and a consortium of British, German and French engineering firms was commissioned to carry out the work.

But while courting Western finance for the Aswan Dam, Nasser was equally impatient for means to equip his armed forces with modern weapons. Promises had been made by the USA and Britain. Egypt's requests would be taken seriously – in time. Meanwhile, Nasser was fobbed off with occasional deliveries of near-obsolete armoury while stores at the canal base, which were otherwise serving no useful purpose but were due for renewal, were denied to the Egyptians and instead shipped back to Britain. In Washington it was amazing to those who were not used to diplomatic delaying tactics to find how many declarations of approval from congressional and other committees had to be secured before arms deliveries could begin.

In June 1955, responding to rumours that Russia might act as an alternative supplier of weapons, Eisenhower finally gave the go-ahead for an arms order worth $27 million, but with financial conditions attached. The Egyptian government offered to pay in cotton, its only substantial revenue earner. Unfortunately, cotton, especially high-grade Egyptian cotton, was the last thing wanted in the USA where its own cotton producers were suffering hard times. The counter-offer of extended credit was dependent on financial restraints that, for the ever sensitive Nasser, were reminiscent of the economic control once imposed by the British occupiers. With negotiations going nowhere Nasser delivered an ultimatum. If he could not buy arms from the West, he told American ambassador Henry Byroade, then a deal with the Russians, who were prepared to accept cotton in part payment, would go ahead.

It was a double shock for Byroade. Taking his cue from his CIA colleagues led by Kermit Roosevelt and Miles Copeland, the ambassador had tried hard, not without success, to persuade Foster Dulles that Nasser was the best hope for Egypt and America's best hope for peace in the Middle East. Now, it seemed, Nasser was about to prove himself deficient on both counts.

Angry and confused, Byroade acted uncharacteristically by consulting his British opposite number, Sir Ralph Stevenson. A busy humming of the diplomatic wires brought an uncompromising reaction from London. If Nasser signed up with the Russians he could expect no further aid from those who sought to be his closest allies. The Egyptian leader was furious. It was bad enough that Byroade had, in Nasser's view, broken a confidence. But that the British should then come on with threats laced with false protestations of friendship was too much. The Russian offer would be accepted and there would be no further talks with the British about arms. Washington remained silent, probably hoping for more encouraging news from Roosevelt and Copeland, both of whom remained convinced that Nasser was clever enough, given CIA counsel, to duck out of the communist embrace.

Confidence in London that Nasser would heed its warnings had evaporated by the last week in September. On the 27th, the newly installed British ambassador, Sir Humphrey Trevelyan, called on Nasser at the office of the revolutionary council to demand a formal explanation. From his window, Nasser watched the approach of the ambassadorial Rolls. With him were the terrible twins of the CIA, who had spent the past three hours persuading Nasser that it would soften the blow to associate his arms contract with Czechoslovakia, where the weapons factories were situated, rather than with Russia and the Kremlin, the font of all Western terrors. If that was mere window dressing so also was the optimistic reference in Nasser's forthcoming speech to an Egyptian–Israeli détente.[16]

With Trevelyan waiting in an outer room, Roosevelt and Copeland went upstairs, where they shared a laugh at Trevelyan's expense. It was not the friendliest of meetings, but at this and in subsequent conversations with Trevelyan, Nasser made his position clear.

He said that he had been increasingly nervous of Israeli intentions. The Israelis were far better armed than the Egyptians and were in the process of gaining a decisive superiority. He quoted a French pamphlet which he insisted was derived from official sources, which gave a list of arms supplied to the Israelis by the British. He printed an extract from a British military intelligence review which his agents had stolen from a British Unit in the Canal Zone, in order to support his claim that the Israelis had arms superiority even over the Arabs as a whole. He enlarged on the pressure continually coming from his younger officers, who had been urging him for months to accept the Soviet offer and thus redress the balance. He put the blame on us and the Americans for our failure to give him enough arms and for our political conditions. He spoke of his sleepless nights and increasing tension. He had no alternative ... He knew the dangers well and would guard against them. He did not intend to get rid of the British only to bring in the Russians.[17]

Trevelyan was equally frank in his response.

I replied that he under-rated the danger of an arms race and of Communist infiltration, that his information about our arms supplies to Israel was not true – the French pamphlet, for instance, was not official and was nonsense – and that even if he were not breaking any agreement, he was certainly not acting in the spirit of the preamble of the Base Agreement, which contemplated the development of friendly relations between us after the end of the occupation.[18]

When news of the latest twist in Egyptian affairs reached Washington, there was no need to spell out the implications for Dulles. In little more than a year – the time it was reckoned that Egyptian forces needed to learn how to press all the right buttons – Israel would be vulnerable. Before then, possibly within weeks, Israel would be tempted to strike first. This might bring in the Soviets on the side of the Arabs. World war loomed.

In the absence of the president, who had suffered a heart attack and was confined to hospital, Dulles jerked into action. Doubtless telling himself that whenever the initiative was left to the Brits something was bound to go wrong, he dispatched his Near

Eastern affairs specialist, George V. Allen, to pull Nasser back onside. It was a hopeless assignment. Nasser was in no position to backtrack on his arms deal, even if the prospect had appealed to him, which it didn't. Anti-American feeling was strong within the revolutionary council, where some of Nasser's more demonstrative colleagues were convinced that the USA was no longer playing an even hand between Egypt and Israel. There were strong indications of substantial deliveries of French arms to Israel, which the USA had done nothing to discourage. At the other end of the scale of grievances – but in Egypt it was often the minor slight which gave greatest offence – it did not pass notice that uniquely for charities operating outside the USA, contributions to Israel were exempt from tax. Clearly the Zionist lobby was gaining strength.

If Nasser had shown any inclination to submit to US demands, his political career would almost certainly have come to an untimely end. There was only one good reason why he should even have considered a retraction. He was still dependent on the USA for the financial guarantees that would enable him to build the Aswan High Dam. It was a chance he had to take.

When Allen, with the much-discomfited Byroade in attendance, arrived for the meeting with Nasser they were kept waiting for an hour or more, 'to cool off', as one of Nasser's secretaries put it.[19] The preliminary humiliation over, they were subjected to an impassioned monologue from Nasser on the double dealing of American diplomacy. After hearing the bad news, Dulles concluded that his special envoy and the ambassador would be better occupied on other duties, well away from the Middle East. Byroade was subsequently appointed US ambassador to South Africa, while Allen became ambassador to Greece.

In London, the advice from Sir Ivone Kirkpatrick at the foreign office was to play the anti-Russian card for all it was worth.

The Russians have deliberately elected to open a new old War front in the Middle East . . . Egypt is the largest of the Arab states and no Western policy in the Middle East which is actively opposed by Egypt will be entirely satisfactory. An effort should be made to prevent Egypt falling completely under Russian domination. If this fails we must try ruthlessly to isolate Egypt. In the meantime we must try to prevent the uncommitted Arab States joining the Egypt–Syria–Saudi combination. Finally we must recognise that it is the Israel–Arab conflict which has weakened Western influence in the Middle East and opened the door to Russia. If we wish to maintain a position of influence with the Arabs we must bring the conflict to an end as soon as possible. This means strong pressure on Israel and also on those Arab states in which we still have influence.[20]

The details of how this was to be achieved were left unstated.

Nasser awaited the delivery of an arsenal valued at around £150 million. By mid-1956, it amounted to some fifty Ilyushin jet bombers, 100 MiG fighters, 300 medium and heavy tanks, more than one hundred self-propelled guns, 200 armoured personnel carriers, two destroyers, four minesweepers, twenty motor torpedo boats, 500 pieces of artillery, rocket launchers, bazookas and radio and radar equipment.[21] It took a little time for the western allies to respond. The temptation to put an immediate stop to the Aswan Dam project was resisted. Dulles feared that a slap-down for Nasser would give the Soviet foreign minister, the convivial Dimitri Shepilov, another excuse for showing how friendly he could be. In fact, while making sympathetic noises, Russia was reluctant to act as an alternative banker for the dam, having too many infrastructure priorities of its own to worry about, but Dulles was not to know that. Dulles also reasoned that if Aswan went ahead, it would at least keep Nasser occupied for the foreseeable future, tying him to a high-prestige enterprise that he was not likely to sacrifice for a military adventure.

The cost of building the dam was huge, starting with $70 million in grants, three-quarters from the USA and a quarter from Britain. The follow-up was a loan of $200 million from the World Bank, plus a loan of $130 million from the USA and $80 million from Britain. But spread over fifteen years, the burden on foreign aid was manageable. The counter-claim held that the Egyptian economy was too fragile to support such a vast scheme. With a trebling of the Egyptian defence budget to a quarter of the country's total revenue, there was a risk that part of the Anglo-American money advanced for the dam might be siphoned off to pay for Soviet weaponry. Dulles also faced opposition in Congress. Handing out fat cheques to foreign clients to increase cotton production, undercutting American producers, did not go down well with representatives from the southern states. There was also resentment that the dam was to be built by a European consortium. The treasury secretary, George Humphrey, saw the whole scheme as a British plot.

With the two sides of the argument in balance, Dulles opted for delaying tactics. When British and American leaders met in Washington at the end of January 1956, Aswan barely rated a mention. In his own account of the Suez crisis, Selwyn Lloyd claims ingenuously that 'we learned, I think for the first time, of doubts about the Aswan Dam project',[22] adding that Eugene Black, head of the World Bank, was having problems in introducing Nasser to economic realities. In fact there were several warning signals of trouble that Eden and Lloyd chose to ignore. On such a sensitive issue they were happy to let Dulles take the decisions. Instead they focused on trying to establish common ground on promoting the Tripartite Agreement to contain the arms race in the Middle East and to prevent violations of the Arab–Israeli frontiers.

But Dulles had no wish to be tied to policies dreamed up in London, the heart of old-style colonialism, especially in a presidential election year. He was cool on imposing restraints on Israel or, indeed, on America's client oil state of Saudi Arabia, which then, as now, was permitted to get away with financing subversion and terrorism throughout the region. Nor was Dulles prepared to add muscle to the Baghdad Pact, still the great hope for Eden of a defence structure that would protect Western interests in the Middle East.

Eden and Lloyd returned home from their prestige trip with

little except a vague promise from Washington to support the British nuclear deterrent. Eden put a gloss on his report to the cabinet, excusing Dulles from holding back on the Tripartite Declaration on the grounds, easily shown to be specious, that while the president might 'move' forces, he might not 'engage' them without congressional assent. The all but outright rejection of the Baghdad Pact was softened to US 'support, moral and material short of membership'.[23]

Subsequently, Eden conceded that he had 'probably overvalued the political results, as one is apt to do at a time of contact with close allies'.[24] Press comment at the time was less charitable. Leading the pack was Randolph Churchill.

> The Washington conference has failed to produce any result which could not have been procured through normal diplomatic channels. This was made abundantly plain by a pompous declaration and uninformative communiqué. When the statesmen and politicians can't think of anything else to say they always drag in God. Last night's declaration did it twice over, both in preamble and in peroration.
>
> It was obvious from the start of the conference . . . that as no planning had been done by either side, no joint plan could be produced. The declaration and the communiqué were full of pious platitudes and impeccable opinions.[25]

This was just the latest of a succession of press attacks on Eden which had started in January when the usually loyal *Daily Telegraph* accused him of failing to live up to his election promise of strong leadership. 'There is a favourite gesture of the Prime Minister's . . . To emphasize a point he will clench one fist to smack the open palm of the other hand – but the smack is seldom heard. Most Conservatives, and almost certainly some of the wiser trade union leaders, are waiting to feel the smack of firm government . . .'[26] To which the *Mail* added, 'The many events are wrapped up in uncertainty and indecisiveness . . . There are few hard-and-fast decisions. The Government's trouble seems to be not paralysis so much as lack of will.'

By-election results showed a drift away from the government by a middle class frustrated by inflation, which ate away at fixed incomes, by domineering trade union bosses (the poor level of management, not least in the newspaper industry, was rarely commented upon) and by formerly respectful foreigners who loaded their grievances on Britain. Terrorism in Cyprus by supporters of union with Greece and riots in Aden were bad enough, but the discord was at its loudest in the Middle East.

> Judged by the only test of a policy – success in the creation of a stable system – British diplomacy in the Middle East has failed lamentably since last May for all the hopes pinned to the Baghdad pact, and this failure is symptomatic of a lack of nerve in high places ... The instruments of British policy are some power, some moral authority and, necessarily in a dangerous world, a great deal of skill and forethought. It is terrifying to think to what extent this last essential has been lacking from the direction of our affairs in the last nine months.[27]

The Spectator followed up with weekly attacks on Eden, accusing him of committing 'almost every possible mistake'. 'It is only the loyalty which attaches to any leader and a certain hold on his party born of years of political apprenticeship which have saved him. Both of these can evaporate.'[28]

Egged on by his equally touchy wife Clarissa (a cousin of Randolph Churchill, incidentally), the highly strung Eden veered between anger and mortification at his unfavourable publicity. But instead of coming out fighting, his tendency was to hide behind his press secretary, William Clark, who had the impossible task of reproducing the glowing coverage Eden had enjoyed in his golden days as Foreign Secretary.

On the face of it, Clark was an inspired appointment. As diplomatic correspondent of the *Observer*, he had travelled the same international circuit as Eden and could talk with him on equal terms. That Clark was to the political left of his employer was also seen as an advantage, since he was expected to tone down the hostile comment from the Labour-leaning newspapers. But the relationship soon foundered. Eden's biographers are inclined to push the entire blame for this on to Clark, who was said to offer the prime minister unsolicited advice. But this is to misunderstand the role of a public relations counsel. Eden had never matured beyond a media world in which journalists were respectful and asked the right questions, usually in a pre-agreed order. It was Clark's job to show that while any government is entitled to put the most favourable slant on its management of events, there had to be some give and take in dealings with the press. When Clark thought that a particular policy was likely to be ill received in Fleet Street he said so, warning that there was little he could do about it. This was incomprehensible to Eden and to those like Alec Douglas-Home, then commonwealth secretary, who, according to Eden's latest biographer, thought Clark was 'getting above himself'.[29]

Maybe Clark expressed himself tactlessly, but to take the word of Lord Home, one of the worst communicators in modern British politics, on the proper function of a public relations adviser is to lose all sense of proportion. The only member of Eden's government capable of getting on with the press was Macmillan. It is no coincidence that he turned out to be a more successful prime minister than either Eden or Home.

After six months in the job Clark was a disillusioned man. It was partly his inability to cope with Eden's erratic mood changes. But he also realised there was nothing he could do about the whispering campaign against the prime minister. Over the clink of establishment glasses the favoured subject of conversation was the state of Eden's health spiced by speculation as to how long he could bear the strain of his job. By mid-January 1956 there was press talk of his imminent resignation, fostered by the carefully worded ambiguity of one of his closest colleagues. Sir Anthony, said Rab Butler, is 'the best prime minister we have', thus trumping his earlier wisecrack that he would 'support the prime minister in all *his* difficulties'.

Eden's frailties had long been a matter of concern. His periods of sick leave were so frequent as to be the subject of bad-taste jokes. At a cabinet meeting presided over by Churchill and during one of Eden's absences the discussion turned on the preoccupation of the minister of agriculture, Thomas Dugdale, who was getting praise from farmers and blame from animal lovers for a plague that was wiping out the country's rabbit population. 'I'm very worried about this myxomatosis,' said the prime minister. 'You don't think there's any chance of Anthony catching it?'[30]

It did seem that Eden was susceptible to every passing germ. Stretches of frenetic work were interrupted by debilitating sickness and lengthy convalescence. As early as the mid-1930s a bumpy European flight had brought on a heart spasm and doctor's orders to rest for six weeks, while a bout of jaundice took him out of the 1945 election campaign. But it was just as likely to be a common cold that would lay him low.

As Eden's private secretary from 1951 to 1954, 'the dominant preoccupation' for Evelyn Shuckburgh 'was the secretary of state's ill health'.

> He was constantly having trouble with his insides. We used to carry round with us a black tin box containing various forms of analgesic supplied by his doctor, ranging from simple aspirins to morphia injections, and we dealt them out to him according to the degree of his suffering. It was understood that if an injection was required the detective was sent to perform it; this task at least the Private Secretary was spared. The truth is that Eden's complaint had not been properly diagnosed and when I expressed concern to his doctor about all these pain-killers, he replied that he was responsible for a very important national figure and conceived it to be his duty 'to keep him on the road'. When Eden acquired a loving wife, Sir Harold Evans was called in and a proper diagnosis was made. But it was very late in the day.[31]

In 1953 Eden had gone into hospital to have his gall bladder removed. In the course of the operation his bile duct was damaged, leaving him with recurring attacks of cholangitis, an inflammation of the bile duct, which led to sudden high fevers and exhaustion. Anecdotal evidence suggests that to overcome the tiredness he was prescribed amphetamines, which can certainly energise the patient but in many cases also cause hyperactivity and aggressive outbursts, side effects that now make the use of amphetamines a rarity.

D. R. Thorpe invokes Eden's medical records held at Birmingham University to refute what he describes as 'many inaccurate statements made about [Eden's] medicines and the "uppers" and "downers" he supposedly swallowed.'[32] But his comments are restricted to the period of the Suez crisis. It is Eden's state of mind – and the medicines that may have affected his judgement in the lead-up to Suez – which are critical.

By the spring of 1956, Eden was vulnerable. Criticised unfavourably (and often unfairly) in the Tory Party as a poor substitute for Churchill, losing support in the country (according to a Gallup poll in the six months up to March 1956, the prime minister's approval rating fell from 70 to 40 per cent[33]), unable to rely on his senior colleagues, who, at best, were unreliable team players, and failing to understand, let alone solve, the economic problems that beset the country, Eden let his frustration and anger show all too obviously. Knocking back the painkillers and energy boosters along with a generous intake of alcohol did not help to steady his personality. Without question he was not the politician to cope with a crisis. But he was in prime condition to create one.

I I

Selwyn Lloyd was in Cairo, dining with Nasser at the Tahera Palace. Joining them at the table were Dr Mahmoud Fawzi ('a smooth and rather slippery character', decided Lloyd[1]), General Hakim Amer, Egyptian commander-in-chief ('Nasser's vacant-faced but staunchly loyal henchman'[2]), Humphrey Trevelyan, British ambassador, and Harold Caccia, one of Lloyd's private secretaries. It was 29 February 1956. During dinner the conversation focused on the Baghdad Pact and the rivalry between Egypt and Iraq. According to Lloyd:

> Nasser said that there was no chance of improvement in Anglo-Egyptian relations unless we gave an undertaking that there should be no new Arab members. Iraq could remain a member, although, as he said that, I had the impression that he meant to have Iraq out by fair means or foul. I said that the trouble was Egypt's propaganda against Britain everywhere in the Middle East, the Sudan, Libya and East Africa. Radio Cairo's broadcasts in Swahili were just incitements to murder. Nasser admitted that this propaganda was put over on his directions. I then said that I was prepared to put to my colleagues the proposition that we would undertake not to try to persuade any other Arab country to join the Pact, provided he would stop his propaganda. He said that he was prepared to agree to that and we should talk more about it when we met again the following morning.[3]

Towards the end of the meal, Trevelyan was called out by one of the embassy staff, who handed him an urgent telegram. It revealed that General Sir John Glubb, who commanded the 17,000-strong Arab Legion on behalf of King Hussein of Jordan, had been summarily dismissed. Trevelyan held back on the news until he was with Lloyd on the way back to the embassy. The foreign secretary was, as Trevelyan recorded, 'greatly upset'.[4] Partly it was irritation at losing a loyal servant to a client state. But Lloyd had known for some time that Glubb's days were numbered. He had been under pressure since the assassination of his mentor, King Abdulla, four years earlier. Hussein, Abdulla's grandson, a twenty-year-old leader with a reputation to make, did not take kindly to inferences that roles had been reversed, that it was Glubb who ran the country on behalf of his young protégé. The Sandhurst-trained Hussein was also at odds with Glubb over strategy. The general had had his work cut out trying to contain Israeli–Arab fighting along 400 miles of open frontier. But as Israeli incursions were stepped up, Hussein called for a more proactive policy. A British officer, even one devoted to the Arab cause, was not likely to adopt the role of aggressor.

So it was not Glubb's retirement which disconcerted Lloyd – the old soldier was nearly sixty, after all – but the manner in which he was sent packing and the timing of his departure.

> Lloyd was convinced that Nasser had known of General Glubb's dismissal and half convinced that Nasser had planned it to coincide with his visit. It put him in a most embarrassing situation. He was being attacked in the British Press for coming to Cairo at all. This would be interpreted as a deliberate affront which he had to swallow. He toyed with the idea of refusing to go to the meeting with Nasser which had been arranged for the morning, but rightly decided to keep the engagement.[5]

The second meeting started badly, with Nasser congratulating Lloyd on having orchestrated the sacking of Glubb as a way of improving Anglo-Egyptian relations. Was this a bad joke? Lloyd failed to appreciate the humour, but he recovered sufficiently to renew his attempt to find some common ground. 'The proposition emerged that there should be no new Arab members of the Baghdad Pact, that Nasser would acquiesce in Iraqi membership of it and stop anti-British and anti-Pact propaganda and that he would at the same time try and revive the Arab League Security Pact with Iraq as a member of it also.'[6] There seemed to be no prospect of a settlement on Israel, but Lloyd was sufficiently encouraged by the meeting to take Trevelyan seriously when, on the way to the airport, he urged the foreign secretary to give Nasser the benefit of the doubt.

> We had the choice of two unpalatable courses. We could make a bargain such as Nasser had proposed. We could not expect genuine co-operation from him in return for it. We should have to look out for Egyptian attempts to injure our interests elsewhere in the Arab world, but we might be able to take the edge off Nasser's hostility and arrive at a modus vivendi of a sort. The alternative was to adopt a thoroughly tough policy against him. We must then expect unrelieved hostility from him. We knew that he had the power to hurt our interests. If we decided on this course, we must hit hard and accept all the serious international consequences which would follow. I recommended that we should try the first course. I was supported by Harold Caccia, who said that it was at least questionable whether we had now got the power to carry through a tough forward policy.[7]

The mood was quite different in London, where Eden was in a panic. Knowing how the press would react to yet another British defeat in the Middle East, his impulse was to tell Lloyd to set off immediately for Amman to persuade King Hussein to reverse his decision. He had already sent a telegram to the king asking for time to consider the situation.[8] 'Go now,' he urged Lloyd. Even the bag carrier was not that compliant. He had endured just as much humiliation as he could take for one trip.

Reckoning that by the time he arrived in Jordan Glubb would already have left the country, Lloyd decided to stick to his schedule, with the next stop Bahrain. There he was met by a demonstration that threatened to turn violent. Following on from Glubb's dismissal, treated by the British press as a national insult with the rotund and avuncular Glubb somewhat bizarrely standing in for a latter-day Lawrence of Arabia, the incident in Bahrain, heavily embroidered by imaginative hacks, filled the headlines. Lloyd was variously reported as having been stoned by the mob, rescued by the police, besieged in the residency and, finally, smuggled out at dead of night to flee his tormentors. A more objective version comes from Donald Logan, who was travelling with Lloyd.

> He was in the first car with Harold Caccia, we were in the second or third, and there was a small group of students by the road. A few stones were thrown, and there were a few boos and cries as the cars passed. We arrived eventually at the Resident's house and swapped impressions.
>
> We were in the Resident's house for some time, because the demonstration went on to block the road, and we had to wait while the police cleared the road. The students were later established to be representatives of the Committee of Education, who were agitating for more local control against the influence of the ruling family.[9]

But it was the torrid accounts favoured by the popular press which stayed in the public mind. These and the accompanying editorials, which put all the blame on the wicked Egyptians. Eden came to the same conclusion. Or, rather, for him, it was Nasser alone who was the enemy. Not for a moment did it occur to the prime minister that in removing Glubb, Hussein had acted not only in his own best interest but in that of Britain also. In restoring his authority, the young king had upstaged Nasser, thus bolstering Jordan's independence, while allowing for further cooperation with the West. Instead, Eden listened to the siren voices of the Suez Group, who chorused that they had been right all along in opposing the evacuation of the Canal Zone. He demanded action to save his dwindling reputation. But to do what? His first instinct was to punish Jordan by freezing the British subsidy, running at some £12 million a year, and by withdrawing all military support, thus exposing the country to neighbouring predators. Arguing powerfully against this was Anthony Nutting, minister of state at the foreign office, a rising star of the Tory Party, who had every expectation of early promotion while Eden remained prime minister. Nutting took the line that hurting Jordan would force Hussein to turn to Egypt, the one thing Eden wanted to avoid. It was a theme that Glubb himself adopted. Writing in *The Times*, he warned against getting tough with Jordan. 'Suddenly to cut off the subsidy would either destroy Jordan or force the King into the arms of friends who would almost certainly ruin him.'[10]

Arguing far into the night of 1 March, Nutting also made the point that blaming Nasser for every British mishap in the Middle East was to play the game as Nasser wanted, elevating the Egyptian leader to the status of ruler of rulers, commanding loyalties across the region. Eden would have none of it.

> I could see no wrong in anything Nasser did, I was told, despite the fact that for months he had been trying to undermine every British interest and ally in the Middle East. 'You love Nasser,' he burst out, 'but I say he is our enemy and he shall be treated as such.' I retorted that I had always tried to avoid taking likes or dislikes for individual foreign leaders and I reminded Eden that it was he who had taught me this salutary rule, even though he did not always obey it himself. 'All I am trying to do,' I concluded, 'is to establish the true facts and to avoid attributing to Nasser victories which are not properly his.'[11]

But Eden was no longer interested in establishing facts. As he saw it, even in the unlikely event that Nasser was not the cause of Glubb's removal, he was just waiting for the opportunity to do some further damage to Britain. 'From now on Eden completely lost his touch. Gone was his old uncanny sense of timing, his deft feel for negotiation. Driven by the impulses of pride and prestige and nagged by mounting sickness, he began to behave like an enraged elephant charging senselessly at invisible and imaginary enemies in the international jungle.'[12] This became clear when Eden had to defend his position in the House of Commons. The debate on 7 March was a disaster for the prime minister. With Lloyd's continuing absence abroad, he decided to wind up for the government, a tactical error since instead of delivering a reasoned opening speech to set the tone for the debate, all he could do was to try to deflect the barbs of his critics, not least those in his own party, whose case was best summarised by Julian Amery in a letter to *The Times*.

> The dismissal of General Glubb from the command of the British-paid Arab Legion and the stoning of the Foreign Secretary in the British Protectorate of Bahrein attest the bankruptcy of the policy of appeasement in the Middle East. These are the ineluctable consequences of the retreats from Palestine, Abadan, the Sudan, and the Suez Canal Zone.
>
> We are now very close to the final disaster. The challenge to our influence in Jordan and on the Persian Gulf, if left unchecked, must lead to the break-up of the Baghdad Pact. Our oil supplies, without which we cannot live, would then be in immediate danger; our communications with other Commonwealth countries would be threatened; and all Africa would be opened to Communist advance.
>
> In the glare of these dangers only a complete abandonment of appeasement can save the situation . . .
>
> In recent months the Government have been charged with failing to give leadership. They now have the chance, as they have the duty, to confound their critics and promote a rescue operation to save Britain from disaster in the Middle East.[13]

In his less than frank memoirs, Eden concedes that as a result of his Commons performance 'my friends were embarrassed and my critics exultant', before going on to claim that 'as diplomacy, the speech served its purpose'.[14] Few would have agreed with him. Whatever he was saying to Nutting and others in private of his determination to be tough, his stance in public was to adopt delaying tactics ('I am not in a position to announce . . . definite lines of policy') and to hope that Jordan would come to its senses, and, he might have added, help to save his premiership. The parliamentary correspondents were unanimously hostile. Unable to contend with the persistent barracking from the opposition, Eden had finally lost his temper, rounding on Alf Robens, the shadow foreign affairs spokesman, for daring to suggest that he

might be unnerved by what was said in the press. To deny what
was so patently true removed from Eden any remnants of sympathy that he might otherwise have garnered. 'Deplorable', 'In-
ept', 'A Shambles' – there was not a kind word to be said for the
premier.

Reeling from this punishing experience, the prime minister
again felt the need to substitute action for words. Nutting
was the first to hear about it. On the Monday after the Glubb
debate he had sent Eden a paper on Middle East policy, suggesting that it was about time the United Nations took over
responsibility for keeping the peace between Israel and her Arab
neighbours.

> My second suggestion was that we should step up our aid, mili-
> tary and economic, to our friends in the Arab world. Bearing in
> mind how our refusal to deliver to Nasser the arms for which he
> asked had sent him shopping in the Soviet bloc, I felt that we
> should do all in our power to ensure that Iraq, Jordan and the
> Persian Gulf sheikhdoms were built up with British aid and
> British arms. Finally, realising that it would be useless to oppose
> head-on Eden's declaration of war on Nasser, I tried to soften
> and divert him with suggestions for neutralising Nasser's attacks
> on our interests. This could be done by, for instance, spelling
> out his proposals for concessions by Israel on frontiers, refugees
> and the Jordan waters problems, as well as by helping Israel's
> Arab neighbours to secure their defences. For by such words and
> deed we would be demonstrating to the Arab world that we
> wished to see justice done for their cause.[15]

The response was quicker than Nutting had expected. That
evening he was at a formal dinner at the Savoy when he was
summoned to the telephone.

> 'It's me,' said a voice which I recognised as the Prime Minister's.
> If his esoteric self-introduction was meant to conceal his identity
> from the Savoy Hotel switchboard, our subsequent conversation
> could hardly have done more to defeat his purpose.

'What's all this poppycock you've sent me?' he shouted. 'I don't agree with a single word of it.'

I replied that it was an attempt to look ahead and to rationalise our position in the Middle East, so as to avoid in the future the kind of blow to our prestige that we had just suffered over Glubb.

'But what's all this nonsense about isolating Nasser or "neutralising" him, as you call it? I want him destroyed, can't you understand? I want him removed, and if you and the Foreign Office don't agree, then you'd better come to the Cabinet and explain why.'

I tried to calm him by saying that, before deciding to destroy Nasser, it might be wise to look for some alternative who would not be still more hostile to us. At the moment there did not appear to be any alternative, hostile or friendly. And the only result of moving Nasser would be anarchy in Egypt.

'But I don't want an alternative,' Eden shouted at me. 'And I don't give a damn if there's anarchy and chaos in Egypt.'[16]

Nutting returned to his dinner guests feeling as if he were in a nightmare. 'Only the nightmare was real.'

Nutting was ready to fight his corner. Lloyd gave in without a murmur. At cabinet on 21 March, he argued Eden's policy as if it were his own. He was satisfied that Colonel Nasser was unwilling to work with the Western powers or to cooperate in the task of securing peace in the Middle East. It was evident that he was aiming at leadership of the Arab world; that, in order to secure it, he was willing to accept the help of the Russians; and that he was not prepared to work for a settlement of the Arab dispute with Israel. Despite the conversations in Cairo, there had been no slackening in the Egyptian propaganda against the British position in the Middle East. It was now clear, said Lloyd, 'that we could not establish a basis for friendly relations with Egypt'. This being so, Britain should stop trying to conciliate Nasser, and rather seek increased support for the Baghdad Pact.

We should make a further effort to persuade the United States to join the Pact. We should seek to draw Iraq and Jordan more closely together. We should try to detach Saudi Arabia from Egypt, by making plain to King Saud the nature of Nasser's ambitions. We should secure further support for Libya, in order to prevent the extension of Egyptian or Communist influence there. We should seek to establish in Syria a Government more friendly to the West. We should counter Egyptian subversion in the Sudan and in the Persian Gulf.

Lloyd also recommended direct action against Egypt, including the withholding of military supplies, the withdrawal of financial support for the Aswan Dam and the blocking of sterling balances. 'In all this we should need the support of the United States Government. The first task would be to seek Anglo-American agreement on a general realignment of policy towards Egypt.'[17]

But Eden was thinking ahead to more drastic action. The Mussadiq regime in Iran had been overthrown by American and British intelligence services working more or less in unison. Could not the same be achieved in Cairo? It was a sign of the change in Eden that when covert operations in Iran had first been mooted he had reacted coolly. Now he was all for disposing of Nasser by whatever means.

At this point British intelligence entered the scene. It was not a good time for MI5 and MI6, the home and overseas branches of the intelligence service, reeling from the scandal of Burgess and Maclean, the two middle-ranking diplomats who had defected to the Soviet Union. There were worries at the highest level of other horror stories unfolding. These fears were realised in April 1956 when Nikita Khrushchev and Marshal Bulganin, the new faces of Soviet communism, made their appearance in Britain to see the wonders of capitalism at first hand.

It was an ill-fated visit with undiplomatic language leading to social gaffes on both sides. But it was the antics of the secret service which caused lasting embarrassment. It appeared that the Admiralty, presumably having nothing better to do, wanted to know more about the *Ordzhonikidze*, the Soviet VIP cruiser anchored in Portsmouth harbour. The specific request was for the dimensions of the propeller, knowledge that would assist the back-room boys in estimating the maximum speed of the ship and thus the setting for the homing device used on torpedoes. Matching the naivety of a naval command that imagined even a million-to-one chance of Britain ever again engaging in a conventional naval war with Russia, MI6 seemingly went out of its way to invest a simple task with maximum risk. The frogman chosen to inspect the Soviet vessel was heavy in nicotine, alcohol and years. But Commander Lionel 'Buster' Crabb was a jolly good chap and, said his superior, 'he begged to be allowed to do the job for patriotic reasons'.[18] So that was all right.

Except, of course, that it wasn't. Crabb was spotted on his second dive and never returned. In a futile effort to muddy the tracks, a senior policeman dashed to the hotel where Crabb had checked in with Mr Smith, an agent whose name really was Smith, demanded to see the registration book and tore out four pages. By now, however, the Russians were spreading the word that their hosts had been up to no good. Khrushchev took particular delight in revealing that the *Ordzhonikidze*, far from being top of its naval class, was an out-of-date vessel used solely for ceremonial purposes. Soon after the Russian leaders returned home, the ship was sold to Indonesia.

When eventually the cacophony of excuses and recriminations died down sufficiently for Eden to learn the truth, he was understandably furious that his bid for world statesmanship – talking to the Soviets on equal terms – had ended in farce. Heads rolled, most of them at a junior level, though the chief of the secret service was sacked. His successor was Dick White, formerly head of MI5, an efficient if not a greatly imaginative administrator.

As was soon to become evident, the British intelligence network in Egypt was an amateurish set-up caught in the headlight beam of communist plotting, most of it entirely illusory. The chief source for this misinformation, codenamed Lucky Break, was said to have a direct line to Nasser and his trusted associates. The identity of Lucky Break is still unknown, but there was surely a link across to the deputy chief of Egyptian Air

Force Intelligence, Squadron Leader Khalil, who was claimed by MI6 to be one of their own. Fed a sufficiency of secrets to satisfy his masters while clearing him of suspicion, Khalil was later exposed as a double agent. The revelation was buried in the Suez debacle.[19]

Even when the communist scare stories were known to be based on flimsy evidence, they were pushed hard in Washington in the hope of gaining CIA support for a covert operation against Nasser, similar to that which had led to the overthrow of Mussadiq in Iran. Foster Dulles was sufficiently interested to approve an operation codenamed Omega, designed to frighten Nasser into working with the West rather than with the Soviet Union. But as with so much else in the Atlantic alliance, opinions on what needed to be done were sharply divided between Washington and London. The Americans favoured economic pressure while setting the diplomats to work on isolating Nasser from the rest of the Arab world. Britain, or, rather, Eden, wanted Nasser out of the way, permanently. Somewhere along the line there was talk of an assassination plot. 'Spycatcher' Peter Wright was brought in to advise on how best to inject nerve gas into the ventilation system of Nasser's office. 'I pointed out that this would require large quantities of the gas and would result in massive loss of life among Nasser's staff.' Wright concluded, 'It was the usual MI6 operation – hopelessly unrealistic.'[20]

Historians have tended to dismiss Wright as 'notoriously unreliable', though it is hard to understand why he should be any less reliable than Dick White, who, post-Suez, had every reason to distance the secret service from dodgy practices.

There is evidence of other 'quick tricks' of varying degrees of lunacy put up by Kirkpatrick. Two of them crossed the desk of Denis Wright. 'One was some idea of poisoning the Nile. He just mentioned this casually, but didn't go into details. I regarded it as ridiculous. And the other one was to sabotage a shipment of radio valves to Egypt. I've forgotten the details of it, but he did ask me about this, and I must have written a minute saying this wasn't practical.'[21] Equally fantastical was a French plot to send in a commando team to blow up the headquarters of the Revolutionary Command Council.[22]

Nasser himself certainly believed that the British and French secret services were out to get him. From KGB files we learn of a request to Moscow for help in updating Nasser's personal security.

> Two senior officers of the KGB Ninth (Protective Security) Directorate flew to Cairo ... Subsequent investigation quickly revealed that Nasser's only security consisted of a group of bodyguards. There was no alarm system in any of the buildings where he lived and worked. His cook bought bread at a bakery opposite the presidential residence, and meat and vegetables at the nearest market. Having rectified these security failings, the KGB advisers were then asked to provide protection against radiation and poison gas. The best method, they explained, was to keep a caged bird on all premises used by Nasser. If any of the birds died, the building concerned should be evacuated. Egyptian intelligence asked in vain for higher-tech systems of detection which the KGB was reluctant to provide.[23]

The CIA stayed clear of the James Bond antics of British intelligence, though it was agreed to mount jointly an Iraqi-led coup against the pro-Nasser regime in Syria, a plan that was overtaken and smothered by the Suez crisis. There was cooperation too in seeking out alternatives to Nasser who could be enlisted to form a government once the dictator had been overthrown. It was an unofficial task taken up enthusiastically by Julian Amery, who claimed to have been acting with Eden's approval. His candidates for office were 'generally liberal and pro-western in the sense of being anti-Soviet and anti-socialist ... a lot of them were ex-ministers'.[24] But in the absence of names, they remain shadows. Who they were and how strong their commitment was is impossible to say.

If American involvement in plots to oust Nasser fell short of Eden's dearest wishes, he could at least take comfort in knowing that the Egyptian leader was no longer held in regard either by the CIA or by the White House. The Soviet arms deal had started Dulles on the downward slope of disillusionment. His descent accelerated sharply in mid-May when he heard that Egypt was about to recognise communist China. That Nasser should take this initiative – a calculated offence against all that Dulles held most sacred – at a critical moment in negotiations for financing the Aswan Dam, suggests a dangerous overconfidence. His ex-cuse was a rumoured East–West embargo on sales of military hardware to the Middle East, which, if implemented, would stop the delivery of arms from Russia. In this event, China might take over as the weapon provider. But Nasser must have realised that the chances for the adoption of the embargo were remote. A likelier explanation for his provocative diplomacy was the simple wish to parade on the world stage as the head of a neutral country with an independent foreign policy. He was not beholden to the USA, the USSR or, least of all, to the UK.

As for the Aswan Dam, Nasser had only to read the newspapers to know that the prospects for an agreement were less than rosy. In Washington, where the make-or-break decisions were made, Republican economy watchers, who had been elected on promises to reverse the 'reckless spending' of their Democratic predecessors, were liable to react unfavourably to any high-cost aid programme that extended far into the future. As a senior staff member of the National Security Council, Chester L. Cooper was among those who learned 'a surefire way to project the image of a sound fellow while killing an idea I was reluctant to criticize on its merits. When the discussion, pro and con, had all but run its course, I would simply ask, "How much will it cost?" When a number – any number – was mentioned, I needed only to raise my ample eyebrows, suck in my breath, and then utter a barely audible, "Wow!"'[25]

Pressure was put on Eugene Black of the World Bank to tie the Egyptians into a straitjacket deal. Tight limits on the country's borrowing capacity outside the Aswan loan were demanded, along with undertakings not to siphon off Aswan money to spend on undeserving causes such as building up the military. Furthermore, the bank demanded the right to advise on Egyptian economic policy and to delay or stop funding if conditions were not met.

Eden was happy for the Americans to take the lead on negotiations with the Egyptians, though there were increasing worries that Britain, with its less than impressive infrastructure, could ill afford to support macro-projects overseas, let alone for a country that was less than friendly. While the Board of Trade worked on a less expensive blueprint, Kirkpatrick declared unequivocally against the dam.

> If the Russians build the Dam they will increase their influence in Egypt and will appear to be benefactors. But if, as I suspect, Nasser is already sold to the Russians this advantage will be purely marginal. On the other hand if we finance the Dam we not only incur expenditure which we cannot afford, but we have to suffer the serious disability of seeming to do more for our enemies than we are prepared to do for our friends.[26]

The friends were Britain's Baghdad Pact partners – Pakistan, Turkey, Iran and Iraq, all of whom were eager for Western aid. Eden and Lloyd, the latter still smarting from his treatment in Egypt, were onside with Kirkpatrick and disposed to reject the message from Trevelyan in Cairo that Nasser 'still believes his interests to be with the West'[27] and that nothing would contribute more to a stable Middle East than a prosperous Egypt. Eden described Trevelyan as 'very gullible'. He might have said the same of Eugene Black. The head of the World Bank remained convinced that mutually acceptable terms could be hammered out.

But Nasser was losing patience. The Aswan Dam was to be his monument to greatness, but if getting it built required him, as he saw it, to hand over control of Egyptian finances to Anglo-American watchdogs, then the dam would have to wait. Black temporised, promising that rights of inspection would be exercised with restraint and with a proper regard for Egyptian sensitivities. But he was no match for the powerful voices in Congress objecting to the cosy relations developing between Egypt and

Russia and to a trebling of the Egyptian defence budget. This was before the cotton producers' lobby weighed in demanding to know why it was that the Eisenhower administration was so intent on destroying its market by subsidising foreign competition. The objection was of dubious validity since it would be twenty years before the economic plan based on Aswan would bear fruit. The effect, however, was to add to a growing chorus of complaint against Dulles and, by association, Eisenhower. And all in an election year. Foster Dulles was never one to throw away votes.

By the end of June, Nasser had given up on Western promises, confiding to Ahmed Hussein, his ambassador in Washington, that if money was not forthcoming he would in retaliation nationalise the Suez Canal Company,[28] the first suggestion that he was prepared to risk confrontation with America, Britain and France to achieve his ends. He was, however, willing for Hussein to have one last try at securing a deal. In fact, Nasser was well aware that his ambassador was on a hopeless mission. It was common knowledge that Dulles was faced with the real prospect of the Foreign Aid Bill being amended by the House of Representatives to exclude aid to Egypt. Since there was no way that the dam funding could be approved, Nasser was risk free in telling Hussein that he could accept all conditions including – a late entry – a readiness to come to terms with Israel.[29] It was Nasser's way of ensuring that after the inevitable brush-off he would be left on the moral high ground.

And that is how it went. Dulles kept his options open until the last moment, hoping that the Egyptian president (the title had been bestowed on Nasser on 23 June after an election in which he was the only candidate) would take precipitate action, making the closing of the Aswan cheque book a fait accompli. Nasser failed to oblige. A meeting between Dulles and Ambassador Hussein was fixed for 19 July.

Two days earlier Selwyn Lloyd had warned his cabinet colleagues of an impending adverse decision on Aswan. He made no comment on the likely consequences. The only link over to the Suez Canal was made by Maurice Couve de Murville, French ambassador in Washington, who had also served in Cairo. He predicted that if Nasser were rebuffed he might well retaliate by seizing the canal. His words were ignored.[30]

There are contrasting accounts of the meeting between Foster Dulles and Ahmed Hussein. Was Dulles curt and ill tempered or correct and polite? The first version has Hussein touching a raw nerve with Dulles by claiming that in the absence of American support the Russians would step in. Dulles is said to have retorted, 'Well, as you have the money already, you don't need any from us. My offer is withdrawn.'[31] Hussein's own account is more in line with conventional diplomatic exchanges and accords with the secretary of state's claim that he was in no way abrupt. Admittedly, Dulles came straight to the point. 'Mr Ambassador, we are going to issue a statement. I am sorry, we are not going to help you with the Aswan Dam.'[32] Dulles then gave his reasons, mentioning in passing that he did not think the Russians had sufficient resources for the project but if they did undertake it, they would have trouble with their satellite countries. He was right in that, at least. The meeting was conducted, however, the deed was done.

Later, when the Suez crisis had run its course, a stock response in British political circles was to put all the blame on Dulles for the way things turned out. Was it not Dulles who had started it all by his summary rejection of the Aswan Dam project? In one interview Lloyd even had the gall to criticise Dulles for handling the Egypt ambassador 'a little harshly', adding smugly, 'but there it was'.[33]

As we now know, Lloyd and Eden were given plenty of notice of what Dulles had in mind.[34] Sir Harold Beeley, who was an under-secretary at the foreign office at the time of Suez, recalls 'a long departmental meeting in London, on whether or not we should go ahead with the Aswan Dam, before Dulles withdrew, and I was the only dissident at that meeting. I don't think I had more than one supporter. I said that it would be a mistake to withdraw our funds, and I recommended that to Kirkpatrick after the meeting. The weight of opinion on the British side was in favour of withdrawing before Dulles actually told the Egyptians

that he was'.[35] In the event, a curt announcement from the Foreign
Office concluded 'that in present circumstances it would not be
feasible to participate in the project'. The satisfaction at having
quashed Nasser was palpable. What could he do but accept
defeat? The answer came a week later.

12

The fourth anniversary of the overthrow of King Farouk was the perfect occasion for President Nasser to confound his enemies and startle the world. Alexandria, a nationalist stronghold, was the ideal setting. So it was that on 26 July 1956 the rostrum, the microphones, the loudspeakers and the searchlights – for Nasser was not due to address the faithful until dusk – were set up in Liberation Square. From the early hours the crowd gathered until it was 100,000 strong. When at last Nasser appeared, strategically placed cheerleaders led a frenzied welcome that echoed across the city. Then he spoke.

Though not a natural demagogue (his early speeches lacked passion), Nasser had quickly learned the art of holding and manipulating an audience. It was all there – the defiant gestures, the dramatic pauses, the gut-rending appeal to the deepest emotions rising to a shrill call to action that could so easily tip over into mob violence. His theme was the evils of imperialism.

> Imperialism attempted to shake our nationalism, weaken our Arabism, and separate us by every means. Thus it created Israel, the stooge of imperialism. The battle in which we are now involved is a battle against imperialism and the methods and tactics of imperialism, and a battle against Israel, the vanguard of imperialism. Now Arab nationalism marches forward, knowing its road and its strength, knowing who are its enemies and who are its friends.

He recalled the days when Egyptians and their Arab brothers were denied dignity and freedom. But those days were over.

Arab nationalism has been set on fire from the Atlantic Ocean
to the Persian Gulf. It believes in its right to life. Here are the
battles which we are entering. We cannot say that the battle of
Algeria is not our battle. Nor can we say that Jordan's battle is
not our battle . . . Our fates are linked. My fate in Egypt is linked
with that of my brother in Jordan, in the Lebanon, Syria and in
the Sudan.

On he spoke into the hot night, lashing the American and British
governments along with the World Bank, linking the building of
the Aswan High Dam with the building of the Suez Canal.

The Suez Canal was dug by the efforts of the sons of Egypt –
120,000 Egyptians died in the process. The Suez Canal Company, sitting in Paris, is a usurping company. It usurped our
concessions. When he came here de Lesseps acted in the same
manner as do certain people who come to hold talks with me.
Does history repeat itself? On the contrary! We shall build the
High Dam and we shall gain our usurped rights. We are determined. The Canal company annually takes thirty-five million
pounds. Why shouldn't we take it ourselves? The company said
they collected a hundred million dollars every year for the benefit
of Egypt. We desire to make this statement come true, and to
collect this hundred million dollars for the benefit of Egypt.

He had been speaking for well over two hours. Now, at the rep-
etition of the codeword 'Lesseps', Egyptian troops who had been
following his words on radio moved in on the Canal Company's
offices in Port Said, Ismailia, Suez and Cairo. With perfect timing,
Nasser reached his peroration. 'Today, O citizens, the Suez Canal
has been nationalized . . . Today, O citizens, we declare that our
property has been returned to us. We are realizing our glory and
our grandeur.' A new Suez Canal Company would be formed.
'And it will be run by Egyptians! Egyptians! Egyptians!'

The crowd went mad with cheering. As reports of Nasser's
speech spread across Egypt, the people came out on the streets
to shout their support. Stopping along the route from Alexandria

to Cairo to receive the congratulations of his adoring public, Nasser took thirty-six hours to return to the capital.

As Eden's recent run of bad luck would have it, when the news came through of the sting in Nasser's Alexandria speech, the prime minister was giving a dinner in honour of Britain's closest friends in the Middle East – the young King Faisal of Iraq and his mentor, the sixty-seven-year-old Nuri el-Said, who had been prime minister on and off for thirty years. The embarrassment of a monumental put-down in front of those he most wanted to impress fuelled Eden's determination to be seen to act decisively. Hugh Gaitskell, who was at the dinner, gave his support. 'I said that I thought he ought to act quickly . . . and that as far as Great Britain was concerned, public opinion would almost certainly be behind him.'[1] Nuri chimed in, urging Eden to 'hit Nasser hard and hit him now'.

Eden needed no encouragement. Cutting the evening short, he set the tone for a national emergency by immediately summoning a meeting of senior ministers and the chiefs of staff. Also invited were Andrew Foster from the US embassy (ambassador Winthrop Aldrich was on vacation) and Jean Chauvel, the French ambassador, who brought with him Jacques Georges-Picot, director general of the Suez Canal Company, who happened to be in London. There was a touch of irony in the fact that the only person with first-hand knowledge of the operation of the canal was not asked for his views. Instead, Georges-Picot was ushered into a waiting room where he could recover from the shock of realising that just six weeks after signing a new agreement with the Egyptian government, he no longer had a company to run.

> It was a good hour later that Jean Chauvel reappeared to tell me the conference was over. Then came the prime minister, who was kind enough to stop and thank me for my trouble and tell me that since the talk dealt only with the political situation, he had not needed my services . . . As I left, I learned from our ambassador that the British government had a vigorous reaction in mind.[2]

Georges-Picot was not alone in his surprise at the turn of events. But that he and the political establishment in Britain and France had failed to anticipate Nasser's bold move says much of the inability of the political old guard to understand the world in which they were operating. It was the insolence of the upstart which generated anger. How dare he? If Nasser was allowed to get away with it, how many other third-rate countries would begin to get above themselves? Later, when a more rational justification was needed for action against Egypt, economic and legal arguments were brought into play. But in the early critical days after the takeover, emotion ruled.

Eden's fury was plain to see. He had been made to look a fool by Nasser, who was always one step ahead in a diplomatic game for which the rules were still being written. If there had ever been any doubt in his mind that Nasser was his enemy, his latest act of defiance was too close to European events of the 1930s for Eden to ignore the parallels. As he saw it, Nasser may not have been as dangerous as Hitler or even Mussolini, but he was of the same aggressive mindset, taking what he could not get by peaceful negotiation.

It fell to Kirkpatrick to remind Eden that the very day of Nasser's nationalisation of the Suez Canal was the twentieth anniversary of Germany's unprovoked and, as it turned out, unopposed reoccupation of the demilitarised Rhineland. A few lonely voices pointed out that the relevance of the Rhineland episode was more tenuous than the government chose to suggest. No Egyptian troops had crossed any frontier, no foreign or disputed territory had been seized and on the canal no British ship had been denied passage or detained. But Eden was not listening. As recalled by Sir Guy Millard, who was one of Eden's private secretaries at the time of Suez, the military option was consistently high on the agenda. 'It was decided that, in default of other solutions, eventually there would have to be a military solution to reverse what had happened. Other solutions would be explored first, but from day one they were committed to a military solution, if all else failed.'[3]

The Suez crisis brought about a dramatic, if temporary, change in Eden's fortunes. On the very day that Nasser went for broke, Harold Nicolson, whose son, Nigel Nicolson, was to wreck his parliamentary career over Suez, was at a party with a mixed bunch of political friends.

> Nye Bevan was there, and talked to me about the 'decay' of the present government. He attributes it entirely to Eden, who, he says, is much disliked, weak and vacillating, and in fact, hopeless. He was not talking as an Opposition leader, but as a student of politics. He said that in his experience the character of a government was determined by the character of the Prime Minister. To choose Eden had been a mistake, since he was not a strong man. He interfered with his colleagues and did not control them, and gave the impression to the House that he did not know his own mind. Now when I hear a man abused like that, I immediately wish to take his side. But I fear that it is all too true.[4]

Less than twenty-four hours later Bevan, the torch-bearer of the far left in the Labour Party, was giving full backing to Eden's resolve to slap down Nasser. As Richard Crossman, another left-winger, put it, 'Nasser really did grab it [the canal] in an intolerable way and, if he got away with that grab, might well launch a war against Israel.'[5]

Cross-party support for the government remained solid throughout the Commons debate on 27 July. Hugh Gaitskell deplored 'this high-handed and totally unjustifiable step by the Egyptian Government' and urged the blocking of Egyptian sterling balances in retaliation. In the parliamentary lobbies members of the Suez Group, formerly reviled for their blimpish mentality, were praised for having foreseen the consequences of the British evacuation of the Canal Zone. They, in turn, resisted the urge to put the knife into the politician who had submitted to the sell-out. The new Eden, action man, deserved unreserved support. From the back benches there were respectful murmurs of approval when the prime minister, speaking of the need for 'firmness and care', told the Commons how the government had thought it necessary 'to take certain precautionary measures of a military nature'.

In a surfeit of patriotic fervour, the press weighed in on the side of the government. It was no surprise that *The Times*, then still the voice of the establishment, was strong on action against 'a clear affront and threat to Western interests'. But the liberal *News Chronicle* also urged 'retaliatory action', while the *Herald*, the mouthpiece of the Labour Party, wanted 'no more Hitlers'. Writing in *The Spectator*, Charles Curran congratulated Eden on regaining 'every yard of the ground he has lost inside the Tory Party during the past year. He has established a hold on Tory loyalties firmer and warmer than he has ever had before. So far he has acted about Suez in complete conformity with one of the basic tenets of Toryism and by doing so he has secured the support of the great majority of British citizens. For the party this result is seen as a vindication as well as an achievement'.[6]

At the heart of the rhetoric was the dreadful fear that Nasser could now hold Britain to ransom. In Eden's lurid imagery, 'The Egyptian has his thumb on our windpipe.' A quarter of all British imports came via Suez. That made the canal significant but hardly dominant in the British economy. But it was the oil which really mattered. Of this precious liquid, three-quarters of British needs were satisfied by Middle East providers using the canal. The accepted, though exaggerated, consequences of an interruption of canal traffic were of petrol rationing within a week and of a run-down of manufacturing industry within a fortnight. But, in 1956, oil accounted for only 13 per cent of Britain's total energy needs. Coal was far more important. On the other hand, the long-term prospects appeared to be more daunting. In his brief occupancy of the Foreign Office, Macmillan had presented a cabinet paper forecasting a trebling of oil imports over twenty years.

> Although some of the extra oil required will come from the Caribbean area, the greater part must come from the Middle East, where the major proved reserves of the world are situated

and where our companies have their greatest interests. There is
no alternative source, as the only other large producing area, the
United States and Canada, has become a net importer. Therefore
supplies of Middle East oil are essential to the economy of this
country. If they were cut off or seriously interrupted irrevocable
harm would be done to our economic position, and a British
investment now valued at some £600 millions would be lost.
Western Europe as a whole is similarly dependent on the Middle
East for its oil supplies, 75 per cent of which came from that
area last year.[7]

The paper made no dramatic recommendations. It simply urged
that a working party be set up to consider action the oil companies
should take.

These civil service ruminations on Britain's dependency on oil
are an early indication of the political myopia that characterised
the entire Suez episode. If the authors of the cabinet paper had
dug a little deeper, they might have discovered that the oil companies were already well ahead with building giant tankers that
were better suited to the Cape route than to the canal. More
pipelines were planned with capacity for stockpiling oil to raise
Britain's reserves above the currently estimated and totally inadequate six weeks. And this was before the promise of discovering
new oilfields was brought into the account. In any case, the ownership of the canal did not make a scrap of practical difference to
European communications with the oil-rich states. The difference, if there ever was one, had been made with the withdrawal
of British troops from the Canal Zone in 1954. If Eden had been
paying closer attention to Foreign Office and defence thinking he
would have heard wise counsel offering an alternative to confrontation with Nasser. The way forward, it was argued, was to reduce
military expenditure in the Middle East (running at around £57
million a year) in favour of economic and technical assistance.

Certain steps are already being taken, but it is essential that we
should intensify our efforts in all possible ways. In particular, we
consider that there is an immediate need to expand and improve

local police forces and intelligence, thereby reducing the need for military intervention. Furthermore we see great advantages in offering training facilities in this country to the military and police forces of the appropriate Middle East States. We also consider that everything possible should be done to prevent further Middle East States from turning to the Communist *bloc* for military equipment and techniques. Measures should also cover the diplomatic, economic and cultural fields; and we should seek to make effective use of psychological and clandestine operations. In addition, in colonial territories and protectorates, we must improve and control educational facilities.[8]

And this was from the recently bullish chiefs of staff. Perhaps the Suez Canal was not the vital artery that Eden and his supporters assumed.

Immediately after the Commons debate on 27 July, there was a cabinet meeting. Butler was the only absentee. After hearing that £2 million held in the Canal Company's bank in Cairo had been confiscated, a Suez Committee, otherwise known as the Egypt Committee and by jokers as the Pretext Committee,[9] was set up, chaired by Eden; the other members included Macmillan, Salisbury and Lloyd, though significantly Macmillan's diary reference relegated Lloyd to the 'other ministers turning up as required'.[10] Later in the week the twin aims of the committee were specified. These were to place the canal under international control and to 'bring about the downfall of the present Egyptian government'. No room for misunderstanding there.

A crowded day (27 July) left Eden much to be pleased about. It seemed that he was leading a united front. But there was yet another confidence booster. It came in a telephone conversation with French foreign minister Christian Pineau, who gave Eden the clear message that in France the determination to end the Nasser regime was every bit as strong as in Britain. In the Gallic imagination the canal was not just a masterpiece of engineering but a tribute to the Napoleonic mission to embrace a world civilisation. On a less elevated level, the Canal Company was the 'last

great international stronghold of French capital'.[11] Its board was
controlled by French directors, it was staffed largely by French
technicians and it provided a modest income to tens of thousands
of French shareholders. All this was now at risk.

Pineau's telephone call was followed by Prime Minister Mollet
and Pineau flying over to London for consultations with Eden
and Lloyd. They found the prime minister in an 'over excited
state', railing against Dulles for his hostility to Britain.[12] In their
eagerness to confirm the Anglo-French alliance against the
Egyptian leader, Mollet came up with the grandest of ideas.

'Why don't we take up the proposal made by Paul Reynaud in
1940 to unite our two countries? French opinion would certainly
favour it.' Pineau recalled: 'the reaction of our English friends
lacked enthusiasm'. 'Excellent idea in substance,' said Eden, 'but
a bit premature. Let's resolve the actual crisis. We will think about
it calmly and in due course.' Pineau added, 'The grimace of
Selwyn Lloyd was less than diplomatic. The idea seemed to him
preposterous, even shocking.'[13]

Nasser was well established as a hate figure in France well
before the Alexandria speech. As the foremost Arab nationalist,
he was portrayed in the popular imagination as the greatest single
threat to what was left of empire, that most visible evidence of
French status as a leading nation. The country had endured a
succession of nationalist uprisings. While Britain was able to
count some successes in preparing colonies for admission to the
Commonwealth, France had so far failed in its objective to incor-
porate its overseas territories into a grand Francophone union.

The first test of French resolve had come in Vietnam, one
of three colonies in Indo-China, the other two being Laos and
Cambodia. A guerrilla war of ferocious intensity pitched China
against the USA with France in the middle. By the autumn of
1953, America was covering almost 80 per cent of the financial
cost of the French war effort in Indo-China. The human cost was
something else. The death list stretched to 23,000 French and
African troops and 14,000 Indo-Chinese, with over 120,000
wounded or missing. The true figures were kept from the French

public. Even so, the distance from Hanoi to Paris was not so great as to make it possible to claim that the army was in control. Of the politicians who were prepared to speak out, the star turn, and the one outstanding leader thrown up by the Fourth Republic, was Pierre Mendès-France, son of a Jewish tailor, a veteran of the Resistance who, pre-war, was France's youngest elected member of the National Assembly. As a left-wing radical, Mendès-France took a severely practical view of his country's capabilities. 'It is absurd to pretend that we are still a world power. We must limit our ambitions and, however painful it may be, live within our means.'[14] Few of his peers were ready to be quite so blunt, but there was a noticeable shift, particularly among young voters, towards support for a settlement in Indo-China that would leave a semblance of French self-respect.

The response from the army was characteristically bullish. The generals had no faith in a weak and vacillating governing class. If negotiations were to take place then it had to be from a position of strength that could only be achieved by first inflicting a crushing defeat on the Viet Minh. General Henri Navarre, commander-in-chief of Indo-China from May 1953, came up with a plan that was as bold as it was foolhardy. An air drop of French forces into the heart of Viet Minh country was intended to draw the guerrilla fighters out into the open, there to be annihilated in a set-piece battle. The problem, as Navarre's critics tried in vain to point out to him, was that guerrilla fighters were not inclined to fight set-piece battles. That was why they were guerrilla fighters.

It did not take long for France's paymasters in Washington to catch on to this essential point. 'You cannot do this,' Eisenhower told a French diplomat, adding that Navarre was 'surely smart enough to know the outcome of being emplaced and then besieged in an exposed position with poor means of supply and reinforcements'.[15] Eisenhower was to be disillusioned.

On 21 November 1953 six French paratroop battalions led by three generals dropped on the isolated village of Dien Bien Phu, deep in enemy-held jungle 170 miles west of the French power base at Hanoi. There they prepared for General Vo Nguyen Giap to respond to the challenge. The wait was not long. Far from being an amateur and ill-disciplined force incapable of facing superior French firepower, the Viet Minh proved superior in tactics and equal in courage. Dien Bien Phu never surrendered, it was overwhelmed. Only 3,000 French out of a total of nearly 17,000 survived the siege or subsequent captivity.

The French army kept its pride. No one could doubt that Dien Bien Phu would enter the history books as a shining example of dedication to duty and noble self-sacrifice to rank with Verdun. But when it came to apportioning responsibility for the disaster, the military was slow to acknowledge that the theory of warfare had moved on since the days of Napoleon. Instead, others were to blame, not least the spineless politicians in Paris and the double-dealing Anglo-Americans who had gone back on promises to mount a rescue operation. The reality was otherwise. Not much could have been done to help the French out of their predicament. A massive air strike by B-29 bombers was briefly on the cards, but what in the end would it have achieved in the absence of back-up by combat troops? As one of Eisenhower's military advisers put it, 'One cannot go over Niagara Falls in a barrel only slightly.'[16] Dulles knew this, and he knew also that sending in the US army was not an option. In Paris, Mendès-France was chosen to head a government pledged to end the fighting in Vietnam within thirty days. The combatants came together at Geneva, where the peace conference was chaired by Eden, Dulles having written himself out of any deliberations that had Red China as a participant.

Geneva was declared a triumph for Eden and in the short run so it must have appeared. The creation of a communist North Vietnam bordered by the 17th Parallel, with the remainder of Vietnam, Cambodia and Laos as independent entities to the south, provided an acceptable exit strategy for France to which Dulles gave his half-hearted approval. But the promised free elections that were supposed to follow the peace settlement never happened. In the USA it began to look like Munich all over again. The same thought must have occurred to Eden. Nothing was calculated to give him more pain than the accusation of being a diplomatic soft touch. It had happened over the withdrawal from Egypt; now it looked like happening over Indo-China. While his friends sought to reassure him, there was a strong lobby urging Eden to toughen up.

The feeling in France was one of relief at having escaped the consequences of Dien Bien Phu. Like his predecessors, who also had to rely on shaky coalitions, Mendès-France was soon out of office, mourned by younger voters who had looked to him to bring France into the modern world. The army took a diametrically opposed view. The generals were glad to see him go. Having been forced out of Indo-China – in the military mind incompetence had nothing to do with it – the shame was intensified by having to stand by while the USA filled the power vacuum. Military aid still flowed into Vietnam but no longer was it routed via Paris. France had been demoted in South-East Asia in the same way that Britain had been downgraded in the Middle East. In both countries anti-American sentiment was widespread in political circles.

Responding to the military rallying call, French politicians soon rediscovered their preoccupation with empire. After the loss of Indo-China, the French in North Africa looked to be dangerously vulnerable. Efforts to divert Tunisia and Morocco from the road to independence had failed. That was hard enough for loyalists to take, but their dread was of a far greater catastrophe in Algeria, though until Dien Bien Phu the prospect was rarely discussed openly. Algeria was different. A retreat from Algeria was not to be contemplated. While Tunisia and Morocco were classed as protectorates, Algeria was part of metropolitan France with its own deputies in the National Assembly. Not only were the two economies closely integrated but there were expectations of tapping into bountiful oil from the Sahara. (The first successful strike came in June 1956, 400 miles south of Algiers.)

Compared to other European rulers elsewhere in Africa, France had in many ways set a good example in Algeria. There was a strong infrastructure of roads and railways and great strides had been made in health and education. Democracy in its most basic form, however, had been slow in coming. Soon after the end of the Second World War, Algerians had extracted a promise from France that they would soon be able to participate fully in the running of their country. A mixed community with a Muslim majority was at last to be governed by Muslims and not by European civil servants appointed in Paris. In 1954, they were still waiting. The obstacle to progress was the one tenth of the population – the million-plus *'colons'* of French ancestry – who were French first and Algerian a very poor second. Successive efforts to find an accommodation between the two sides culminated in February 1955 with the appointment as governor general of Jacques Soustelle, a left-wing politician with impeccable democratic credentials. At this point the seeds of mass revolt had barely taken root. Soustelle came with an open mind, intent on finding a way to integrate the two communities. Opposed by the *colons*, who equated even modest reforms with revolution, and by the emerging National Liberation Front (FLN), which made its point through assassination and sabotage, he put his faith in a 'third force' of loyal Muslims whose moderation would pave the way to a peaceful settlement. But first there had to be an end to terrorism. Soustelle gave the job to the military. It was his biggest mistake.

The French army had moved on since Dien Bien Phu, but not in any sense that gave comfort to the civil government. Finding in defeat justification for taking a political stance, the generals saw themselves as the last line of defence against communism and anarchy. After Indo-China, they were not about to give up on Algeria, no matter what orders came through from Paris. Invited by Soustelle to take out the extremists, the army responded in kind. Extremism was countered by yet greater force. The effect was cumulative. Whenever an Arab village suffered a heavy-handed police search, the FLN gathered recruits. In April 1955 the people of the Constantine region in eastern Algeria rose in revolt, killing seventy-one Europeans. Many more Algerians died in a ruthless exercise of retaliatory justice.

France had yet another government and a new prime minister.

Secretary-general of the Socialist Party from 1946, Guy Mollet was a teacher of English, a back-room politician, noted as a power broker, whose sole experience of office was as mayor of Arras, the coal-mining area north of Paris. Having no clear-cut ideas on the future of Algeria but having an urgent need to establish his authority, he decided to make his mark where Soustelle had patently failed, by reconciling the Muslim population to a lasting association with the mother country. The manner in which he went about this said much for his inexperience. A state visit to Algeria was planned, the first by a French prime minister since 1930. The day chosen, 6 February 1956, was the twenty-second anniversary of riots on the streets of Paris, an occasion that encouraged the more aggressive *colons* to contemplate a repeat performance. There was even talk of holding Mollet hostage until the government had acceded to French rule by force. It did not quite come to that, but the reality, a carefully orchestrated demonstration that quickly descended into mob violence with Mollet rushed away to the government residence under a barrage of agrarian missiles, brought home the hopelessness of his mission. Like Soustelle before him, Mollet submitted to the settler and thus military lead.

His first choice as governor general of Algeria, the seventy-nine-year-old General Catroux, a progressive despite his age, was told to step down. In his place came Robert Lacoste, the government's contact man with the *colon* lobby in the Assembly, known for his distinctly unprogressive opinions. A few weeks later, the National Assembly voted extraordinary powers to force a settlement on Algeria. Regiments stationed in Germany were transferred to North Africa, 70,000 reservists were called up and military service was extended to twenty-seven months. By July 1956 there were close on half a million French servicemen in Algeria. The rebel force was put at 25,000. Even so, the French army failed to seize the initiative. Setting itself up as the civil authority, its clumsiness and insensitivity destroyed the faith of ordinary citizens in French decency, driving them into the arms of the FLN.

There are many starting points on the road to the Suez war, but for France it has to be Algeria. Quick to apportion blame for a conflict that had no obvious resolution, the Mollet government fastened on to President Nasser as the evil genius behind the rebellion. An avowed nationalist and pan-Arabist, Nasser made no secret of his support for the Algerian insurgents. During the first half of 1956 all the Algerian leaders who had escaped death or imprisonment had fled to Cairo, where they formed a Committee for National Liberation. Cairo Radio pumped out invective against the colonial powers. No attempt was made to counter rumours (mostly unfounded) of Egyptian readiness to share its bounty of Russian arms to support rebel operations – or, indeed, French arms, since the sale of weapons to Egypt continued up to the time of the canal nationalisation. An outrage, thundered *Le Figaro*. 'The French are not respected in the Middle East when they send arms to those who insult them every day.'[17]

For the army, Nasser was perfectly cast as the scapegoat for the failure to restore peace. Egypt's role in Algeria matched that of China in the war in Vietnam. But unlike China, Egypt could be defeated by determined action by France alone. There were those in the Mollet government who were prepared to follow this faulty logic to its terrifying conclusion. Robert Lacoste was convinced that the overthrow of Nasser would demoralise the rebels, giving France the opening for a settlement favourable to the *colons*. 'One French division in Egypt is worth four divisions in Algeria,' he declared.[18]

Lacoste's strongest backing came from his Gaullist partners in Mollet's socialist-led coalition. Ostensibly in retirement, de Gaulle himself was given insider reports on government affairs by Jacques Chaban-Delmas, minister without portfolio, who made weekly visits to Colombey-les-deux Eglises. But he brought back nothing in the way of constructive advice. Rather, de Gaulle was looking for the signals of impending collapse of the Fourth Republic, a regime, as he called it, of 'mediocrity and chloroform' floating on the surface of France 'like the scum on the sea'. All would be different, ran the message, when de Gaulle made his triumphant return to the Elysée. Meanwhile, his allies in government followed what they imagined de Gaulle would do in the circumstances, which was to support the Algerian *colons*. Of their number, the most influential voice was that of Maurice Bourgès-Maunoury, the minister of defence, who came out strongly against Nasser and his baneful influence in North Africa. Bourgès-Maunoury had held several ministerial jobs before taking on defence. Though described as a 'serious, steady and level headed' politician, his experience in the Resistance had made him over-sensitive to any suggestion of 'another Munich'.[19]

Though susceptible to the romance of the imperial tradition and the renewal of French *gloire*, Christian Pineau was more cautious, at least at the start of his turn as foreign minister. An economist by training, a member of de Gaulle's wartime government in exile, Pineau had also served in earlier governments. But this was his biggest job so far. He wanted time to work his way in. Encouraged by the recommendation of a conference of French ambassadors to the Middle East to attempt a rapprochement with Egypt,[20] he gambled on direct talks with Nasser. After all, he reasoned, they had something in common to start their conversation on the right track. Both were fiercely opposed to the Baghdad Pact, recognising it as a blatant promotion of British self-interest.

Pineau arrived in Cairo a week after Selwyn Lloyd's fateful visit. Doubtless he felt he had the advantage over the British foreign secretary. This impression remained with him throughout the talks. There is no record of the use made of interpreters, but given the misunderstandings that subsequently emerged, it is likely that the critical exchanges were in English, a language Nasser and Pineau had in common but spoke imperfectly. In any event, when Pineau departed Cairo on the next leg of a Middle East tour, it was with the mistaken conviction that a deal had been struck. In return for France continuing to attack the Baghdad Pact, Nasser would distance himself from the Algerian insurgents.[21]

Even if, improbably, Nasser had accepted this one-sided agreement, it was soon to be rescinded by Mollet, for whom a closer relationship with Britain counted for more than pacifying Egypt. On a flying visit to London, he agreed to accept the Baghdad Pact. For his part, Eden was ready to back French claims on Algeria. Pineau, however, ever optimistic, waited hopefully for Nasser to deliver a reduction in rebel activity. When instead the fighting intensified he assumed a betrayal. He might just as reasonably have judged that Nasser had less influence in Algeria than had been supposed. But by now almost the entire French government believed that Nasser was the source of all their colonial troubles.

They had the public on their side. The call for immediate action against Nasser was taken up by the press. A writer in *L'Express* summed up the general view when he condemned the '*coup de poing*', warning that it could lead to further acts of economic terrorism throughout North Africa and the Middle East.[22] The only member of the government to stand out against the crowd was Mendès-France, who had joined the administration having credited Mollet with progressive views. When he proved to be wrong, Mendès-France did the decent thing and resigned, the first of the few dissenting politicians on either side of the Channel who were ready to live up to their principles. For his former colleagues, the nationalisation of the Suez Canal was the confirmation of all they had feared. It was time to act. The *entente cordiale* was about to show its muscle. The trouble was, the muscle turned out to be distinctly flabby.

Of all the shocks that Eden had to endure over the next four months, one of the greatest was the revelation that given Egypt's pride of place in British military thinking, there was no plan for the reoccupation of the Canal Zone. Or, rather, the consideration given by the Joint Planning Staff (JPS) to a possible reoccupation had led to the disturbing conclusion that it was no longer a practical proposition since it would take 'at least six months'[23] to reactivate the Canal Zone base. This was assuming that the Egyptians, with their Soviet arsenal, would be ready to cooperate, an unlikely prospect. Furthermore, 'a base of this size and concentration is undesirable in the face of nuclear threat'.[24] This was in February.

By July, when the canal was nationalised, the base barely figured in military thinking. If this came as a setback to Eden's determination to be seen to act decisively, even more frustrating was the belated realisation that with defence taking 10 per cent of the national budget and with a military establishment 750,000 strong, there was no chance of high-speed action to retake the canal. If Eden had wanted to engage in all-out war in Europe he would have been accommodated, but rapid response was not yet part of the military vocabulary. The army, in particular, was weak on firepower and mobility. There was no provision for sending a force overseas for a limited war without calling up and retraining reservists – all of which took time. If this sounds like ineptitude on a monumental scale – it was.

Eden's hopes that it could be otherwise were raised at his first emergency meeting of ministers and military chiefs. As acting chairman of the chiefs of staff (Sir William Dickson was ill) and as First Sea Lord, it fell to Admiral Earl Mountbatten to suggest what immediate military action could be taken. He reported that the fleet was assembled at Malta and could sail within a few hours. The Royal Marine commandos could be picked up at Cyprus, and Port Said occupied within three or four days. 'The Prime Minister', Mountbatten recorded drily, 'was delighted – almost too delighted – with this information.'[25]

In later years, Mountbatten embroidered his version of events to blame Eden for not taking up his plan for a lightning strike. But it was Mountbatten himself who ditched the idea almost within breathing space of raising it by conceding that while 1,200 marines could seize the causeway along the canal, they would have difficulty in maintaining their position in the face of Egyptian opposition, unless troops could be moved in quickly to give the necessary back-up.[26]

There was no chance of that happening. The British troops nearest to Egypt were two armoured regiments in Libya, but it was unthinkable for an Arab state to be used to launch an attack on another Arab state. The next-best choice for a jumping-off point was Cyprus, 250 miles north of the Egyptian coast. Eight infantry battalions and three parachute battalions were based in Cyprus, but they were fully occupied with holding down the rebel forces of EOKA. Moreover, since drops were not part of their current mission, the paras were short on specialist training. To complicate matters further, the air bases in Cyprus were in a poor state, while Famagusta, the only serviceable port, had restricted berthing space and a shallow harbour. The nearest port with generous loading capacity was Valletta on Malta, but that was over a thousand miles from Port Said.

The French military was also beset by logistical problems. The best part of the Mediterranean fleet was at Toulon, two weeks' sailing from Egypt. The two brigades of paratroops in Algeria were, like their British counterparts, otherwise engaged than in their main function, and would thus need at least two weeks' retraining. Long-range jet fighters in Germany could not be moved to the Mediterranean in less than ten days.

It took some time for the generals to absorb these unpalatable facts. As Sir Frank Cooper, who was head of the air staff secretariat at the air ministry, points out, 'One of the problems with a peacetime military operation is that the military don't think it is going to happen. This was just as true before the Falklands.'[27]

As the military machine lumbered into action, an ever watchful Nasser calculated that the risk of war fell with every week that passed. He shared his thoughts with Mohamed Heikal, who jotted down notes of their conversation.

> Peak danger time . . . 80 per cent at beginning of August, decreasing each week through political activities. How can we make the political situation swim? Fawzi can do that. He is an expert in floating things. Second week in August, danger 60 per cent. Third week, 50 per cent. Fourth week, danger 40 per cent. End of September, danger 20 per cent. Can we gain two months by politics? If we succeed we shall be safe. So much will depend on Fawzi.[28]

He made one other calculation. 'Participation of Israel in this operation to be ruled out. Eden would not accept. Israel may try but Eden will refuse. He will prefer to keep it European.'[29]

But there he was wrong.

13

At the end of July, Chester L. Cooper, a senior CIA man in London, noted that 'some of my colleagues in British intelligence and in the Ministry of Defence . . . suddenly "left town". One of them told me, with more or less a straight face, that he was off for a "summer holiday"'. Cooper was amused to observe that when his friends returned to their desks they were 'surprisingly pale and fatigued for people who, presumably, had been resting in the sun'.[1]

The real story, as Cooper was well aware, was of British and French military planners setting out their wares in a hastily renovated complex of offices and conference rooms under the Thames, the core of Churchill's wartime administration. Before long there were over a hundred staff officers crammed into these subterranean quarters. General André Beaufre, over in London for preliminary consultations, was not impressed:

> The first meeting of the planning committee took place in the underground wartime accommodation of the Air Ministry. One left one's car on the Embankment near Westminster, penetrated into a shelter at the far end of a garden and, going down a rather insalubrious staircase, reached the underground offices constructed during the war; they consisted of a series of tiny rooms, lit by electricity and with fresh air pumped in through air ducts as in a ship's cabin. My own staff together with the British was destined to spend 2½ months in this uninviting cellar, where much work was done but much time wasted also.[2]

The allocation of top jobs was determined by the balance of resources. Britain had most of offer – 50,000 men, of whom nearly half were reservists, as against 30,000 from France; 100 warships with thirty from France and five aircraft carriers with just two flying the tricolour. It did not go down well with the French military, but it was the destiny of their staff officers at Suez to have 'deputy' attached to their rank. De Gaulle warned of trouble to come. 'I approve of the operation,' he declared, 'but not for putting an English general in charge.'[3] When the post-mortems of the campaign came to be written it was a popular refrain of French commentators that had roles been reversed it would all have turned out quite differently. The probability is that they were right, though not necessarily for the accepted reasons.

Commander-in-chief of allied forces was General Sir Charles Keightley. Son of a clergyman, fifty-five years old, educated at Marlborough and Sandhurst, Keightley had the ruddy face, bristling moustache and voice that stretched into a long drawl, which made him the very model of a British general. Cast in that role in a movie, commented an American journalist, 'critics would protest that the character was overdrawn'.[4] But appearances of a bluff, simple soldier belied an impressive military record. One of the few tank officers to emerge with credit from the fighting in France in 1940, he had commanded the 6th Armoured Division in Tunisia in 1942 and 1943. Immediately prior to the Suez crisis Keightley was commander-in-chief of Middle East land forces.

Two other attributes marked him out as the natural choice to head up the Suez campaign. The bearer of the Légion d'honneur and Croix de Guerre, he was in credit with the French while, as the officer who had organised a smooth handing over of the canal base, he was forthright in his view that the evacuation had benefited no one but the Russians.

Keightley's number two was Vice-Admiral D'Escadre Barjot, who was short, round and hyperactive, a bon vivant 'with a paunch which projected so suddenly you could almost have stood a glass on it'.[5] The war had interrupted his naval career. An opponent of the Vichy regime, Barjot had made a living as a journalist before rejoining the navy in 1945. In contrast to Keightley, he had close contact with his political masters and was

certainly better informed than his commander-in-chief, who 'was
in the impossible position of being asked to do things with both
hands and both feet tied'.[6]

Eden's obsession with secrecy and his refusal even to spell out
clear objectives for the military planners frustrated the 'bureau-
cratic . . . neat and tidy'[7] Keightley, whose uncertainties about the
whole operation translated into an over-cautious approach to his
assignment. This in turn infuriated Eden, who was all for speed.
So too were the French. But unsure as to the true purpose of his
mission, to take and hold the canal or to take and hold Egypt
until a post-Nasser government was in place, Keightley opted for
a slow build-up to maximum force, covering all eventualities. He
was supported by Sir Gerald Templer, chief of the imperial
general staff, who had the additional worry that the supply
of Russian arms to Egypt had created a formidable fighting
machine.[8] He insisted on putting off D-Day until the allies could
be sure of delivering a knockout blow in the first round.

It was the first of a succession of potentially catastrophic mis-
calculations. Though much of the blame was subsequently to be
put on faulty intelligence, the blunder was really that of the top
brass, who were disinclined to take into account anything that did
not fit their preconceived view on how to fight a war. Their
only excuse was that 'they and their generation of senior British
commanders had all experienced disasters during the Second
World War through underestimating opponents and they had
learnt the principles of war the hard way'.[9]

Still, they might have given closer attention to the information
that was to hand. It was known, for example, that Egypt had been
supplied with at least two hundred Soviet jets, and this was the
figure that stuck in the military mind. But it was also known that
only a third of these planes were operational.[10] To then argue that
the shortage of trained Egyptian pilots might be compensated by
an inrush of Eastern bloc 'volunteers' was close to suggesting that
the whole operation should be called off. Why risk a Third World
War for a stretch of water?

As with fighter jets, so it was with the three hundred or

so Soviet tanks and the rest of the advanced weaponry in the Egyptian arsenal. Even with Russian technicians and other support staff on hand (up to eight hundred in all) there was simply not a sufficient number of trained personnel to make full use of the hardware.

The manpower figures put out by the Egyptian defence ministry were impressive at first glance. As commander-in-chief, General Abdel Hakim Amer claimed to be able to mobilise half a million men. Even he, however, had to admit that the majority were part-time, often reluctant recruits to the National Guard and the Liberation Army. There was a ready supply of the latest Czech semi-automatic rifles, which must have been galling for the British forces, who had to make do with the breech-loading rifle used in the Second World War. But again, advanced weaponry was only effective with advanced training, and in this the Egyptians were weak.

Taking all these factors into account and drawing the wrong conclusions, the strategists emerged from their Stygian cells to deliver their verdict. Nasser was to be overthrown and the canal secured by an air and naval bombardment of Port Said to prepare the way for a seaborne invasion supported by paratroops.

A week had gone by since Nasser's nationalisation speech, but it was only now that the designated commander of land forces, Lieutenant General Sir Hugh Stockwell, arrived from Germany to take up his new job. Described by his French deputy, General Beaufre, as 'tall, elegant with a small white swept back moustache, lively and intelligent but nervy and as volatile as a continental',[11] Stockwell was a hands-on leader who had an aversion to paperwork and prided himself on straight talking. It was said that he was the only four-star general never to have been through staff college.

Many stories were told of Stockwell's aplomb under fire. In 1940 he had fought a difficult rearguard battle at Pathaus in Norway. 'Having hidden in a slit trench and fearing his position was being given away by a mooing cow whose udders were heavy with milk, he enticed her closer and milked her into his steel helmet.'[12] As their retreat continued the cow followed him all the way to Narvik.

If Stockwell was 'open and impulsive,' as General Jacques Massu described him, Beaufre was more imaginative, 'reserved and cerebral'. Massu went on, 'these personalities should have been complementary. In reality they made a poor team. Stockwell was as stubborn as a mule, refusing to accept any of Beaufre's ideas. On the other hand, Beaufre, who was intellectually superior and knew it, could not accept a command structure which, from the outset, put him in the subordinate position'.[13]

The Port Said plan did not impress Stockwell. For one thing, he pointed out, Port Said was an island at the end of a 27-mile causeway, 'like a cork in a bottle with a very long neck'. Once troops had landed, assuming that they *could* all land since Port Said was ill equipped to receive an armada, they would be at the mercy of saboteurs who would destroy the bridges that had to be crossed before the troops could fan out. In characteristically bluff manner, Stockwell called for a rethink. 'Like the good little soldiers we were, we wrote an appreciation laying out all the facts, and produced the conclusion that we preferred to launch this operation through Alexandria. There were many military factors to our advantage.'[14]

Not least of the plus points was that Alexandria had three times the docking capacity of Port Said and a superior airport. The amended plan called for a two-day bombing strike to dispose of the Egyptian air force before British and French commandos staged a pincer attack on Alexandria. Supported by a naval bombardment, the Royal Marines were to secure the port while the French were to attack over the beaches to commandeer the west and south-west exits from the city. Simultaneously, French and British parachutists were to drop close to the short causeway connecting to the desert road to Cairo.

Led by two tank battalions, the infantry would then break out to meet the concentration of Egyptian armour around Giza. A further parachute landing would support the crossing of the Nile to put Cairo within reach and to open the way for a two-pronged drive for Suez and Ismailia, followed by the occupation of Port Said.

The operation was down as Hamilcar until it was realised that in French this was Amilcar. Since it was thought to be confusing to have an H and an A as the identifying symbols on military vehicles the codename was changed to Musketeer (said to be inspired by Stockwell's moustache). It required the deployment of 80,000 troops. Justifying such military largesse, Stockwell commented, we could not afford to lose nor risk a setback'.

This was essentially a British plan. So far the French contribution had been limited to observations on broad principle. When Beaufre arrived in London on 10 August, he was presented with Stockwell's conclusions on Alexandria as the obvious focus for attack. D-Day was to be 15 September. Eden agreed the plan on 10 August; Mollet on 18 August. But there was much detailed work still to be done.

Irritated by the inability of the military to come up with a quick solution to what he saw as a simple problem, Eden was further disconcerted by the breaking of ranks among his own closest advisers. As the top civil servant at the foreign office, Kirkpatrick was strongly in favour of confrontation ('We cannot possibly risk allowing Nasser to get away with it') but he was offset by the senior legal adviser to the FO. Sir Gerald Fitzmaurice delivered a forthright judgement. There was no legal basis for armed intervention of a neutral state to protect property or to guarantee freedom of passage through a canal or to prevent further violence.[15] No international court was likely to take Anglo-French claims seriously. The canal company was registered in Egypt and was subject to Egyptian law. Moreover, its concession had only twelve years to run. Whether or not there would be an extension was open to question, but pre-empting negotiations could hardly serve as an excuse for resorting to force.

Fitzmaurice was supported by the attorney general, Sir Reginald Manningham-Buller, who wrote directly to the prime minister warning him that he had a weak case to argue. Eden was not persuaded. Ignoring the advice of Fitzmaurice and Manningham-

Buller, he opted instead for the guidance of Lord Kilmuir, the Lord Chancellor, who took the line that Egypt had broken the 1888 Convention. 'By her invasion of the rights of the signatory powers under the Convention of 1888, Egypt has been guilty of a crime of aggression against those powers.'[16]

Intervention was therefore justified to protect foreign property. But where was the aggression? Nasser had not confiscated the canal. Rather he had brought it under state control with fair compensation for the shareholders. The niceties of legal debate were lost on Eden. Nasser was an enemy who had to be destroyed. To argue a contrary case was tantamount to treason. Sensing that Fitzmaurice was not without his supporters in the foreign office, Eden made a conscious decision to cut the diplomats from his inner circle. It was an extraordinary action for a prime minister to take, suggesting arrogance of a high order or a fear of contradiction that bordered on the pathological, or both.

Ignoring his opponents was no way to contain dissent. Frustration in the Foreign Office soon spread to other departments of state. In the corridors of Whitehall, the gossip was of a prime minister who had taken leave of his senses. As Richard Powell, permanent secretary at the ministry of defence at the time of Suez recalls, 'without too much fear of exaggeration no civil servant, from Norman Brook [Cabinet Secretary] downwards, was in favour of the operation'. He goes on, 'we felt that ministers who were keen on it had just not thought the thing through and assessed the consequences'.[17]

There were some critics too powerful for Eden to ignore. One of them was the First Sea Lord, Earl Mountbatten, who, of all the senior officers involved in Suez, was closest to Eden. Mountbatten was not liked by his colleagues. As a member of the royal family (he was Prince Philip's uncle) he was inclined to behave as if the other chiefs of staff, indeed everyone short of the monarch and the prime minister, were his underlings. 'Mountbatten was on the make,' declared Sir Frank Cooper. 'He was a great man but a shit. He was always out for Mountbatten . . . no one trusted him.'[18] In typically earthy language Templer told Mountbatten that he was so crooked, 'If you swallowed a nail you'd shit a corkscrew.'

But if, to his peers, Mountbatten was a monster of insensitivity, his experience as the last viceroy of India gave him the advantage of recognising the strength of nationalist ideology. He was convinced that war with Egypt would do nothing for the problems it was supposed to solve. More probably it would make them worse. Responding to Templer's call for 'resolute action', Mountbatten wrote:

> If we were fighting a visible enemy who was trying to dominate the Middle East by force of arms I should back you to the limit . . . But there is no such enemy . . . The Middle East conflict is about ideas, emotions, loyalties. You and I belong to a people which will not have ideas which we don't believe in thrust down our throats by bayonets or other force. Why should we assume that this process will work with other peoples? . . .[19]

Mountbatten drafted a letter to Eden to try to convince him that instead of armed intervention 'our trump card is a reasonable, constructive offer [to Nasser], backed by as many nations as we can collect and one that the Americans, as well as the countries of Asia . . . could not conceivably condemn as being "imperialistic"'.[20] The letter was never sent. Mountbatten was persuaded by his political masters, Walter Monckton, minister of defence (who was himself increasingly sceptical of Eden's policy) and Lord Hailsham, the minister responsible for the navy, that he had no business giving unsolicited advice to the prime minister. But with the chiefs of staff, Mountbatten kept up his opposition to the use of force, much to Templer's irritation, and it must have been plain to Eden that his First Sea Lord was a powerful source of disaffection which was liable to spread to General Keightley and his military planners beavering away under the Thames.

For the moment, however, they were more concerned with putting together a credible force. The military build-up was supposed to be secret, but a casual glance at the newspapers revealed much of what was happening. Almost immediately after the crisis began two aircraft carriers, *Theseus* and *Bulwark*, were taking on ammunition and supplies at Plymouth. In early August they were reported to be loaded with troops and sailing for 'somewhere in the Mediterranean'. A third aircraft carrier, *Ocean*, left Devonport with troops from Scotland and the north of England on the day that schools were told that their army cadet camps had been cancelled because the regulars who organised them were 'wanted for other duties'.

Other duties included the retraining of 20,000 reservists, most of whom had lately completed their two years' national service but who were now expected to go through the whole grizzly business all over again because they happened to have the know-ledge, mostly in engineering, that was thought to be handy for the invasion of Egypt.

The call-up was of dubious legality. The National Service Act of 1948 granted no specific right to the government to summon reservists without parliamentary approval. But in 1956 Parliament was not consulted. The reservists were told to get back into uni-form on the authority of an Order in Council signed by the Queen. That the government was not entirely confident of its position may explain why those few reservists who refused to accept their recall papers – sending them back with an expletive scrawled across them – escaped prosecution. The other possibility is that the authorities had too much else to worry about to chase after reluctant soldiers.

Those who did answer the call were not best pleased to be summoned to duty. Ken Chambers was twenty-two when the War Office telegram was delivered to his door.

I thought it was a practical joke at first but with a War Office stamp and my army details on it (number & regiment), my world was suddenly transformed. It read, 'Report within 48 hours to Coopers Lane Camp, CAD Bramley, Hampshire. Railway warrant attached.' I went to the nearest pub for a stiff whisky and the landlord said, 'Alright mate?' I replied, 'Look at this.' I showed him the telegram and he said, 'This one's on me and good luck!'

I had to explain to my family and tried to answer questions, but the most difficult part was to tell my fiancée, Gladys, that I had been recalled to the army, as we were planning our wedding in September but because of the uncertainty over Suez, our plans had to be cancelled. This was a huge disappointment and put a lot of stress on my fiancée to cancel various appointments and other plans were quickly talked about.[21]

With a twenty-four-hour pass to help him on his way, the wedding took place as arranged on 29 September. Ken was back in camp by nightfall and by midweek was on his way to Cyprus.

Brian Henderson was three months married and building up his career as an architect when he received his recall papers. A lieutenant in the Engineers who had finished his national service two years earlier, he and his men, who were of the same vintage, were badly in need of retraining. Instead they were put on board the *Empire Parkeston*, 'an old, rattly vessel better suited to the Woolwich Ferry than the open seas'. Having landed in Gibraltar, where Lieutenant Henderson's men were refused access to the shooting ranges ('Sorry, old boy, it's the naval shoot this week'), they re-embarked, this time for Malta. By now the reluctant soldiers were thoroughly fed up with cramped conditions, poor food and a ship that rolled so vertiginously as to be reminiscent of a fairground rollercoaster. They also took a fierce dislike to their sergeant-major, who was obsessed with inspections. Brian Henderson could see that trouble was brewing. It came after the *Empire Parkeston* anchored at Grand Harbour and the men departed to sample the delights of Malta. When they returned dead drunk, the RSM decided to reassert discipline by ordering everyone to lie to attention in their bunks. The response was to carry him shoulder high out on to the deck with the idea of throwing him over the side. It took all of Brian Henderson's persuasive powers to secure the release of the martinet. There was more discontent in Cyprus, their next port of call. 'The ex-coal miner in charge of the kitchens knew next to nothing about food. I remember being served fishcakes which turned out to be a mix of anchovies, oatmeal and cochineal. When a senior officer came round to ask if there were any complaints he was greeted with a fusillade of plates zimmed across the room.'[22]

The dissatisfaction extended to the regular troops, even to the war-hardened French paratroops, who were beginning to arrive in Cyprus. Pierre Leulliette was among their number.

> Under new tents, already discoloured by the sun, on camp-beds with no legs, level with the ground, we waited. Each of us had a pair of sheets. Oh, English comfort! But the heat woke us in the afternoon, still very drowsy. We got up and tried to find a little breathable air outside the tents. Unfortunately, everywhere the sun was relentless; the sky was grey with heat. There was no vegetation, as far as the eye could see.
>
> We had to stay there for a fortnight, parked on a few acres of sand, and surrounded by high barbed-wire fences. All contact with the outside world was strictly prohibited. No letters, even to our parents: we were a secret. The days were torrid and the nights freezing. We shivered beneath our thin blankets from the first day, though we slept in our clothes, like beggars caught napping by winter. What was more, all our food came by special plane, so we had to endure hunger, like prisoners of war. Half a mess-tin of beans! Only half per man per meal. Little bread. Hardly any water. The prospect of living in such conditions for even a fortnight made us feel sick.[23]

For Brian Henderson the final indignity was the order to stay put on the island. He and his men never did reach Suez. Insubordination was so common among reservists as to raise fears of a mutiny. In the period up to the outbreak of war, incidents ranged from a mass protest meeting of the Grenadier Guards on Malta to the desertion of up to four hundred reservists who, returning from Germany for a week's leave, failed to make a reappearance.

On board the SS *Marshall*, 'a desperate old rust bucket', Martyn Habberley and his friends soon put paid to the traditional spit-and-polish tradition of the British infantry by throwing all their cleaning kit overboard. When their commanding officer threatened to clap the offenders in irons he was told he had been reading too many Hornblower books. The voyage was a nightmare.

> We ran into a storm for several days in the Bay of Biscay. While the ship was being loaded there had been a strike by the riggers so the loaded trucks in the holds were not properly fastened down. When we started rolling badly, over forty degrees in fact, the trucks started breaking loose. Every time the ship rolled there was a shuddering crash as everything in the holds went from one side to the other, and on deck the ammunition (I think 20 lb-er) was jumping out through the truck canvases and rolling around the decks, where the petrol in the jerry cans was leaking out steadily. Luckily there was plenty of seawater washing around as well. After the worst rolls there was a long wait before the ship righted herself, the crew all looked terrified and we were definitely in real danger of foundering. The Bosun went below in the early stages to attempt to lash the cargo, but broke a leg fairly quickly, so after that they decided to head into the wind and just let it roll, and we did this for three or four days.[24]

They did eventually get to Suez, but after the fighting was over. The abiding memory of Martyn Habberley of this last phase of an unwanted adventure was of his CO returning to the ship via a violently swinging Jacob's ladder while his men lined the deck rail shouting, 'Drown, you bastard, drown.'

The rebellious mood among reservists was also apparent in France, where those called up were never sure, until the last moment, whether Algeria or Suez was to be their destination. Several troop trains were derailed, a shipload of reservists broke loose in Marseilles and hid themselves in the Old Port and there were protests, often violent, in Paris and Le Havre.

For regular and reservist alike the abiding memory of the Suez build-up is of the lack of any information as to what was really going on. With hindsight, it is easy to understand if not to sympathise with the political reasons for trying to keep everything under wraps. The surprise is that Eden or anyone else in the know really believed that they could move men about as if they were markers in a war game and still command blind loyalty. Minor irritations caused by official indifference could easily turn into lasting resentment.

Petty Officer Evans serving on the aircraft carrier HMS *Ocean* had just started married life in an Admiralty flat in Weymouth. After a weekend of moving in he set off back to Portland, where *Ocean* was anchored, telling his wife Kate, 'I'll see you this afternoon.'

> On arriving on board, there seemed to be a lot of unusual activity and it wasn't long before I discovered I'd got the afternoon watch in the forward engine room, and that we were going to sea! It turned out that we were going to Plymouth, but I couldn't let Kate know of course, so it would be another step in Service wives' education. Later that day she was in Weymouth shopping . . . and met the RN Housing Officer. He asked how we liked the flat and Kate told him she was getting something for my tea. He told her not to bother and explained why, but she didn't believe him till she went to look out towards Portland and saw that the ships had gone.[25]

In Plymouth the men were told all leave was cancelled. A week later *Ocean* and *Theseus* were on their way to Cyprus. Since both ships were supposed to be in the Home Fleet Training Squadron 'it was not very popular with the lower deck – especially the married ones'.

Where there were efforts to give servicemen some relevant information, but not too much, the results could be farcical, as national serviceman Tony Thorne discovered one morning parade.

> When the CO arrived, he was accompanied by the whole complement of the camp's officers. They marched onto the parade ground and then stood rather awkwardly behind the colonel.

This was serious stuff. 'Must be war,' muttered someone in the ranks . . .

He was right on the button. The colonel told us that that same morning another colonel, called Nasser, had helped himself to one of our canals without so much as a by your leave. The whole camp was to be put on a state of high alert and we were to be watchful for any threats of enemy action. The guard was to be doubled and sentries would be posted around the camp day and night.

We had not seen that many Egyptians when we had ventured into the ancient city of Canterbury, but this was not all.

The colonel continued by telling us that there was a distinct possibility that we (the Brits, that is) might declare war and invade Egypt to get our canal back. In this case it was possible that we might be hurled into action. He said that he had heard from the War Office that, even though we had not yet completed our basic training, we were on stand by. He then marched off the parade ground, leaving us to ponder our fate.

We were brought down to earth by the gentle Sussex voice of the sergeant major.

'Right, you lot. You all heard what the officer said. Now get a grip. You could be lucky enough to be amongst the shock troops. I don't know about the fockin' Gippos, but, by God, you would shock me! And now go back to your duties and pray to the Almighty that we can get back our Panama Canal. Dismiss.'[26]

If the troops were in a poor state of readiness, the military hardware was in an even sorrier condition. Trucks and armoured vehicles stored away at the end of the Second World War were taken out of 'mothballs' only to find that most of them were scarcely roadworthy. Flat batteries could be replaced but when, as was invariably the case, wireless aerials, canopies, ammunition racks and other essential fittings were missing the chances of rehabilitation were slight. There were simply not enough spare parts to go round. There was some relief in borrowing equipment from the NATO reserve in Germany, but there was a limit to what could be done here without letting the Americans in on the Anglo-French plans.

Efforts to make do and to cover up deficiencies made matters worse. It was not unusual to see lorries being towed to embarkation to be dispatched in the sure knowledge that they were no better than scrap metal. But they were at least sand coloured. Hundreds of former national servicemen can testify to their military duties as paint sprayers. In France, so much yellow paint was used that supplies ran out. Of course, once everything in sight was converted to yellow, it was not to be too long before the order came to restore the traditional army green.

The failure of army administration showed up most obviously in preparing the armoured brigade for battle. Centurion tanks were too heavy to be transported by rail, and on roads their tracks were liable to tear up the surface. Since giant transporters were in short supply, the only solution was to call in Pickfords, a removal firm that used massive roadsters to carry heavy items of engineering. The drawback for the army was in having to submit to the rules for civilian transport.

> Transporter crews, tied to trade union hours of work and restrictions never intended to cope with an emergency or the needs of the Services, took a week to do a journey which a military unit would have covered in three days, and behind each convoy trailed a fantastically disproportionate number of empty spare transporters which the regulations of the British Road Services said must always be held in reserve. Between the time that the first tank was loaded on to its transporter and the last tank was stowed in its LST [tank landing ship], there was a lapse of four weeks; valuable time, which could have been spent in hard training, had been lost.[27]

More seriously, there were not enough LSTs. Of a total strength of thirty-two only two were in service. Those that came out of mothballs needed extensive repairs before they could be deemed seaworthy. When the 6th Royal Tank Regiment sailed for Malta, three of its Centurions had to be left behind.

Even where the army had modernised it was not always with sufficient thought to fighting efficiency. A case in point was the replacement for the all-purpose American jeep. Four times more expensive to produce, the Champ was bigger and heavier than its agile predecessor. It was also useless for the 16th Parachute Brigade preparing for the Suez campaign at its base in Cyprus. It was too bulky to be carried in the Hastings aircraft but, slung beneath the machines, the load prevented the landing wheels from touching the ground. The search began for decommissioned jeeps.

> The consequence was that officers with briefcases stuffed with money had to be despatched to accost local farmers around the Middle East Command, who were astonished and gratified to discover that their battered second world-war runabouts were worth a fortune. The vehicles so acquired were rushed to workshops where a crash programme rendered them fit for an airborne operation.[28]

There were too few transport aircraft for paratroops and those that were able to get into the air were the old side-loading type, whereas modern equipment and vehicles were designed for backloading planes.

The news was a little better from France, where the annual holiday trek to the south was hampered by straggling military convoys heading for Toulon. As early as 2 August, the French and British press were giving out details of the strength of the French fleet with pride of place going to the 35,000-ton battleship *Jean Bart*. Not all the ships were ready for battle – the *Jean Bart* had only one of its guns in place and the sole carrier could boast just twenty-five modern planes capable of taking on Nasser's MiGs – but the general effect was of a massive show of force. Equally impressive was the turnout of the French paras.

> The aircraft which carried them into battle were French, as were the parachutes which each soldier packed himself. As yet unseen by most British soldiers, if not undreamed of, were their SS10

wire-guided ground-to-ground missiles, the revolutionary anti-tank weapon which the French took to Suez. Even their medical packs were pre-sterilised and standardised for single treatments, the envy of the British medical officers.[29]

First impressions could be deceptive. General Beaufre had his work cut out to bring his troops and their equipment up to scratch.

> The troops themselves were in need of re-training; the regiments were first-class but had been employed on anti-guerrilla operations for months . . . In addition . . . regiments had to familiarise themselves with equipment not used in Algeria, in particular the 106 SR anti-tank gun, which was new to them . . . The staff of Force A, the signals, the whole air support system, the services and the base, all of which had been hurriedly thrown together, had to be organised and trained. Regimental parachute jumps had to be carried out, range practice, tactical training, loading and landing exercises – and all this in fifteen days![30]

Beaufre began to wonder whether he would be ready in time. He was not alone in his doubts. In 10 Downing Street, the stress level was mounting. Increasingly disillusioned with the military, aware of growing disaffection within his own ranks (Walter Monckton at defence was the first of the ministerial doubters), Eden was nervous of giving the impression of 'order, counter-order, disorder'. After one midnight meeting, the PM's press secretary, William Clark, was driven home by Norman Brook, who, as cabinet secretary and head of the civil service, was one of the most powerful members of the administration.

> He came in for a drink and began by saying that he had felt he must warn the PM that the idea of using force was growingly unpopular. 'How do you do it in this age? Call together Parliament, send in the troops and get a positive vote of perhaps forty-eight in Parliament, and a vote against you in the UN? It just isn't on.' We agreed that Britain now found herself almost isolated, the Arab world against us, Asia against us, America

wobbly, the Old Commonwealth wobbly, only France as an ally and she is a definite liability with world opinion. Clearly Brook is advising against aggressive action, but I don't know if he'll win. As he said, the bluff etc. is all very well until this Armada sails, then we are committed because it can neither turn back nor sit offshore. As he left, Brook sighed, 'Our Prime Minister is very difficult. He wants to be Foreign Secretary, Minister of Defence and Chancellor. Of course if there is war,' he added, 'he will have to be Minister of Defence.'[31]

America was certainly wobbly, as Brook suggested, but it was on the special relationship that Eden now pinned his faith that all would be well in the end. Just hours after Nasser had made the speech of his life, Eden dispatched an urgent appeal to Eisenhower:

Dear Friend

You will have had by now a report of the talk which I had last night with your Chargé d'Affaires about the Suez Canal. This morning I have reviewed the whole position with my Cabinet colleagues and Chiefs of Staff. We are all agreed that we cannot afford to allow Nasser to seize control of the Canal in this way, in defiance of international agreements. If we take a firm stand over this now, we shall have the support of all the maritime powers. If we do not, our influence and yours throughout the Middle East will, we are convinced, be irretrievably undermined.

Eden went on to stress the threat to oil supplies, but 'it is the outlook for the longer term which is more threatening'.

The Canal is an international asset and facility, which is vital to the free world. The maritime powers cannot afford to allow Egypt to expropriate it and to exploit it by using the revenues for her own internal purposes irrespective of the interests of the Canal and of the Canal users. Apart from the Egyptians' complete lack of technical qualifications, their past behaviour gives no confidence that they can be trusted to manage it with any sense of international obligation. Nor are they capable of providing the capital which will soon be needed to widen and deepen it so that it may be capable of handling the increased volume of traffic which it must carry in the years to come. We should, I am convinced, take this opportunity to put its management on a firm and lasting basis as an international trust.

Dismissing legal quibbles as to Egypt's right 'to nationalise what is technically an Egyptian company', Eden was ready 'to use force to bring Nasser to his senses' should economic and political pressure fail to produce results. He added an urgent request for Eisenhower to send a representative to an Anglo-French meeting in London on 29 July.[32]

Eisenhower had a more excitable version of the same message from Christian Pineau via the US embassy in Paris. Nasser's action was 'an outrage' that warranted strong action. Otherwise, 'the inevitable result would be that all Middle East pipelines would be seized and nationalised within the next three months and Europe would find itself totally dependent on the goodwill of the Arab powers'. Obviously, said Pineau, this was an 'unacceptable situation'.[33]

Eisenhower was thrown into a mild panic by these missives. Crisis was written all over them but the president was hazy on the details of the canal and its importance to Britain and France, as his diary entries make plain.[34] Still recovering from a serious heart attack, he more than ever needed Dulles to front up for him. But the secretary of state was in South America, and it was not thought politic to pull him back so abruptly. Instead, it was the under-secretary of state, Robert Murphy, who set off for London. 'Just go over and hold the fort,' Eisenhower told him.[35] He was to express the president's 'grave concern' but to give 'no hint as what we are likely to do'.[36]

Murphy's hosts, however, had quite other ideas in mind. Their aim was to convince him of their government's resolve and to squeeze from him some expression of US support for recovering control of the canal by whatever means. A campaign of gentle intimidation started with a lunch at No. 10, as Harold Macmillan recorded.

Bob Murphy arrived yesterday . . . It is clear that the Americans are going to 'restrain' us all they can . . . We had a good talk, and the PM did his part very well. The French are absolutely solid with us, and together we did our best to frighten Murphy all we could . . . We gave him the impression that our military expedition to Egypt was about to sail. (It will take at least 6 weeks to prepare it, in fact.)[37]

The follow-up with Murphy was a dinner hosted by Macmillan, whose association with the American diplomat went back to war days when they were both in North Africa. Adopting the role of prophet with grave tidings, Macmillan laid onthick Britain's determination to rise to Nasser's challenge. To do otherwise was to relegate Britain to the world's also-rans ('another Netherlands'), a prospect too dreadful for Macmillan, the hardliner, to contemplate.

Murphy 'shared British indignation over Nasser's high-handed action' but he knew very well that 'United States policy opposed the type of eighteenth century strategy which was in the minds of our friends'.[38] His fear was that Britain and France would be tempted to go it alone with potentially catastrophic consequences for the whole of the Middle East. Immediately following the dinner with Macmillan, who expressed himself delighted with the results ('It seems that we have succeeded in thoroughly alarming Murphy'[39]), the president's emissary cabled Eisenhower 'a strictly factual account of the evening's conversation'. It was enough to persuade Eisenhower that it was time for Dulles to show an interest.

It was precisely what London and Paris most wanted, a sign from Washington that the Suez crisis was receiving attention at the highest level. But Dulles was disinclined to play that game. When he returned from his South American tour, his first instinct was to try to lower the tension by authorising Murphy to keep talking with Lloyd and Pineau while holding off on any firm decisions.

Eisenhower saw it differently. He insisted that Dulles should get involved. At a White House conference on Suez only one voice, that of Admiral Burke on behalf of the joint chiefs of staff, was raised in support of Anglo-French direct action. But he stopped short of proposing US participation, instead urging a search for 'means of splitting off Egypt from other Arab and Moslem groups'. The president responded tartly that 'we have been trying to do this for several months'.[40] In Eisenhower's view only Dulles had the stature to make clear American opposition to the precipitate use of force. Eden had to be disabused of the impression that the USA would go along with anything Britain and France did. As Murphy put it:

> As is often the case among allies, the material interest of the United States was not identical with that of either France or the United Kingdom. France and Britain had very substantial holdings in the Canal Company. American holdings were insignificant. France and Britain were directly dependent on the flow of Middle East oil. The United States was not.[41]

But if diplomacy and economic pressure failed, then what? 'Even though our commercial interests were not as vitally affected as those of our British and French friends, we certainly were fully aware of the importance of Western prestige in the Middle East.'[42] Dulles believed he had the answer. A conference of maritime powers would be called to secure an 'international regime to operate the Canal'.

Arriving in London on 1 August, Dulles played tough and tender, asserting that Nasser had to be made to 'disgorge' his ill-gotten gains while promoting the expectation that his conference would produce a peaceful settlement. British and French hopes of drawing the USA into preparations for military action were dashed. The negotiating route had to be taken first, however long it turned out to be.

Pineau was furious and made no effort to conceal his contempt for what he called American naivety. But for the moment Eden was not prepared to move without American support. Dulles was able to reassure Eisenhower that he had made no commitment to a 'military venture by Britain and France which, at this stage, could be plausibly portrayed as motivated by imperialist and colonialist ambitions'.

He had also made clear that an operation without at least the moral support of the United States would 'be a great disaster'.

> Egypt was much stronger militarily, and was getting moral and material support from the Soviet Union and Egypt's prestige and influence in the Arab world was [*sic*] much greater. I said they would have to count not merely on Egyptian reaction but on Egyptian reaction backed by assistance from the Soviet Union at least in the form of military weapons and supplies, and perhaps 'volunteers'. All the Arab and parts of the Moslem world would be arrayed against the United Kingdom and France. Also they would be in trouble in the United Nations. I could not see the end of such an operation and the consequences throughout the Middle East would be very grave and would jeopardize British interests, particularly in the production and transportation of oil even more than the present action of Nasser. I felt that it was indispensable to make a very genuine effort to settle this affair peacefully and mobilize world opinion which might be effective.[43]

Meanwhile, reasoned Dulles, if Nasser was to finance his Aswan Dam from canal tolls, he would not move against Britain and other prime users of the canal. So why the hurry? He might have added that given the state of British and French military unpreparedness, immediate action was, in any case, out of the question. The pencilled-in D-Day was still six weeks away.

Later, Dulles was accused of inconsistency. The charge is unfair. In public, Dulles felt that he had to stand alongside his allies. To show an apparently united front, he was ready to go along with a joint communiqué from the three foreign ministers condemning the 'arbitrary and unilateral seizure by one nation of an international waterway'. In private, however, he was unequivocally against bringing in the military. If it appeared otherwise the problem was with the sabre-rattlers who were giving close attention only to what was pleasing for them to hear.

The pressure for Dulles to adopt a stronger line was kept up in Paris, where Mollet, in a 'highly emotional state', told the American ambassador that Nasser was 'acting in close accord with the Soviet Union,' and though comparisons with Hitler might seem banal, Nasser had adopted a familiar tactic in 'always talking peace after each aggression'. Mollet wound up with a thinly veiled threat.

> As I got up to leave Mollet said he wished to tell me one more thing in greatest confidence which he had not mentioned previously. He said that it was made clear to him by the Soviet leaders when he was in Moscow that they were prepared, in concert with Nasser, to agree to bring about peace in Algeria on a basis acceptable to his government provided he would agree to come part way to meet their views on European matters. They did not ask that France make any dramatic moves, such as the abandonment of NATO, but only that she be less faithful to the West and become in effect semi-neutralist. Mollet said I must realize the temptation that such an offer regarding Algeria offered to any French statesman. He hoped that I would understand when he said that he felt that his firm rejection of this Soviet offer gave him the right now to speak frankly of his fears for the Western position and to request a sympathetic hearing by the US Govt.[44]

But Eisenhower and Dulles were not to be bullied. The message back from the president was for the world to be shown that 'every peaceful means to resolve this difficulty' had been exhausted before military action was contemplated.

Eden and Mollet gave way with as much grace as they could muster. Invitations to a conference in London went out to those nations that had signed the 1888 Convention and others with shipping interests. Deliberations would begin on 16 August. The date was a matter of contention. Having little faith in the ability of the conference to come up with a solution, Pineau was keen to get the whole business out of the way as quickly as possible. According to the French timetable Anglo-French forces should by mid-August have been well on the way to Cairo. Oblivious to such plans, Dulles argued that time was needed for serious deliberations; 16 August was the eventual compromise between the French and American preferred dates. By then, Eden had put his signature to Musketeer.

The busy congregation of diplomats and the approaching military drumbeat did little to disturb the placid surface of life in Egypt. Douglas Stuart, the BBC correspondent in Cairo, observed the scene near his back-street parking place.

> Most days I park the car in the same spot in the centre of Cairo and then walk to my various appointments. Over the weeks, I've got to know the people near the parking place quite well, particularly the steady customers of the small soft-drinks shop. We smile at each other, say good day and exchange platitudes about the weather; then they sink back into their chairs on the pavement and return to their newspapers and gossip . . . I've not encountered hostility anywhere; on the contrary, I've found a great deal of friendliness and enjoyment of even the slightest of jokes.

On the other hand: '. . . the Egyptian government is doing its best to stir up popular indignation against the West'.[45]

The newspapers and the radio played up the 'Anglo-French military threat to Egypt'. Everywhere there were preparations to meet 'imperialist invasion'. Schools became recruiting centres for the new National Liberation Army. Every day the newspapers carried pictures of veiled Egyptian women holding sub-machine guns. Children were not excluded. Douglas Stuart saw army instructors showing six-year-olds how to drill.

> . . . Colonel Nasser's military dictatorship, with all the skill of modern propaganda techniques, is seeking to create a martial mood among the people. The streets of Cairo are decorated with huge photographs of their leader in army uniform. An enormous silver eagle, the symbol of the revolutionary regime, blazes across the Nile at night in neon-lit splendour. A giant plywood

soldier straddles one of Cairo's main shopping streets. In the air-conditioned cinemas the people watch films glorifying the Egyptian Army. From time to time there's a little clapping.[46]

Of a more practical nature were the preparations for putting the Suez Canal out of action, should this prove necessary. A retired and rusty tank landing craft was moored some 200 yards from the jetty at Ismailia. The *Akka* was loaded with cement and scrap iron. No one had to be told why it was there. Nonetheless, there were still close observers, including the British ambassador, Humphrey Trevelyan, who were struck by the absence of jingoism. 'For weeks Mars presented a warlike face, blood red and looming large in the Eastern sky. Surely, we thought, this must be a good omen; for the Heavens would not foretell war in such an obvious way.'[47]

President Nasser shared this optimism. For now, he was prepared to wait on events.

14

On 8 August Eden went on television to put the black spot on the Egyptian leader. 'The pattern', he declared, 'is familiar to many of us . . . we all know this is how fascist governments behave and we all remember, only too well, what the cost can be in giving in to fascism.' He promised that 'an act of plunder which threatens the livelihood of many nations will not be allowed to succeed'.

Allowing for the uneven production values in a medium that had yet to come to terms with the political broadcast, it was a stilted and unconvincing performance. Because Eden could not help but appear as a very superior person, his attempt at cosy familiarity, addressing his audience as 'my friends', struck a false note. Here was a prime minister who seemed to be unsure of his ground, a salesman with a dodgy product. 'Our quarrel', he told his audience, 'is not with Egypt – it is with Nasser.' Really? Could anyone be so naive as to believe that Nasser had been visited on the Egyptian people without popular support? Anyway, following Eden's unlikely proposition, unless he had in mind a duel at sunrise, going to war with Nasser meant going to war with Egypt, bringing death and destruction to those with whom, apparently, we had no quarrel.

Listening to the confused message at his home in Stansted was Rab Butler.

I remember leaning out of the bow window into the garden and smoking one of the last cigarettes I ever had. My mood was one of deep misgiving and anxiety on hearing this analogy with fascism and this personalization of Nasser. I thought the Prime

Minister had got that part of it wrong. I admired his courage, his gallantry, his wartime record and his Foreign Office achievements. He seemed thoroughly in character in standing up for British rights in the Middle East and I supported him. But it was surely unwise to use in 1956 the language that ought to have been used in 1936. The circumstances had altered. The cast had changed.[1]

His misgivings were shared at all levels in the administration. Denis Wright, who was an assistant under-secretary at the foreign office, heard nothing of comfort in the broadcast. The next day he wrote an indignant letter to his Conservative member of parliament, protesting at the government's action. He also consulted a senior colleague, Paul Gore-Booth, who showed him a minute he had sent to Ivone Kirkpatrick complaining of being kept in the dark and asking for information. Kirkpatrick's response was to call a meeting of all under-secretaries for later that morning. It resolved nothing.

> Kirkpatrick had only two things to say. One was that there was a complaint about lack of information, but there hadn't been any. The other was that the Foreign Office had not been consulted. Kirkpatrick said that Ministers were never obliged to consult their departments. If they wished to, they expected the best advice, but to assume that Ministers have to rush to their departments for advice, we must get that out of our heads.[2]

Kirkpatrick also spoke of the need for foreign office officials to defend the policies of their ministers. Denis Wright came away feeling as much in the dark as ever and with a low opinion of Kirkpatrick.[3] It was an opinion widely shared.

The permanent secretary seemed to imagine that if he barked loud enough all those within hearing would remain silent. But there was no stopping the gossip of a disaster in the making, much of it originating with those who had first-hand knowledge. Here is Patrick Reilly, who, home from Paris in mid-August, spent 'four absolutely miserable weeks' at the foreign office.

I was offered a lift down to Suffolk one Saturday evening, where my family were on holiday, by [Major-]General John Cowley, who was then Vice-Quartermaster-General, and whose family were holiday-making close to mine. All the way down to Suffolk, he talked with great frankness about the situation. He was in despair about the muddle and confusion that was going on. Ships, I remember him complaining, were being loaded and unloaded, and the whole thing he obviously considered a great mess.[4]

Few could be found to take an opposing view, as Evelyn Shuckburgh discovered when, on release from the foreign office, he embarked on the less exacting role of a lecturer at the Imperial Defence College. Young officers from the Commonwealth and allied states 'couldn't understand what on earth the British government was up to'.

So they turned to me and said: 'What's the Foreign Office up to? You're a Foreign Office man.' So I went over there to try and find out. And I remember I couldn't see Kirkpatrick, but I saw [Patrick] Dean [Deputy Under-Secretary of State at the FO], and I didn't think I was given a very clear picture. It was very hard to explain to these American, Canadian, Australian officers what we were up to. And it wasn't greatly helped when the First Sea Lord, Lord Mountbatten, came and lectured to us, and over drinks at the bar after the lecture – this was at the height of the operation – said he thought it was bloody awful nonsense too. So it really was a shambles.[5]

A just-retired senior civil servant, Sir Edmund Hall-Patch, expressed the general impression of Whitehall that 'we are in the hands of a weak man who is trying to prove that he is a strong one'.[6]

In the pause before the canal users' conference could begin, various ideas were mooted for keeping up the pressure on Nasser. A suggestion from Jacques Georges-Picot, the managing director of the unloved canal company, was well received. He wanted his remaining employees to give immediate notice and to leave the country. This would deprive Nasser of the services of the European pilots who were judged to be essential for handling the large volume of traffic on the canal. In this as in so many other matters, Georges-Picot was misinformed. The pilots were not essential to the smooth running of the canal. But he and the politicians had to wait on this revelation. For the moment, it was thought unwise for Britain and France to incur blame for the very disruption they were seeking to avoid. They wanted Nasser to make the first move.

There was not much else they could do to give Nasser a hard time. The freezing of Egyptian assets outside Cairo's control had already been brought into play and, for what it was worth, a ban imposed on arms exports to Egypt. In Eden's dream world, Egypt's economy, heavily dependent on the export of cotton, would be brought crashing down by dumping cheap American cotton on to the world market. But Washington was better served by economists who understood the knock-on effect of a trade war on developing countries, not least India, another country for which cotton was a prime export. In any case, where was the justification for such drastic action?

Nasser was behaving impeccably. With the long-established exception of Israel, he stuck by the letter of the 1888 Convention guaranteeing freedom of access to the Suez Canal for all countries. He made no attempt to retaliate against the freezing of assets or to attempt to countermand instructions to shipowners to pay canal dues into blocked accounts. To meet one of Dulles's frequently voiced objections to the manner in which Nasser had gone about the canal nationalisation, he lifted his threat of imprisoning foreign employees of the company who refused to work.

It was inevitable that Nasser would refuse to attend the London conference even before Eden's television appearance on 8 August labelled him as an implacable enemy. He gave his reasons for staying away when he met ambassador Byroade on 3 August after 'spending the day with his children on the beach and going to a movie to "clear his mind"'.

Having been put under threat of invasion and starvation (a reference to the freezing of Egyptian assets), Nasser found himself wondering whether the British 'were not deliberately making it impossible for him to be represented'. Then again:

> He thought the choice of nations was very strange and composed for the large part of 'satellites' of the Big Three. How for instance was Ethiopia chosen? The combination of Commonwealth and close friends and allies of the United States left little doubt that conference would be pro forma. The British would put in a 'paper' and a great majority of the others would quickly agree with very little discussion or consideration of Egypt's case.[7]

But Nasser was, so he claimed, 'ready to sign a new international agreement . . . guaranteeing freedom of passage and uninterrupted use of Suez Canal facilities'.[8]

To add to Anglo-French frustration at failing to detect a fault line in Nasser's strategy, the other maritime nations were beginning to show distinct signs of acquiescence in the changes to canal management. As an increasing proportion of shipowners paid their dues to the nationalised company (35 per cent by mid-August), the financial markets steadied and the insurance premium imposed by Lloyds of London on vessels taking the canal route was lifted.

Washington was not entirely convinced by Nasser's exercise in smooth diplomacy. Nothing could remove Dulles's sense of grievance over the Soviet arms deal and his aversion to Egyptian persistence in courting Russia as an ally. The Pentagon led the way in urging the Secretary of State to consider 'the desirability of taking military action in support of the UK, France and others as appropriate', the aim being to placing the Suez Canal 'under a friendly and responsible authority at the earliest practicable date'.[9]

This was followed on 3 August by a warning from the joint chiefs of staff that 'as Nasser's influence spreads it may be anticipated that other Arab states . . . will use his successful act of nationalisation as justification for themselves expropriating US

and Western enterprises'.[10] And not only Arab states. The status
of the Panama Canal was a sensitive issue in Washington. Mention
of a possible takeover was liable to make Eisenhower sound like
Eden in his worst mood, threatening on one occasion that 'if we
left the Panama Zone we would take the locks with us'.[11]

As a special assistant to Dulles, one with a close knowledge of
the Middle East, George Russell was convinced that 'the possibility of our establishing a cooperative relationship with Nasser
no longer exists'. There were too many signals of hostile intent
starting with:

> Nasser's efforts to build a solidarity of the Arab countries, especi-
> ally Egypt, Saudi Arabia and Syria, even at the expense of econ-
> omic progress in Egypt; his rage at Iraq's participation in the
> Baghdad Pact; his lip service in private talks to a Palestine settle-
> ment while exacerbating the problem in public speeches; his firm
> insistence upon obtaining the entire Negev; his skill, for a period
> at least, in playing off the Soviet bloc against the West; his
> shrewdness in attacking at one time Britain and at another time
> the US but rarely the two at the same time; his public dispatch
> of Ambassador Hussein to accept the US offer to assist on the
> Aswan Dam, after having shown no interest for six months, at a
> time when he was aware that the Secretary of State was no longer
> in a position to make firm arrangements; and, finally, using the
> 'turn down' as a pretext for seizing the Canal and thus, if success-
> ful, putting Egypt in a position to affect the economy of Western
> Europe, the countries of South Asia and elsewhere.[12]

Dulles took note but did not respond, choosing instead to stick
to his policy of exploring peaceful ways of achieving a settlement.
But 'this divergence of initial approach between us and the British
and French does not by any means imply that we will not be
solidly with them if the conference method breaks down'.[13]

The assumption here was that Britain and France would do
their best to make the conference work. In fact, they showed no
inclination to do so. In France, further bad news from Algeria
hardened opinion in support of war with Egypt, come what may

at the London conference. A debate in the National Assembly on 2 and 3 August concluded with a massive vote of confidence for Mollet – 422 to 150 – with only the communists standing out against the government.

The leading French press continued to weigh in on Mollet's side, calling for the toppling of Nasser even if this had to be done by France acting alone. 'In throwing down this challenge,' roared the normally left-leaning *Le Monde*, 'the Egyptian government is testing the cohesion of the West's diplomatic and military machinery. Everything will now depend on the speed and determination with which the western nations are able to take retaliatory measures.'[14] Chauvinistic editorials were heavily laced with anti-Americanism, the charge being that while post-war France had remained loyal to American leadership, now when help was needed the USA was selfishly holding back.

While opinion in France remained firm, British resolve was showing further signs of vulnerability. Despite earlier protestations of harmony, Labour was now out of tune with government strategy. Hugh Gaitskell was in a difficult position. His instinct was to give Eden as much support as was needed to bring about a settlement. He had no liking for Nasser or his nationalist aspirations. Most of his parliamentary colleagues agreed. But across the country there were party divisions opening up between the left-wing libertarians who felt that Nasser was entitled to do whatever he wanted in his own back yard and those working-class supporters who had unpleasant memories of military service in the Canal Zone and were only too keen for their successors to have 'a bash at the wogs'.

In trying to hold the balance, Gaitskell was constrained by not knowing all the facts. On 30 July, after Eden had made a short holding statement to the Commons, he met with Gaitskell to assure him that a full-scale military operation was not in prospect. This was on the same day that orders were drafted for the requisitioning of civilian transport, a sure sign for those able to read it that the country was building up to a national emergency.

Gaitskell had only rumours to work on and he refused to believe them. As a shadow treasury spokesman with close connections with Fleet Street, Douglas Jay had failed to persuade Gaitskell to take seriously the warnings of impending disaster emerging from the Foreign Office. 'I went to see him with John Hynd MP before the debate on 2nd August, saying that I heard rumours in my *Daily Herald* office, via the Diplomatic Correspondent [W. N. Ewer] from the Foreign Office, that plans were going forward for armed force. Gaitskell said he didn't believe it, [because] Eden couldn't be so reckless and foolish.'[15]

Eden might be forgiven for withholding sensitive information but in dissembling quite so blatantly in his dealings with Gaitskell he was simply putting off the day when the opposition leader would take his revenge on government duplicity. When the invasion force was finally on its way, Gaitskell, according to Douglas Jay, 'launched a whole series of attacks that were the most powerful speeches I had ever heard in the Commons'. In conversation with Jay, he added, 'I shall never believe anything that Eden says to me again, in public or in private.'[16]

In the early days of the crisis, however, Eden could at least count on a sympathetic hearing from Gaitskell.

The Commons debate on Suez on 2 August went reasonably well for the government. Eden made no mention of the moves towards creating an Anglo-French invasion force except to refer vaguely to 'precautionary measures of a military nature' and announcing the call-up of some reserve units. Gaitskell's response raised smiles of contentment from government supporters as he equated Nasser's takeover of the canal with the territorial snatches of Mussolini and Hitler. Moreover, he had no objection to Eden's 'precautionary measures'. But – and in subsequent debates his proviso was invariably forgotten – 'while force cannot be excluded, we must be sure that circumstances justify it and it is . . . consistent with the UN Charter'.

The following day, Gaitskell gave a clearer indication of his thinking in a letter to Eden.

In view of the reports in the Press this morning, which I gather came from the Foreign Office, that Britain and France intend if necessary and without active American participation to use force – even if there is no further aggressive action by Nasser – I feel I must repeat to you publicly the warnings I have already uttered privately. While one or two members of our Party indicated in the debate that they would support force now, this is, I am pretty sure, not the general view.

Naturally our attitude in the event of this situation arising would depend on the exact circumstances. If Nasser were to do something which led to his condemnation by the United Nations as an aggressor, then there is no doubt, I am sure, that we would be entirely in favour of forceful resistance. But I must repeat, what I said in my speech yesterday, that up to the present I cannot see that he has done anything which would justify this.[17]

This 'friendly warning', as Gaitskell put it, was 'to avoid any possible misunderstanding in future'. But just in case there *was* any misunderstanding, Gaitskell wrote again, yet more emphatically, on 10 August:

Lest there should still be any doubt in your mind about my personal attitude, let me say that I could not regard an armed attack on Egypt by ourselves and the French as justified by anything which Nasser has done so far or as consistent with the Charter of the United Nations. Nor, in my opinion, would such an attack be justified in order to impose a system of international control over the Canal – desirable though this is. If, of course, the whole matter were to be taken to the United Nations and if Egypt were to be condemned by them as aggressors, then, of course, the position would be different. And if further action which amounted to obvious aggression by Egypt were taken by Nasser, then again it would be different. So far what Nasser has done amounts to a threat, a grave threat to us and to others, which certainly cannot be ignored; but it is only a threat, not in my opinion justifying retaliation by war.[18]

The Labour-leaning newspapers were yet more outspoken, starting with the mass-circulation *Daily Mirror*, which devoted a whole front page and two centre pages to arguing four basic propositions.

1. Nothing that has yet happened over the Suez Canal justifies war or the threat of war.

2. Regardless of the outcome of the Conference, British public opinion would not support a Government which pursued a policy of force at this stage.

3. Sir Anthony Eden's desire or intention to overthrow Nasser as Egypt's leader is blatantly unrealistic. Eden cannot talk to Nasser in 1956 as Churchill talked to Mussolini in the 1940s.

4. Britain must not 'go it alone' over Suez. We must deal with the crisis through collective international action, referring the result of the London Conference to the United Nations.[19]

Item four was precisely what Eden and Mollet wanted to avoid. The longer the talking went on, the greater the chances for Nasser to win the last round. In a letter to Eisenhower, Eden drew a limit on Anglo-French patience.

> Nevertheless I am sure you will agree that we must prepare to meet the eventuality that Nasser will refuse to accept the outcome of the conference; or, no less dangerous, that he, supported by the Russians, will seek by stratagems and wiles to divide us so that the conference produces no clear result in the sense we both seek. We and the French Government could not possibly acquiesce in such a situation. I really believe that the consequences of doing so would be catastrophic, and that the whole position in the Middle East would thereby be lost beyond recall. But by all means let us first see what the conference can do – on the assumption that Nasser commits no further folly meanwhile.[20]

Eisenhower made do with a gentle stand-off reply, saying how good it was of Eden 'to send me so promptly your thinking on the subject', adding that he 'was glad to hear from Foster that you are looking so well'. Whatever Eden's outward appearance he was certainly not *feeling* well. His mood changes were more erratic and were no longer reserved for those closest to him. Richard Freeborn was an interpreter for a Soviet delegation invited to the Commons to meet Eden and other members of the cabinet led by Selwyn Lloyd.

> [Eden] appeared to me extremely nervous and somewhat uncontrolled in his address to the Soviet delegates. He spoke quickly and at some length, forgetful of the need for translation, it seemed, and though I took notes I could not convey the full extent of what he said when he had spoken for 3 or 4 minutes (as I recall) before allowing a pause for translation. I managed to express the gist but I know I was not adequate to the task of full translation. He then spoke at length again and I noticed that Selwyn Lloyd had gone quite puce in the face. The Soviet delegates were beginning to glance at each other, aware that they were in the presence of someone whose behaviour was abnormal. I made a further stab at translation but was interrupted by Eden starting again. Shortly afterwards the meeting closed on Eden's departure accompanied by Selwyn Lloyd and the other cabinet members.[21]

The prime minister's fragile temper and contradictory behaviour lost him many friends. Air Chief Marshal Sir William Dickson, chairman of the COS, confessed to John Colville that he 'had never been spoken to in his life in the way the PM spoke to him during those tempestuous days'. Freddy Bishop, Eden's principal private secretary, concurred, adding that he had 'finally given up making allowances for AE or feeling sorry for him'.[22] The liberal use of amphetamines almost certainly accounts for Eden's frenetic energy. Often, said Dickson, he was 'like a prophet inspired' sweeping the cabinet and chiefs of staff along with him, 'brushing aside any counter arguments and carrying all by his exaltation'.[23] But the possible side effects, including anxiety and paranoia, may

also have affected Eden. Signs of him cracking up were observed
even by junior colleagues such as Anthony Nutting at the foreign
office, and Nigel Birch and Christopher Soames at the air ministry.[24] But their outspoken criticism of the prime minister was
restricted to table talk. Their assumption at this stage was that if
action were called for it would surely be taken by those farther
up the political pecking order.

As it happened, resistance to Eden was beginning to emerge
within the cabinet. Among the six waverers identified by the
Cabinet Secretary were R. A. Butler, Heathcoat-Amery (agriculture minister) and, more critically, Walter Monckton, the minister
of defence, who was the only senior minister to come out against
the use of force.[25] Macmillan quickly marked him down as one
of the 'weaker brethren' and noted, after a fraught meeting of
the Egypt Committee on 24 August, that Monckton was 'calm
but obviously distressed'.[26] But he remained at defence until
18 October, when instead of leaving the government he was made
paymaster general, a ministerial position with nebulous responsibilities, but with cabinet status. As such Monckton was to be
landed with the task of coordinating the government's propaganda
and information during Suez, a reminder of his wartime days
when he did the same job but from Cairo.

How did Monckton square his conscience? In retirement he
claimed not to have been 'fundamentally troubled by moral considerations'. His anxieties had more to do with 'allying ourselves
with the French and the Jews . . . [who] were bound to bring us
into conflict with Arab and Muslim feeling'.[27] But at this early
stage in the crisis, Israeli involvement was not an option; indeed,
it would have been strenuously opposed by the whole cabinet
with the exception of Macmillan. It seems then that Monckton's
initial anger was directed against France, though fuelled by an
objection to 'taking warlike action against Egypt behind the back
of the Americans'.[28] As to resignation:

> Naturally I anxiously considered whether I ought not to resign.
> Resignation at such a moment was not a thing lightly to be

undertaken. I felt that I was virtually alone in my opinion in the Cabinet and that I had not the experience or the knowledge to make me confident in my own view when it was so strongly opposed by Eden, Salisbury, Macmillan, Head, Sandys, Thorneycroft, and Kilmuir; for all of whom I had respect and admiration. I knew that if I did resign it was likely that the Government would fall, and I still believed that it was better for the country to have that Government than the alternative. What the Labour people had in mind was a kind of rump of the Tory Government led by Butler, which they would support. This could not last. Moreover, far more than I knew at the time, the ordinary man in the country was behind Eden.[29]

The tortured rationale of this excuse for inactivity hardly bears examination. That Monckton believed his resignation would sink the government suggests a level of self-delusion to match that of the prime minister. But there was more to the story. Personal circumstances limited Monckton's freedom of action. A messy divorce had deprived him of his chance of becoming Lord Chief Justice and had left him short of money. There was only one other attractive prospect for a post-parliamentary career. But an acrimonious departure from the government would have taken him out of line to be the chairman of the Midland Bank. In other words, Monckton sold out. He was not the last to do so.

On 16 August representatives of twenty-two nations gathered at Lancaster House close by Buckingham Palace. Only two of the original invitees to the Canal Users' Conference failed to turn up; Greece cited its grievance against Britain for holding out against the demands of the Greek Cypriots while Egypt declined for reasons of self-interest already spelt out by Nasser to the US ambassador in Cairo. As a senior politician of the host country and, according to Dulles, because 'he so desperately wanted it', Selwyn Lloyd took the chair. He did not have an easy time of it. Many of those seated around the table in the Long Gallery, hot and stuffy in a humid London summer, were not at all sure why they had taken the trouble to come.

Under Egyptian management, the canal was providing the shipping companies with a service that was in no way inferior to that delivered by the Canal Company. There was no indication that Nasser was about to interrupt the flow of oil. Why should he, since he needed the revenue from canal tolls? The act of nationalisation had been well received by most countries and, indeed, acclaimed by thirty-two governments ranging from China to Spain and representing two-thirds of the world's population.[30]

Now it was up to Britain and France to show why other states should be compelled to give their blessing to what was beginning to look uncannily like the last throw of old-fashioned colonialism. Eden was aware of the risks, which was why he opposed having Russia along to peddle the inevitable anti-colonial rhetoric. But, as Dulles pointed out, to exclude Russia would be to add to the already loud chorus of complaint that the conference was weighted in favour of the Western bloc. Not that he expected Russia to toe the Anglo-French line. In a pre-conference talk, foreign minister Shepilov made clear to Dulles that, in his view, 'under international law and historic precedent Egypt have the right to nationalise the Canal', though he had the company rather than the waterway itself in mind. When it came to guaranteeing freedom of navigation, 'military preparations undertaken by the UK and France were not warranted'. Friendly negotiation was the way forward.[31] These comments were made less than three months before Russian invaded Hungary. But in swallowing the large doses of hypocrisy, Shepilov was saying no more than was in the minds of Dulles and Eisenhower, the latter having stated categorically, at a press gathering on 8 August, that he could not conceive 'of military force being a good solution, certainly under conditions as we know them now'.

Once the conference was under way, Eisenhower was urging Dulles 'not to allow the British and French to insist on too rough a line with Nasser'. Maybe, mused the president, 'supervision' rather than 'control' could be exercised by a 'commission of smaller countries' including Egypt. Disagreements on tolls or investment in maintenance could be referred to the World Court 'or other suitable body'.[32]

Eisenhower was right to concentrate on the precise wording of any joint proposal that was to be put to Nasser. Dulles understood the point. The purpose of the conference was to come up with a formula for the management of the canal which gave right of way to the maritime powers without compromising Egyptian sovereignty. To produce a document that satisfied both sides was a matter of delicate drafting. Britain and France wanted a Canal Authority capable of imposing its will on a recalcitrant Nasser. But that was to throw away any chance of conference unanimity and to invite certain rejection by Egypt.

Offering himself as the advocate of reasonable compromise, Dulles edged the Western allies towards supporting the setting up of a Suez Canal Board, with an international membership, to work in partnership with Egypt to secure the 'maintenance and development of the Canal'. Vague as it was, the document failed to win the approval of Russia. This was wholly predictable since Soviet best interests demanded that Western influence on Egypt should be eradicated. But while Shepilov left Dulles in no doubt as to his views, he was uncharacteristically withdrawn in the conference debate, deferring to India's Krishna Menon to act as spokesman for Nasser.

Menon was a curious and in many ways a contradictory character. Though an ardent left-wing Indian nationalist, he spoke no language but English, rejected spicy Indian food and was more inclined to sport a tweed jacket and flannel trousers than traditional Indian dress. Most of his political career, including ten years as a Labour councillor, had been spent in Britain where, as Nehru's trusted adviser, he had risen to be Indian high commissioner and representative at the United Nations.

Menon was much disliked, even by those who were counted among his closest allies. A self-righteous arrogance combined with long-winded oratory caused resentment not least in Cairo, where there was anger at Menon's assumption that he could speak on behalf of Nasser without prior consultation.

All that said, Menon was the only delegate to the Canal Users' Conference to come close to a practical solution to the Suez crisis. Instead of handing over authority to a Canal Board requiring Nasser to rescind his act of nationalisation (the equivalent of political suicide), Menon suggested an international 'advisory' committee backed by a new version of the 1888 Convention. Any breach of the terms of the Convention would be subject to UN sanctions. The scheme had the virtue of treating Egypt as an equal, not as a renegade nation in need of strict paternalism.

Unfortunately, Menon made his debut late in the proceedings when delegates had long since given up any pretence of glancing at their watches. Bad timing was aggravated by a truly awful speech 'delivered from notes, rambling and repetitive'.[33] Predictably, the British and French dismissed Menon as a mischief-maker unworthy of serious attention. Less predictably, Dulles was equally unimpressed.

> At our session this afternoon, Menon made a long speech and introduced his proposals which were all right as generalities but which could be accepted by Nasser without there being any assurance whatsoever that the Canal could not be one hundred per cent operated purely in the political interests of Egypt as an instrument of its national policy. There are references to international bodies but they are pure scenery.[34]

The following day, eighteen of the countries represented lined up behind Dulles. They included Ethiopia, Iran, Pakistan and Turkey, 'so that . . . the programme becomes not just a western programme but one with African and Asian support'.[35] A minority of four – the Soviet Union, India, Indonesia and Ceylon – supported the Menon plan. There was only one other pressing decision. Who was to carry the message to Cairo? Eden had no doubts on that score. Dulles was the only candidate to lead the five-nation delegation. It was, after all, Dulles who had put most into the plan. To make it stick, he had to be seen to be giving it his full backing.

But this was not the prime consideration. Neither Eden nor his closest colleagues in the British and French governments really expected Nasser to submit placidly to the dictates of the London conference, even with Dulles leading from the front. If there was to be a rejection, it was important for Dulles to receive it at first hand. It would then be hard for him to disassociate the USA from what Eden and Mollet saw as the inevitable next step – a show of force to make Nasser toe the line or, better still, to bring about his downfall.

The omens did not look good to at least one young national serviceman. On 20 August Lieutenant Peter Mayo of the Royal Marines noted in his diary:

> We are preparing to go to war if the need arise in the next few weeks, though no-one has really understood that yet. The excitement of the move and the vague and vaguely romantic notion of going to defend one's country's 'rights' still prevail. I imagine a few weeks of the sunny aridity of Malta will cure this. I was just thinking of what little consequence it would be if I were to end my life next month in some obscure brush with some obscure Egyptian. The whole thing would be senseless and insignificant, and I doubt it would make much difference to the world.[36]

15

The charm offensive now mounted on Dulles to persuade him to go to Cairo was shamelessly outrageous. Eden set the tone with frequent references to Dulles's 'masterly performance' at the conference, while going out of his way to tell senior US diplomats, whom he knew would be reporting home, 'what a wonderful job Foster has done here' and that the Secretary of State was 'the only one who stands a chance of negotiation with Nasser'.[1]

But it was Macmillan who stretched the bounds of ingratiation beyond embarrassment. As Dulles recorded for Eisenhower's benefit:

> As I was leaving Sir Anthony Eden's Reception last night, Harold Macmillan said he would like to speak to me privately. We went into one of the private rooms. Macmillan asked first of all whether I planned to stay on as Secretary of State. He said that he was thinking of perhaps going back to take over the Foreign Office in the reasonably near future and that his decision in this matter would be influenced by whether I would be his vis-à-vis in the United States. He spoke of the very happy relations we had together when we were both Foreign Ministers and that he would very much like to renew this.[2]

Dulles was not to be seduced. He had no intention of finding himself trapped in what could soon be a war zone. His worries on this count were well founded. Along with the protestations of peaceful intent from Eden and the others came the frequent threats of force if they did not get their way. Two days before Macmillan urged Dulles 'most strongly to take on the negotiation with Nasser' he was telling the secretary of state that if 'we accept Nasser's refusal ... Britain is finished'. He added that in this event 'I will have no part in it and will resign,' but there was a clear implication that before it came to that the troops would be sent in.[3]

The message from Paris was put more bluntly. Pineau was not one to lose a single opportunity to impress on Dulles that 'military action would be inevitable in the Suez dispute'. This was also the uncompromising line taken by Ivone Kirkpatrick. As the chief adviser on foreign affairs to Selwyn Lloyd, he might have been thought to have exceeded his brief when, at the very same Downing Street reception used by Eden and Macmillan to praise Dulles to the skies, he spelt out his creed to a bemused US embassy official:

> He said in effect that we would, as he put it, 'have to have a row' with Nasser. He said we might as well have it early as late. He compared Nasser to Hitler and the Rhineland and said it was just a question of how long all of us would have to go along appeasing Nasser 'before we had the inevitable row'. I do not know to what extent Ivone was speaking in the official British view; but if he was, then the British like the French feel sure that force is the only answer. I did say to Ivone that I did not believe that public opinion in the United States, or for that matter in Great Britain, would support a resort to force at this time. He snapped back that he did not care about public opinion, that it was the business of informed leaders to lead their countries in what they thought was the right course of action and not merely to 'follow public opinion'.[4]

With Dulles having put himself out of the running as fall guy for the Cairo negotiations, the search was on for a credible replacement. The choice fell on Robert Menzies, prime minister of Australia, who had given strong support to the eighteen-nation proposals for settling the Suez issue. He was also on record as being among the first major politicians outside the Anglo-French circle to declare against Nasser.

Trading on his credentials as a lawyer and statesman, Menzies argued that those who regarded the problems as purely academic, that Egypt as a sovereign power had the right to nationalise an Egyptian enterprise, ignored 'two salient facts':

First, for historical reasons ... the concession had an international character recognised by an international convention. It could not, therefore, be regarded as a merely domestic enterprise under the sole control of the Egyptian Government. Secondly, what Egypt did was to repudiate this contractual concession twelve years before its due date without consultation and without agreement. If such a repudiation is not a breach of international law then there is no international law.[5]

Having made his points at the London Conference, which he judged to be a success, Menzies spent what he imagined would be his last night in London before returning to Canberra.

At about 2 a.m., the telephone rang, and woke me up. On the line was Winthrop Aldrich, the American Ambassador ... He said: 'I want you to come up to my house (in Regent's Park).' 'When?' I asked. 'Right away. Anthony, Selwyn and Foster are here, with some others. They want to discuss a matter with you!' I protested, and asked whether it would not keep till the morning. He said that it would not, and that he would send a car down to the Savoy at once. I got up, dressed, and arrived at the Residence at about 2.30 a.m.

They explained that they were now contemplating a Committee of five, to get a properly balanced result. Anthony Eden then said to me, 'We all want you to be a member of the Committee.' Dulles interjected, 'No, Anthony, not a member, Chairman. We want him as our chief spokesman, because he knows how to put a case!'

I at once demurred ... I should be at my post in Australia. They kept at me. I suggested some other names, but they would not have them. 'If you say "No", we will re-think the whole matter of the Committee.'[6]

Having cabled Arthur Fadden, his deputy prime minister, to secure the agreement of colleagues that 'I should be available for the Committee', Menzies said 'yes'.

From Eden's point of view, the Australian prime minister was by far the best second choice to fill the role marked out for Dulles. An Anglophile of Churchillian passion and proportions, Menzies could be relied upon to warn Nasser of the consequences if he failed to accept international control of the canal. Still lacking approval from Washington for his strong line, Eden sought to strengthen the Menzies delegation with one of his 'Dear Friend' letters to Eisenhower showing how the Russians were exploiting allied weakness in the Middle East.

> I have no doubt that the bear is using Nasser, with or without his knowledge, to further his immediate aims. These are, I think, first to dislodge the West from the Middle East, and second to get a foothold in Africa so as to dominate that continent in turn. In this connexion I have seen a reliable report from someone who was present at the lunch which Shepilov gave for the Arab Ambassadors. There the Soviet claim was that they 'only wanted to see Arab unity in Asia and Africa and the abolition of all foreign bases and exploitation. An agreed, unified Arab nation must take its rightful place in the world'.
>
> This policy is clearly aimed at . . . our Middle East oil supplies. Meanwhile the Communist bloc continue their economic and political blandishments towards the African countries which are already independent. Soon they will have a wider field for subversion as our colonies, particularly in the West, achieve self-government. All this makes me more than ever sure that Nasser must not be allowed to get away with it this time. We have many friends in the Middle East and in Africa and others who are shrewd enough to know where the plans of a Nasser or a Mossadeq would lead them. But they will not be strong enough to stand against the power of the mobs if Nasser wins again.[7]

Considering how, subsequently, Britain and France heaped all the blame for the Suez reversal on Eisenhower for giving a misleading impression of US intentions, his response to Eden's red scare letter should be kept as a ready reference. As a model of clarity it is hard to fault.

> Now that the London Conference is over, our efforts must be concentrated on the successful outcome of the conversations with Nasser. This delicate situation is going to require the highest skill ... I share your view that it is important that Nasser be under no misapprehension as to the firm interest of the nations primarily concerned with the Canal in safeguarding their rights in that waterway ... and of course there should be no thought of military action before the influences of the UN are fully explored. However, and most important, we believe that, before going to the UN, the Suez Committee of Five should first be given full opportunity to carry out the course of action agreed upon in London, and to gauge Nasser's intentions.

> If the diplomatic front we present is united and is backed by the overwhelming sentiment of our several peoples, the chances should be greater that Nasser will give way without the need for any resort to force ...

> I am afraid, Anthony, that from this point onward our views on this situation diverge. As to the use of force or the threat of force at this juncture, I continue to feel as I expressed myself in the letter Foster carried to you some weeks ago. Even now military preparations and civilian evacuation exposed to public view seem to be solidifying support for Nasser which has been shaky in many important quarters. I regard it as indispensable that if we are to proceed solidly together to the solution of this problem, public opinion in our several countries must be overwhelmingly in its support. I must tell you frankly that American public opinion flatly rejects the thought of using force, particularly when it does not seem that every possible peaceful means of protecting our vital interests has been exhausted without result. Moreover, I gravely doubt we could here secure Congressional authority even for the lesser support measures for which you might have to look to us.

I really do not see how a successful result could be achieved by forcible means. The use of force would, it seems to me, vastly increase the area of jeopardy. I do not see how the economy of Western Europe can long survive the burden of prolonged military operations, as well as the denial of Near East oil. Also, the peoples of the Near East and of North Africa and, to some extent, of all of Asia and all of Africa, would be consolidated against the West to a degree which, I fear, could not be overcome in a generation and, perhaps, not even in a century particularly having in mind the capacity of the Russians to make mischief. Before such action were undertaken, all our peoples should unitedly understand that there were no other means available to protect our vital rights and interests.[8]

He might well have added, *sotto voce*, 'Is that plain enough for you, Anthony, or should I come over to spell it out in capital letters?' Maybe he should have done just that, for Eden persisted in believing that it was only the threat of force, with the real prospect of carrying out the threat, which would secure British and French objectives.

It was made clear to Menzies that he had no power to negotiate. His job was to persuade Nasser to accept, without amendment, the formula agreed by eighteen maritime nations. If this proved impossible, Nasser should be left under no illusion as to the inevitable consequences. Having set out the terms of engagement, Eden was keen to get the business over quickly. His frustration with those who had to prepare the groundwork for the mission to Cairo was palpable. 'He is obviously worried and perplexed,' reported Walworth Barbour of the American embassy. 'When I told him we had decided to depart Friday morning [31 August] he clasped his head and groaned, "Oh these delays. They are working against us. Every day's postponement is to Nasser's gain and our loss." He went on to urge a speedy resolution. "If the UK was to meet disaster it was preferable it should come as a result of action rather than inaction."'[9]

For the confrontation with Nasser, Menzies assumed the role

he knew best, that of the bluff man of the world who could be trusted to speak his mind, which only went to show how little he understood the Arab mentality. At their first meeting, he was all affability. Addressing Nasser directly, he surprised his host with an opening gambit.

> 'I know you,' he said. Somewhat taken aback, Nasser asked how – had they met before? 'No,' said Menzies. 'But before I left London I went to the BBC and asked them for all the film footage they had on you. So, Mr President, I sat down and watched you for hours, and in particular your Alexandria speech about the canal. So I know you well.' 'I'm glad you do,' said Nasser.[10]

Menzies tried to set the agenda with two meetings each day followed by jointly agreed press statements. Nasser demurred. Each should have their own press spokesman and, as for the meetings, after the opening session there could be only one daily, and that in the evening, since 'it looks as if I may have a war on my hands and in the morning I must be preparing for it'.[11]

The talks got nowhere. What Menzies saw as international cooperation to operate the canal, Nasser interpreted as domination in a light disguise. And he reacted badly to the Menzies slap-on-the-shoulder style of diplomacy, complaining of having to deal with 'this Australian mule'.[12] Sensing that he was losing the game but reluctant to give up without playing his last card, Menzies engineered a one-to-one meeting with Nasser to offer, as he saw it, a friendly warning from one who 'knew something of the state of opinion in London . . . and . . . something of the French state of mind'. It would be a mistake, he told Nasser, 'to exclude the use of force from your reckoning'.[13] Menzies later claimed that Nasser reacted calmly and that 'we parted in a most amicable way'. Egyptian sources credit Nasser with a more robust response to a clear threat. Whoever was right, Nasser now had the perfect excuse to break off the talks, which he did by accusing Menzies of trying to impose 'collective colonialism in regulated form'. It is almost certain that he never had any intention of doing otherwise, but this way he could appear as the man of peace refusing to deal with imperialist bullies.

Menzies could not bring himself to admit that from the very start his mission was hopeless. There had to be someone to blame. The obvious candidate was Eden, who was expecting, even hoping for, a failure to justify stronger measures. How could Menzies have succeeded when he had no authority to bargain? But ever loyal to the British flag, Menzies excused Eden and instead directed his wrath at Eisenhower, who had used his weekly press conference to repeat 'what I have said each week before this body', that 'we are committed to a peaceful settlement of this dispute, *nothing else*'. According to Menzies this 'gave the final power into the hands of Nasser'.

Why this should have been so is hard to say, unless Menzies assumed that Britain and France would not act against Egypt without US support. If so, in this as in much else to do with Suez, Menzies was sadly misguided. Not least of his illusions was the conviction that his pro-British sentiments would win approval at home. Even while he was in Egypt the unanimity of his government was breaking up. Dick Casey, his foreign minister, who had been resident British minister in Egypt in the Second World War, came out strongly against military action. On 11 September, on the eve of Eden's critical Commons debate, he aligned himself with Lester Pearson, his opposite number in Canada, who asserted that the use of force would be futile in the face of American and Asian disapproval, the absence of NATO support and at the risk of censure by the UN.

Eden failed to recognise that he was losing friends in the Commonwealth. All would be well, he calculated, if, following the Cairo slap-down, America could at last be persuaded that Nasser was not open to reason. The eighteen-nation proposals, master-minded by Dulles, had been summarily rejected. At his desk in the Foreign Office, Patrick Reilly caught sight of a telegram on which Eden had scribbled, 'Foreign Secretary, this may give us the pretext for which we are looking'.[14] Now, surely, the Secretary of State would stand alongside his Anglo-French colleagues to demand retribution. But Dulles had other ideas. Thinking things through at his holiday home on Lake Ontario, it occurred to him that perhaps too much attention had been paid to Egypt's presumption of its right to control the canal. The 1888 Convention had made it an international waterway. What was against the canal users coming to their own arrangements to manage the flow of traffic on a non-profit basis? 'As to pilots, why do the ships have to hire pilots through Egypt? Why cannot the British, French or others supply pilots? There are some physical problems but could not these be handled, if need be, through the naval craft authorised to be stationed at each end of the Canal?'[15]

While Eden thought it a 'cook-eyed' idea, he conceded that it had merit as part of the diplomatic game. Although Nasser had successfully undercut the work of the London Conference, there was still nothing that Eden could pin on him that would justify sending in the troops. The setting up of a Canal Users' Association that made its own rules without reference to the Egyptians might just provoke Nasser into taking action that would validate military intervention. Moreover, reasoned Eden, it would be military action sanctioned by the USA, since it was surely inconceivable that Dulles could bear the humiliation of abandoning his own scheme without putting up a fight. Eden was no stranger to misunderstanding the way Dulles's mind worked, but on this occasion he was so far wide of the mark that the shock of realising his error was to send him reeling. Mollet and Pineau urged against wasting more time in fruitless discussion. Eden tried to reassure them. Patience was justified if it produced an unequivocal demonstration of American support.

The prime minister was in buoyant mood when he led the House of Commons in its first Suez debate after the lengthy summer recess. The message was of steady progress towards US, French and British unity of purpose, culminating in the Canal Users' Association.

I must make it clear that should the Egyptian Government interfere with the operations of the Association or refuse to extend to it the minimum co-operation, then that Government will once more be in breach of the 1888 Convention. I must remind the House that what I am saying is the result of exchanges of views between three Governments. In that event Her Majesty's Government and others concerned will be free to take such steps as seem to be required; either through the United Nations or by other means for the assertion of their rights.

This was just what the Tory backbenchers wanted to hear. At last here was the firm smack of government. But it was not what Dulles wanted to hear. As reports of Eden's speech came in on the tape, he realised that his efforts to find a peaceful solution were having the opposite effect. He had already been warned by his embassy in Cairo that Nasser would refuse [to] permit pilots employed by association of users formed without Egypt's consent to enter what is considered as Egyptian territory. Furthermore Egypt would ignore any decisions taken unilaterally by such association for setting up traffic and convey systems and would certainly insist that tolls be paid to it – not to an association residing abroad'.[16]

Moreover, it was difficult to see how repair and construction work could be carried out without Egyptian consent. But here was Eden publicly declaiming that if (which every informed observer took to mean 'when') Egypt challenged the premises of the Users' Association, the USA would join Britain and France in forcing obedience. It is not hard to understand Dulles's anger. It may have been a mistake to offer a simplistic plan that was so obviously open to misinterpretation. But with a presidential election barely two months away, Dulles was under more than usual pressure to come up with an idea that would at least keep in prospect a peaceful solution. It was also reasonable for him to assume that after all the signals to Eden that the USA was not ready to embark on a Middle East war, the prime minister might have thought twice or more before assuming a dramatic change in policy.

Dulles had to move fast to correct the misleading impression.

Gathering together the Washington press corps, he offered a weak justification for the Users' Association as an 'interim solution' which could not be imposed on Nasser. He went on, 'If we cannot work out a programme for getting ships through the Canal on acceptable terms . . . the alternative . . . would be to send our vessels around the Cape.' Then came the *coup de grâce*. 'We do not intend to shoot our way through.' Eden was devastated. Where could he go from here?

At this point Lloyd made a rare attempt to assert himself. While he was wholeheartedly with Eden in the belief that Nasser was a grave threat to British interests, he argued for one more nod towards conciliation, an appeal to the United Nations, which just might wrong-foot Nasser. Recourse to the UN had been on the cards for some time. Lloyd had put the suggestion to a meeting of the Egypt Committee on 27 August and to Dulles ten days later. 'We must set the stage,' he told Anthony Nutting, but when asked whether his stage setting was for war he avoided a direct answer, 'merely saying that he felt sure that Nasser would in due time commit some act of provocation'.[17]

At first, Lloyd was without allies. No one in the government, least of all Eden, expected anything to come from a UN debate. Russia was certain to veto any practical suggestions for meeting British and French concerns and the move was vigorously opposed by Pineau and Mollet as just another delaying tactic. In what the US ambassador to Paris described as a 'disturbing interview', Pineau made no secret of his conviction that there was no way out 'save use of military force'.[18]

More surprisingly, Dulles was also opposed to UN involvement. He feared an unseemly division in the Western ranks if, as was likely, the USA stopped well short of unqualified support for an Anglo-French resolution. Lloyd was warned by Lester Pearson that neither Canada nor the USA would allow the UN to be used as a cover for war.[19]

But having been slapped down by Dulles over the Canal Users' Association (SCUA), Eden was more amenable to Lloyd's idea for going to the UN. At the very least it would keep the show on the road until Anglo-French forces were ready to strike. Returning to the House of Commons for the second day of the Suez debate, however, Eden was unable to present the UN option as anything but a climb-down. Those Tories who, a few hours earlier, had praised Eden as the strong leader now feared the return of the prevaricator. Policy had shifted from resolute action to long-winded debate should Egypt, as expected, refuse to cooperate with SCUA.

With a week to go before a second London conference of canal users to discuss the setting up of SCUA, Eden and Mollet met in London to consider what else could be done to keep up the pressure on Nasser and, fond hope, goad him into provocative action. First on their list of options was the withdrawal of the European pilots who guided ships through the canal. Note had been taken of the boast by Jacques George-Picot, the chief executive of the canal company, that he could paralyse traffic if he chose to order a repatriation.

The offer had so far been resisted chiefly because the French and British governments did not want to seem to be the first to put canal navigators at risk. Also, they were nervous of too close an association with the canal company. The lofty ideals of freedom of navigation and commerce were liable to be tarnished if they were seen to be linked to sordid commercial interests. Among the maritime nations, the canal company was nobody's best friend. It performed efficiently within its limits and posed as a model employer, paying well above standard wages and providing staff with social services that were out of reach for the average Egyptian. But it was nonetheless a lacklustre operation that put more money into promoting its international image to share-holders than on improving its service to its customers. Despite promises going back a century, the canal had never been widened to allow two vessels to pass in transit. Deepening the canal had proceeded in slow motion. The company acquired its first suction dredger in 1950, ninety years after its invention.

Ironically, the first major improvement since the canal opened was pencilled in for 1956–60. This was to double the width of the waterway, after a belated realisation that new bypasses such as those at Port Fuad and Kabrit were inadequate to handle the hoped-for increase in traffic.

The company had raised the proportion of Egyptians on its staff from 24 per cent in 1949 to 42 per cent at the time of nationalisation.[20] But most of the best jobs were reserved for outsiders. This was particularly true of the pilots, an elite group each of whom, on employment, had to boast of ten years' experience on the high seas, including two as a master mariner. Even then, two years' training was thought essential before they were let out on their own. Only 17 per cent of pilots were Egyptian, and although the company, as part of a renegotiation of terms in early 1956, had promised to take on more, the impression put around was that simple natives were not up to such onerous duties.

Those with first-hand experience of the canal were less taken with company pretensions. 'I was stationed in Ismailia in the war,' commented Sir Frank Cooper, who was at the Air Ministry at the time of Suez. 'I had seen the ships going through. Any fool could steer a ship through.'[21] Georges-Picot later claimed to have known all along that the pilots 'entertained exaggerated notions ... of their indispensability'.[22] But this was not his line in the weeks after nationalisation. The Egyptians, he argued, could not run the canal without European assistance. It was an opinion he promoted at every opportunity, in part sustained by sending unsolicited cheques to French newspapers that might otherwise have been tempted to criticise the canal company. This particular exercise in public relations came to an abrupt stop when it was exposed by the left-wing *Libération*. Georges-Picot earned a few laughs when he protested that the cash was for 'out of the ordinary expenses'.

Ignoring their first instincts and wiser counsel, Eden and Mollet decided that when it came to the role performed by the Suez pilots, Georges-Picot knew what he was talking about. Given the risk of international condemnation for interrupting what up until now had been the smooth running of the canal, they looked to the advantage of showing that Egyptian ineptitude was the real danger.

The European pilots steered their last convoys on 14 September. Over 150 of them departed at midnight, leaving the canal to be kept open by seven Greeks and twenty-six Egyptian pilots supported by nine newly trained Egyptians. Middle East correspondents hovered over their typewriters, eager to be the first to report to the world a canal log jam, maybe a collision, even a sinking. They were soon led to conclude that good news is no news. Working up to seventeen hours a day, the forty-two pilots who remained on duty escorted forty-one ships through the canal on 15 September and thirty-six more the following day.[23] Their task was eased by the decision of some shipping lines to go round the Cape, but this turned out to be a short-term measure. As more pilots were recruited traffic increased, and by the end of October it was as if the canal company had never been. The only consequence of any note following the retirement of the European pilots was the change in the weekly holiday for canal personnel from the Christian Sunday to the Muslim Friday.

Mollet and Pineau were inclined to shrug off what they saw as a minor diplomatic setback. Nasser was up to operating the canal. So what? His offence against France was as serious as ever – the hijacking of a French enterprise and his support for the Algerian rebels who threatened the integrity of the Fourth Republic. Eden saw it differently. He needed no persuading that Nasser was a threat to British interests but, in the absence of American backing, to move against Egypt with popular support required more than a single act of nationalisation that, so far, had not led to the awful consequences predicted back in July.

A war was still widely anticipated – a *Times* leader on 12 September assumed it to be imminent – but while the military was building up for a major operation there was increasing concern that the whole business was getting out of hand. Without stronger provocation from Nasser, the proposed attack on Alexandria had all the appearance of a juggernaut out to flatten a molehill. This was certainly the view of Mountbatten. At a critical meeting on 7 September attended by Eden, Monckton, Keightley and the chiefs of staff, Mountbatten held forth on the casualties that would follow a heavy bombardment of Alexandria and a protracted land campaign against fervent nationalists. Eden's claim that 'the Egyptians were yellow and would crumble immediately' prompted Keightley to speak up in support of Mountbatten.

At a cabinet meeting that afternoon, Eden conceded that the risk of heavy civilian casualties was unacceptable. There had to be a strategic rethink. As it happened the French too were unhappy with Musketeer, but for different reasons. As General Beaufre noted:

> If the appearance of allied forces in front of Cairo did not suffice to topple Nasser, we should have to force a crossing of the Nile, no light undertaking in September; the capture of the port of Alexandria might well be a tough job and, moreover, might entail major damage to the town – I was not averse to seeing the British keep this task to themselves. Finally the assault landing was not without its difficulties and dangers: the main beach was being mined and a secondary beach, of great importance for the capture of the western exits to Alexandria, was dangerous, being covered by a line of submerged reefs. In addition the parachute dropping zone south of Lake Mariut was some way off and Egyptian tanks might well arrive there before our own. The early stages of the operation were therefore fairly risky.[24]

If, however, as the British and French governments maintained, the aim was to topple Nasser, Alexandria was the obvious landing place for a forward push to Cairo. It therefore came as a shock to Beaufre when he found that his commander-in-chief, Admiral Barjot, with his chief of staff, General Gazin, was giving thought to Port Said as the better option. As far as Beaufre could understand (he described Barjot as having become 'somewhat muddle-headed with age'[25]), the idea was to leave Alexandria to the British while giving French forces their own show in Port Said. Beaufre was, as he put it, 'dumbfounded'.

Could this be true? After thirteen days of studies and conferences, with planning under way and only twelve days from the
'off', here we were, proposing an entirely new concept! This was
definitely irresponsible ... Moreover at first sight his new concept seemed to me highly dangerous. I had already referred to my
conclusions on the necessity of going to Cairo – or threatening to
do so. A limited operation could lead only to political defeat and
Port Said as a hostage would give us no bargaining position –
UNO, the US or the Russians would soon find ways and means
of forcing us out of it. Moreover, what would happen to the
remainder of the Canal which would be left to the Egyptians?[26]

Beaufre achieved a compromise. Barjot agreed to Port Said featuring in a reserve plan to be implemented only if 'the landing at
Alexandria proved to be too dangerous'. When this was put to
Keightley and Stockwell they readily agreed to hold the proposal
in reserve without much expectation of it ever being pulled out
of the file. But this was before the meeting with Eden and Mountbatten on 7 September had highlighted the risk of heavy civilian
casualties in and around Alexandria. Three days later Mollet and
Pineau were in London, where they agreed with Eden to abandon
the attack on Alexandria and instead to prepare a new plan for
an attack on Port Said. It is unclear whether at this time Eden
realised that he was throwing away his best chance of bringing
about Nasser's downfall. Almost certainly, Mollet and Pineau
understood the implications of switching the invasion from Alexandria to Port Said. But they also had another plan which they
were not yet prepared to reveal. If it worked out the way they
expected there would be no need for Anglo-French forces to
enter Cairo. Other pressures could be brought to bear on Nasser,
pressures that could only lead to his destruction.

One of the close observers of the Anglo-French predicament
was David Ben-Gurion, lately restored as Israel's prime minister.
Since Israel was denied entry to the Suez Canal and would presumably remain so whoever was technically in charge, the management of the waterway was not his immediate concern. What
did worry Ben-Gurion was Egypt's accumulation of Soviet
weaponry and the use to which Nasser was likely to put it. He
had long held to the doctrine that attack is the best form of
defence, a policy that in relation to Egypt found increasing favour
with Israeli politicians of all parties. But Ben-Gurion was also
aware that for Israel to act alone was to invite the charge of
unprovoked aggression followed by an international embargo on
arms sales. If this were to happen, Israel would be vulnerable to
counter-attack by Egypt in alliance with other Arab states.[1]

Above all else, Ben-Gurion needed dependable allies. With
hindsight, the USA might be judged to have been the best prospect. But while there was popular support for the Israeli cause
and a powerful Jewish vote, the Eisenhower administration
favoured an even-handed approach to Middle East problems.
Eisenhower himself was suspicious of Israel's territorial ambitions
and was inclined to judge Arabs and Jews as equally culpable in
fomenting unrest in the region. The best that Ben-Gurion could
expect from the USA was benevolent neutrality.

Britain was, if anything, a more dubious proposition. Still
bruised by the humiliating departure of its troops from Palestine
in 1947, Britain put more store in its alliances with Jordan, Libya,
Iraq and the Gulf States than in friendship with Israel. While
Churchill was an avowed Zionist and Eden was prepared to back

the Alpha peace initiative, designed to guarantee Israel's borders, the mindset in the foreign office was distinctly pro-Arab. This found unequivocal expression in a paper from Evelyn Shuckburgh and Harold Caccia on the implications of Egypt's purchase of Soviet arms. Arguing that 'if we lose Egypt we lose the rest of the Arab world', the authors concluded with a 'firm belief that the continued support of Israel is incompatible with British interests'.[2] Macmillan, who was then foreign secretary, recoiled from such partisanship, but an alternative policy was hard to come by. An agreement to vacillate was the best on offer.

> The surest way of limiting Iron Curtain supplies [of arms to Egypt] would probably be to increase supplies from the West (particularly if this included US aid). But this would be difficult (a) because Israel would demand more and (b) because it would show that blackmail had paid off. On the other hand a cessation of or reduction in our supplies would increase Egypt's dependence on the Soviet bloc and a denial of training facilities to the Egyptians would almost certainly afford the Communists a splendid opportunity of penetration. If our ultimate intention is to keep the Soviet Bloc out there is something to be said for continuing to give training facilities and arms on about the same scale as previously. Israel is better armed than Egypt and our arms would not for some time anyway tilt the balance against Israel. The difficulty would be to resist Israeli demands for compensatory increases.[3]

Nothing much had changed by the time that the canal was taken into Egyptian ownership. Subsequently, voices were raised in favour of at least an understanding with Israel. When Eden shared with Churchill his aim of overthrowing Nasser it was to be told, 'Unless we bring in Israel, I don't think it can be done.'[4] And Macmillan weighed in with the proposition that 'we must make use of Israel against Egypt if the military operation is actually undertaken'.[5]

In seeking a cause, or pretext, for action that went beyond the nationalisation of the canal, it did not pass notice that Egypt was in violation of a 1951 UN resolution which called for the freedom of navigation for Israeli vessels. It was, as a *Spectator* leader put it, 'the one point on which the Western powers could force Nasser to yield without being accused of colonialism and also the one point on which his yielding would do most to disable him for the post of uncrowned king of Arab nationalism'.[6]

But there was a downside to this argument. Egyptian defiance of the UN went back a long way and no country, Britain least of all, had been prepared to act on fine words. To protest now on behalf of Israel while threatening to back up the UN resolution with force would inevitably look very much like opportunism and, in any case, would simply complicate the issue. Eden's instinct was to regard any involvement with Israel as just another obstacle in the way of achieving his objective. Voicing Britain's official position, Lloyd declared that it was 'imperative to keep Israel out of the situation, as much in Israel's interests as anyone's'.[7] Clearly, Ben-Gurion could not expect much sympathy from London.

Then there was France. Israel occupied a special place in the affections of the Mollet government. While the Quai d'Orsay kept up a polite but firm front against treating Israel as in any way different from other Middle East states, Mollet and his senior ministers were seasoned by their experiences in the Resistance. Having themselves suffered persecution under the Vichy regime, they were naturally drawn towards others who had reasons to hate fascism. Seated at a dinner next to the wife of General Paul Ely, the thirty-two-year-old Shimon Peres discovered that she had spent much of the European war in a concentration camp.

> She told me of her meetings with the Jews there, what had happened to most of them, and how she still kept in touch with the few friends who had survived. People like her could never again maintain an indifference to international politics. As she said, 'you can't return from the edge of the abyss and resume a light-hearted existence of not caring'.[8]

Peres was one of Ben-Gurion's Young Turks, a peripatetic diplomat whose job it was to buy weapons from whatever source available. France offered a golden opportunity. It was not simply that there was a mutual sympathy. Hard economics favoured an arms deal. Galvanised by colonial warfare the French armaments and aviation industries looked to foreign markets to achieve economies of scale. Israel had a long shopping list and was ready to pay the going prices without demands for extended credit. When such an opportunity presented itself joint pledges with the USA and UK to limit arms sales to the Middle East were quietly jettisoned. And there was Algeria to take into account. Peres did all he could to reinforce the conviction in Paris, based on none-too-solid evidence, that Nasser was the evil genius inciting the Algerians to rebel.

By the end of 1955 modest deliveries of French tanks and aircraft had been welcomed by Israel but had done little to lighten the siege mentality that followed the early shipments of Soviet arms to Egypt. Peres was under pressure to come up with a breakthrough deal, such as the delivery of the Mystère Mark IV, the new advanced fighter plan favoured by NATO. It was now that his patient diplomacy paid off. His strongest ally in French political circles was Maurice Bourgès-Maunoury. As minister of the interior responsible for Algeria he had struck up a friendship with Peres based on their shared distrust of Nasser. But his support for arms for Israel took an added force when, following the elections that brought Guy Mollet to power, Bourgès-Maunoury was made minister of defence. It was the moment to submit a new shopping list.

This time Peres went for broke, asking for sixty Mystère IV, thirty-six Vautour, a new fighter-bomber not yet off the drawing board, 2,000 tanks and a large quantity of anti-tank missiles. In all, the bill came to around $100 million.

Bourgès-Maunoury was immediately attracted to an accord that would not only fortify an ally on Nasser's eastern flank but would also finance the manufacture of helicopters and light armour which the French army needed to fight the guerrilla war in Algeria.[9] But the agreement in principle required government backing. Mollet was onside, having assured Peres that 'Israel is developing the very model of a socialist society to which we in our French party aspire'.[10] To Ben-Gurion he wrote, 'Now you will see I am not Bevin.'[11]

Christian Pineau, however, was not such an easy touch. New to the job of foreign minister, he was, at this stage, still listening to his officials who wanted him to make his mark by persuading Nasser to drop his support for the Algerian insurgents. At the very least, Pineau needed time to make his own assessment of Middle East policy. So it was that in the evolving relationship between Peres and Bourgès-Maunoury, the Quai d'Orsay was kept at a distance.

In early 1956, General Harkaby, head of Israeli intelligence, travelled to Paris to meet Pierre Boursicot, his opposite number at the Service de Documentation et Centre de Espionnage. Harkaby brought with him useful details about the movements and contacts of FLN leaders, promising more as information became available. Boursicot was impressed, and since he was able to deal directly with Mollet, a plan for Franco-Israeli collaboration, bypassing the Quai d'Orsay, began to emerge. In Tel Aviv, the Israeli Defence Force (IDF) chief of staff, General Moshe Dayan, and Shimon Peres were made responsible for negotiating a far-reaching agreement with France 'on the basis of equal and joint responsibility'. Ben-Gurion told colleagues, 'Alongside an ally such as France, Israel will be ready to go a long way.'[12]

On the weekend of 23/24 June, a month before the canal nationalisation, an Israeli delegation led by Dayan, Peres and Harkaby arrived in Vermars to settle in at the chateau of the Perrier magnate, Fernand Levin. They were joined by a French group headed by Pierre Boursicot and General Maurice Challe, deputy chief of staff. The Quai d'Orsay and the Israeli ambassador to France were not represented.

The Vermars conference had momentous results, including an agreement worth $80 million for the immediate delivery of eighty-two Mystère Mark IV, 120 AMX tanks, forty Super-Sherman tanks and eighteen 105 mm mobile guns, together with generous allocations of ammunition and spare parts. The aircraft were to be flown by Israeli pilots directly to Israel with a refuelling stop at the Italian naval base of Brindisi. The Italian authorities made do with a tall story that the planes had been returned to France for maintenance and remodelling. American intelligence was less gullible.[13] Eisenhower noted, 'Mystère fighter bombers for Israel show a rabbitlike capacity for multiplication.'[14]

Ben-Gurion was at the airfield to welcome the first Mystère arrivals. Also there was Pierre Eugène Gilbert, France's ambassador to Israel, whose efforts to advance the military kinship between the two countries earned him the nickname Monsieur Mystère.

The leap in confidence enjoyed by the Israeli command as they faced the Egyptians on equal terms raised the tantalising prospect of further cooperation with their new best friend. The exchange of intelligence, endorsed at the highest level, was soon to lead to a cooperative venture that extended to joint military operations against Algerian rebel bases along the eastern shores of the Mediterranean.

More was in prospect. The Suez crisis set off another round of talks. With Dulles clearly set against confrontation with Nasser and with Eden ambivalent on whether or not to move without US acquiescence, an idea took hold in the French Ministry of Defence for a joint French–Israeli action against Egypt. As the strongman in the Mollet government, Bourgès-Maunoury was all for it, as Peres discovered when he was in Paris in early August.

'How much time do you reckon it would take your army to cross the Sinai peninsula and reach Suez?' the French Minister asked outright. Peres replied that the accepted assessment in Israel was between five and seven days. Bourgès shook his head sceptically. In France, he said, it is usual to accord an operation like that about three weeks. He went on to ask whether Israel was planning to act one day on her southern border and, if so, when? Peres answered that 'our Suez is Eilat. We will never reconcile ourselves to a blockade, and that would be the reason for an Israeli action – if ever there is one.'

Then another French participant in the meeting laid all his cards on the table: 'If France goes to war against Egypt, will Israel be prepared to go with us?' 'Yes!' Peres replied immediately. As they were walking out of the meeting, Yosef Nachmias mumbled to Peres, only half in jest: 'You should be hanged for such a commitment! Who gave you the authority to make it?'

'If I had said no,' Peres explained, 'that would be the end of the tie with France. On the other hand, it is clear that such an operation requires the approval of the Israeli Government. We can always change our minds.'[15]

Ben-Gurion reacted cautiously. It was one thing to puncture Egyptian pretensions to Arab leadership, but not at the cost of being seen by the rest of the world as an aggressor. Like Eden, Ben-Gurion needed Egyptian provocation to justify action. On the other hand, Israel was in need of friends. The French offer was not to be lightly dismissed. Mollet was also cautious. He had invested too much political capital in the Anglo-French joint command to be able to switch allies at this late stage in the game. But he too was ready to continue exploratory talks.

On the afternoon of 24 August Ben-Gurion chaired a meeting of army general staff with French envoys led by Robert Lacoste. 'I agreed to French planes using our airfields and [proposed] that any assistance they may need be extended to them. Then Gilbert turned to Lacoste with a radical proposition; that Israel conquer the Sinai Peninsula thereby de facto turning the Canal into an international waterway.'[16] It was clear that France was prepared to go much farther than Ben-Gurion or any of his colleagues had dared to hope.

To move things along, and to test just how far the French would commit themselves, Peres put in a request that left his fellow negotiators open mouthed. Would the French defence ministry please supply Israel with a 1,000-kilowatt atomic reactor? There was no immediate response except for diplomatic puffing and panting, but a deal to transfer nuclear technology eventually became part of the broader agreement to coordinate action against Nasser.[17] The handing over of that small reactor would enable Israel to establish its first atomic pile at Dimona. It certainly helped to swing Ben-Gurion towards a partnership with France. On 21 September he cabled Peres on support for a military operation to topple Nasser. 'If they act at their convenience, we will back them to the best of our ability.' To those of his ministers who voiced reservations he said, 'This is the birth of the first serious alliance between us and a western power. We can't not accept it.'[18]

The second Canal Users' Conference opened in London on 19 September. Selwyn Lloyd was again chairman. Dulles made a united front with his Anglo-French allies (Lloyd regarded his speech as the best he had heard from the secretary of state[19]). But privately Dulles despaired of a positive outcome. As he cabled the president after the first day:

> My general impression is that the British and the French have quite isolated themselves even from what are naturally their closest friends. The Norwegians, whom the British habitually count upon, are worried; and also Italy, which since the war has worked closely with France, is worried. The fact is that the United States is the only bridge between the British and the French and the rest of the countries here. I do not yet know whether that bridge is going to hold. The Egyptians are making an enormous effort to make it appear that the Users' Association is a device to lead the members down the path to war for which the British and the French are preparing, and Egyptian propaganda in this sense is having a definite impact. Doubt that we shall make as much or as rapid progress this week as the British and French have wanted, but we will know better by tomorrow.[20]

But tomorrow came and went and so did the rest of the week without any resolution of the outstanding issues. In Washington, the combined talents of the CIA and military intelligence concluded that while Britain and France were 'convinced that the elimination of Nasser is essential to the preservation of vital Western interests in the Middle East and North Africa . . . military action is likely only in the event of some new and violent provocation'.[21] On this occasion, American intelligence was wrong. A misleading impression of Anglo-French intentions had been created by an apparent softening of the French position. While Pineau insisted to Dulles that 'if the negotiation with Nasser does not produce results, we shall resume our freedom of action',[22] he was now happy to go along with the British appeal to the UN. Though Dulles was still opposed to the move, the willingness of France to continue talking was judged to be a good sign. What he did not know was that most of the critical talking was with Israel and the question was not whether force would be used but when.

Eden must have suspected that something was going on in Paris and that he was being deliberately excluded. Certainly there were worries in London that the ties of the Anglo-French alliance were loosening. An opportunity to clear up misunderstandings was on offer at the end of September when Eden and Mollet were to meet in Paris. Subsequently Eden and Lloyd referred to this get-together as a spur-of-the-moment arrangement, but the date had been fixed long before. While the Middle East was high on the agenda there were British concerns other than Suez, notably Jordan, where King Hussein was under threat from Egypt and Israel, the latter having ambitions to strengthen its frontier by occupying west Jordan.

Knowing that the talks would not be easy, Eden cast about for ways of demonstrating to Mollet his unwavering dedication to the Anglo-French alliance. What about taking up Mollet's suggestion for a common citizenship?[23] Anthony Nutting, who was told to frame a proposal, found it hard to take the suggestion seriously. Eden presented it as his own idea, failing to mention Mollet and Pineau's visit to London immediately after Nasser's Suez speech. No wonder Nutting was puzzled. Since Eden had succeeded to the premiership he had set his face against continental involvement, rejecting involvement in a European army and membership of the European Canal and Steel Community and remaining aloof from the talks at Messina fifteen months earlier when the Common Market was first mooted. In the end Eden himself must have recognised the inconsistency, for he and Lloyd set off for Paris on 26 September armed with nothing but their powers of persuasion.

The French ambassador in London, Jean Chauvel, put up warning signals of the visitors giving 'too strong an impression of the British government's firmness towards the Suez matter', quoting Eden's private remark to him: 'Make sure they understand that I completely agree on the substance, but I must take my public opinion into account.'[24] Mollet was not greatly worried. He now had another and more dependable ally. And as he made clear to Eden, he was not about to put at risk his relations with Israel by telling Ben-Gurion to ease off Jordan. But nothing was said of a possible Franco-Israeli attack on Egypt.

The news that there might be an alternative French plan for disposing of Nasser came through to General Beaufre while he and Stockwell were wrestling with the challenges of switching the line of attack from Alexandria to Port Said. Beaufre now realised why Barjot had enthused over the Port Said option in the first place. When it had originally come up for discussion, Barjot had known of a possible Israeli assault across Sinai. Nasser would be caught in a pincer movement. By holding back on the second half of the plan, Barjot had given his ground forces commander the impression that he was losing his mind. Now all, or nearly all, made sense. But Beaufre was still not convinced. It seemed to him that France was having to concede too much.

The Israeli plan that was beginning to emerge called for a blitz attack on the Egyptian forces in Sinai followed by a diversion north to take the Gaza Strip and south to open up the Gulf of Aqaba. Beaufre had no doubt that the Israeli army would dispose of the opposition in short order, but French support was essential in helping to destroy the Egyptian air force before it was able to attack Israeli cities. All this was pretty risky, thought Beaufre, and for what? 'Acting alone with the Israelis, our political cover would be extremely precarious; collusion with the Israelis would be very dangerous both in the Middle East and in North Africa – and all these risks would be run simply to take Port Said, a ludicrous "hostage" which could under no circumstances bring about a decision.'[25] There were other problems soon to become apparent but for the moment Beaufre had his work cut out balancing the demands of his political masters to accommodate the Israelis and cooperating with the British command without letting them know of the possible Israeli involvement.

The day after Eden and Lloyd returned to London, Moshe Dayan, along with foreign minister Golda Meir, transport minister Moshe Carmal and Peres, flew to Paris. Their first formal session with their French hosts was at the Montparnasse home of Louis Mangin, the political aide to Bourgès-Maunoury. Pineau, who was now fully informed of the Israeli connection, was there, along with Bourgès-Maunoury, Abel Thomas, director general of the defence ministry, and General Challe. Much to the disappointment of the Israelis, Mollet chose to keep his distance (citing a political crisis as an excuse), and it was Pineau who led the discussion, making clear that France was determined to take back the Suez Canal by whatever means.

> Pineau spoke for about forty-five minutes, and then our delegation presented Israel's position. First, we agreed with the French view that relations with Nasser could no longer be regularized by diplomatic means. There was now no alternative to military action. Second, we regarded France as our friend and ally and agreed wholeheartedly to act jointly with her. Third, we had to be certain of Britain's stand if she stayed out of the campaign. Would she invoke her treaty with Jordan and go to her aid if Jordan should attack Israel, or if Israel should move into the West Bank in reaction to the entry of Iraqi forces into Jordan? If she would, we could find ourselves in a situation whereby we were allied with France in a military operation against Egypt on one front, while Britain was fighting at the side of Jordan and Iraq against us on another. Fourth, what was the United States likely to do? During our War of Independence she had declared an embargo on arms to the Middle East. Now America might declare an economic embargo, which would be a

grave hardship. And finally, what of the Soviet Union? Was she likely to send her forces to the aid of Egypt?[26]

Cautious if optimistic responses were made to these queries. Much depended on how the forthcoming debate at the UN turned out for the Anglo-French case against Egypt. But one important conclusion was arrived at. France alone did not have the air strength to bomb the Egyptian air force out of existence. British support was essential. An effort was made on the French side to minimise the problem. If Israel opened the campaign and France committed her troops, Britain was bound to join in. Dayan was not so sure; neither was Ben-Gurion. They both distrusted the British, who 'hated the very idea that [their country] might possibly be smeared as partners with Israel in military action against Arabs but, at the same time, would welcome the chance of exploiting Israel's conflict with the Arabs to justify their action against Egypt'.[27]

While the French and Israeli military were edging towards a coordinated plan for the invasion of Egypt, the French and the British military were putting the finishing touches to Musketeer Revise, their latest plan for the invasion of Egypt. The objective of Musketeer Revise was to break down 'Egyptian resistance to Western operation of the Suez Canal and enable Allied forces to secure the Canal Zone'. This was to be achieved in three phases. In phase one, a surprise allied air attack would destroy the Egyptian air force before it could get off the ground. In the next phase key military targets would be taken out while submitting the Egyptian citizenry to a barrage of propaganda urging them to dispose of their leader. After Nasser's fall, British and French troops would land at Port Said to take possession of the Canal Zone before moving on to Cairo to set up a puppet government or at least one that was sympathetic to Western interests. The invasion force was to be held in a state of readiness with Keightley and his commanders expecting, at most, ten days' notice for the action to begin.

When told about Musketeer Revise, Walter Monckton, who

was in his last days as minister of defence (he resigned on 11 October to be succeeded by Anthony Head), voiced what everyone was thinking but hardly dared say. 'Very interesting, but how do we actually start this war?'[28]

There were two other vital questions attached to Musketeer Revise. The first was the impact on Egyptian morale of a sustained air attack. Air Marshal Sir Denis Barnet, air task force commander, was supported by the chief of staff in his belief that Egyptian resistance would crumble as soon as the bombs fell. It was a theory that had been found wanting in the Second World War. Saturation bombing had done little if anything to shorten the conflict. But this was different. No one was suggesting that the civilian population should be made to suffer. On the contrary, targets were to be carefully monitored for their military and economic value. Advances in aircraft design had raised the accuracy rate of precision bombing and, anyway, the Egyptians lacked the fighting spirit of the Germans.

These arguments were not rock solid. There were those who believed that the Egyptians under Nasser's charismatic leadership might well put up tough opposition. Keightley and Stockwell were not inclined to take chances, hence their insistence on putting together a seaborne invasion force to rival the Normandy landings. This drove Beaufre to distraction. Where was the British sense of urgency?

Another question that hovered over Musketeer Revise had to do with the power of psychological warfare. Its foremost exponent was General Templer, who had made heavy use of propaganda in the closing stages of his campaign against insurgents in Malaya. On 2 August he produced a memorandum calling for an all-out attack on Egyptian morale.[29] The result was the setting up of an information coordination executive made up of representatives from a range of government departments, from the cabinet office to the ministry of defence, together with the BBC controller of overseas services.

If these diverse talents could agree on anything it was the fundamental difference of mounting a war of words in Malaya, where Templer was able to hold out the promise of forthcoming independence to persuade guerrilla fighters to surrender their arms, and in Egypt, where it was nigh impossible to think of any Anglo-French offer that could possibly win converts. Appeals to Egyptians to overthrow Nasser were unlikely to carry conviction when there was no clear or attractive alternative.

The choice of front man for the psychological war fell on the unfortunate Brigadier Bernard Fergusson, a friend and former colleague of Templer, whose career spanned Burma and Palestine. Fergusson was all that a soldier should be, but otherwise he was not well suited to his role. 'My only assets were my knowledge of the Middle East, my ability to speak French and the fact that I was available.'[30]

The manner of his recruitment should have warned Fergusson that this was not the way to win promotion. His account of what happened reads like something out of a John Buchan novel.

It was some time in late August. I had arranged to catch the night train north, and my wife was to meet me at Perth first thing in the morning. I had boarded the train, and was sitting down to a pink gin in the restaurant car before dinner with two fellow-travellers whom I happened to know when I felt the crook of an umbrella handle steal round my upper arm from behind. I looked round, and there was 'Pooh' Hobbs, my former Number Two at COHQ, now a major-general and Commandant at Sandhurst. He was smiling, but he left no room for argument when he said: 'I have to tell you to get hold of your luggage, get off the train and come with me'.

In the taxi, he explained that he had been to look for me at White's Club, where he had picked up my trail to King's Cross. There was the possibility of a military expedition to recover the Suez Canal; it had been decided to set up a special planning staff, and both he and I were to be on it. It was of course ultra-secret. The thing was in its infancy, and he himself didn't know much about it yet; but over a couple of drinks in White's he told me what little he did.[31]

Richard Hannay could not have put it better.

Fergusson's self-deprecating conviviality, together with a talent for disbelieving the worst, helped him to endure the tribulations that he was about to experience. British and French radio for Arab consumption had been pushing the anti-Nasser line from late July.[32] A 'Free Egyptian' station transmitted from France operated at a frequency close to the opposition Voice of the Arabs, while British radio was pumped out from Libya, Cyprus and Aden. The longest-established and most professional radio operation was Sharq-al-Adna, based in a collection of Nissen huts near a Cypriot village appropriately named Polymedia. Blessed with a medium-wave transmitter powerful enough to reach all parts of the Middle East, Sharq-al-Adna broadcast a popular mix of music and drama which allowed for the almost imperceptible insertion of pro-British comment.

Just as effective, and for the same reason that it did not overplay its hand, was the British government-funded Arab News Agency, which 'operated the most comprehensive service in English and Arabic available in the Middle East with branch offices in Damascus, Beirut, Baghdad, Jerusalem and Amman and representatives in fifteen other cities including Paris and New York'.[33]

But these advantages had been thrown away when, prompted by British intelligence, the decision had been taken to raise the stakes, in effect to match Nasser's Voice of the Arabs radio with an equally virulent campaign of 'black' propaganda. The first move was to attach to the staff of the Arab News Agency in Cairo two of the more ludicrous characters to emerge from the wartime Special Operations Executive, the body that had dropped agents and saboteurs behind enemy lines in the Second World War, usually with tragic consequences for the agents and saboteurs. William Stevenson was accompanied by Sefton Delmer, his former assistant in SOE. Delmer was seconded from his job as foreign correspondent of the *Daily Express*, where his byline photo with Sam Spade hat pulled low over his forehead supported his image as a man of mystery. They were no match for the home team. In August, Egyptian intelligence denounced the Arab News

Agency (ANA) as a cover for an MI6 spy ring. There were thirty arrests. Of the four Britons rounded up, James Swinburn, the business manager of ANA, lightened his sentence to five years by cooperating with the authorities. Those expelled from the country included Stevenson and Delmer and two bona fide journalists who had proved troublesome, Ann Sharpley of the *Evening Standard* and Eileen Travis, an American writing for the *Daily Mail*. Having gained the initiative, Egyptian intelligence now began to put pressure on other press correspondents who were known to be none too friendly towards the Nasser regime. Clearly, Fergusson would have his work cut out to make a favourable case for Allied intervention in Egypt.

While Fergusson struggled with the demands of shaping mass opinion, the man who was indirectly responsible for landing him with his unenviable task had his own difficulty in winning friends. Following his summit in Paris, Eden returned to what had become a regular chore – writing to Eisenhower to urge a tougher stance against Nasser. His immediate aim was to persuade the president to put pressure on American shipowners, whose vessels sailed under the Panamanian and Liberian flag, to pay their canal dues to the SCUA account. The Soviet threat was yet again called into play to reinforce Eden's plea. Dispatched on 1 October, his cable brought a dusty response from Dulles, who by now was thoroughly alarmed at all the talk of forcing Nasser to submit to the dictates of SCUA. Rounding on a journalist who suggested that Dulles was deliberately undermining the SCUA set-up by depriving it of its power to bite, the Secretary of State professed amazement: 'What is this talk about teeth being pulled out of the plan? I know of no teeth. There are no teeth in it, so far as I am aware.'

Anthony Nutting was with Eden at 10 Downing Street when the news came in. 'Eden read the Dulles statement quickly and then, with a contemptuous gesture, he flung the piece of paper at me across the table, hissing as he did so, "And now what have you to say for your American friends?" I had no answer. For I knew instinctively that this was for Eden the final let-down. We had reached breaking-point.'[34]

Eden refused to take comfort from messages fed back from Washington by Macmillan, who was there on IMF business. Eisenhower was sure that Nasser had to go, claimed the chancellor. Moreover, Dulles recognised Britain's right to use force. Macmillan was repeating Eden's frequent mistake of hearing only what he wanted to hear. Eden failed to respond. He knew at last that there could be no prospect of the USA standing alongside Britain and France. The disappointment and the pressure were too much for him. Visiting his wife in hospital, where she was recovering from a dental operation, Eden himself became a patient when he collapsed with a high fever. Back in Downing Street after a few days' rest, he seemed strangely calm, a personality adrift, functioning, as Chester Cooper observed, 'on a level 10 per cent removed from reality'. It was a critical 10 per cent, Cooper added, and 'virtually guaranteed that his Suez policy, flawed as it was, would turn into a grave national and personal tragedy'.[35]

17

The same day that Eden fell ill, 5 October, Lloyd and Pineau took their places at the horseshoe table of the UN Security Council, to all appearances intent on finding a peaceful solution to the Suez crisis. The debate was initiated by an Anglo-French draft resolution endorsing the majority proposals of the London Canal Users' Conference, including the setting up of an international board to run the canal. Predictably, the Soviet Union, represented by Shepilov, denounced the scheme as a capitalist plot, but Dr Mohammed Fawzi was more accommodating. Hinting at a compromise on some degree of user participation that acknowledged Egyptian sovereign rights, he called for a fair system of tolls with a reasonable share of canal revenue allocated to infrastructure. What counted as fair and reasonable was left open for a discussion over which Dag Hammarskjöld, the UN secretary general, was happy to preside. 'I will be acting merely as a chaperon,' he told Dulles, who retorted: 'My understanding of a chaperon is a person whose job is to keep two people apart. Your job is to get the parties together.'[1]

Over three days from 9 to 11 October, Hammarskjöld sought the common ground. It turned out that there were six broad principles acceptable to all parties, starting with unrestricted movement through the canal. Any agreement had to respect Egyptian sovereignty, protect the canal from the political interference of any one country, fix a level of tolls acceptable to Egypt and SCUA, decide on how much was to be spent on development, and determine the level of compensation to be paid to the defunct Canal Company.

Temporarily free of the stream of advice that Eden was accustomed to throw at him, Lloyd felt close to a diplomatic break-through. Though distrustful of Fawzi, he saw strong hints that Egypt was ready for a settlement. The leaders of other Arab states, notably Saudi Arabia, were leaning on Nasser to accept some form of user participation in the management of the canal. The last thing they wanted was for the Egyptian leader to promote his nationalist credentials at the expense of their oil-exporting economies. But while Lloyd was full of the joys of optimism, Pineau was cast down. With his government colleagues having made up their minds to teach Nasser a lesson, Pineau could not expect to be well received in Paris if he returned with a draft settlement that was anything but a climb-down by Egypt. Recognising the nuances, Hammarskjöld expected the split between Britain and France to widen, the more so after Pineau began telling everyone, including the press, that the talks were going nowhere.

Lloyd took a more positive line. The rush of confidence brought on by the experience of at last coming into his own persuaded him that he was close to achieving the substance of what was needed to guarantee the efficient running of the canal. The proposition was at best dubious. Fawzi later claimed that he knew all along that Pineau was negotiating in bad faith.[2] If this is true, it made it all the easier for him to play a double game that would have met with Nasser's approval. Egypt stood forth as the innocent party, ready to compromise on the unreasonable demands of the imperialist powers while knowing full well that there was next to no risk of these professed good intentions ever being put to the test. French intransigence would see to that. Fawzi must have known that Nasser would never allow Israel to be included in the 'unrestricted movement through the Canal' or accept the participation of SCUA, already rejected as an infringement of Egyptian sovereignty. Yet he encouraged Lloyd to believe that a serious offer on both counts was within reach.

The view in Washington was closer to reality. Dulles had the advantage of direct contact with Ali Sabri, chief of Nasser's political cabinet, who was installed in a suite at New York's Waldorf

Astoria. Putting it bluntly, Sabri warned that 'the policies of the Western governments made it extremely difficult for the Egyptian Government to foresee a solution of the Suez controversy, since obviously it could not accept a settlement which was designed in part to bring about its own collapse'.[3] The only way forward, thought Sabri, was for Britain and France to accept a loose association between a users' association and the Egyptian government on the lines suggested by Krishna Menon at the first London conference. No chance. The plan had already been turned down once, and though Menon was tireless in arguing his case, his persistence, not to mention his hectoring manner, had repelled those he was trying hardest to impress. Fawzi in particular could not bear Menon, whom he suspected, almost certainly correctly, of trying to upstage him. Much to his chagrin, Menon was excluded from the UN-sponsored talks between Fawzi, Pineau and Lloyd.

All this was very confusing for Dulles, who was beginning to feel that he was losing track of events. Signs of exhaustion and irritation, which may also have been the first symptoms of the cancer that was to kill him three years later, showed up in official communications. 'Never before, in recent years,' he declared at a meeting of the National Security Council on 4 October, 'have we faced a situation where we have no clear idea of the intentions of our British and French allies.'[4] Yet those same allies banked on unconditional support for whatever they had in mind while using the USA as a scapegoat for their ineptitude.

In the long term, Dulles surmised that 'their answer is to be found in increased European unity so that they will have together the strength which they need to be a powerful force in the world comparable to that of the Soviet Union and the United States, and more able to carry out their own policies'.[5] Meanwhile, the best that Dulles could hope for was to 'keep the lid [on the Suez crisis] a little longer', in the hope that a compromise plan would emerge.

On this last point at least, Lloyd would have agreed with him. He felt sure that an arrangement to ensure that the interests of the canal users would be safeguarded was almost within reach. Eden was having none of that. Restored to energy, he reminded Lloyd that it was not his job to bargain away what he most wanted – a decisive victory over Nasser. An order was given. Lloyd and Pineau emerged from behind closed doors and, without further reference to Fawzi or to Hammarskjöld, tabled a resolution for the Security Council which revived the Eighteen Power proposals that Menzies had tried and failed to sell to Nasser a month earlier. Fawzi reacted coldly, giving Russia the perfect excuse to use its veto. Eden was delighted. Applying the twisted logic that underpinned British policy in the Middle East, the prime minister concluded that he was now close to justification for military intervention.

On the morning of Sunday, 14 October, the day after the Anglo-French resolution had been vetoed by Russia, Eden cabled Lloyd.

> Should not we and the French now approach the Egyptians and ask them whether they are prepared to meet and discuss in confidence with us on the basis of the second half of the resolution which the Russians vetoed? If they say yes, then it is for consideration whether we and the French meet them somewhere, e.g. Geneva. If they say no, then they will be in defiance of the view of nine members of the Security Council and a new situation will arise.[6]

But Eden was misinterpreting the Security Council majority (nine votes to two) for the Anglo-French resolution. There was no indication of support for tougher action, only for further negotiation.

What Eden had failed to register was Fawzi's freshly acquired status as the voice of reason. There is no way of knowing whether Fawzi anticipated this outcome of the private talks, but everybody knew that he had offered concessions that had been rejected. Whether or not he had gambled on an Anglo-French, but particularly French, determination not to be reasonable was irrelevant. The fact was, he had not been called upon to deliver on his concessions. Even if this came as a relief, because there was no guarantee that Nasser would have backed him, he could safely proclaim that his efforts to achieve a peaceful settlement were entirely genuine. Dulles for one thought there was value to be had in persevering with Fawzi. He urged Hammarskjöld to reopen talks. As late as 24 October, the secretary general outlined a plan for operating the canal in cooperation with a body representing the canal users. Fawzi waited until 2 November to send a genial response. This was four days after the Suez fighting had started.

In mid-October the Anglo-French alliance was back on track save for one complication: Jordan. The Hashemite kingdom was showing signs of falling apart, a prospect that excited Israel with the anticipation of territorial gain. On 10 October an Israeli attack on the border village of Qalqilya had left 100 Jordanians dead. Invoking the Anglo-Jordanian Defence Treaty, King Hussein had called on Britain for support. The response was muted. A promise to honour the pact with Jordan was limited to a robust protest at Israeli behaviour. It was not enough to satisfy Hussein, who knew that the sword as wielded by Ben-Gurion was a good deal mightier than diplomacy. It was only natural that Hussein, casting around for help elsewhere, should turn to Israel's prime enemy. An urgent appeal went to Cairo. Eden must have despaired of receiving anything but bad news from the Middle East. The thought of diverting troops from the forthcoming Suez campaign was bad enough, but the nightmare was having to fight on two fronts, defending one Arab state while attacking another.

There was only one way out of the quandary, a friendly occupation by Iraqi forces. As Hussein's cousin, King Faisal could be expected to sympathise. He knew too that if Jordan fell, Iraq would not be far behind. Faisal's Anglophile prime minister, Nuri el-Said, was happy to accede to Eden's wishes, the more so because he shared the belief that Nasser had to be cut down to size. Why did Hussein not think of all this before? The probability is that he did but a falling out over a failed plan for merging Iraqi and Jordanian forces under a joint command may have deterred him from asking favours. In any event, happy relations were now restored and the Iraqi offer of a brigade to bolster Hussein's rule was accepted with relief.

The news was not well received in Tel Aviv. The presence of Iraqi troops was no guarantee of Jordanian independence. On the contrary, Iraq would be in a strong position to take over the whole country, so frustrating Israeli designs on Jordan and posing a direct threat to the Zionist state. Nuri had to be told to pull back. There was only one person he would listen to and that was Eden. And there was only one person Eden would listen to and that was Mollet. For Ben-Gurion, the time had come to test the strength of the French connection.

Mollet's warning that the movement of Iraqi troops would precipitate one conflict too many in the Middle East was taken seriously by Eden. Against the advice of Anthony Nutting who, in Lloyd's absence, was in charge of the foreign office, Eden sought to allay Israeli fears by urging Nuri to keep his troops well away from the Israeli border, and when this proved to be not enough, to reduce his armed force to a single infantry regiment. In vain Nuri argued that it was not Iraq but Israel which threatened the peace. The generous supply of arms crossing from France to Israel was now common knowledge, convincing Nutting that an Israeli move to capture the west bank of the Jordan river was imminent. He was close to the mark. What he did not know was that for the moment Jordan was an unwelcome diversion for Ben-Gurion, who was intent on joining with his French allies to score against Nasser. The carve-up of Jordan could wait as long as Iraq could be contained. Ever suspicious of the British, Ben-Gurion failed to be reassured by Eden's placatory moves. Realising that the entire Suez operation, as conceived by Paris, was at risk, Mollet decided to come clean with Eden on the likelihood of Israeli involvement, should circumstances be favourable.

On the morning of 13 October, Mollet cabled Eden to say that two French emissaries would be arriving the following day with an urgent message for the prime minister. Secrecy was essential. Albert Gazier, minister for social affairs, and, more significantly, Pineau's deputy, and General Challe were flown to the wired-off military sector of Northolt Airport and then driven, not to Downing Street but to Chequers, the prime minister's country residence. It was, recalls Nutting, a 'glorious autumn day, radiant with sunshine and crisp as a biscuit'. The most eventful day of his life started with a tête-à-tête with Eden.

> I told the Prime Minister that we had just heard that morning from Sir Michael Wright, our Ambassador in Baghdad, that Nuri had taken our last request reasonably well, but was puzzled by our sudden concern for Israeli susceptibilities. In view of this reaction, I hoped we would not press him for any more reassurances for Israel, no matter what our French visitors might demand of us. Eden smiled and said that from his knowledge of Nuri he would proceed very cautiously and would probably not move at all for the next day or so. This would give us time to discover what the French had to tell us and to make our plans accordingly.[7]

The French party arrived at three o'clock. Eden was waiting for them in his study. The door closed on a meeting of just five – Gazier, Challe, Eden, Nutting and Eden's private secretary, Guy Millard. Assuming that he was there to take minutes, Millard had his writing pad at the ready. Eden told him to put it away. 'There's no need to take notes, Guy.'

> After the initial courtesies had been disposed of, Gazier opened the discussion with a further appeal that we should halt all Iraqi movements into Jordan. We were playing with fire, he said. The French Government were in much closer touch with Tel Aviv than we were, and they knew that the Israelis were in a highly nervous state about the Iraqis. It would not be safe to write off their threats as mere bluff. Did we really want to risk provoking a situation in which we were on the opposite side to France at a time when our two countries should be at one in every sphere, and most especially in the Middle East?
>
> I jumped in at this point to say that we had already pushed Nuri far enough. We had persuaded him to station his troops in

north-east Jordan, to issue strict instructions that they were not
to cross to the west bank of the Jordan River or in any way to
present the smallest 'threat' to Israel, and finally to send only a
token force. We could not now forbid him to move at all. After
all, the idea of sending Iraqi troops to reinforce Hussein had
sprung from us and not from Nuri. But my arguments were
in vain. For Eden, whose antennae had begun to sense that
Gazier's appeal might be the prelude to some further and more
'positive' proposal for joint Anglo-French action, cut me short
by saying that he would, at any rate, ask Nuri to suspend his
move temporarily.[8]

Having conceded this much, Nutting felt it was the moment for
the French to reciprocate with a promise not to send any more
Mystère fighter planes to Israel. He passed a note to Eden, who
put it aside. He was 'all agog to hear what Gazier would have to
say next'. It was a question. 'How would Britain react if Israel
were to attack Egypt?' Eden needed to think about that. There
was the Tripartite Declaration to consider. Britain was obligated
to resist any attack across the armistice lines of Israel and the
Arab world. But this did not apply to Egypt. Gazier could quote
Nasser's public announcement that he did not recognise the declaration or the assumed rights of its signatories to send troops
into Egypt.

> 'So that lets us off the hook,' Eden said excitedly. 'We have no
> obligation, it seems, to stop the Israelis attacking the Egyptians.'
>   I thought for a moment of arguing the obvious point that our
> obligations stemmed from the Tripartite Declaration itself and
> that, whatever Egypt might say, this meant that we had a peace-
> keeping role to play in the Middle East. But it seemed more
> important to find out what lay behind the French enquiry. So I
> asked Gazier what, if any, information he had that Israel was
> contemplating an attack on Egypt.[9]

It was Challe's turn to speak. Avoiding a direct answer to the
question of Israeli intentions, he proceeded to an outline of what

became known as 'The Plan' for taking back control of the Suez Canal, starting with an Israeli attack on Egypt across the Sinai Peninsula. Then:

> France and Britain, having given the Israeli forces enough time to seize all or most of Sinai, should order 'both sides' to withdraw their forces from the Suez Canal, in order to permit an Anglo-French force to intervene and occupy the Canal on the pretext of saving it from damage by fighting. Thus the two powers would be able to claim to be 'separating the combatants' and 'extinguishing a dangerous fire', while actually seizing control of the entire waterway and of its terminal ports, Port Said and Suez. This would not only restore the running of the Canal to Anglo-French management, but, by putting us physically in control of the terminal ports – a position which Egypt had hitherto always held – it would enable us to supervise all shipping movements through the Canal and so to break the Egyptian blockade of Israel.[10]

The details of the plan were left for further discussion. Challe had in mind a combined seaborne and paratroop invasion, the timing and division of responsibilities for which had to be decided quickly. But it was uncertain just how far the Israelis had committed themselves. The answer, as became clear in the next few hours, was not far at all.

When, a day after the Chequers meeting, Ben-Gurion was told of the plan, his reaction was 'violently negative'.[11] Though aware that it was French inspired, he detected a British plot to reconcile the many contradictions in that country's Middle East policy. As he saw it, Israel was required to face grave military and political risks in the service of France and Britain without being recognised or even talked to by the British before winding up branded an aggressor and forced into submission by an Anglo-French ultimatum. It fell to Shimon Peres to calm the prime minister, persuading him to leave room for further negotiations. A cable to this effect was sent to Paris.

Eden, meanwhile, was in a state of high excitement. Nutting

was convinced that he had already made up his mind to go along with the Challe proposal.

> We were to ally ourselves with the Israelis and the French in an attack on Egypt designed to topple Nasser and to seize the Suez Canal. Our traditional friendships with the Arab world were to be discarded; the policy of keeping a balance in arms deliveries as between Israel and the Arab States was to be abandoned; indeed, our whole peace-keeping role in the Middle East was to be changed and we were to take part in a cynical act of aggression, dressing ourselves for the part as firemen or policemen, while making sure that our fire-hoses spouted petrol and not water and that we belaboured with our truncheons the assaulted and not the assaulter. And all to gain for ourselves guarantees for the future operation of the Suez Canal which had only a day or so before been substantially gained in Lloyd's negotiations with Fawzi in New York.[12]

Lloyd was telephoned in New York to be told to return on the next flight. He arrived back at London Airport shortly before noon on Tuesday, 16 October, and was driven to Downing Street to meet Eden. Nutting was waiting to intercept his boss. 'Drawing him aside, I told him what was afoot and what advice I had given . . . His reaction was spontaneous. "You are right," he said. "We must have nothing to do with the French plan."'[13] Nutting assumed that Lloyd was in ignorance of the plan, but this is unlikely given the communication he had already had with Eden. In any event, whatever his reservations, once Lloyd was ensconced with Eden he was soon following the line of least resistance. 'Short of resignation,' says his biographer, 'Lloyd had no option but to comply.'[14] But why was it that resignation was not considered an option? Every insider account of Suez credits Lloyd with voicing severe reservations, on occasion outright opposition, to the unfolding plot for disposing of Nasser. If he had resigned, or even threatened to resign, British involvement in the Suez operation would have come to a halt. Yet he stayed on. The plain fact was, Lloyd liked his job with all its trappings and he was prepared to do anything to hang on to it.

On the afternoon of the 16th, the day of Lloyd's return from New York, he and Eden were on their way to Paris for a meeting with Mollet and Pineau. Ben-Gurion was keen to make it a tripartite get-together so that he could test British intentions, good or otherwise. But before going farther Eden wanted clarification on the extent of French planning with Israel.

The Anglo-French summit at the Palais Matignon continued long into the evening. It was a closed session. The four leaders were huddled together without the benefit of advisers or interpreters. No minutes were kept. Gladwyn Jebb, an ambassador who was more than commonly mindful of the importance of his role, was furious at his exclusion. If it is at all possible to be sympathetic to Lloyd it must be at a time when the jet-lagged foreign secretary had to face up to an incandescent ambassador who was temperamentally incapable of hiding his disdain for a lesser being. The flavour of their conversation can be gleaned from Jebb's subsequent put-down.

> I do not complain, but it is, I believe, a novel arrangement for diplomatic business of the highest importance to be conducted by the Principals without any official being present, even to take a note. I am sure that you feel that this is a good method of proceeding, and anyhow it is for you to say. But however great the advantages of the new system, it has one very considerable disadvantage so far as your representative on the spot is concerned. This is that, although he has to live with one of the Principals and has to continue negotiations with him in the absence of his own Principal, he has no means, apart from a few remarks which the latter may let fall, of knowing what actually happened when the Principals met.[15]

Jebb was not alone in his innocence. In both London and Paris, senior diplomats who were accustomed to seeing everything were cut out of the information loop.

Nothing was finally decided at the Palais Matignon meeting but both sides were left with much to think about. Not surprisingly, Eden was nervous of coming out too strongly in support of Israel while Jordan was still at risk. But he was ready to talk to Ben-Gurion and he made known that if Israel and Egypt went to war, Nasser could expect no help from Britain. Moreover, Eden was taken with the idea of acting as a sort of umpire with the threat of intervention to protect the canal. This got through to the Israelis in a diplomatic note purporting to be dictated by Eden but more probably set out by Mollet as a record of their meeting.[16]

In the event of any threat of hostilities in the neighbourhood of the Canal, the French and British Governments would call the belligerents to halt and to withdraw from the immediate vicinity of the Canal. If both agreed, no action would follow. If one or both refused, Anglo-French forces would intervene to ensure the free passage of the Canal.

In the event of hostilities developing between Egypt and Israel, Her Majesty's Government would not come to the assistance of Egypt, because Egypt was in breach of a Security Council Resolution and had moreover repudiated Western aid under the Tripartite Declaration.

Different consideration would of course apply to Jordan, with whom Her Majesty's Government had, in addition to their obligation under the Tripartite Declaration, a firm treaty.[17]

Back in London, Eden summoned the cabinet. The formal record shows that for the first time ministers who were not on the Egypt Committee were made aware of the crisis building up in the Middle East. But while coming clean on the likely Israeli participation, Eden held back on the efforts that had gone into persuading Ben-Gurion to shoot first.

With hindsight, now was the time for Eden's colleagues to begin asking questions. Conventional wisdom holds that the 'collective responsibility' of the cabinet means that vital decisions are arrived at by consensus. In fact, as recent experience of an increasingly presidential style of government tells us, it rarely happens that way. Ministers have enough to do keeping track of events in their own departments without intruding on the affairs of their political neighbours. When a prime minister dedicates himself to a mission, it is almost impossible for any but his closest associates to learn enough to be an informed critic. Add to this the Churchillian tradition that regarded loyalty to the leader as the first article of Tory faith and it is easy to imagine how most members of the cabinet managed to stifle any doubts they might have felt about Eden's Suez policy or his capacity to carry it through. Butler, the second- or third-most powerful government figure depending on where one ranks Macmillan, is a case in point. Instinctively opposed to force, he struggled with his conscience but could not bear thinking of the consequences of openly defying the prime minister. Not for nothing was Butler known as the great ditherer.

Having acknowledged the chorus of murmured support from around the cabinet table, Eden was ready to move on with The Plan. Not so Ben-Gurion. Looking like an Old Testament prophet and seeing himself in that tradition, he was deeply conscious of Israel's destiny and his own role in bringing it to fruition. He was ready to take risks but only when there was a 90 per cent chance of success. The Plan, in his view, came in well below that. Then there was the emotional factor. Sensitive to anything but wholehearted support for Israel, he was disinclined to do any favours for Britain, even when there were side benefits.

But setting aside his general aversion to the Challe scenario, Ben-Gurion fastened on to three practical issues to be decided. While there was confidence that Israel could win a land war against Egypt, Ben-Gurion needed a guarantee that the Egyptian air force could not retaliate. This called for an Anglo-French air strike to be launched simultaneously with an Israeli advance into the Sinai Peninsula. Second, he wanted a clear assurance that Iraq would stay out of Jordan and that Jordan would not join forces with Egypt. Finally, if Israel was to go to war it was with the expectation of territorial gains. Would the allies stand for Israeli claims to the straits of Eilat and Sharm el-Sheikh, which would give access to the Red Sea?[18]

Clearly, another top-level meeting was called for if there was to be any chance of a tripartite deal. Mollet was the first to act. His impatience with the lengthy preliminaries to action against Egypt was intensified when on 18 October a French naval patrol in the Mediterranean boarded the *Athos*, a cargo vessel flying under a Sudanese flag. Found to be carrying over 70 tons of arms and ammunition, the *Athos* was on its way from Alexandria to Algiers. There was no doubt that the weaponry was for the rebel cause. Though only the first arms delivery that could be traced directly to Egypt, it served to fuel popular indignation against Nasser. Unless Mollet could soon recover the initiative, his government would be at risk.

An invitation to Paris was sent to Ben-Gurion. He could hardly refuse. With French arms arriving by the day, it would not have been wise to snub Mollet. But his response dampened expectations. 'The British idea of an Israeli attack and of British interference as umpire is out of the question.' He was ready to fly to Paris if Mollet considered it necessary 'in spite of the disqualification of the British idea'.[19]

In an attempt to soften him up Ben-Gurion was given star treatment. The DC-4 that had been presented by President Truman for de Gaulle's diplomatic jaunts was sent to collect the Israeli delegation. General Challe and Louis Mangin, an adviser to Bourgès-Maunoury, were on board. Arriving in Tel Aviv, they made straight for the office of Moshe Dayan, who was known to be among Ben-Gurion's more bullish advisers.

> The talk was tough. I asked them if the French Air Force would come to our aid if our cities were bombed within the first twenty-four hours – when our own planes would be needed over the battlefield. They answered in the negative, adding that the British were opposed to this idea as it would spoil the 'scenario'. At this point I just blew up, perhaps as much for the tiresome use of the word 'scenario' as for the reasoning. Shakespeare, I said, was a genius of a scenario writer, but I doubted whether any in the British Cabinet had inherited his qualities. I, for one, would not support a partnership proposal based on the condition that one

would do the job and the other two would come along and kick him out. If we had to fight the Egyptians alone, we ourselves would decide when and how to do so, being governed by what suited us best. In a partnership, however, if Egyptian planes bombed Tel Aviv because our own planes were away preparing the path for the Anglo-French conquest of the Canal Zone, it was inconceivable that our partners would not come to our aid so as not to spoil the 'scenario'![20]

The compromise offer was to station French squadrons in Israel ready to go into action should need arise.

Dayan had a better idea. Israel would carry out small-scale land attacks near enough to the canal to give the Allies sufficient cause to intervene but not so near to Cairo as to prompt an Egyptian counter-attack on Israeli cities. The French could well understand the attraction of the plan to the Israelis. It involved them in the minimum of risk for the maximum of gain. Clearly, negotiations would not be simple.

The Israeli delegation – Ben-Gurion, Shimon Peres, Dayan and his *chef du bureau*, Mordechai Bar-On – began what turned out to be a seventeen-hour flight to Paris at dusk on the evening of Sunday, 21 October, the date on which Musketeer Revise was supposed to have got under way. Up to the last moment there were doubts that Ben-Gurion would agree to travel, though doubtless his apparent reluctance had more to do with proving to his French escort that he was no easy touch than with any wish to back away entirely from a joint operation. Waiting to board the plane, he told Challe, 'If you are thinking of pressing the British proposals on us, the only useful thing about this trip will be the opportunity to meet your prime minister.'[21] It was not much of a start but at least it got the show on the road. The challenge now facing Mollet was to persuade Eden to join the party.

A sixth sense must have told Eden that he would be chancing too much to put in a personal appearance. His simply being in Paris would excite press comment and he could hardly travel incognito. But keen as he was to see The Plan advance, it was open to him to send a representative. Selwyn Lloyd was the obvious choice. It has been said that Lloyd was picked so that he would become irretrievably linked to any plot that might be hatched in Paris.[22] Eden was certainly capable of such devious practice. It is more likely, however, that Lloyd went for no stronger reason than he was foreign secretary. While he still had to be convinced that Eden was on the right track – the dismissal of his efforts at the UN must have rankled – he was his master's voice. Moreover, if the occasion should arise, his visit to Paris could be explained away without arousing too much suspicion.

Lloyd was in his Wirral constituency for the weekend when the call came. With him was Donald Logan, his assistant private secretary. They travelled back to London on the overnight train. Early on Sunday morning Lloyd was at Chequers listening to Eden's briefing on the forthcoming Anglo-French-Israeli rendez-vous. It was to be a secret mission. For foreign office consumption it was to be put about that Lloyd had gone down with sinus trouble. For the story to hold, Lloyd's official driver was stood down. Donald Logan was deputised to drive him to the airport and to accompany him to Paris. But Lloyd drew the line at dressing up for the part.

> The idea that he arrived wearing a false moustache arises from the fact that he did say, as a joke, that he did not like all this secrecy, and that he felt he ought to be wearing a false moustache. The story was put around that he was wearing a dirty raincoat to go to Sèvres. If he was, it was not intended as a disguise, as he probably wore the raincoat all the time when he was going to the House of Commons. There is nothing in that at all.[23]

Another myth relates to Lloyd's office diary. Deleting the engagements for 22 October, Logan substituted a note recording: 'A day, marked among other things, by a nearly fatal car accident – for which my driving was not responsible.' For the same date, Lloyd's personal diary refers simply to 'SL's journey'. His biographer claims that 'for a man who was normally so punctilious about keeping written records this entry in itself speaks volumes about his inner feelings'.[24] As Logan explains, it does nothing of the sort.

> We were being driven pretty fast by a [French] military driver, when we came to a crossroads that had no light or policeman on it, and another car being driven equally fast came straight across our nose. It was perhaps my own concern, rather than anything else, that made me think, if we had an accident, what explanation could we have given. That was the only significance in the near-accident.
>
> I may have made a mistake when compiling the diary of Selwyn's engagements for that week. It would obviously have been awkward to have a gap, and thinking of putting something innocuous in the diary to remind Selwyn of what he was doing, in case the date was not as significant as it later turned out to be, I put in a reference to the incident, to remind him in cryptic form of the date of our clandestine visit to Sèvres. I had no idea that this scrap of paper would get into the public archives. I ought not to have been so flippant. I thus drew more attention to the incident than it merited.[25]

The need for secrecy was taken more seriously by the Israelis. Ben-Gurion arrived with a hat pulled down to hide his mane of white hair while Dayan wore dark glasses to cover his eye patch. Nonetheless, they were nearly caught out. A worker at Villacoublay military airfield had no trouble in identifying Ben-Gurion. He promptly contacted a reporter for an Israeli newspaper, who passed up a scoop when he refused to believe such an improbable story.[26]

The Israeli party was driven to a diplomatic safe house, the Villa Bonnier de la Chapelle in the Parisian suburb of Sèvres. The stately residence had powerful associations for hosts and guests. One room was set aside as a memorial to the only son of the Bonnier de la Chapelle, a hero of the Resistance who, in 1943, had led the assassination plot against General Darlan in Algiers. Caught and executed by the Vichy regime, the eighteen-year-old symbolised a struggle against oppression that brought back memories for French and Israelis alike.

Their discussions started on the periphery of the big topic, partly to ease their way to hard decisions but also to fill the three-hour gap before Lloyd was able to join the meeting. The talk ranged from Poland and Hungary, where there was growing hostility to Soviet dominance, to Jordan, where pro-Nasser candidates had scored a resounding victory in the recent election. The latter gave Ben-Gurion the opportunity to expound his theory that Jordan was unsustainable as an independent state. It should be split between Israel and Iraq, the first stage of a comprehensive restructuring of the Middle East that had Britain taking care of Iraq and the Gulf States while France with Israel oversaw the affairs of Lebanon and Syria.

As Ben-Gurion rumbled on, there were signals on the French side of the table that they were eager to get down to business. In trying to solve all problems at once, declared Pineau, none would be solved.[27] It began to dawn on Ben-Gurion just how eager the Mollet government was to secure a deal. The political temperature in Paris was rising sharply. The capture of the *Athos* gun runners had set off another burst of anti-Nasser rhetoric in the press and in the Assembly. Now there was the Ben Bella incident to quicken Mollet's sense of urgency.

That very afternoon a plane carrying Ben Bella and four other leaders of the Algerian National Liberation Front had been hijacked by the French air force. Justification for this act of piracy was hard to find. Ben Bella had been on his way to Tunis in the expectation of having proposals for a compromise peace in Algeria brokered by Tunisia and Morocco. Mollet had approved the initiative, but not so the French military command in Algeria. In defiance of political orders, General Lorillot had done nothing to foil the plot and may actively have encouraged it, as too may some of Mollet's closest colleagues. Mollet himself was outraged but went along with the majority view of his cabinet that since nothing could be done to reverse what had happened without revealing a dangerous weakness in the political fabric, it was best

to put up a united front. What Mollet needed now was a resounding victory over Nasser to recover his authority.

Lloyd and Logan arrived in Sèvres at 7 p.m. From here on the
memories of those present are at variance, sometimes wildly so.
Poor recollection is unlikely to have been the problem. Rather,
each of the participants wished to put the best possible interpretation on their involvement in what came to be seen as a very
dodgy business. On one point there is broad agreement. Lloyd's
account, in which he gives himself credit for keeping a clear
head while raising solid objections to The Plan, can be safely
discounted. That Lloyd would rather have been somewhere else
was made plain as soon as he joined the meeting. Dayan noted:
'Britain's foreign minister may well have been a friendly man,
pleasant, charming, amiable. If so, he showed near-genius in con-
cealing these virtues. His manner could not have been more
antagonistic. His whole demeanour expressed distaste – for the
place, the company, and the topic.'[28]

Logan was more understanding.

> He did not like the job that he had been sent to do. So naturally
> he did not go in smiling. He was not pleased with the task ahead
> of him. He was not a man to go into a situation like this in a very
> affable way. He had a difficult task to do, and was there knowing
> that the French and the Israelis were already close together. He
> was to find, in the conversation, that they were even closer than
> he thought, so he had an uphill task. He had a marked lack of
> enthusiasm for what he had to do. Of course they thought he
> was po-faced. Moreover, what he said was not agreeable to them,
> and that encouraged them to think that he was unhelpful.[29]

Ben-Gurion and Lloyd took an instant dislike to each other, the
first seeing in Lloyd everything that drove him mad about the
British, starting with the tendency to say one thing while meaning another. Lloyd, on the other hand, resented the pushiness
of the Israeli leader, who failed to show proper respect for the
representative of a major power. Not surprisingly, their opening
manoeuvres put them at opposite poles.

Dayan again:

Lloyd's opening remarks suggested the tactics of a customer bargaining with extortionate merchants. He said that in fact it was possible to reach agreement with Egypt over the Suez Canal within seven days. His talks in New York with Egypt's Foreign Minister Fawzi had been fruitful, and the Egyptians agreed to recognize the Suez Canal Users' Association, to set the Canal fees in advance, to guarantee international supervision of the operation of the Canal, and to accept the imposition of sanctions, in accordance with the UN Charter, if they broke their commitments.

If all was so well and good, why, then, was he here? Because, he explained, such an agreement would not only fail to weaken Nasser, but would actually strengthen him, and since Her Majesty's Government considered that Nasser had to go, it was prepared to undertake military action in accordance with the latest version of the Anglo-French plan. This called for the invasion of Sinai by the Israeli army, whose units were to reach Suez within forty-eight hours . . . Some time during those forty-eight hours, the Anglo-French ultimatum would be issued to both sides, ordering them to withdraw from the Canal. If Egypt rejected it, the Anglo-French attack would be launched to capture the Canal Zone and overthrow Nasser.

Britain would not go to the aid of Egypt following the attack by Israel nor would she go to the help of Jordan, despite the Anglo-Jordanian defence treaty, if Jordan attacked Israel. But Britain would aid Jordan if she were attacked by Israel.

Ben-Gurion's reply was firm and brief. He said he had already rejected the plan as outlined by Lloyd. Israel was not anxious to be branded as an aggressor and to be the recipient of an ultimatum to evacuate the Canal area. If Israel were to attack Egypt under this plan, Egypt might react by bombing Israel's cities. With Israel fighting alone, one could not rule out the prospect that Soviet and Czech 'volunteers' would be dispatched to stiffen the Egyptian Air Force. Ben-Gurion's answer, therefore, was that

Israel would not start a war against Egypt, neither now nor at any other stage. If she were attacked, however, she would defend herself and eventually defeat Egypt, even at the cost of heavy casualties.[30]

At this point it fell to Dayan to explain what Israel *was* prepared to do. This consisted of a limited action, open to interpretation as a reprisal raid should plans go awry, close enough to the canal to justify an Anglo-French demand that Egyptian and Israeli forces be evacuated from the Canal Zone. If, as expected, Egypt rejected the ultimatum, British and French air forces could start bombing Egyptian airfields. When asked to elaborate, Dayan refused more detail.

> Being a wise military man, he did not give away military secrets easily. He made no secret of the fact that what the Israelis were most interested in were the Straits of Tiran, and that their objective was to dominate Sharm el-Sheikh. This was a long way from the Canal, and we pointed out that it was in no way a threat to the Canal. He would not go much further, but he did agree that there could be a significant military action in the vicinity of the Mitla Pass [about 30 miles from the canal]. The back of an envelope was produced, and he drew maps. And in the end, we felt that we had gone as far as we could in getting him to say there would be something significant around the Mitla Pass. That was all we could get out of him.[31]

Lloyd and Ben-Gurion were now a long way from their starting positions. In a few short hours, Ben-Gurion had come to recognise two essential facts. First, the alliance with France was too important to be sacrificed; second, since France would not move against Nasser without Britain, he had to concede enough to persuade Lloyd that a coalition could work.

In the end, the only sticking point was the timing of the air attack on Egyptian airfields. Ben-Gurion wanted it to coincide with an Israeli attack; Lloyd held to intervention when there was clear evidence of a 'real act of war'. This would take at least forty-eight hours, argued Lloyd. Dayan gambled on a final settlement of thirty-six hours.

No further progress could be made until Eden had spoken. Lloyd returned to London. He left behind a bag of mixed feelings. Could he be trusted to play the forceful messenger? Pineau for one thought not. Following closely on Lloyd's heels, he sought his own rendezvous with Eden. He was right to be worried. The more Lloyd thought about The Plan, the less he liked it. As he revealed to Nutting when the junior minister cornered him at the foreign office, 'Since the essence of the Anglo-French role in the plan was to intervene only after Egypt had refused to withdraw her forces to the west bank of the Canal, we could not undertake to destroy Nasser's Air Force simultaneously with the Israeli invasion of Sinai.'[32]

But Nutting's sense of relief was tempered by Lloyd's confession of impotence in his relationship with Eden. 'I am so confused and exhausted that I honestly have no advice to offer any more.'[33] The only surprise in this was his imagining that he had ever had much advice to offer in the first place. A hurriedly summoned cabinet was told by Lloyd 'from secret conversations which have been held in Paris with representatives of the Israeli government, it now appeared that the Israelis would not alone launch a full scale attack against Egypt'. Researching a television documentary on Suez, Peter Hennessey described this as the 'smoking minute' which showed that ministers knew more than they were subsequently inclined to admit.[34] They were certainly made aware that whatever the Israelis did, Lloyd had lost faith in achieving a negotiated settlement with Egypt. France would not go along with it and, in any case, it would be impossible to keep up for much longer the military pressure needed to persuade Nasser to compromise.

The tone of the foreign secretary's report must have caused Eden to boil with frustration. That evening he joined an after-dinner session with Lloyd and Pineau at Carlton Gardens. Here, as his sympathetic biographer concedes, 'Selwyn was a bystander in his own home'.[35] Eden swept aside Lloyd's objections to The

Plan, insisting only that Britain should not be put in the position of *asking* Israel to take any particular action. Rather, the success of The Plan would revolve around an Anglo-French response to Israeli strategic decisions independently arrived at.

The next move was to reconvene the three-power meeting at Sèvres. This was simple enough since the French and Israeli delegations were still at the Villa Bonnier de la Chapelle waiting for Lloyd to put in a reappearance. Eden had other ideas. His foreign minister was clearly not up to his appointed task and anyway had shown an aversion to going on with it. An envoy was needed who would get on with the job and stop wasting valuable time. Since no minister fitted the role, Eden fell back on unelected officials who knew how to obey orders. The first choice was Richard Powell, permanent secretary at the ministry of defence. It was not a task that appealed to him, wary as he was of Eden, who 'wasn't really 100% in control of himself'. Powell searched for a graceful way of backing out. 'I can't remember what I said, but I suppose I said that this was a matter for a diplomat to handle, and this is why Pat Dean was chosen.'[36]

As Lloyd's deputy under-secretary of state, Patrick Dean was said to be 'the only chap who knew everything'.[37] As chairman of the joint intelligence committee, which linked the foreign office with the military and MI6, he was certainly better informed than most of his colleagues, but as Dean subsequently pointed out, 'We knew roughly what was going on, but we did not know exactly what policy was anywhere until it was more widely known within the foreign office.'[38] And, of course, Eden was taking good care to keep the foreign office, with the exception of Kirkpatrick, out of the loop. So it was that when Dean was told to be on his way to Sèvres, he was grateful for having Logan to go along with him. The time on the flight was spent with Logan briefing his colleague on all that had happened over the past fortnight, starting with General Challe's visit to Chequers.

In Paris, the two civil servants were met by Challe, who accompanied them to Sèvres. By now, Dean was clear on his objective, to ensure that the Israelis understood that only a threat to the canal would trigger British involvement. That required a 'real act of war'. Dayan gave the necessary assurances while insisting to Ben-Gurion that in the event of France and Britain failing to live up to their part of the bargain, Israel could convincingly reinterpret their act of war as a retaliatory raid. Ben-Gurion confided in his diary: 'I think we have to undertake this operation. This is a unique opportunity that two "not so small" powers will try to topple Nasser, and we shall not remain alone against him while he becomes stronger and conquers all Arab countries.'[39]

With a consensus reached, Logan and Dean prepared to go home. But there was still one remaining formality. Ben-Gurion wanted a record of what had been agreed. As Logan recalled:

> We had been sitting in the room all afternoon, and the first thing that Pat or I heard about any document being produced was towards the end of the afternoon, when we heard the sound of someone typing in a neighbouring room. Three copies of the Protocol were produced for us, with the comment: 'This is a record of what we have been discussing. Do you agree?' That was the first indication that we had that anybody intended to make a record of the conversation. It must have been done by both the Israelis and the French, judging by the way the document was put together and its style. Part of it must have been drafted by a French assistant and part by an Israeli, and then put together. It was an accurate account, and seemed to us to be a useful record to take back to the Prime Minister, to show that we had got the Israelis to agree to a significant military move against the Canal.[40]

The terms of the protocol were to remain strictly secret. The main provisions were:

1. The Israeli forces launch in the evening of 29 October 1956 a large-scale attack on the Egyptian forces with the aim of reaching the Canal Zone the following day.

2. On being apprised of these events, the British and
   French governments during the day of 30 October
   1956 respectively and simultaneously make two
   appeals to the Egyptian government and the Israeli
   government on the following lines:

   A. TO THE EGYPTIAN GOVERNMENT

   (a) halt all acts of war
   (b) withdraw all its troops ten miles from the Canal
   (c) accept temporary occupation of key positions
        on the Canal by the Anglo-French forces to
        guarantee freedom of passage to the vessels of
        all nations until a final settlement

   B. TO THE ISRAELI GOVERNMENT

   (a) halt all acts of war
   (b) withdraw all its troops ten miles to the east of
        the Canal

   In addition, the Israeli Government will be notified that the
   French and British Governments have demanded of the
   Egyptian Government to accept temporary occupation of key
   positions along the Canal by the Anglo-French forces.

   It is agreed that if one of the Governments refused, or did not
   give its consent, within twelve hours the Anglo-French forces
   would intervene with the means necessary to ensure that their
   demands are accepted.

   c. The representatives of the three governments agree that the
       Israeli Government will not be required to meet the
       conditions in the appeal addressed to it, in the event that
       the Egyptian Government does not accept those in the
       appeal addressed to it for their part.

3. In the event that the Egyptian Government should fail
   to agree within the stipulated time to the conditions
   of the appeal addressed to it, the Anglo-French forces
   will launch military operations against the Egyptian
   forces in the early hours of the morning of 31 October.

According to Dayan the Israeli and Anglo-French objectives were different but parallel. The Anglo-French goal was to hold the Suez Canal to ensure free passage while Israel intended to take control of the western shore of the Gulf of Aqaba and Sharm el-Sheikh to secure freedom of shipping. The first objective was a temporary measure, the second permanent. The first was to be achieved with Israeli support, the second by Israel alone.[41]

At 10.30 p.m. on 24 October Dean was at Downing Street where he was ushered in to see Eden and his senior ministers, including Butler, Macmillan, Lord Home, secretary of state for commonwealth affairs, Anthony Head, the newly installed minister of defence, and Mountbatten. A copy of the Sèvres Protocol was handed over to Eden, who showed surprise and then anger that secret diplomacy was no longer a matter of a handshake between gentlemen. It was the defining moment of the Suez crisis. Whatever justification was later advanced for Eden's policy on Suez, it foundered on this simple fact – that the prime minister was thrown into a panic by the risk of his actions becoming known outside a closed circle of senior colleagues who could be trusted to keep quiet or whose word could be challenged if it ever came to a dispute over his selective version of events.

Dean and Logan were ordered back to Paris the following day, where they were to seek out and destroy all copies of the protocol.

> We flew over that morning, and arrived with Pineau in the middle of the day, and told him of the Prime Minister's request. He said that he had to think about it, but it would be difficult as the Israelis were already on the way back to Israel with their copy. We were asked to wait in the reception rooms of the Quai D'Orsay, which we did. Then, feeling a bit hungry and thirsty, we found that the door was locked! It was late afternoon before we were taken back to Pineau, who told us that the French Government did not agree that the document should be destroyed, and that in any case the Israelis had their copy.[42]

Four days later, on 29 October, the Israelis launched their attack.

18

An abridged report of what was afoot in the Middle East was given to the full cabinet by Eden and Lloyd on 25 October. The minutes recorded an agreement:

> In principle that, in the event of an Israeli attack on Egypt, the government should join with the French government in calling on the two belligerents to stop hostilities and withdraw their forces to a distance of ten miles from the Canal; and should warn both belligerents that, if either or both of them failed to undertake within twelve hours to comply with these requirements, British and French forces would intervene to enforce compliance.[1]

No mention was made of the Sèvres Protocol. One or more cabinet members (they are not identified) voiced disquiet that 'our action might do lasting damage to Anglo-American relations'. They might have pitched their concern more strongly had they been aware of the efforts that had gone into disguising Anglo-French intentions towards Egypt.

Among the many in the higher reaches of government who found it hard to understand what was going on was Sir Roger Makins, Britain's ambassador in Washington until 15 October, when he took on a new job as head of the Treasury in London, serving under his old friend Harold Macmillan. Makins was puzzled on several counts. There was no explanation as to why it was thought necessary for him to take up new responsibilities at such a critical period in Anglo-American relations, responsibilities moreover for which he was not over-qualified. Dulles, who could make no sense of it, was further irritated when he discovered that Makins's successor, Sir Harold Caccia, was proceeding at a leisurely pace towards Washington, having been permitted to travel by transatlantic liner. The suspicion had to be that Eden wanted a suspension of top-level diplomacy while his Suez plot unfolded. He was to deny this most vehemently. Eden's latest biographer quotes him as putting the onus on Caccia. 'I wanted him to fly, but he wanted a rest and asked to be allowed to go by sea . . . I regretted this.'[2]

Even assuming this to be true, and there is only Eden's word for it, a prime minister who was ready to permit such indulgence at such a time has to be classed as a fool. The likelier explanation, that it was all a ploy to keep Dulles guessing, is more to Eden's credit as a tactician if not to his sense of propriety.

By the last week in October Dulles was registering a 'deliberate British purpose of keeping us deliberately in the dark as to their intentions with reference to Middle East matters generally and Egypt in particular'.[3] To clear the air, thought was given to 'inviting Eden and Mollet and their foreign ministers to this country for a tripartite discussion toward the end of November'.[4] Meanwhile, reports from London and Paris were studied with more than usual thoroughness. Ambassador Winthrop Aldrich was assiduous in keeping Dulles abreast of affairs at Westminster, though he put too much emphasis on Lloyd as a source of intelligence. The failure to assert the authority of the Canal Users' Association had driven Britain 'into closer alliance with France and away . . . from the US, which [Lloyd] deplores'. It explained 'to a certain extent some of the brittle attitudes which are now being taken by the British'.[5]

The cosy feeling that come what may the Anglo-American special relationship would soon be back on track was shattered when reports started coming through of a military build-up in Israel, along with rumours that somehow Britain and France were involved.

The Israeli armed forces were strong on improvisation and flexibility. A small country, short of 2 million people, could not afford a large standing army. Instead, a core of professionals, 11,000 strong, was supplemented by some 40,000 conscripts, men and women, who served for two and a half years and two years respectively. This was national service of a calibre unknown in Europe. Whereas, say, in Britain, young soldiers devoted their time and energy to the archaic rituals of military discipline such as marching up and down, stomping their feet in unison, in Israel the stress was on fighting skills, the art of survival against heavy odds.

'The actions of those days developed combat doctrines and methods of combat still in use in the Israel Defense Forces today,' wrote General Raful Eitan in 1991.

> The ideas were revolutionary and innovative. We developed ways to penetrate mine fields, break through fences and fight in trenches and built-up areas. We trained in land-sea maneuvers and engaged in special parachuting exercises. We reached a high level of cooperation and coordination with the Air Force and Navy. The great sense of readiness we felt as a result of our skills contributed to the ability of each soldier to dare bravely and believe that the capability of each soldier has no bounds.[6]

The system had its drawbacks. For one thing, there were not enough full-time soldiers to nurture all the recruits to an acceptable level of training. For another, a largely conscript army which prided itself on the absence of formality was not the easiest to manage. It was one of the frustrations of Moshe Dayan, then the only serving officer with the rank of general, that his best-laid plans were liable to be thrown into disarray by subordinates who thought they knew better. His problem was exacerbated when the rebel had an impressive record of reprisal raids against the fedayeen strongholds. A young parachute commander called Ariel Sharon was a prime example.

But whatever the failings of the Israeli military, compulsory service, including a period in the reserve, made certain that the entire rising generation of Israeli military put the defence of the country above all other priorities. Within days a full mobilisation was calculated to bring army strength up to around 200,000. For Operation Kadesh – a biblical reference to the wanderings of the children of Israel in the Sinai Desert – a part-mobilisation summoned around 100,000 reservists. That this was achieved without neighbouring countries realising immediately what was happening was a tribute to the army's organisational skills. Key officers were notified by telephone or telegram. It was then up to them to gather in those under their command, chiefly by going around knocking on doors. All this took less than a day. In the final hours of assembling twelve brigades, fully armed and ready for action, word went out for vehicles of whatever make or age but capable of carrying men and equipment across rough terrain.

> The vehicles trickle in, as and when their orders reach them, accompanied by their civilian drivers. If a driver – no matter his age – says that he wants to go to war along with his vehicle, he is allowed to do so. After all, it is his property, and sometimes his only property; and he knows best how to coax it into mobility or to persuade it to negotiate the thick sand or punitive rock of a tricky passage.[7]

By now, of course, even the most laid-back observer realised that something was up. But what? As Donald Logan recalled, even for those with insider knowledge of the likely sequence of events it 'was a very uncomfortable period, knowing what was going to happen, but knowing that very few people knew what was going to happen and wondering if it really was going to happen, or if something would prevent it'.[8] For those at a distance from the decision-making there was a surfeit of rumours being bandied about, but few could take them seriously. On 27 October, at a reception at the Iranian embassy in Paris, the Egyptian ambassador joked with Pierre Maillard of the Afrique-Levant section of the Quai d'Orsay.

> 'Monsieur le Ministre, you are going to attack us soon it seems?' Maillard, embarrassed, didn't say anything and the Ambassador continued: 'No, no, I am teasing you. You know two diplomats from a communist country have come to tell me that you are going to attack us at the same time as Israel. But this is ridiculous. If this

was true, you would not be able to stop the repatriation of your citizens. These stories of invasion are completely false and I have underlined this in the despatches that I have sent to Cairo . . .'[9]

The shared assumption of Israeli watchers was of an impending attack on Jordan. This was suggested by the move north away from the Sinai border of Colonel Ariel Sharon's 202nd Parachute Brigade. That they were travelling overland instead of by air caused some comment, obscuring the more relevant detail that the force was one battalion short. The deception relaxed the Egyptian high command, which was, in any case, already persuaded that the Sinai was an unlikely battleground of Israeli choosing. Twenty-four thousand square miles of not much except sand and rock was inhospitable country for all except the itinerant Bedouin, who were noble or savage according to romantic inclination. Running the length of Egypt's eastern border, the defence of the Sinai was concentrated at four communication points. Elsewhere Egyptian troops were light on the ground with at least half the normal garrison occupied in putting up a show of strength in Cairo and other urban centres. Thus over the whole of Sinai, Egyptian forces numbered no more than around thirty thousand.

Two battalions of the Desert Frontier Force guarded the southern pass, otherwise known as the Pilgrim's Way, across a ridge of high ground about 45 miles to the east of the Suez Canal. At its higher levels the Pilgrim's Way was pretty well an impenetrable barrier except for a series of narrow gorges of which the most important was the Mitla Pass. The best part of the rest of the Egyptian garrison was deployed in the north-east triangle formed by El Arish, Rafah and Abu Ageila.

The war started with a spectacular display of low-level flying. On 29 October at 1500 hours, four Israeli piston-engined P-51 Mustang fighters swept over the Sinai Desert, descending to little more than 12 feet above the ground to slice through the overhead wires connecting Egyptian forces with their headquarters at Ismailia.[10]

In the late afternoon a 395-strong battalion of the 202nd Para-troop Brigade led by Lieutenant Colonel Raful Eitan dropped 15 miles to the east of the Mitla Pass. It was some time before the Egyptian defenders realised that they were under threat. Sixteen Dakota transports had flown in low under Egyptian radar, rising to 1,500 feet just minutes away from the jump area. Assembling his troops, Eitan led the march towards the Mitla Pass. In gathering darkness they dug themselves in, covering the road in both directions. At 2100 hours, eight jeeps, mortars and other weapons, ammunition, water, food and medicine were parachuted in. Along with the supplies came an order to stay clear of the Mitla Pass itself.

By now the Egyptians were aware that Israeli forces were in the area. A chance encounter with three troop carriers of the Frontier Regiment, two of which escaped an Israeli ambush, raised the alarm. But Cairo remained calm. When Nasser heard that Eisenhower had ordered a general evacuation of American nationals he expressed surprise.

> Nasser was friendly and relaxed and said he was unable to under-stand what all the turmoil was about. He had just taken vacation of four days and something seemed to have happened during that time of which he was completely unaware ... Could it be that Israel really wanted war? If so, he could not see why. It is true that in monitoring Israeli radio a certain change in tone had been detected about five days ago but he had not attached any particular significance to it. What is it all about?[11]

A day earlier, when Israeli mobilisation had become common knowledge, part of Sharon's 202nd Brigade had concentrated near Eilat close to the far tip of the Israeli border with Jordan. Sharon was not best pleased with his task. 'Some other unit could have done it equally well, and it would add an extra 65 miles to our race to link up with the battalion at Mitla.[12] The thought occurred to him that this might be Dayan's ruse to keep him out of the limelight when the real fighting started.

No attempt was made by Sharon to hide his troops. Indeed, he was determined to be seen. Lookouts at the British base at Aqaba, just across the border, had no difficulty in spotting Israeli army vehicles on the move. How could anyone doubt that Jordan was the intended victim? The pundits were wrong. As the paratroops prepared to drop over the Mitla Pass, Sharon made a smart about-turn from Jordan to dash across Israel, from its eastern to its western border, there to begin a battle drive into Sinai. Nine hours later, having lost many of his vehicles to breakdowns or sand drifts, Sharon was close to the border town of Kuntilla, his first target.

> That evening we took Kuntilla, moving the attacking unit around to the rear so they could come in out of the setting sun. On the radio we heard the Israeli military spokesman announcing a 'raid to eliminate terrorist bases in the Sinai', part of the ruse to paint what was happening as a reprisal rather than the opening moves of a fully-fledged war (in fact there were no terrorist bases in the Sinai). By dawn the next morning we were in position in front of Themed, a Bedouin oasis that had been heavily fortified with mine fields and perimeter defenses and was held by two companies of Egyptian infantry. We arrived without most of our tanks. Along with almost sixty other vehicles they had broken down in the treacherous dunes and wadis. With no road, there were places where the brigade's tractors had had to tow every single truck and half-truck.
>
> But we were there. With the rising sun at our backs this time I sent in a battalion-size attack under Ahron Davidi, who crashed forward in a fast-moving arc of half-tracks, jeeps, and the remaining tanks. Huge whirls of dust clouded the desert from the charging vehicles, illuminated from behind by the bright morning glare. Emerging from the cloud, at the last moment we formed a single line and smashed into the middle of the Egyptian defenses. Themed too fell quickly.[13]

Making do with what was left of his tanks and trucks, Sharon pressed on to the Mitla Pass, where Eitan's paratroops were taking heavy punishment. 'At ten that evening one of our searchlights picked out a big homemade sign by the side of the desert track. It read in Hebrew, 'Border Ahead. Stop!' Just beyond, Raful's battalion was waiting, dug into the hard dirt on the flatlands of Mitla's eastern approaches. It had taken us thirty hours to reach them.'[14]

Heavy shelling by the Egyptian 2nd Infantry Brigade had pinned down the Israelis where they were vulnerable to air strikes. This undeniable plus for the Egyptian air force was later magnified to suggest extensive follow-up attacks on Israeli airfields. Sporadic raids were carried out but in contrast to Nasser's version of events published in the *Egyptian Gazette*,[15] they were largely ineffective. However, fiction should not detract from one of the few successes of the Egyptian MiG17 fighters. At the Mitla Pass, they were powerful enough to add a sense of urgency to Eitan's appeals for help from the rest of his brigade as it made its way across Sinai for a planned link-up. It was a race between Sharon and Egyptian reinforcements moving in from Fayid for what the Egyptian high command expected to be a decisive victory.

A major problem for Sharon was the absence of reliable communications. Ground-to-ground link-ups were sporadic and, in any case, much of the equipment had been lost or damaged in the breakneck advance. But help was on hand. Sharon's saviour was a young reservist, Erich Reich.

Imagine my surprise to discover I had become a communication officer. That really was a joke. What did I know of those cumbersome walky-talkies I had seen other soldiers lug around? As I was being hustled towards a Piper plane waiting to take off I was informed that I was to make contact with the brigade that had just jumped on to the slopes of the Mitla Pass in the middle of the Sinai desert. This is the first I had heard that the 1956 war had begun. 'Your pilot is an experienced navigator so you shouldn't have too many problems.' That proved a rather inaccurate statement. 'And who am I communicating with?' I queried. 'The Boss, Ariel Sharon!' was the curt response.[16]

What he knew of Sharon made Reich even more nervous of his mission.

> Sharon was already then a pretty well known character, impetuous, brave and someone who didn't suffer fools lightly. His orders had to be obeyed immediately, if you didn't want to find yourself the recipient of one of his famous tongue-lashings. Orders he was given, on the other hand, could be disregarded, if he didn't believe them to be right. As far as he was concerned, plans he was provided with were only guidelines to be improved upon as and how he deemed necessary. A sort of Israeli malaise, 'I can do anything better than you and I am always right.'[17]

While his pilot was waiting for take-off he gave Reich basic instruction on using the radio monitor. Then they were on their way.

> We were hardly above the clouds when the radio crackled into life and a rasping voice came through loud and clear, 'Where the hell are you?' 'On our way,' I replied. Talk about being impatient. In that department, I would say Sharon takes the honours. It must have been about an hour or so later just as I was becoming a little anxious, I noticed bright lights looming ahead. 'We've flown too far,' I pointed out to the pilot. 'We're about to cross the Suez Canal.' We made a sharp u-turn heading into a northerly direction. It was at the break of dawn and after numerous one-sided radio conversations we finally made contact with the battalion at the Mitla Pass and landed beside them.
>
> It was then we learned of the casualties suffered in the ambush. I still remember the hill we crawled up to find out how they were faring after the jump and subsequent fighting. Most seemed tired but in pretty good shape. After reaching them it was time to communicate with the armoured regiment on its way to Mitla. Our orders were pretty clear, 'Get back on the plane and return to base, now!' We said our goodbyes and couldn't have been more than about fifty meters from the plane, when suddenly two Egyptian Mystère aircraft came screaming across the sky towards

us. Everyone ducked, behind rocks, bushes or anything vaguely appearing safe. A couple of seconds later bullets strafed along the ground, hitting among other things our poor little Piper plane, which burst into flames. My immediate concern wasn't, 'Wow, that was close' but how strong the curses were going to be for not departing earlier.[18]

But there was no time for recriminations. When the 202nd Brigade was reunited, Reich was recruited into the infantry and made a platoon leader.

The latest intelligence of the Israeli move into Egypt set off frenetic activity in Washington. Eisenhower was in the last fortnight of his campaign for re-election. It was hard to imagine a worst time to become embroiled in an Arab–Jewish conflict. His immediate thought was to call into play the 1950 Tripartite Declaration whereby America, France and Britain had pledged opposition to the use of force to settle Middle East disputes. The way forward, suggested Dulles, was for the three powers to move a UN Security Council resolution calling for a cessation of hostilities. But this proved difficult. In the absence of a British ambassador who was still enjoying a first-class ocean voyage at the taxpayers' expense and with the French ambassador unaccountably preoccupied with other matters, Dulles was obliged to press his case with two embassy subordinates who turned out to be masters of prevarication.

Frustrated on one diplomatic front, Dulles turned directly to the UN, where Cabot Lodge, the American representative, called for a meeting of the Security Council. This put his British and French colleagues on the spot. Both Sir Pierson Dixon, who was known for his opposition to the use of force against Egypt, and Bernard Cornut-Gentille were disposed to support a Security Council call for Israel to withdraw. First, however, they had to check with their governments. The response was a clear indication of an imminent Anglo-French intervention which would be jeopardised by a restraining order from the UN. At this point Cornut-Gentille sensibly collapsed with the strain of it all and departed the scene. It was left to Dixon to tell Lodge that any move against Israel would be without Anglo-French support.[19]

Doing his best to speak for his government while disguising his true feelings, Dixon may have expressed himself too forcefully. At any rate, Eisenhower was 'astonished to find that he [Dixon] was completely unsympathetic, stating frankly that his govern-ment would not agree to any action whatsoever to be taken against Israel. He further argued that the tripartite statement of May 1950 was ancient history and without current validity'.[20] This was in a letter to Eden in which the president asked, sadly and almost plain-tively, 'as to exactly what is happening between us and our Euro-pean allies – especially between us, the French and yourselves'.

More forthright with his advisers, Eisenhower spoke harshly of his 'double crossing' allies. With increasing evidence of Anglo-French preparations to join the war against Egypt, the president dispatched a succession of messages, including two to Ben-Gurion, urging restraint. From Eden came a response so utterly and obviously devoid of candour that it must have served only to confirm Eisenhower's worst fears.

> When we received news of the Israel mobilisation, we instructed our Ambassador in Tel Aviv to urge restraint. Soon afterwards he sought and obtained a reassurance that Israel would not attack Jordan. This seems to me important, since it means that Israel will not enlarge the area of conflict or involve us in virtue of the Anglo-Jordan Treaty. In recent months we have several times warned the Israel Government, both publicly and privately, that if they attacked Jordan we would honour our obligations. But we feel under no obligation to come to the aid of Egypt. Apart from the feelings of public opinion here, Nasser and his press have relieved us of any such obligation by their attitude to the Tripartite Declaration.
>
> Egypt has to a large extent brought this attack on herself by insisting that the state of war persists, by defying the Security Council and by declaring her intention to marshal the Arab States for the destruction of Israel . . .

We have earnestly deliberated what we should do in this serious situation. We cannot afford to see the Canal closed or to lose
the shipping which is daily on passage through it. We have a
responsibility for the people in these ships. We feel that a decisive
action should be taken at once to stop hostilities.[21]

The last line quoted was the only sentence that matched the facts.
On 30 October the British cabinet, including those ministers such
as Butler who subsequently tried to distance themselves from
Eden, approved 'subject to the forthcoming consultation with the
Prime Minister and the Foreign Minister of France, the terms of
notes to be addressed to the governments of Israel and Egypt,
calling on them to stop hostilities, to withdraw their forces to a
distance of ten miles from the Suez Canal and to allow Anglo-
French forces to occupy temporarily key positions on the canal'.[22]

The ultimatum was sent out that evening, though it took longer
than expected to get through to the people who mattered. Ronald
Higgins was a political officer at the British embassy in Tel Aviv.

After a long day the ambassador and his deputy drove away
through the blackout to their homes on the hill at Ramat Gan. I,
the junior, was left holding the fort for the night shift.

Late that evening the telephone rang down in the embassy's
bleak foyer. It was the Deputy Head of the Israeli Foreign Office.
Had we got anything for him? Any message? Puzzled, I said no.
What then, he asked, was all this press agency talk about an
ultimatum? Heavens, I said, had he not received it from his
embassy in London? No, nothing.

I gasped, outlined the content from memory and warned him
that several of the twelve hours granted had already elapsed.
Asking him to hold on, I rushed up the four floors to the strong
room for the definitive text. I carefully read this to him, with
such solemnity as a sense of history demanded and my puffing
allowed. Then I remarked that something must have gone drasti-
cally wrong with Israeli communications. To play safe with our
own, I must ask him to try to obtain his government's response
within an hour. So far as I knew, the Royal Air Force's Canberra

bombers were already warming up on our airfields in Cyprus, just over the horizon.

I sent an emergency telegram at once to the Foreign Office to report this extraordinary situation, telephoned the ambassador at home to tell him the form and then waited for the Israeli to come back. About an hour later he did so, saying he had his government's answer. Impetuously I asked if it was yes or no, thinking I could get that off at once to London and send the full text later. He declined. It was not, he said, the way diplomacy was done.

He started to dictate the text and comedy broke in. After a few sentences, me scribbling away, he broke off. That wording was not right, was it? Should it be 'not however unless' or 'always providing'? What did I think? The rival variations seemed of little significance and the minutes were ticking by.

By this time I had been joined in the grimly sandbagged lobby by a senior but non-political colleague who, worried about his children, was begging me to get a quick plain answer out of the Israelis. I asked the ministry to hold on, turned to my colleague and said that was not the way diplomacy was done. Somewhat later, with the whole text before me, I was at last able to flash it to London.[23]

It was some weeks before Higgins discovered what had gone wrong. Assuming the ultimatum to be secret, the Israeli embassy in London had decided to send it in their cipher, which meant translating it into Hebrew. Poor radio transmission caused further delay. Once received it had to be deciphered and then, because it was a secret document, brought from Jerusalem to Tel Aviv by road. There was a fog. Mused Higgins, 'Through such series of unpredictable mistakes and accidents can the course of history be altered.'[24]

Another 'accident' that might have altered history, or at least the official interpretation of events, was the premature action of the French navy. Two and a half hours before the ultimatum expired, the French destroyer *Kersaint* cruising off Haifa fired on an Egyptian frigate, *Ibrahim al-Awwal,* which, in a half-hearted way, was trying to shell the Haifa oil refinery. Reluctant to get in too close, the Egyptian gunnery was off target, achieving little more than sending up showers of seawater close to the quayside. When the *Kersaint* responded, the *Ibrahim* made haste to escape, chased by two Israeli destroyers and several French Mystères, which used the now disabled vessel for rocket practice. The *Ibrahim* was eventually boarded and towed into Haifa, where it was declared a prize of war and recommissioned in the Israeli navy. While the excitement lasted US navy ships were standing by off Haifa, waiting for any US evacuees. A misplaced shell might have started something more than a localised war.

In Cairo, Ambassador Trevelyan spent 30 October helping to burn papers. 'We had no time to separate the confidential from the rest; we burnt the lot, inside the chancery and outside on the lawn, until we were inches deep in ash and had showered the neighbourhood.'[25] At 9 p.m. he was with Nasser to hear the Egyptian rejection of the ultimatum. 'Whatever one thinks of him,' Trevelyan recorded, his 'prompt and decisive refusal [to comply] required courage.' No restrictions were imposed on embassy staff until 2 November, when the compound was sealed by Egyptian police.

The ultimatum was, said Dulles, 'as crude and brutal' as anything he had ever seen. Not surprisingly, it was cheerfully accepted by Israel in the sure knowledge that Egypt would refuse to withdraw from its own territory. As Evelyn Shuckburgh, Eden's one-time private secretary, noted in his diary, 'The [ultimatum] seems to have every fault. It is clearly not genuinely impartial, since the Israelis are nowhere near the Canal; it puts us on the side of the Israelis; the Americans were not consulted; the UN is flouted; we are about to be at war without the nation or Parliament having been given a hint of it. We think AE has gone off his head.'[26]

Eisenhower winged off a remonstrance to Eden (no longer 'my dear Anthony' but solemnly 'dear Mr Prime Minister') and to Mollet.

I have just learned from the press of the 12-hour ultimatum
which you and the French Government have delivered to the
Government of Egypt requiring, under threat of forceful intervention, the temporary occupation by Anglo-French forces of
key positions at Port Said, Ismailia and Suez in the Suez Canal
Zone. I feel I must urgently express to you my deep concern at
the prospect of this drastic action even at the very time when the
matter is under consideration as it is today by the United Nations
Security Council. It is my sincere belief that peaceful processes
can and should prevail to secure a solution which will restore the
armistice condition as between Israel and Egypt and also justly
settle the controversy with Egypt about the Suez Canal.[27]

At the UN, where there was already talk of a three-power collusion to bring about Nasser's downfall, an American-led Security
Council resolution calling for an immediate ceasefire was vetoed
by Britain and France. Pierson Dixon could hardly bring himself
to believe that it had come to this, that Eden, one of the principal
architects of the UN, should now be seeking to destroy its legitimacy. He found himself repeating the dismal performance of
imposing a veto when the Russians weighed in with a single
censure motion on Israel. The next move, sparked by Nasser's
friends in the Yugoslavian delegation, was to refer the whole issue
to an emergency session of the General Assembly, where the veto
could not be exercised.

At Westminster, Eden's announcement of the ultimatum set
off a hurricane of protest. Gaitskell accused the prime minister
of abandoning the three governing principles of British foreign
policy – Commonwealth solidarity, the Anglo-American alliance
and the UN Charter. Eden was at his worst, protesting his peaceful intentions in waging war. The blatant inconsistencies drove
the opposition to fury. Long memories recalled the Munich
debates of 1938 to find a parallel. At one point the Speaker sus-
pended the House to give a respite to overworked tempers, the
first time that had happened in over thirty years.

When Lloyd rose to speak, it was to utter the first of the Suez lies that were to bedevil his and Eden's reputations for the rest of their lives. 'It is quite wrong to state that Israel was incited to this action by Her Majesty's Government,' he declared, and then, more damningly, 'There was no prior agreement between us about it.' His defence, after years of trying to square his conscience, was to argue that his duty to Parliament and to the electorate to give an honest account of himself was secondary to his responsibility to help save British lives and protect British property, 'particularly when active hostilities were taking place or there was an inflammatory situation'.[28] Considering who it was who had put British lives and property at risk, the excuse takes some stomaching.

The deadline for the ultimatum came and went. According to the Sèvres Protocol, military operations against Egyptian forces (specifically attacks on Egyptian airfields) were to begin in the early hours of 31 October. Lloyd urged a delay, however, to allow American nationals to be evacuated and in the forlorn hope of persuading America to adopt the Anglo-French military initiative as its own. It was yet another case of going through the motions of the peacemaker to win over the doubters in the Tory Party. The government was showing signs of breaking up. Walter Monckton was telling anybody who cared to listen that Eden was 'a very sick man' on the verge of a breakdown.[29]

Even Macmillan, the cabinet hawk, was having doubts. With gold and dollar reserves 'falling at a dangerously rapid rate' the government 'could not afford to alienate the US government more than was absolutely necessary'.[30] But America *was* alienated, as evinced by the threatening moves of the US Sixth Fleet into the Mediterranean, where it was liable to impede the Anglo-French invasion force. At 10 Downing Street, Eden's press secretary (for a few more days before he resigned) met with a 'cheerful FO character' who remarked, 'It's rather fun to be at No 10 the night we smashed the Anglo-American alliance.'

When Ben-Gurion learned of the postponement of the Anglo-French attack on Egypt's air bases, he immediately suspected a double-cross. His biggest fear was of Nasser's Soviet-made jets crossing the Israeli border on a mission of mass destruction. Ill with influenza, Ben-Gurion allowed his fevered imagination to conjure up nameless horrors. It was left to Dayan to reassure his prime minister.

He was very worried about the effect this delay might have on the position of our men at Mitla. His immediate reaction was to ask that they be withdrawn that very night. He was concerned that the Mitla paratroops might be trapped deep in enemy territory. I tried to reassure him. Even if the British and French cancelled their invasion, I was confident that we could proceed with our campaign and emerge victorious. I argued that rather than withdraw from Mitla, our forces there should be strengthened, and I hoped we would be able to do so. With great reluctance Ben-Gurion dropped the evacuation idea, but I could see that military logic did little to reduce his anxiety.[31]

Dayan had good reason to be confident. He was already well ahead with the second phase of his plan of attack. This brought the Central Task Force under Colonel Yehudah Wallach into action; the objective being to destroy Egyptian positions in the north of Sinai in and around the area of Abu Ageila. A succession of tank battles, marked by confusion on both sides, ended in stalemate, broken only by the Israeli decision to bypass Abu Ageila. That the Egyptians fought bravely is undeniable, and subsequent Israeli claims to outright victory can be sustained only in the light of Nasser's order to begin a withdrawal to meet the threat of the Anglo-French invasion.

Meanwhile the fighting at the Mitla Pass was hotting up. Having joined the early arrivals, Sharon took issue with a defensive position in the open desert. With a shortage of workable armoury and the nearest Israeli reinforcements 150 kilometres away, he was eager to move to higher, more easily defendable positions closer to the eastern entrance of the pass. GHQ turned down his request. Dayan had no wish to provoke the Egyptians into a major counter-attack at a time when Israeli forces had enough to contend with at Abu Ageila. This left Sharon, ever the exponent of attacking first, a frustrated officer.

> I now had twelve hundred men with me, together with a few field guns, the three AMX light tanks, and several new French recoilless rifles that had been airdropped to Raful. With these it would be impossible to fight off an armored brigade. And we were alone, far behind Egyptian lines with no possible relieving forces to call on. Beyond that, the area where Raful's men had dug in was completely open, a vast tableland that offered no natural defenses against tanks and armoured infantry. The only way I could see to defend ourselves was to move into the pass and take up positions there, where the steep cliffs and narrow defiles would give the oncoming Egyptian tanks no room to maneuver.
>
> Again I asked headquarters for permission to move into the pass. But again it was refused.[32]

Convinced that the pass was largely unoccupied after a sup-posedly devastating assault by Israeli air power on the Egyptian positions, Sharon suggested that he prove his point by sending a reconnaissance patrol into the defile. Permission was granted. The subsequent debate on justification for Sharon turned on his interpretation of what it needed in men and weaponry to constitute a patrol. According to Dayan:

> The unit that set forth was not a 'patrol' but in fact a full combat team, quite capable of capturing the pass. It consisted of two infantry companies on half-tracks, a detachment of three tanks, the brigade reconnaissance unit on trucks, and a troop of heavy mortars in support. Commanding the unit was a battalion com-mander [Motta Gur]. The deputy commander of the brigade went along too.
>
> As soon as the convoy entered the defile, it was fired on from the hillocks flanking it on both sides. The full combat unit con-tinued through the defile on the assumption that it was held only by light Egyptian forces. As the spearhead of the convoy

penetrated deeper into the narrow pass, the firing grew in intensity, and the half-tracks – and the troops they were carrying – were hit. The commander of the unit rushed forward to rescue them, but he, too, found himself trapped, unable to advance or to retire. Nevertheless, the forward portion of the convoy, totalling more than one company, succeeded in breaking through and reaching the western end of the pass, despite the murderous fire poured into the defile. The rest of the force remained pinned down, their casualties mounting under the continuous heavy fire from the heights above.

From one o'clock in the afternoon until eight in the evening, the paratroopers fought a tough and bitter battle until they finally overcame the Egyptian opposition and captured the pass. Not even a veteran combat-hardened unit like this one had ever experienced such a battle. Their casualties, too, were unprecedentedly heavy: 38 killed and 120 wounded.[33]

Eitan blamed a failure of intelligence, Dayan blamed Sharon. Sharon was unapologetic.

The Battle of Mitla Pass created anger and dissension both within the ranks of the paratroopers and also between myself and General Headquarters, in particular Dayan. The internal criticism was mostly stimulated by Motta Gur, who believed I should have taken personal command of the battle in the pass instead of remaining at the entrance to organize the defense and evacuate the wounded. At the same time, Dayan accused me of disobeying orders by sending a large force into the pass instead of a reconnaissance patrol and of engaging in a battle, although my orders were to avoid any fighting.[34]

At the subsequent inquiry Sharon refused to make excuses. Ben-Gurion was reluctant to take sides. 'I don't feel', he said, 'that I'm in a position to judge between two commanders on this issue.'[35]

Dayan had to swallow his pride. Sharon's men had proved their valour and were therefore to be applauded. The chief of staff led the congratulations. At the same time he knew, and Sharon came to know, that the capture of the Mitla Pass was a victory without purpose. It might have been different if the Israeli objective had reached as far as Suez. But the grand plan stopped well short of that. 'For their mistaken judgment and tactical errors, the paratroop unit paid heavily in blood. As for the breach of my orders and my forgiving attitude, the truth is that I regard the problem as serious when a unit fails to fulfil its battle task, not when it goes beyond the bounds of duty and does more than is demanded of it.'[36]

Whatever plaudits were garnered by Sharon as a bold and daring commander, the truth was that he had made a serious misjudgement. The Israeli air attack had failed to dislodge defenders cocooned in rifle pits dug along the tops of ridges and in caves cut into the steep walls of the pass. For the Egyptians it was like shooting at a fairground target. Faulty strategy was compounded by bad luck.

> At the very start of the battle the paratroopers' fuel truck went up in flames, to be followed by the ammunition truck and three other vehicles. The company commander who jumped from his half-track was killed on the spot. The supporting heavy mortars were knocked out of action. Enemy fire also hit and immobilized four half-tracks, a tank, a jeep, and an ambulance. The paratroopers were forced to scramble up to the hillside caves occupied by the Egyptians and in hand-to-hand fighting capture one position after another. They had no other course of action, for it was the only way they could end the battle as victors and extricate the scores of wounded and killed.[37]

Dayan's attention switched to Abu Ageila, where the rest of the Egyptian Sinai defences were concentrated. He was not at all happy with the progress made. In particular, he wanted to know why it had not been possible to capture Um Katef, an essential road junction and the only remaining Egyptian position that barred the way to central Sinai. Dayan did not find his meeting with brigade officers at all agreeable. 'True, they were not a crack formation . . . they were a reservist brigade of insufficiently trained infantrymen of above average age'.[38] The problems of a largely volunteer army were beginning to show. A half-hearted attack turned to farce.

The Egyptians were already into a planned withdrawal towards the canal, having destroyed most of their heavy equipment, while the Israeli 7th Brigade kept up the pressure on what they assumed to be a heavily fortified barrier. Early in the morning of 2 November, two Egyptian prisoners were sent into Um Katef to demand a surrender. They were given a captured Egyptian jeep and a large white flag. Unfortunately neither of them could drive. A brief lesson on how to work the gears was all they had before they set off. Since by now Um Katef was clear of Egyptian forces, the two envoys in search of a surrender drove through the fortifications and out the other side before encountering a company of the Israeli 37th Brigade making its approach from the opposite direction.

Unwilling or unable to explain their mission, the Egyptians were made prisoners again while the 37th Brigade tanks rolled on through Um Katef, expecting to make contact with the 7th Brigade at Abu Ageila. They did, but not in the way they had hoped. Seeing the approach of a column of tanks but no flag of truce, Colonel Adan of the 7th assumed a break-out attempt and opened fire. Eight of twelve Israeli tanks were knocked out before the mistake was realised.[39]

Despite setbacks, there was no longer any doubt that Israeli forces would prevail. Like all successful commanders, Dayan was adept at spotting the weaknesses in the enemy (something the allied forces would patently fail to do). The Egyptian strategy was defective on two counts. First, heavily defended positions such as that at Abu Ageila were of limited value unless they were at the centre of fortified zones. In the absence of huge concentrations of artillery and anti-tank weapons they could be bypassed or bombarded into submission. Second, lack of mobility also made Egyptian forces vulnerable.

Abu Ageila could play a decisive role in the defence of Sinai only if it served as a solid base for mobile forces who could go out and engage an enemy seeking to break through to the Canal. In desert terrain like Sinai there is no alternative to armour, aircraft, paratroopers and motorized infantry. The defending force must be able to meet such attacking units with its own counterpart mobile units. The Egyptians made a fatal assumption in thinking that their fortified defence positions of Abu Ageila, Rafah and El Arish would prevent our penetration into Sinai and would protect the Canal without requiring their armoured and air forces to join in blocking our breakthrough, and without their men having to go out and fight us beyond the perimeter of their posts.[40]

But assuming for a moment that the Egyptian military had been better prepared to fight a desert war, there was still every reason for Dayan to feel confident of success. For however hard he and Ben-Gurion tried subsequently to minimise the Anglo-French contribution, once the allied forces were engaged there was no way that Egypt could triumph on two fronts. It was Nasser's conscious decision to allow the Israelis an easier ride than they might otherwise have enjoyed by withdrawing forces from Sinai to meet the threat of an Anglo-French invasion.

That threat became real at dusk on the evening of 31 October. It was then that 200 Canberras, Venoms and Valiants with forty French Thunderstreaks, operating from aircraft carriers and from Malta and Cyprus, swept in over Egyptian airfields and ports. Just before the bombs fell an American U-2 spy plane passed over Cairo military airfield. All was calm and quiet. Ten minutes later, the U-2 made a second sweep. This time there were craters, smashed buildings and burning planes Eisenhower remembered the two sets of photographs as the most dramatic visual intelligence ever put before him.[41] They came with his breakfast on the morning of 1 November. 'Bombs, by God!' he declared. 'What does Anthony think he's doing?' With confusion all around him Anthony may himself have wondered what he was doing. The only thing he did know was that on the afternoon of the 31st he had pressed the red button. Operation Musketeer was on.

19

In what was to become standard practice throughout the short-lived Suez campaign, Eden had no sooner made his decision than he had a change of mind. British and French bombers were already in the air when Eden had word from the embassy in Cairo that 1,300 US nationals were being evacuated to Alexandria along the Desert Road next to Cairo West airfield, one of the top Anglo-French targets.[1] A frantic appeal went off to Keightley to call back the planes. It was too late for that, but he was successful in ordering a reprieve for Cairo West.

The air assault achieved its prime objective – to remove the Egyptian air force from the military reckoning. Upwards of one hundred aircraft were destroyed on the ground. There was little opposition. In many cases the bombers were guided in by lights blazing on the runways. The surprise, which was total, derived from a genuine disbelief that this could really be happening. Alone of the Egyptian high command, Nasser took the threat of an Anglo-French invasion seriously, and then only after forcing himself to accept what seemed a ludicrous proposition, that France and Britain, but Britain in particular, were ready to sacrifice their remaining Arab friends for the sake of a strip of water.

The damage caused by the air strikes was played down by Egyptian propaganda. Cairo Radio put out the reassuring message that the airfields could be easily repaired (true) and that the attackers had been fooled by decoys (not true) after the pride of the Egyptian air force had long since departed to havens in Syria and Saudi Arabia (party true), though what they were supposed to do from their refuge to protect the homeland was never explained. Ironically, the illusion of triumph in the midst of devastation was supported by allied warnings to civilians to keep away from military installations, thus ensuring that the evidence of destruction had few witnesses.

The British aim of minimising civilian casualties was commendable and largely effective. Unfortunately, this claim was about the only success that could be marked down to the information and propaganda division. At the start, expectations were pitched at an unrealistic level. As Frank Cooper at the air ministry put it, 'There was a popular theory that if you bombed something and coupled it with propaganda everyone would pack in and give up.'[2] It was not to be. As Brigadier Bernard Fergusson, who was in charge of this side of operations, cheerfully acknowledged, 'if anyone likes to say that the performance of my Psychological Warfare Branch was ludicrously bad, they will find nobody agreeing more fervently than I'.[3] Ill fortune combined with poor management to defeat the best intentions, the poor management starting with the failure to bow to French army experience in Algeria, where indoctrination had been raised to a fine art.

The centrepiece of Fergusson's propaganda empire was Sharq al-Adna, the radio station transmitting from Cyprus. Remembering the director, Ralph Poston, from pre-war days in Palestine, Fergusson did not anticipate any objection to intensifying the station's anti-Nasser output. In the event, there were very serious objections, not least on the argument that a frontal attack on one Arab leader was likely to bring all other Arabs rushing to his defence. More, it turned out that the 150 or so Arab staff of Sharq al-Adna were not at all ill disposed towards Nasser, who they thought was rather good news. They were certainly in no mood to attack him over the airwaves. Poston was at one with his staff, denouncing Eden's Suez policy and the 'disastrous situation' it had caused. He then went on air to warn listeners against British plots, at which point Fergusson had him arrested and sent back to Britain.[4] Most of his colleagues resigned in sympathy. Desperate to recruit malleable Arabic speakers, Fergusson went first to known enemies of Nasser, none of whom were ready to take the risk of reprisals against their families. He ended up with 'a scratch lot . . . not one of whom was Egyptian. Their accents were recognisably Palestinian or Algerian, and I learned afterwards that their Egyptian audiences had decided they must be Jews – which was hardly calculated to "win friends and influence people." [5]

It was the same problem with the British-subsidised Arab News Agency, where, recovering from the spy scandal of the previous August, staff were keen to prove that they could still offer a reasonably balanced version of the news. Tom Little, who headed the ANA Cairo team, was convinced that Eden had got it wrong on Nasser. Pro-government reports from the London office were frequently spiked, and Little remained on friendly terms with Nasser, who fed him the occasional exclusive.

If relationships between communicators were bad, the practical arrangements for delivering propaganda were even worse. The first bright idea to fizzle out was that of dropping tons of leaflets over Egyptian cities urging citizens to turn on Nasser. This was to be achieved by means of a clever device sensitive to barometric pressure dropped from cruising height. The propaganda bomb was set to explode at 1,000 feet, scattering the leaflets over a wide area. To reinforce the message a 'voice aircraft' would then fly low over the ground, urging surrender before battle commenced.

Fergusson's nightmare started when the printing press in Nicosia broke down and was declared a write-off. Flying over a replacement from the UK wasted several vital days. He then discovered that the fiendish device for distributing the leaflets had only ever been tested in Britain. The barometric pressure in the Middle East was such that instead of exploding at 1,000 feet, the leaflet container held together until it was about 6 feet above the ground. Fergusson had no trouble in imagining the consequences if innocent Egyptians were wiped out by a bulk consignment of messages of peace. He solved the problem by adding a weight of sand to the container, thereby acquiring the distinction of being the only person ever to dump sand on Egypt. Thereafter, five leaflet drops were cancelled one after the other largely because the transport aircraft had been delegated for other, presumably more important duties.

Before long, leaflets were the least of Fergusson's problems. Great store had been set on notching up the level of radio propaganda until it drowned out the voices in praise of Nasser. The plan was for Sharq al-Adna, now renamed Voice of Britain, to take over the wavelength of Cairo Radio after the Egyptian transmitters had been put out of action by a few well-placed bombs. But where were the bombers? They were well on their way when an order from London cancelled the raid.[6]

> It was Tom Prickett, whose title was Chief of Staff, Air Task Force, talking with me in the Operations Room somewhere about the third day, who suddenly said: 'I wonder if they could possibly think that Cairo Radio is actually in Cairo, and are forbidding us to bomb it for fear of civilian casualties?' I buzzed off a signal at once, and his guess was right.[7]

It had not occurred to anyone in London that the transmitters for Cairo Radio were out on the edge of the desert, well away from urban centres. Air Chief Marshal Denis Barnett put the blame squarely on the politicians.

> Throughout the execution of Phase I there were considerable political restrictions imposed from Whitehall, and attempts to reorganise the programme of this key phase. For example . . . the attack on Cairo Radio at ABU ZABAL, which had been planned to take place at the earliest daylight opportunity in Phase I (i.e. concurrently with the first strikes by the ground attack forces) was cancelled and was not re-inserted until 2nd November . . . When the attack did take place it was only semi-successful and clearly required a repeat attack. But the trend of events had then reached a stage at which further attack was prohibited. Had the attack been delivered in its planned position in the programme there would unquestionably have been time for a decisive re-attack.[8]

Selective memories of the air campaign rate it a great success because it reduced Egyptian fighting strength and removed the danger of retaliatory raids against Israel. The failure to bring about a collapse in civilian morale is generally forgotten. So too is the failure to achieve another key objective – the protection of the canal.

> At first light on 1st November shore-based and carrier-based aircraft attacked Egyptian airfields. The Naval aircraft also attacked the blockship [*Akka*] lying off Ismalia, but it was not sunk. A re-strike was ordered, but when the aircraft arrived over the target the blockship had been towed by tugs and was almost in position at the entrance to the Canal. The ship was again attacked but not sunk, and the Egyptians succeeded in towing the ship into a position blocking the Canal. The blockship operation cannot therefore be considered a success. Detailed study of the armament required to sink the blockship had showed that 12 Seahawks carrying rockets should succeed, but despite that, half the aircraft were sent off with bombs.[9]

The 5,000-ton *Akka* was not left to do its job alone. The next day, the ocean-going tug *Edgar Bonnet*, loaded with cement, found its resting place on the canal bed. It was followed by the frigate *Abu Kir*, which was scuttled 2 miles north of Suez. She was raised and towed clear on 8 April 1957, the last of some fifty wrecks that had blocked the waterway. It was Nasser's boast that in closing the canal he had received invaluable help from Allied planes when they destroyed the rail and road bridge at Ferdan, thus depositing on the canal bed a hefty load of stone and scrap metal.[10]

Oil tankers then had no choice but to go round the Cape, a disaster for European energy supplies according to Eden when he was merely speculating on the prospect, which raised a few eyebrows among those who were beginning to doubt his sanity. Little more was heard from the air task force on the inaccuracies of its marksmanship. Instead, attention focused on the achievements of precision bombing. In addition to the Egyptian aircraft put out of service direct hits were scored on the Gamil bridge carrying the only road connection between Port Said and the mainland, and on the Huckstep arms dump east of Cairo. 'Not one bomb or rocket aimed at this massed target fell outside the target area.'[11]

Nasser was with the Indonesian ambassador when the raids started. 'I heard the aeroplanes and I said to the ambassador that these were bombers, so they were not Israelis because the Israelis don't have jet bombers . . . I went to headquarters. The members of the Revolutionary Council came . . . I said to General Amir, "We have only one way open to us; the withdrawal of our troops from Sinai within two nights. We have to begin this very night." '[12]

Missing from this account is the reaction of the revolutionary council to a war on two fronts. According to one of Nasser's closest confidants there were voices urging submission. Foremost among them was Abd al-Hakim Amir, who as war minister and commander in chief might have been expected to be more bellicose. Instead, he warned that 'the continuation of the war means the destruction of the country and the killing of many civilians'. He was supported by Salah Salem, known to the Western press as the 'dancing major', having been caught by photographers in an undignified cavort. This was just one more service Nasser could perform for the country, said Salem. 'Sir Humphrey Trevelyan is still at the British embassy. Go and give yourself up to him for they want only you.'[13] That was the extent of the challenge Nasser had to face.

Popular demonstrations demanding a stand against imperialism and Israeli aggression brought offers of help from other Arab rulers. These stopped short of a general declaration of war against Israel, but the sabre-rattling gave cause for concern to the oil-buying countries already made nervous by Anglo-French belligerency. The general worry intensified when the Syrian army, in a dramatic gesture of unity with Nasser, blew up the three big pumping stations on the Iraq petroleum line to Tripoli. In Iraq there were fierce mutterings of an attack on Syria to protect its oil outlets. So far there was not much on the credit side for Anglo-French intervention.

In Cyprus, relations between French and British commanders were increasingly strained. While the French were under pressure from their politicians to get a move on, the British were only too aware of the climate of nervous restraint in London. For Beaufre it had been sheer agony trying to speed up the decision-making. It seemed to him that Stockwell and Keightley were deliberately looking for problems. The weather was uncertain, the parachute drops were too risky, the Egyptian roads were in too poor a state to carry tanks, the sea was too rough for landings. But the differences went deeper than that. The French military made no secret of its fierce dedication to its self-appointed role as the protector of the French soul. For many serving officers, the army *was* France. They did not take well to direction by any external authority, least of all a foreign one. Reading the memoirs of French generals such as Beaufre and Massu, the sensitivity to apparent or real if minor slights by British commanders stands out conspicuously. Respect had to be shown but respect – or at least its visible demonstrations – did not come easily to such as Keightley and Stockwell, whose own tradition of winning the most important battles bestowed on them a confidence, not always justified, in giving the orders. The two navies and air forces did these things better – relations between the French and British services were generally amicable – but it was the army which counted, and it was here that differences over objectives and strategy proved fatal to the Suez campaign.

Musketeer was essentially a British plan foisted on the French. The many changes and refinements to changes that were made (seven revised plans and five postponements) from late August on, largely in response to political prevarication, had been a source of ever increasing frustration for Beaufre, who was at odds with Stockwell from the moment that Musketeer had transmuted into Musketeer Revise and Port Said had replaced Alexandria as the focal point for attack. As Beaufre saw it,

> The entire success of the operation depended on a rapid break-out from Port Said on to the mainland and this must be done along the narrow Canal embankments which formed the sole means of access towards the south across Lake Menzala. The smallest demolition at any important point could hold us up for days. Moreover at the end of our 12 miles along the embankment,

during which we should be moving with vehicles in single file, the enemy might well be awaiting us in force at El Qantara with tanks and artillery; we could be in a very difficult position.[14]

Everything depended on speed. A combined parachute and armoured attack would capture El Qantara before the Egyptian defenders knew what was happening. But Stockwell, prompted by Keightley, who, in turn, had to refer constantly to London, seemed intent on losing any element of surprise. Even so, it came as a shock to Beaufre when he was told that the air attack was to be extended beyond the forty-eight hours needed to dispose of the Egyptian air force. The idea was to follow up with a combination of psychological and aerial warfare lasting up to eight days, designed to break the Egyptian will to fight. 'Indubitably,' wrote Beaufre, 'we were now in cloud cuckoo-land.'[15]

A succession of postponements in the timetable led to further changes that included a cutting back of the air campaign, much to Beaufre's relief. But his blood pressure rose again when he failed to dissuade Stockwell on following up a two-day air attack by ferrying a vast, slow-moving invasion force across the Mediterranean. Five or six days at sea, argued Beaufre, would give too much time for the opposition, already winning over world opinion, to harden against the allies. In any case, the military response was out of all proportion to the challenge. Schooled in the experience of European conflict, Keightley and Stockwell were unyielding proponents of overwhelming force as the only means of gaining victory with minimum losses. But Egypt was not Germany, even if Stockwell was led to believe that there might be a correlation. Because senior Egyptian officers had been trained at Sandhurst and other British military establishments, Stockwell exaggerated their competence. He also overestimated the influence of Nasser's German advisers, Second World War veterans, who were said to have applied the lessons of Rommel's desert campaigns. Then there was all that Soviet weaponry, which potentially reduced British arms to the capacity of peashooters. That advanced weapons were virtually useless if not handled by professionals and that the mass forces boasted by Nasser were in part weak and demoralised fugitives from the Israeli campaign made no impression on Stockwell. His ADC was more realistic:

> It was very difficult to assess exactly how big the Egyptian Army was, because they had 70,000 to 80,000 infantry in their Army, they had a lot of tanks, a lot of Centurions, a lot of Russian equipment, and they had a hell of a lot of MiGs too. But the whole question was whether they could fight with them. We had an Intelligence Officer, whose name I have conveniently forgotten, who was, I believe, useless. He was a Colonel, who assessed their potential on numbers, rather than on what they could do on the day. I only saw two of what one could call tanks, they were SU100s, Russian self-propelled guns, and I think they were the only sophisticated weapons that turned up in the actual fight.[16]

For Roy Fullick, a paratroop major at Suez, it was all one with the tale of the imaginary city of Talata. In the early 1950s a military intelligence review had misinterpreted the identification of signal stations along the canal. Arabic numerals (*wahid, itnein, talata*, etc.) had been taken as names of towns. Thus the city of Ismailia was faced across the canal by the equally large township of Talata.[17]

Beaufre was right in urging a rapid response using paratroops supported by elite infantry units carried in the fastest ships available. Too risky, argued Stockwell. Memories of Arnhem would not go away. The war of words hotted up when the campaign started for real with the Israeli attack into Sinai on 29 October. As soon as it became clear that the Israeli troops would prevail, Paris and the increasingly agitated Admiral Barjot took up the call for Musketeer to be revised yet again, allowing for the landing of an advance allied force within twenty-four hours. This could only mean sending in paratroops after the first air assault on the Egyptian airfields. Stockwell was backed up by Durnford-Slater in an adamant refusal even to contemplate such a bold move. It appeared that the latest reconnaissance photographs showed that

Port Said and the Canal Zone were being reinforced. Paratroops
in relatively small numbers could not be exposed to a determined
enemy with advanced weaponry. Anyway, even if they were permitted to go in, they would inhibit the use of naval gunfire to
soften up the landing area for the infantry.

Barjot and Beaufre fell to arguing with each other as to who
was to blame for the British inability to act decisively. In the end
they agreed between themselves on three parachute drops to test
resistance at Port Said and Port Fuad. The dropping zones would
be narrow strips of land protected by water against tank attacks.
Support weapons would be flown in by helicopter. If Egyptian
defences crumbled, all well and good; if not, the paratroops would
be safe until the arrival of reinforcements. It was a plan, codenamed Telescope, that Stockwell accepted reluctantly, albeit with
amendments. There would be just two parachute drops to take
place twenty-four hours before the scheduled arrival of the allied
armada.

The emphasis now was on cutting down the time needed to
cross the Mediterranean. The seaborne force could not leave
until it had been shown that the air attacks were not enough in
themselves to finish the job. But there was nothing to stop
Stockwell and Beaufre adopting the strategy of anticipation.
Under cover of training exercises their forces were ready to sail
as soon as the Anglo-French air attacks were launched on
31 October.

For the fighting force this meant a lot of activity without knowing what precisely was intended. Second Lieutenant Peter Mayo
of 42 Commando Royal Marines was among those who were told
on Sunday, 28 October to get ready for embarkation.

> There at once started an absolute wave of speculation. Were we
> going to Jordan, Hong Kong, Singapore, or to be sent through
> the Canal with a convoy just to see what happened? The whole
> thing seems pretty shambolic to me, and nobody will tell anybody
> anything at all definite. As far as I can make out it is merely an
> exercise in getting organised, packed up and on board at short

notice ... Someone voiced the solution that it's all a typically cumbersome idea for getting us all out of camp for a few days to let the water supply catch up with consumption.

The next day:

Like everyone else I have spent most of the day packing. How I loathe and abhor packing. However all is now accomplished. There has been great activity all over camp, with ammunition arriving all morning and being sorted out, everything being crated up in the troop stores, etc. Over all there is a rather fairy-tale, Christmassy, unrealistic atmosphere. Rumour and counter-rumour continue to follow in quick succession in spite of the fact that the Colonel cleared the lower decks this morning and told us that it was an exercise called for by the Force Commander to see if we could mobilise quickly and efficiently. Everyone I think is in his secret heart rather hoping it will turn out to be something more interesting, though I am afraid this is extremely improbable. 'A' troop leaves at 10 o'clock tomorrow to embark on HMS *Simla*.[18]

Lieutenant Mayo was to be surprised. As the first bombs exploded on Egyptian airfields, the leading vessels in Stockwell's invasion fleet, including HMS *Simla*, were steaming out of Malta's Valletta harbour on a dummy run that was quickly upgraded to the real thing. The flotilla was soon joined by a French contingent already on its way from Algiers. The next day, the 16th Parachute Brigade Group, led by Brigadier Mervyn (Tubby) Butler, set off from Cyprus with their LSTs (tank landing ships) to meet up with the main fleet on 6 November. In the general confusion of a hurried departure many stores and items of equipment were left behind for later delivery. In the event, most of it turned up at Port Said as the brigade was preparing to re-embark for Cyprus.

By anticipating orders, if only by a few hours, Stockwell in Malta and Beaufre in Algiers had saved sufficient time for them to advance their planned assault date from 8 November to

7 November. But there was no getting away from the unpalatable
fact that a week on the high seas was a week too long. There was
near-panic in Paris and London as it finally dawned on the chief
protagonists that they were stuck with a timetable that could no
longer be amended by committee. Those who had been excluded
from the magic circle now began to realise the enormity of what
was being undertaken. As first lord of the admiralty, Lord Hailsham was aware of some contingency planning but was not told
what it was or in what circumstances it would be activated. When
the ships did get under way, 'I was misled ... and given to
understand that these were precautionary measures in case we
might have to act in our capacity as a guarantor of Jordan.' When
he realised he had been misled and threatened to resign, Eden
came clean. 'A young naval captain high up in the operations
section of the Admiralty was duly instructed to brief me ... I
heard him out, and then asked one question, "What do you think
of it?" I said. "I think it is madness," was his reply. "So," said I,
"do I" and I took steps to see that my view was passed on to the
right quarters.'[19]

Not that it did any good. There was to be no turning back.
Nor indeed was there any way of moving forward more speedily.
Commanding an amphibious warfare squadron, a motley collection of nineteen tank and vehicle carriers, Captain Ronald Brooke
experienced the frustration of a string of orders to increase speed
when he knew that the brink of his capacity was just 10 knots.
'The ships were in a poor state. They had been docked in their
home ports on the principle that one day they might come in
handy. Well, when the day did come they needed a major overhaul
to get them going. Maintenance had been patchy, they had no
regular crews and there was a shortage of essential machinery.'[20]
Brooke's HQ was a river-class frigate last used for anti-submarine
warfare. 'It was an old ship even then.'

The inadequacy of the British fleet showed up most obviously
in the mutations of the aircraft carriers *Ocean* and *Theseus*,
formerly of the home fleet training squadron, which underwent
three sea changes. Refitted to allow for more troop accommoda-

tion, they were each then equipped with a hospital and operating theatre. When that job was finished Rear Admiral Sayer was told that his ships were also to act as helicopter carriers. With commendable understatement he noted that 'the combination of all three tasks, particularly where they had to be carried out simultaneously, tended to prejudice the efficient conduct of some of them', adding, 'In some cases the gap between success and failure was marginal.'[21]

Sayer was surprised, as well he might have been, that the royal navy could not call on a single hospital ship. When it came to the challenge, the surgical teams on *Ocean* and *Theseus* performed wonders, but they were 'heavily overworked' and 'the arrival of seriously wounded casualties had a marked lowering effect on the morale of the second-line troops waiting to land'.
As to the helicopters:

> Each ship carried some 30 vehicles which had to be stowed either on the flight deck or in 'B' hangar . . . To ensure full serviceability, helicopters had to be stowed below during passage to Port Said, and the vehicles on deck. For the operation, a clear flight deck was required and the vehicles had to be struck down, thus occupying space which should have been available for parking unserviceable aircraft . . . The job of shifting round helicopters and vehicles was a long one, fortunately carried out in good weather and in daylight, but under full darken-ship conditions or if there had been motion on the ship, it would have been extremely hazardous and, in certain weather conditions, impossible.[22]

Loaded with helicopters, flight crews, RAF support staff and 420 marines of 45 Commando, *Ocean* and *Theseus* sailed on 3 November. With so much equipment on board there was barely room for the men. 'We were crammed into tiny mess rooms just under the flight deck. Incredibly, the whole of Support Troop, about 60 or so, had to squeeze into a single mess no larger than, say, 15 feet by 40.'[23]

Lieutenant Peter Mayo, on board HMS *Simla*, was experiencing the same feeling of claustrophobia. 'It has been pretty calm all day, but even so life is hell on this ugly tub. One perspires the whole time one is below, and I feel frowsty and enervated most of the time. How they survive in the engine room is more than I can fathom. There is a lot to think about . . . but how to think on this throbbing, juddering, heaving, humming crate?'[24] Inevitably, his mind was on the forthcoming battle. 'I wish I were happier about the cause we are to fight for. The legal rights of the case are fairly plain. But even so, where does it all lead? Is our civilisation really worth fighting for? I begin to doubt it. I begin to lose faith in all but the individual.'[25]

The confusion of a highly intelligent and articulate twenty-year-old (after national service Peter Mayo was to take up a classical scholarship at Pembroke College, Cambridge) was a portent of the malaise that was to affect many of the younger generation after Suez. For now, however, the gut reaction, as recalled by Marine Ashton, was to smother any doubts with a thick coating of patriotism.

Even as I took a closer look at 45 Commando, it was beginning to take on an increasingly aggressive and combative appearance . . . The way they talked, walked and bore themselves communicated the fact that they were psychologically winding themselves up for a battle, the seriousness of which they were only beginning to comprehend. Sten gun magazines were being taped end to end to enable a quick change under pressure. Mysteriously – for they were not official issue – blue steel Commando knives appeared from nowhere; their unmistakeable hilts protruding menacingly from magazine holders and other makeshift scabbards. Our boot-blacked webbing was camouflaged with strips of Hessian and scrim; brasses and cap badges were dulled; desert-warfare goggles issued; grenades primed with short fuses; ammo compressed carefully into Bren and Sten magazines; gun-cotton slabs taped to pole charges; detonators fitted; fuse lengths matched and cut, and all this carried out in the most cramped of living conditions. One could not escape the fact that this was for real. This was no exercise.[26]

What with overcrowding, lack of ventilation and a nightly black-out, the voyage was tediously uneventful except for one unexpected incident. Captain D. M. J. Clark, a reservist officer who was called up for the Suez campaign, tells the story:

'Action stations!'

The ship was blacked out, so we were not allowed on deck. Above our heads we could hear the sound of running feet as the crew hurried to their stations. We could do nothing but sit where we were and use our imaginations as to what was happening outside. Suddenly the main lights went out, and the dim, secondary ones came on . . .

'Bloody eerie, isn't it?' whispered Neville . . .

For ten long minutes we waited, and then the lights came up. The broadcast started to cackle, and the Captain spoke. 'I apologise for that; and I'll tell you what happened. The convoy was suddenly illuminated by searchlights from warships. The Admiral challenged; got no reply. He challenged a second time, and they identified themselves as the American Sixth Fleet, which we know has been making a sweep between the mouth of the Canal and ourselves. The Americans altered course away from us after the Admiral had sent the following signal . . . Number One, have you got a copy of that signal yet? . . . Yes? Thank you . . . It reads "Get out of my way you . . ."' The voice faltered in disbelief. Then 'On second thoughts, I'd better not read this over the broadcast.' The microphone clicked off, hurriedly, and then came on again. 'That is all,' said the Captain. 'Carry on.'[27]

What was the Sixth Fleet up to? Admiral Durnford-Slater could only speculate.

During the early stages of the operation the US Sixth Fleet were operating very close to our carriers and, indeed, on two occasions their carriers penetrated our screen. This caused me acute embarrassment. I was aware that they were probably in the area to cover the evacuation of American nationals from Egypt, but considered it quite feasible that an ultimatum to stop operations might be issued by the American Government, placing me in an impossible position. In addition, there was the ever-present possibility of our aircraft mistaking American aircraft for Egyptian, thus creating an international incident . . . I considered it quite possible that they were obstructing us on purpose as their aircraft flying in the area rendered our air warning radar virtually useless. Fortunately there were no 'incidents' and eventually the American Fleet withdrew to the north west.[28]

The apprehensive Durnford-Slater would have been yet more worried had he known of the order to the Sixth Fleet to be ready for action. On 3 November Admiral Arleigh Burke, chief of naval operations, signalled: 'Situation tense; prepare for imminent hostilities,' to which Admiral Brown responded: 'Am prepared for imminent hostilities, but whose side are we on?' The return signal left the question unanswered. 'Keep clear of foreign op areas but take no guff from anybody.'

As it happened, the closest the Sixth Fleet came to taking any guff was off Haifa when the evacuation of American nationals coincided with an exchange of fire between the French destroyer *Kersaint* and the Egyptian *Ibrahim el-Awal*.

With the allied invasion force still six days off Port Said, the battle to overthrow Nasser was still very much on the Israeli front, where the centre of fighting had shifted to the southern end of the Gaza Strip. The Israeli plan was for a two-pronged attack across minefields and barbed wire to envelop the Egyptian forces at Rafah before breaking through to El Arish on the Mediterranean coast.

Israeli engineers began clearing a way through the minefields on the night of 30/31 October. A French and Israeli naval bombardment of the Rafah defences began at 0200 hours and lasted for half an hour. It was followed by another bombardment, this time from the air. But for all the battering they received, the Egyptian defenders (in effect a rearguard force since a general withdrawal had begun several hours earlier) were able to inflict damage on the Israeli tanks as they made slow progress through the minefields. Whenever a vehicle was hit and started burning, the fire illuminated other targets which then came under sustained attack from Egyptian artillery and machine guns.

With only an hour until sunrise, the Israelis had no choice but to press on. Leading the way on foot were the sappers, probing for mines in the glare of the headlights of the following vehicles, which also made them visible to the Egyptian gunners. But by 0900 hours, the Rafah road junction was in Israeli hands.

When the lead tanks of the 27th Brigade approached the vital crossroads that would enable them to advance toward El Arish, they received the most joyous greeting from the infantrymen of the 1st Brigade, who had just captured it. Scattered shooting still continued, and from time to time the heads of Egyptian soldiers would pop up behind the cactus hedges. But the infantrymen could barely restrain their feelings. They came out of their positions and rushed forward to meet the oncoming tanks. Within minutes, tanks and half-tracks jammed the crossroads and huge grins lit up the dust-covered faces of the enthusiastic troops. Even hardened veterans fell upon their comrades in spontaneous embrace. I had followed the 27th Brigade throughout this attack, and my particular victim was the second in command of the 1st Brigade. We fell into each other's arms in the classic tradition of a Russian movie.[29]

The fall of Rafah isolated the Gaza Strip, making it only a matter of hours before Gaza itself was captured. The assault began shortly before dawn on 2 November. The city surrendered in the early afternoon.

The Gaza Strip had been held by between 7,000 and 8,000 Egyptians. It was captured at the cost of 10 men killed. Not many Egyptians were killed on this occasion and no great number was taken prisoner. Many of them buried their weapons and uniforms in the sand and wandered back in their underclothes, 150 miles to Egypt. Israel let them go. One pathetic group of Palestinian soldiers did the round-trip. When they got to Egypt, they were

turned back for failing to be Egyptian although they were serving
in the Egyptian Army; and in due course they returned disconso-
lately to the shelter of the prisoners' camp at Gaza.[30]

For Dayan, the chief problem in Gaza was the collection of enemy
weapons. There was no difficulty about the heavy weapons left
by the Egyptians but most of their small arms had disappeared.

> So far about one thousand pieces have been given up – machine-
> guns, rifles and revolvers; but there is no doubt that a great
> number are still being withheld. We have been told that in Jordan
> the price of rifles and ammunition is very high, and Bedouin as
> well as just plain smugglers undertake gun-running trips night
> after night to Mount Hebron ... The interesting part of this
> business is that our men, who have had so much experience over
> so many years of fruitless arms searches conducted against them
> by the British ... now find themselves in Gaza repeating the
> same methods – and, of course, getting the same results![31]

By now El Arish had also fallen. As the Israelis mounted an
unstoppable advance, the Egyptian defenders made good their
escape, not always in the best order.

> At dusk, two trains arrived from Egypt, but these could take only
> an insignificant part of the retreating force. Nor could the narrow
> road from El Arish to Kantara handle all the vehicles crowding
> to use it. The railway line and the road were accordingly reserved
> exclusively for the officers; other ranks were ordered to retreat
> on foot. In the event, the men on foot were more fortunate, for
> the vehicles on the highway received the attention of our Air
> Force, whereas our planes did not bother to attack the troops
> moving across the dunes.
>
> These troops, abandoned by their officers, immediately shed
> all they wore and carried which hampered movement – weapons,
> military pack, uniform, and even their heavy army boots. They
> gathered in groups and made their way slowly westwards, in the
> direction of Egypt. Drinking-water was drawn from wells they
> came across, and hunger was satisfied by dates. The date plan-

tations, stretching for miles along the coast, were now at the height of the season, and it was enough to cast a stone at a ripe cluster high on the palm to gather handfuls of fruit. From the air these troops looked like an endless procession of pilgrims, their white underwear conspicuous against the background of golden sand.[32]

Those left behind were the dead and the wounded.

The hospital offered a gruesome sight. On the operation table lay the body of a dead Egyptian soldier with a leg just amputated. He had been abandoned in the middle of the operation without a doctor or a nurse stopping to bandage him, and he died from loss of blood. The hospital wounded, some of them in the wards but most of them trying to hide in the courtyard and garden, told us that when the medical personnel were informed that ambulances awaited them, they ran from whatever they were doing, pushed their way into the vehicles, and vanished. Not even a single male nurse remained behind to treat the wounded, and casualties who were in need of immediate attention – eighteen men – expired during the night. They lay in the same position in which they had been left when the flight started.[33]

With the battle for the northern axis all but over, Israeli forces were soon on the move along the coastal route towards the canal.

There was only one more Israeli objective, the capture of Sharm el-Sheikh down at the southern tip of the Sinai Peninsula. The job of breaking the Egyptian blockade of the Gulf of Aqaba, 'the most ambitious mission in the Sinai campaign', according to Dayan,[34] went to the 9th Brigade, led by Colonel Avraham Yoffe, which began its trek down the coast from around Kuntilla on the morning of 2 November. Using mostly requisitioned civilian vehicles, the desert track, some 10 miles inland from the coast, proved heavy going. Later in the day, Dayan decided to strengthen his attack with two paratroop companies. They were dropped at E-Tor on the Gulf of Suez. Having secured and repaired the airfield, Dayan was able to air-shuttle in an infantry battalion. Leaving nothing to chance, further reinforcements were summoned from Ariel Sharon's 202nd Brigade at the Mitla Pass.

On 3 November Israeli fighter-bombers destroyed two of the four 3-inch guns at Ras Nasrami overlooking the Straits of Tiran. But one of the planes was shot down, and from the captured pilot Colonel Rauf Mahfouz Zaki, commander of the garrison at Sharm el-Sheikh, learned of the two columns converging on him from the north-east and north-west. He had time to prepare an ambush for the advance guard of the Israeli 9th Battalion and to concentrate his forces behind heavily defended emplacements.

The first major attack at 0200 hours on 5 November faltered, with an Israeli withdrawal under intense fire. At 0530 hours the attack was renewed with mortar and air support. Four hours later, the wounded Colonel Zaki left it to his second-in-command to surrender Sharm el-Sheikh.

Among those who took advantage of the lull – at this stage no one knew whether it was the end of Israeli–Egyptian fighting – was Erich Reich, soon to be discharged from his duties as a reservist.

> I had met up with a couple of my kibbutz friends, who like myself, decided to use the opportunity of discovering an area we weren't sure would be open to Israelis in the future. So we nicked a jeep which appeared superfluous to requirements and headed off towards Mount Sinai. Looking back, it was a rather dangerous venture. For a start none of us had a licence or for that matter could drive properly. Manoeuvring tractors in the field was the limit of our expertise. Nor were there any maps available to guide us if we took a wrong turning.
>
> The road gradually deteriorated into a winding dirt track along which we had to drive with extreme care to avoid slipping down the steep embankments on either side. Amazingly we did remember to fill up with petrol before setting out and still more miraculously we didn't get lost. The monks who opened the gate at St Katherine's Monastery must have thought that God had sent

three holy ghosts, to punish them, when they found themselves confronted by three filthy, dust covered Israeli soldiers armed with sten-guns. After the initial shock however they proved very hospitable, showed us around, gave us food and lodgings for the night and even volunteered a guide for the following day.[35]

For Rafel Eitan, the campaign ended with drama of a different sort.

We were flying over the Kuntilla area on a patrol flight when we spotted a group of men waving their shirts rather desperately. We immediately landed close to them and to our horror learned that they had stumbled into a mine field and that we too were inside its parameters. It was a miracle that our plane had not been blown up as we landed. We told the group that they should stay exactly where they were and that we would go and call for help. Our dilemma, of course, was how to take off without blowing ourselves up. After discussing it with my co-pilot, I decided the only thing to do was to take the chance that there were no mines directly around the airplane. I took the nose of the plane, which was facing south, and walked it around so that it was facing the north. Once this was successfully accomplished, I rode the plane on the tracks we had made while landing. Although miracles are not in the habit of occurring twice in a matter of moments, our luck stayed with us and we took off safely.[36]

The Israelis' celebratory mood was topped off by the rescue of a Mystère pilot who was shot down in an attack on Sharm el-Sheikh. Having baled out, he landed close to a Egyptian defence post, injuring his knee in the fall. Unable to walk, Major Benny Peled dragged himself to the top of an incline, where he waited for help. Just 200 yards away was an Egyptian guard hut. Peled was not at first spotted when a Piper circled over the burnt-out Mystère but he was lucky second time around. The Piper landed on the seashore, watched by the Egyptian soldiers at their guard hut. 'Throughout the entire protracted operation – signalling, waving, identification, landing, crawling, loading and take-off –

these two men sat, leaning on their rifles, in stoic silence, following with keen interest, and with intense passivity, all that was happening.'[37] The Israeli–Egyptian drama was played out with Israeli forces halting 10 miles to the east of the canal. Three hours before the fall of Sharm el-Sheikh, the Egyptians had turned their attention to another, more formidable enemy.

20

The defeat of Sinai created only a minor dent in Nasser's confidence that in the end all would be well for him. He would have been more optimistic still had he known more of what was happening behind the political smokescreen thrown up in Paris and London. Faint hopes of a softening of tone in Washington finally dissolved when on 1 November Dulles rose to speak in the UN General Assembly. With a 'heavy heart' he disowned two of America's oldest and closest allies, calling for an immediate ceasefire. To his embarrassment, the Soviet Union joined in the condemnation of the 'aggressors', while conveniently ignoring its own troubles in Hungary, where a ruthless disregard for liberal principles made the Suez operation seem almost respectable. There was some justice in the Anglo-French complaint that while the General Assembly could devote as much time as was needed to debate Suez, the nationalist revolutionaries in Hungary barely rated a mention. But as Dulles was at pains to point out, more was expected of Britain and France, two countries that had led the way in creating the UN and now gave every impression of wanting to destroy it.

Replying to Dulles, Pierson Dixon put up a dismal performance which doubtless reflected his torment at having to speak against his own principles as much as having to work to a brief that for blatant hypocrisy took some beating. Having tried to involve Korea as a precedent for Anglo-French action in the Middle East (an argument that was unlikely to impress Eisenhower, who had made the pull-out of US troops from Korea a vote-winner in his first presidential election), Dixon had the gall to complain of the USA that in mounting its General Assembly attack on Britain and France, no warning had been given to the defendants or consultation offered. His only justification for starting a war (or, rather, to use the preferred phrase, 'police action') in the Middle East was the weakness of the UN in failing to come up with a solution to the Suez crisis.

At the end of a marathon session, the ceasefire resolution was approved by sixty-five votes to five with broad agreement on a proposal from Lester Pearson, Canada's foreign minister, for setting up an international force to supervise the peace. Eden could hardly repudiate a perfectly sensible suggestion from one of the principal members of the Commonwealth. Instead, he blurred the lines between Anglo-French aims and those of the UN. Until the peacekeeping force was in place, Anglo-French forces would stay the course. In this way, Britain and France could be said to be doing no more than the job the UN should have taken on when the canal was nationalised. The allied landings would go ahead.

But there was still a problem of timing. With the Anglo-French force still chugging its way across the Mediterranean, its progress could be interrupted at any moment by determined international action involving, for example, the US Sixth Fleet. The risks were highlighted when, having achieved nearly all its military objectives, Israel responded positively to the call for a ceasefire 'provided that a similar answer is forthcoming from Egypt'. This came as a huge shock to Israel's covert allies. If both combatants ceased fire, what justification could there be for Anglo-French intervention? French influence was brought into play. Ben-Gurion was irritated by Britain's devotion to what a senior French officer called derisorily its 'hundred ship plan'. Israel had played its part. Why should it now risk further international admonition by keeping up the pretence of a battle it had already won?

There were two answers to that. First, the battle was still engaged. Ben-Gurion had been mistaken in thinking that Sharm el-Sheikh was already in Israeli hands. It was nearly so, but not quite. More compellingly, Ben-Gurion could not refuse a plea from his French friends. In fact, he was prepared to extend the fighting if France so required. A face-saving delaying tactic at the UN demanded an Egyptian renunciation of the state of war with Israel with a pledge to end terrorist activity and the blockade of Israeli shipping. At the same time, Ben-Gurion readily agreed to a French plan for hastening their arrival at Port Said by moving Israeli troops closer to the canal to cover a paratroop drop that was supposed to make the support of the seaborne force unnecessary.[1]

As it happened the plan was a non-starter. British politicians and their military would have none of it, and France did not feel strong enough to act alone. But at least, with Israeli compliance in rejecting a ceasefire, the allied landings could go ahead, assuming, of course, that the British government held to its resolve. That was by no means certain. The French establishment and popular sentiment was still broadly in Mollet's favour, though interestingly, while opinion polls in France showed a clear majority against Nasser, it was in Britain that military action attracted the strongest support – 33 per cent as against 20 per cent in France. The discrepancy is explained by French enthusiasm for trying economic sanctions while keeping up the threat of force.[2] The fact remained that few in France questioned the right to put maximum pressure on Nasser. Eden, on the other hand, searched in vain for a semblance of unity. Divisions in the country were matched by differences at the power centre.

Among his immediate advisers the discordant note was struck loud and clear by Mountbatten. Having led the campaign to save Egyptian lives by substituting Port Said for the heavily populated Alexandria as the centre point for the war plan, he remained opposed to the operation in any guise. After the UN call for a ceasefire, Mountbatten made one last bid for common sense.

> I am writing to appeal to you to accept the resolution of the overwhelming majority of the United Nations to cease military operations, and to beg you to turn back the assault convoy before it is too late, as I feel that the actual landing of troops can only spread the war with untold misery and world-wide repercussions. You can imagine how hard it is for me to break all service custom

and write direct to you in this way, but I feel so desperate about what is happening that my conscience would not allow me to do otherwise.[3]

To no avail. On 3 November, Eden spoke on television and radio, his latest effort to turn a vendetta into a national emergency. Those who watched or heard him split down the middle. His admirers were moved by his passionate sincerity ('All my life I have been a man of peace, working for peace, striving for peace, negotiating for peace . . . I could not be other, even if I wished'). Opponents denounced a demonstration of ham acting.

That the attempt at sincerity was less than genuine is suggested by the desperate efforts made by Eden to stem free debate by putting the media under government control. Restricting information on the grounds that to do otherwise was liable to imperil the men who had been sent to fight made some sense, but not to the extent of trying to force the BBC to tailor the news to government wishes. Relations began to deteriorate as early as August when Eden telephoned his old friend and former colleague Lord Cadogan, chairman of the BBC board of governors, in an attempt to influence programme policy.

The one-time senior man at the foreign office and first British representative at the UN, was also a director of the Suez Canal Company, a sinecure that suggested a clash of interests which the distinguished Cadogan studiously ignored. His prime responsibility was to guard the independence and impartiality of the BBC, but his declared sympathy with Eden's refusal to 'appease' Nasser led him to interfere in programming to support the government case.

Reminded by Eden of the governors' 'burden of responsibility', Cadogan agreed to stick to 'straight news', which meant anodyne news or news that suited the government. At a meeting on 13 September the governors agreed 'that the BBC should do nothing to underline the existence of party division and disunity at a time of crisis'.[4] The professional broadcasters saw matters quite differently. As the battle lines were drawn between government and the BBC, William Clark, Eden's press secretary, warned Harman Grisewood, the director general's chief assistant, that extreme measures might be taken to bring the corporation into line. 'I doubt', wrote Grisewood, 'if any career civil servant could have done what Clark did by tact and initiative both in restraining Eden and calming the BBC.'[5] It would not be long before tact and patience ran out.

In the last week of October an attempt was made to 'shock the corporation into collective obedience'[6] with a threat to cut the overseas services budget by one fifth. At this even Cadogan was moved to protest, though he acceded to the demand for a foreign office liaison officer to be installed at Bush House, the head-quarters of the overseas services, 'to advise the BBC on the content and direction of their overseas programmes'. J. L. B. Tichener, popularly known as Tichener of Tartoum, was treated as a joke by the broadcasters, but he managed to outstay the Suez crisis and was assiduous in feeding current events programmes with news filtered by the intelligence and propaganda divisions.[7] The prime mover in trying to muzzle the BBC's external broadcasts was R. A. Butler, who later was to insist that he always had doubts on the wisdom of Eden's Suez policy.

When military operations were about to begin, Harman Grisewood and the acting director general, Norman Bottomley, were summoned to the ministry of defence, where they were told to prepare for the revival of wartime measures including censorship.

> The officials who spoke to us understood very little of the requirements of broadcasting and, it seemed to me, had had no experience of the elaborate system which had been dismantled about ten years before. It would be quite impossible for the BBC itself to establish a wartime system without a Ministry of Information and without the many months of detailed planning which had preceded the outbreak of war in 1938.
>
> Bottomley and I left Whitehall with heavy hearts. We were all the more apprehensive because we knew that Eden relied on his

personal contact with Cadogan to a degree that took little or no account of the way the BBC worked or was meant to work.[8]

It was now that William Clark became Grisewood's best contact inside the government structure, warning him of the reaction to broadcasts that attempted a fair commentary on the divisions of opinion in the country. Came the day when in discussion with Clark, Grisewood 'found him more deeply disturbed than usual'.[9]

> I could see that some sort of crisis was near at hand. He told me that Eden's reserves of patience with the BBC was [sic] fast running out; Clark was finding it harder and harder to prevent the PM's anger from taking the form of sweeping changes. I asked what changes. William told me that the Prime Minister had instructed the Lord Chancellor to prepare an instrument which would take over the BBC altogether and subject it wholly to the will of the Government.[10]

Grisewood found himself in an awkward position. If he shared his knowledge with the director general, then Cadogan would have to know and Grisewood had doubts that the chairman would do enough to resist the pressure. He was saved from making an immediate decision by news from Clark that Eden had found Lord Kilmuir's draft too accommodating to the BBC and had demanded something stronger.

Fortunately for the BBC Eden's broad-brush policy on censorship was suddenly reduced to a single issue when he took to the airwaves on 3 November to present himself as a Churchillian leader, the voice of the nation at its meeting with destiny. The question was, could the opposition led by Hugh Gaitskell be denied the right of reply? There was some thought of allowing Gaitskell to broadcast but to cut him from overseas bulletins which could be heard by British troops as they prepared to go into action. Cadogan thought an all-stations broadcast to be akin to treachery, but as Grisewood explained it was simply not practical to transmit Gaitskell on a selective basis. More to the point, to muzzle the voices of opposition to the Suez campaign was to abrogate the BBC's duty to inform. Grisewood was sure that the whole staff backed the traditional policy of the BBC. 'If the Board had decided to side with Eden the BBC would have broken into revolt. If Eden had had his way, it would, in my view, have been the end of the Corporation as it had been known up till then. I believe most of the senior people would have resigned rather than try to carry out orders of suppression.'[11]

Gaitskell's broadcast on behalf of the opposition was transmitted on the evening of Sunday, 4 November as the leading ships of the Anglo-French armada were nearing Port Said. He was later criticised for attempting to undermine the morale of British forces as they prepared to go into action, but to have remained silent would have been an even greater dereliction of his political duty. By failing to consult the Labour front bench, as he failed to consult anyone whom he suspected of holding opinions that differed from his own, Eden invited the worst possible interpretation of his policy, and on 4 November Gaitskell gave it to him, with both barrels.

As a preliminary to demanding full support for an immediate ceasefire and a UN force to police the Arab–Israeli borders, Gaitskell spoke of 'a tragic terrible week . . . by far the worst week, for the world and for our country, since 1939'. He went on:

> Make no mistake about it – this is war – the bombing, the softening up, the attacks on radio stations, telephone exchanges, railway stations, to be followed, very, very soon now, by the landings and the fightings between ground forces.
>
> We're doing all this alone, except for France. Opposed by the world, in defiance of the world. It is not a police action; there is no law behind it. We have taken the law into our own hands. That's the tragic situation in which we British people find ourselves tonight.

The message was endorsed at a mass rally, said to have attracted up to thirty thousand, in Trafalgar Square, where Aneurin Bevan raised the biggest cheer of the day when he declared of Eden, 'If [he] is sincere in what he says – and he may be – then he is too stupid to be Prime Minister.' The meeting ended with a march on Downing Street, where a force of 700 foot and mounted police struggled to hold back the crowd. Inside No. 10, where the chorus of 'Eden Must Go' was clearly audible, a full cabinet was in session to decide whether or not to press on. It was a bit late to decide the issue. British and French forces were within hours of landing on Egyptian soil. Ministers who had been told little if anything of the military build-up to Suez were now invited to give a verdict on Eden's stewardship of Middle Eastern affairs. Not surprisingly, those who had been kept in ignorance bowed to those in the know and Eden got his endorsement, albeit one that was given grudgingly by up to half the cabinet.[12]

The one minister who had made up his mind that Suez was a dreadful mistake now declared himself openly. Anthony Nutting left the government. His timing aroused some interesting questions of political protocol. His resignation had been handed in on 31 October but he had deferred an announcement 'in view of the imminence of military operations'. When the *Mail* got wind of the undercover resignation and splashed it across the front page, the story was officially denied. Then, of course, the government had to retract. The impression of bungling at every turn was hard to dispel.

Though he was not in the cabinet, Nutting's departure caused dismay in the Tory Party and attracted more press headlines. Over the weekend, Nutting visited his sons at their schools to explain what had happened. John, the eldest at fourteen, was at Eton. Over lunch, his father told him that all was well, that whatever he heard, he mustn't worry or feel ashamed. John found it all very bemusing. But the significance of the conversation was borne in on him the following day when he found himself in a row with another boy, who, quoting his family newspaper, declared Anthony Nutting to be a traitor. The next thing John remembers was being held down by four older boys while his adversary was slumped in a corner with blood on his head. John was dimly aware that a few minutes earlier he had snatched up a poker.[13]

The family newspaper was the *Express*, and the young Eden loyalist was Jonathan Aitken. Forty-three years later, when Aitken pleaded guilty to perjury and attempting to pervert the course of justice, he was represented, without fee, by Sir John Nutting, QC.

The resignation of Anthony Nutting, at thirty-six one of the most promising of rising Tory politicians, brought an end to his parliamentary career. Whatever hurt he felt at the treatment meted out to him was intensified by the stories put around that he had been prejudiced by a romance with an American woman, who, in fact, had no influence or interest in politics. The thriving rumour market, which Eden did nothing to constrain, gave a whole new meaning to the 'sincerity' of the prime minister.

The British and French governments still insisted they were not at war with Egypt. They were simply engaged in police action. The military found it hard to get their heads round that one. On Cyprus, the journalist James Cameron confronted Keightley with the contradiction.

I said, well I'm buggered if I'm going to call it a Police Action, I'm going to call it a war. And Keightley said, 'If you do, we'll hold up your reports forever.' Which they did.

But then, during a Press Conference, General Keightley himself used the expression 'limited war'. So I said: 'I see it *is* a war at last.'

'No it's not,' said Keightley.

'But you just said it was.'

'Did I?' asked Keightley. 'Did anyone else hear me say that?'

'Yes,' shouted about two hundred correspondents.

'The General never used the words "limited war",' insisted his staff.

'Yes, he did,' insisted the correspondents.

'Well, if you think this is a war,' General Keightley concluded amiably, 'you'll bloody well have to prove it' – and left.

'So I decided to leave too – to go back to London where I could call a war a war and really blow my top. But they wouldn't let me. They kept me there till it was all over.'[14]

Clashes between press and official spokesmen became ever more frequent. After Keightley's sole unhappy appearance before reporters, the job of putting over the military story was handed over to 'a delightful but utterly vague colonel', who opened one conference with the memorable words, 'Yesterday, I promised I would get you the answers to some of your questions. I will start by giving three answers. And the answer to Question One is "I don't know".'[15]

The French were more open with information, but it was assumed that journalists would put a favourable gloss on whatever the military had to say. When this turned out not to be so, the repercussions could be serious. The editor of the anti-Suez weekly *L'Express* was called up as a reservist and packed off to Algeria while *Le Monde* was put under financial pressure by a government-inspired charge of 'illegally increasing' its price under a law designed to combat inflation.[16]

Even with censored reports, the opinion leaders in the British press were beginning to catch on to the realisation that the country was embarking on a dangerous adventure. *The Economist* referred to a 'strange union of cynicism and hysteria' in government; the *Spectator* warned of a 'terrible indictment' that Eden would face; while the *Observer* spoke of 'folly' and 'crookedness'. 'Not since 1783', thundered an *Observer* leader column, 'has Britain made herself so universally disliked.' The *Guardian*, then known as the *Manchester Guardian*, urged readers to protest to their MPs, while in *The Times*, so recently encouraging Eden to stand up for all that was great in Britain, the editorial line softened to a wish for compromise.

The public reaction to press comment highlighted the divisions within the country. But there was no doubt that Eden still commanded strong support from a sizeable minority, maybe even a majority, of voters who thought it was about time that the upstart Arabs should be taught a lesson. The *Observer* and *Guardian* lost readers; so too did the *News Chronicle*, a liberal newspaper that was soon to fold as a result of falling circulation.

In the Tory Party, giving Eden the benefit of the doubt was

still the prevailing tendency. A rebel group of fifteen Conservative MPs, headed by Sir Alec Spearman, made known their concerns to Ted Heath, then chief whip and himself one who doubted the wisdom of the official handouts. But as Nigel Nicolson was to point out after losing his parliamentary seat in the Suez aftermath, there was no concerted action to force a change in government policy. After Anthony Nutting's exit, the only other immediate resignation was that of William Clark, who could no longer square his conscience with acting as Eden's spokesman to the media. He was thus spared from denying rumours, soon to be substantiated, that hostilities had started with a naval engagement.

While the invasion convoy proceeded unmolested, there was limited dramatic action in the Gulf of Suez. HMS *Newfoundland* and HMS *Diana* were part of an Anglo-French force patrolling the gulf to protect any merchant vessels that might inadvertently have strayed into Egyptian waters. The *Diana*'s commanding officer was Captain John Gower:

> Darkness fell as *Newfoundland* with *Diana* entered the Gulf of Suez and made a sweep to the north. Both ships were darkened and the ship's company was at action stations, the first time in earnest for most of them. There was no moon but the night was fine and cool, a welcome change after the sticky heat of Aden, and the long watch at guns was relieved for some by the sight of lighted ships as they steamed south. Some hours were passed, still steaming northwards, in identifying merchant ships and checking radar consuls, until at 0100 the behaviour of one ship in particular aroused our suspicion. The ship was to port following a small group of merchant ships on an opposite course to *Newfoundland* and *Diana*, with her navigation lights burning but otherwise darkened. As she came abeam, *Newfoundland* decided to investigate.

In the illumination of the *Newfoundland*'s searchlights, the mystery vessel was revealed as the Egyptian frigate *Domiat*. The signal from *Newfoundland* 'Stop or I fire' was acknowledged, but when ordered 'Report when stopped' the *Domiat* switched off her navigation lights, increased speed and trained her guns on the British cruiser. At 1,500 yards the *Newfoundland* opened fire just before the *Domiat* began firing with all her guns. 'When only a few hundred yards away, the frigate turned in an apparent bid to ram the *Newfoundland*, but *Newfoundland*'s fire was so accurate and effective that the attempt to continue the action was hopeless. Both ships stopped firing together and *Domiat*, badly damaged in the blaze, capsized and, after floating bottom up for three minutes, sank.' The silence that followed the noise of the guns, the sight of the burning ship and of the survivors struggling in the water had what Captain Gower described as a 'sobering effect' on his young and inexperienced ship's company, one hundred of whom were under twenty years of age. 'Any feelings of anger during the action were replaced by sympathy for the Egyptian sailors, many of whom had been trained in England.' Six officers and sixty ratings were picked up by rafts from a choppy sea or were hauled in over the side by ropes and scrambling nets. British casualties were five injured and one killed.[17]

Two days after the *Domiat* incident came the first casualties from mistaken identity. HMS *Crane*, patrolling off the Straits of Tiran, was attacked by four Israeli jets. One of them was shot down.

Meanwhile, aboard his command ship HMS *Tyne*, Stockwell was under pressure from Beaufre to bring forward the paratroop drop on Port Said. Long and arduous were their discussions. Beaufre was increasingly frustrated by the delays imposed by the methodical and, as he saw it, unimaginative British commanders, delays for which he was carrying the blame in Paris. At one point, the impatience of Barjot became so great that the admiral requested permission of the French government to take over direct control of the paratroops, a 'completely lunatic' idea, decided Beaufre, who could see that his own authority was under threat.[18] Barjot did not get his way, but Beaufre succeeded in persuading Stockwell to discount the air photographs that showed a concentration of Egyptian troops at Port Said and along the canal. There would be no postponement. The drop would go ahead as planned.

The British 3rd Parachute Battalion, led by Lieutenant Colonel Paul Crook, was to land 668 men with seven jeeps, four trailers, six anti-tank guns and 176 containers on Gamil airfield, 3 miles west of Port Said.[19] Fifteen minutes later, the French 2nd Colonial Parachute Regiment under Colonel Pierre Chateau-Jobert, better known by his Free French pseudonym 'Conan', would drop on Port Fuad, a residential suburb of Port Said on the east bank of the canal. Both landing zones challenged the skills of the assailants. Roy Fullick, who was with 3rd Para, recalls that Gamil airfield 'only just merited the description of airport'.

> It was a strip of land running between the sea and the brackish Lake Manzala, never more than 800 yards wide and consisting of a pair of runways and a simple control tower . . . Between the airfield and Port Said lay the town's sewage farm, surrounded by half-drained marshland and then a series of cemeteries reflecting the diverse creeds of their inhabitants. Nearer still to Port Said were several blocks of high flats and the coastguard barracks and then on the edge of the town proper an area known as Shanty Town, whose inhabitants were to suffer most from the invasion.[20]

As for the French paratroop force, their landing was even more hazardous. To drop with any accuracy on a zone barely 300 yards long and only 150 yards across, bounded by the sea, roads, the canal and trees, the planes would have to fly in at a height of 450 feet, almost 200 feet less than the accepted minimum.

Brigadier Butler, who had overall command of the British paratroops, was with the French in wanting an even bolder plan, a brigade-strength drop at Ismailia and another at Port Tewfik to coincide with a sea landing at Port Said. In this way, all three key points on the canal would be seized at one blow.[21] On paper, the plan had everything going for it; in reality, however, Stockwell felt that there were too many hostages to fortune. There was no shifting from what was codenamed Operation Telescope save for the addition of a second French parachute drop south of Port Fuad on the afternoon of the 5th.

In the twenty-four-hour countdown to Operation Telescope,

the Port Said defences came under heavy air attack. While preparing for take-off from Cyprus, French and British paratroopers had the chance to compare notes. From the beginning it was clear that the advantage was with the French, as Air Marshal Sir Denis Barnett conceded:

> . . . In general the equipment supplied to the French Air Force for tactical operations was so superior to that available in the Middle East that at times the Royal Air Force looked almost Victorian. This equipment varied from modern tentage in the French Air Force compared with ancient marquees available to the Royal Air Force, to highly modern mobile photographic equipment which the French had and which was not available to the Royal Air Force.[22]

There was also a contrast, unfavourable to the British, in the suitability of the aircraft used to carry the paratroops. While the French were blessed with the rear-loading Nord Atlas 2501 which could accommodate thirty-five paras with their equipment and support weapons, their partners in war had to make do with the Hastings and the Valletta, veterans of the Second World War. Both were side-loading, which meant that heavy equipment had to be slung under the aircraft instead of taken on board and dropped from a tailgate. A rear-loading plane, the Beverley, was due to come into service but it was not ready for Suez.

The loudest complaints were reserved for the interior design of the twin-engined Valletta, which had a main spar about 18 inches high across the fuselage in the middle of the aircraft. Half of those on board had to climb over this obstacle to reach the door. This could prove difficult for a paratrooper carrying a parachute, kitbag, weapon and ammunition amounting to a load close on twice his weight.

In terms of experience there was not much to choose between the two allies. Action in Algeria (and in a few cases Indo-China) could be equated with action in Cyprus, though there were those on the British side who noted a sharp difference in professional attitude. 'There had been an embarrassment in Cyprus when a young English officer informed a French colleague that he had done twenty-seven jumps. The French older captain was puzzled and said he had only done three. The French only counted their operational jumps into real war, regarding keeping a tally of exercise jumps as a bit childish.'[23]

The British drop was at 7.15 a.m. local time; the French drop a quarter of an hour later. The flight from Cyprus took ninety minutes. As the aerial convoy passed over the ships steaming towards Port Said, fighters were shuttling to and from attacks on Egyptian anti-aircraft guns that might otherwise have upset the schedule.

> The plane I was in was a Hastings heavy-drop aircraft, carrying fourteen men, all very relaxed, who for most of the flight lay about the floor of the aircraft, reading magazines and paperbacks. We were flying in fairly low as we approached the Egyptian coast, and the British and French fleets were an impressive sight in the early morning sunlight. It all looked very peaceful, with a line of breakers pounding on the sandy shore. Then we turned into the sun to make our approach round over El Gamil for the drop. Standing in the door provided a fine view of the delta, with little flashes of ack-ack fire from the Egyptian batteries.[24]

There were those who were slightly unnerved by the absence of reserve parachutes. But with a drop height of less than 600 feet, they would have been virtually useless. Anyway, Crook had decided to allow for extra ammunition and still save on weight. For three soldiers the drop, frightening enough in itself, was especially memorable.

> Private Peter Lamph of 'B' Company – he was No. 20 in a Valletta, and got his strap wrapped round his leg as he crossed the spar ... As the plane turned for home, he dropped and landed in the sea. As he came down, he came under heavy small-arms fire and his personal weapons' container was hit several times. He feigned dead and, as time passed, 'B' Company began attacking, and he made his way towards the beach and

was picked up by a patrol later in the day. The happy ending came when Group Captain Macnamara sent him a crate of beer with the compliments of Transport Command to compensate him for his wetting.[25]

Private Pugsley was the first to arrive at his platoon objective, the airfield control tower.

> He landed in one of the only two ornamental palm trees by the tower and hung there muttering: 'Cor, fuck me!' as Sergeant Legg and a platoon raced to secure the tower and the adjacent building. As Private Looker of B Company was still at about 200 feet, with his kitbag swinging beneath him, he saw that he was about to land in a slit trench. The Egyptian occupant obviously thought so too, scrambled out, and stood on the edge of the trench, pointing his rifle at Looker. The fates intervened and Looker's 80 lb kitbag swung into the Egyptian, knocking him into the trench. Looker landed on top of him and quickly despatched him.[26]

The final tally was four dead, with one soldier landing in a mine-field, and thirty-six wounded. One of the latter was a *Daily Mirror* journalist, Peter Woods, later better known as a television news-caster. He it was who managed to persuade Colonel Crook's brigade major that he knew all there was to know about jumping out of aircraft. When he came to admit that this was something of an exaggeration it was too late and he was out of the door. He broke both ankles on landing but he had his story. The *Mirror* ran it under the headline 'I Jump with the Red Devils'.

There were two other unusual casualties. One was a staff officer who had a half-bottle of whisky in his hip pocket. Having per-formed a fast back landing, he cut himself painfully.[27] The other, more serious, was the regimental medical officer, who lost an eye. This caused consternation in Cyprus. Major Frank King was told to do something about it.

> I couldn't find a single doctor on the island who was parachute-trained. So we got three young Air Force doctors from a nearby

hospital and said, 'One of you is going to parachute into Egypt.'
None of them was very thrilled, so we drew lots. Fortunately,
however, we got another message saying a replacement was not
required. The officer who lost his eye had a very good sergeant
who patched him up, and he carried on. He was subsequently
awarded a well-deserved M C.[28]

The French landed with guns blazing, the advantage of having
weapons that could be employed during the drop as opposed, in
the British case, to having to wait for the landing before 1940-
vintage Sten guns could be unstrapped and called into service –
assuming, of course, that they did not jam in the effort. The drop
was spot-on but the landing zone had the distinct disadvantage
of being occupied by a contingent of Egyptian infantry. Pierre
Leulliette was there.

> Lightened, I rose from the ground, clutching my automatic rifle.
> I saw my companions surge up, like myself, from every hole.
> Immense confusion. The ground didn't seem very safe: water,
> humps and hollows everywhere. But a few hundred yards off
> was a green belt of magnificent palm trees. Behind it were some
> large, dazzlingly white buildings: the reservoirs, our first objec-
> tive. They were firing machine-guns at us from behind the trees:
> through binoculars, you could see the crews busy round their
> guns.
>
> We dashed over to them in confusion, jumping, falling and
> getting up again, the captain at our head. But it was a long way,
> several hundred yards at the double, our legs bruised by the
> jump, and bullets flying. From time to time, one of our lot pitched
> on to his face in the sand. You couldn't tell if it was fatal, but it
> was forbidden to stop; there were orderlies in our wake. Stopping
> during an attack, even to pick up a wounded comrade, was
> considered desertion.
>
> Then some field-guns opened up on us. It wasn't a biblical
> deluge of fire, as imagined by people whose idea of war comes
> from the cinemas. No, just a bullet here and a shell there. That
> was all. But it was enough to fill the air. Eventually, as we ran,

we realized that this confused noise wasn't stopping us. We were so beside ourselves, it didn't even frighten us.

Yet, in a flash, I took in an image which I shall never forget: hanging from the top of a palm tree by the straps of his parachute, Sergeant B.'s body was slowly dripping blood into the sand. He had apparently been one of the first killed, before reaching the ground, shot in full flight. His large body was swaying in the palm fronds, sharp as spears. Ten yards away, in a hedge of flowering rose trees, in the shade of the palm trees by the reservoirs, among the damaged stalks, another body caught my attention: the small khaki body of an Egyptian soldier. The contrast between the vitality of the flowers where he'd crashed and his bloodless face took my breath away.[29]

A great benefit to the French paratroops was an unlikely secret weapon, directed by a 'rough tongued, one-eyed veteran of colonial wars'. General Gilles had an aerial command post. Flying above the battle with sufficient height to give a superior radio signal, he was able to direct air fire on to enemy positions.

The immediate objective of the French was to secure the two Raswa bridges, the vital link in the Port Said–Suez route. One bridge had been destroyed but the second, the Treaty Road bridge over the Junction Canal, was intact. It was defended by 30 mm field guns firing from trenches between the iron girders of the bridge, which also gave protection to infantry who showed every indication of knowing how to use modern automatic weapons.

Low-level air strikes, coming in at little over 30 feet, helped to silence the field guns, though blanket bombing was inhibited by the need to protect the bridge. In the end the defenders were drawn out by a mass assault on guns and trenches.

Shots, confusion. The Egyptians, encircled, surrendered. They emerged one by one from their pillboxes, hands in the air. Like us, they were wearing magnificent red berets. They were Nasser's famous 'death commandos'!

But the bridge was still in their comrades' hands, and they would not give in. They were still firing from beneath huge iron girders which protected them from the air. A heavy barrage. Losses on both sides. Then they slowly began to fall back.

While his comrades withdrew, covering each other, one Egyptian remained more than a quarter of an hour by himself at the entrance to the bridge, defending it with his one gun against our entire company, furiously and hopelessly. He was a real death commando. Then a bullet struck him. He slumped back grotesquely, like all heroes.[30]

The whole operation had been concluded in an hour and a half, well ahead of schedule. The troops having dug in to await reinforcements to be parachuted in, probing patrols were sent out towards Port Said and down the canal towards Ismailia. They found no sign of the enemy and the road was clear of mines. The explosives stored by the roadside suggested a plan for craters to serve as vehicle traps. But the defenders had run out of time.

Back at El Gamil, the airfield had been cleared rather more quickly than Crook had anticipated. The drums filled with concrete that were distributed across the runway were presumably there to deter troop carriers from landing. But for 3rd Para they were a positive help in providing cover for a successful attack on Egyptian machine gunners firing from two pillboxes. Another strong defence position was the nearby cemetery, which was dealt with by Crook calling in air strikes. More of a problem was the sewage farm, 'also home to thousands of mosquitoes who proved to be more irritating than the Egyptians'.[31]

The last obstacle before Port Said, the coast guard barracks on the beach road, was also set alight.

These barracks had been turned into a strong point by the enemy, and rocket fire proved ineffective against it due to its size and construction. After . . . a rapid change of armament Wyverns armed with 2 × 1,000 lb and 1 × 500 lb bombs apiece, fused 30 seconds delay were launched and destroyed this target. Ground observation after the Cease Fire showed that this strike was so accurate that adjacent buildings were untouched.[32]

One Wyvern was hit by flak. The pilot bailed out but was picked up by helicopter.

By 1 p.m. 3rd Para was running short of ammunition and the order was given to dig in. Here was an opportunity to check out captured weapons. Many an unreliable Sten gun was thrown aside in favour of a brand-new Czech-made automatic side arm.

In the afternoon 3rd Para was reinforced by a second drop. They were also visited by a French Dakota, which managed to find a landing strip at Gamil. On board was Colonel de Fouquières, who was under orders to see whether it would be practical to fly in French ground forces. The consensus on the British side was that any assumption that the Egyptians were finished was premature. Beaufre was later to claim that this had been a missed opportunity to advance at all speed on Port Said. In both their sectors the paratroops had achieved more than they had been called upon to do. Most critically, the French were in control of the freshwater reservoirs that supplied Port Said. Thus they had a weapon to hand that was more powerful than any explosive.

But it would have taken an audacious ground commander to have pre-empted the infantry heavy armour landing scheduled for the following day. Whatever else can be said about the Suez campaign it was not one that allowed for flexibility or encouraged subordinate officers to use their initiative. In any case, communications with Stockwell on his command ship were all but impossible. Vital wireless equipment that had dropped with 3rd Para – three old and unreliable long-range sets – had fallen to bits on impact. The alternative low-powered sets were near useless for any but the shortest messages until the naval convoy was closer to shore. So it was that Colonel de Fouquières departed without a promise of further action until the next day. But he did take with him a full load of casualties, including the medical officer who had carried on doing his job despite his own wound, together with the female war correspondent from *Le Monde* who had come along to view the battle from the British side.

French expectations were again disappointed later in the afternoon when, under a flag of truce, Brigadier Salab ed-Din Moguy, commander of the Port Said garrison, appealed to Colonel Chateau-Jobert for permission to repair the freshwater pumping station that had been damaged in the fighting. Chateau-Jobert naturally concluded that here was an opportunity to negotiate a general ceasefire. To lead the talks, Brigadier Butler was flown in by naval helicopter. Belying his nickname 'Tubby', Butler was a tall, slim, red-headed Irishman of decisive views and a firm sense of what was needed to satisfy the allies' minimum demands. This amounted to an unconditional surrender, which Moguy, who had lately returned from a gunnery course in Britain, seemed ready to consider. But in late evening, apparently on orders from Cairo, he rejected the terms decisively. Among the French commentators it became the received wisdom that Butler was short on negotiating skills, that had Chateau-Jobert been left to do the job he would have taken a more flexible approach, allowing Moguy the chance to declare peace with honour. Massu, who was an admirer of Butler, agrees that he may have been too brusque but, in the end, this made no difference since any agreement to end the fighting would have depended on Nasser's willingness to surrender, and there is no evidence to suggest that he was ready to give up.[33]

According to his friend Abd al-Latif al-Bughdadi, a member of the Revolutionary Council, Nasser had moments of despair. Witnessing at first hand the wreckage of trucks and tanks in the wake of what should have been an orderly withdrawal from Sinai, Nasser mourned, '103 million pounds down the drain' and railed against his senior officers ('I have been defeated by my own army').[34] But his mood soon changed to defiance as he prepared his fellow citizens for a guerrilla war. 'We shall fight a bitter battle . . . from village to village, house to house.' Boxes of small arms appeared on street corners where anyone who could pull a trigger was invited to help themselves. When Moguy called for reinforcements, Nasser readily assigned three National Guard battalions and three battalions of infantry reservists to bolster the Port Said garrison.

Messages of encouragement to Egyptians to defend their homes were relayed over loudspeakers. The flights of propaganda even took in the promise of Soviet aid and the assurance that Russian planes were already on their way to bomb Paris and London. But however fanciful the claims, the spirit of defiance was unmistakeable. No one should have been surprised when Moguy backtracked on offers to consider a truce. The best that could be achieved was a local ceasefire at Port Fuad where, by nightfall, French paratroops were pretty much in control of the whole town.

There was manifold disappointment in London at the failure to secure an easy victory. Over-eager expectations as much as faulty communications were responsible for Eden's premature announcement to the House of Commons that a ceasefire had indeed come about. The government benches erupted in shouts and cheers of vindication tinged with relief, an emotional outpouring that made the inevitable retraction all the harder to bear. The demands, increasingly voluble at home and abroad, were now for Eden to declare a unilateral ceasefire. If rational argument had had anything to do with it, this is precisely what would have happened, since the pretext for the invasion had disappeared when the last shots had been fired at Sharm el-Sheikh. The war that the Anglo-French action was supposed to stop had stopped anyway.

The chorus of international disapproval for what Britain and France were up to was almost deafening. In Washington a new and louder voice was raised against the two powers. Shortly after addressing the UN General Assembly, Dulles complained of severe stomach pains. It was put out that he was suffering from acute appendicitis, but at Walter Reed Hospital in Washington he was diagnosed with colon cancer. A five-hour operation was deemed a success but there was no question of Dulles returning to work for at least two months. In his place advising Eisenhower was the Under-Secretary of State, Herbert Hoover Jr, an oilman and Middle East expert, that same Herbert Hoover who, after the fall of Mossadeq, had made sure that Britain would lose her exclusive right to exploit Iranian oil. Unlike Dulles, who, whatever his shortcomings in Anglo-French eyes, had a regard for the Atlantic alliance, Hoover could barely disguise his contempt for

European pretensions. With Eisenhower just two days away from the presidential election, he was encouraged by Hoover to get tough with Eden. The sense of urgency was sharpened by the sudden prospect of confrontation with the Soviet Union.

The day before the British and French expeditionary force landed at Port Said, another mission was getting under way in eastern Europe. At daybreak Russian tanks entered Budapest. Moscow's soft words of reassurance for the liberal reformers who had taken over the government of Hungary, delivered only a week before, were forgotten as the Soviet hardliners imposed their will. The conjunction of Suez and Hungary made it impossible for Eisenhower to come out openly against Russian oppression without at the same time throwing petrol on the flames that were shooting up in the Middle East. His frustration was palpable. Putting through a call to Eden, he skipped the small talk. 'I can only presume that you have gone out of your mind' was his opening line to the rattled prime minister.

The president had every reason to be furious. Events in Hungary had been seen in Washington as the first sign of the break-up of the Soviet empire. Now Bulganin and Khrushchev could hardly believe their luck. Here was a golden opportunity to divert world attention from their own troubles and to frustrate Hungarian calls for support from the West. They made the most of it. Letters went off to Ben-Gurion warning the Israeli government that it was 'criminally playing with the destiny of its country and people – which raises the question of the whole existence of Israel as a state'. If that were not provocative enough, Mollet and Eden were treated to a lecture on the 'dangerous consequences' of their action, 'for the cause of general peace', and threatened with rockets. No doubt they would call this barbaric, wrote Bulganin, 'yet in what way does the inhuman attack made by the armed forces of Britain and France on the nearly unarmed Egypt differ from this?'

But the tour de force of Soviet diversionary tactics was the tongue-in-cheek appeal to Eisenhower for joint American–Soviet military action to 'curb aggression' against Egypt. The suggestion was dismissed out of hand, but as Emmet Hughes, a presidential adviser, noted, the Oval Office discussion prompted by the Moscow correspondence was 'sombre'.

> No stern and indignant rhetoric could make the moment less perilous, less precarious. For the obvious danger existed that Moscow might be irresistibly tempted toward aggressive action, on a massive scale, by *both* hope and fear – the hope that Egypt signified a deep division of the West, and the fear that Hungary threatened a kind of earthquake within the Soviet sphere. The combination looked explosive. And the President described it pithily: 'Those boys are both furious and scared. Just as with Hitler, that makes for the most dangerous possible state of mind. And we better be damn sure that every Intelligence point and every outpost of our Armed Forces is absolutely right on their toes.'[35]

Eisenhower's big fear was that the Bulganin message was the opening gambit of an ultimatum. 'We have to be positive and clear in our every word, every step. And if those fellows start something, we may have to hit 'em – and, if necessary, with *everything* in the bucket.'[36]

Against the threat of world war there was yet another bleat from Downing Street appealing for understanding of the Anglo-French position. Eden had now managed to persuade himself that from the very beginning his sole motivation for getting involved in Egypt was to help the UN out of a tight spot.

> I am convinced that, if we had allowed things to drift, everything would have gone from bad to worse. Nasser would have become a kind of Moslem Mussolini and our friends in Iraq, Jordan, Saudi Arabia and even Iran would gradually have been brought down. His efforts would have spread westwards, and Libya and all North Africa would have been brought under his control . . . We and the French were convinced that we had to act at once to forestall a general conflagration throughout the Middle East. And now that police action has been started it must be carried through

... You will realise, with all your experience, that we cannot have a military vacuum while a United Nations force is being constituted and is being transported to the spot. This is why we feel we must go on to hold the position until we can hand over the responsibility to the United Nations. If a barrier can be established in this way between the Arabs and the Israelis we shall then be strongly placed to call on the Israelis to withdraw. This in its turn will reduce the threat to the Canal and restore it to the general use of the world. By this means, we shall have taken the first step towards re-establishing authority in this area for our generation.[37]

As an exercise in self-deception this took some beating. Eisenhower recognised it for what it was. But he was now painfully aware that on the very day that American voters went to the polls, the crisis in the Middle East would reach its climax.

21

On board his command ship 15 miles offshore, Stockwell spent the last hours before D-Day trying to reconcile the political demands with military expediency. His task was to take back control of the canal, but he was also under orders to spare lives and to cause minimum damage. Reasoning that the safety of his troops came before the protection of Egyptians, he had planned a naval bombardment of Port Said's coastal defences. Hearing of this, his political masters in London were thrown into panic as they visualised widespread death and destruction. Stockwell was told to hold back on fire power; only 4.5-inch guns were to be deployed. This cut out the heavy cruisers, including the *Jean Bart*, the pride of the French fleet. It must then have occurred to someone that no matter what size, shells could not discriminate between soldiers and civilians. If the political aim took priority, there was no option but to call off the naval bombardment.

This was not at all to Stockwell's liking. In his view there had already been too many uninformed intrusions on his job. His way out was to plead the ambiguity of his instructions. Denying him his naval bombardment did not put a stop to 'naval gunfire support', and as Stockwell knew very well there were degrees of gunfire support that would make a bombardment look like a firework display. Even so, when the limit on shell size became current gossip among those who were to lead the assault, it was greeted with derision. One marine spoke for all. 'It's all right for those bloody stupid politicians in London, but what about our lads standing by to go ashore? So what's a few dead Marines as long as we don't hurt any Arabs or bust a few windows.'[1] One young officer voiced his surprise that his troop was not being sent in armed with water pistols and woolly balls.

Ironically, there was also pressure from the French to scale down the sea offensive, but not for any wish to give the opposition an easy time. Indeed, at one stage General Jacques Massu, commander of the 10th Parachute Division, whose iron-fist reputation preceded him from Algeria, anticipated up to 40 per cent casualties among his own, mostly foreign legionnaire troops. Described as 'very clever, in a foxy way ... with the instincts of a peasant ... very brave and loved by his men',[2] Massu was disinclined to worry overmuch about civilian casualties. But to his way of thinking, as to that of Beaufre and Barjot, after the French paratroop success in gaining and holding Port Fuad, there seemed no obvious reason why another paratroop landing could not finish the job in quick time. But Stockwell was not about to give up his set-piece battle. A French paratroop landing at Qantara was postponed and then cancelled.

On 6 November, at 4 a.m., the marine commandos who were to be in the first-wave attack on Port Said's beaches sat down to breakfast. Meanwhile, the destroyers *Jamaica*, *Duchess*, *Diamond* and *Decoy* steamed ahead until they were in sight of the coastline. *Jamaica* then began a stately 90-degree turn to port followed by the other destroyers until all four were parallel to the shore line. The range was between 1.5 and 2 miles.[3] As the battle ensigns were hoisted, the gunners took the measure of their targets, as placid a set of sitting ducks as was ever to be lined up for slaughter.

At 6 a.m. the British destroyers opened fire. Jet fighters screamed overhead. On the deck of his LST Angus Jones was struck by 'the most beautiful sky I have ever seen'.

It was dawn, not sunset, yet the whole sky looked a reddish orange. This gave a pink reflection from the grey hulls of some of the ships, but many of the ships were like black silhouettes against the reddish background. It really was a beautiful sight. Looking towards Port Said, the buildings in the distance did not appear as tall as I had expected. On one side of the city was a column of smoke about 1000 ft. high . . . Out here it seemed very noisy and it seemed to stink of gunpowder.[4]

Marine commando troops in green berets with Royal Marine crews in blue berets clambered into their assault craft, known as LCAs or Buffaloes.

> The LCAs were suspended from the davits, like lifeboats on a liner, which were then lowered into the water and unhooked. In almost no time at all, the LCAs from both sides of our ship had formed a line, parallel to the beach, and now began to head in that direction. My position in the LCA was at the rear of the centre row. This meant I would be 10th out of this craft. As the men jumped into the sea, they would be jumping alternately left and right, to avoid a concentration of men in front of the ramp.[5]

Brigadier R. W. Madoc was not entirely dependent on landing craft. On board *Theseus* and *Ocean*, his commandos had been preparing to go ashore in helicopters. It promised to be an uncomfortable ride. The Whirlwinds had no seats, doors or windows and few handholds. They were also very noisy. Communications, if any, were by sign language. The Sycamores were even more hazardous. Of the first three passengers, two had to sit at the door edge with their legs dangling over the side. The third, in the centre, had to balance six mortar bombs on his knees.

Each commando carried about 85 pounds of equipment, including two mortar bombs, a gas mask, a water bottle and a twenty-four-hour 'iron' ration pack. Marine Ashton was dismissive of the 'pathetic' inner-tube lifebelt, but he wound it round his chest as instructed.

> Someone steadied the pack whilst I slipped into the harness. I then returned the favour, and in this careful manner, sixty or so overburdened men 'saddled up' in their confined and cluttered quarters.
> I adjusted my belt, with the extra weight created by pouches bulging with spare .303 ammo for the Bren, slung a 50-round

bandolier around my waist, picked up my rifle and made my way as if in slow motion to the marshalling points in the hangar below. It was still pitch dark and we had heard or seen nothing outside the dim claustrophobic red-lit world below decks.

We stood in 'sticks' like paratroopers, each allocated to a helicopter as previously rehearsed. Even the order of climbing in and jumping out was carefully pre-planned. With our enormous bulk it was difficult to move quickly in any direction, and particularly arduous to get up and down from a sitting or lying position. Both the mortar and machine gun crews were more heavily laden than the rest of us. Right in front of me, one of the latter, Eric Trickey, was carrying well over 100 lbs, with the two legs of the Vickers tripod sticking forward like antennae over his shoulders. Clenching his pipe between his teeth, he was forced to ground his load to make an adjustment; later, it took two hefty naval ratings to lift it high enough for him to regain a vertical position. For this reason, if for no other, we stood patiently like donkeys, bent slightly forward from the waist; moving like deep-sea divers on the ocean floor, and then only when absolutely necessary. The mood was subdued but expectant.[6]

By now, the first wave of landing craft was close to the beach. Captain Douglas Clark was a naval artillery observer in one of the first buffaloes to be launched from HMS *Suvla*.

Above the ramp I could see a strip of blue sky. It was the beginning of a glorious day. But as the ramp lowered and I could see more, the impression altered. We were close to land – far too close for an invading convoy. Barely half a mile away was the water's edge and the beach, blotted out by rolling clouds of smoke; grey smoke from shell bursts and brown smoke from fires. As shells landed, the smoke was pinpricked with flashes, while here and there, fierce red flames showed where the lines of wooden beach huts were on fire.[7]

Just as his buffalo was setting off there was an almighty crash and Clark was knocked sideways by a vicious blast of air.

I ducked below the gunwale, thinking that a shell landed on *Suvla*'s bows. Everybody else in the buffalo was already sitting down, unable to see what was going on, so my precipitate dive closely following the crash could not have re-assured them; and it was some seconds before I'd recovered myself sufficiently to realize that the blast and noise had been caused by the forward turret of HMS *Decoy*, which had crept level with *Suvla* and then stopped only twenty yards to starboard to fire her main armament. An unexpected multi-gun salvo from naval 4.5's just sixty feet from one's right ear is liable to be a little stupefying; but even this didn't prevent me from feeling extremely foolish.

When he stood up again something of Clark's feelings must have conveyed itself to the marine training major who was in command of this first wave of the assault. 'When I looked behind me I saw he had joisted himself up in the stern of the buffalo and was sitting there, unconcernedly smoking a cigarette. As he saw me look at him, he gave a huge grin and a thumbs-up sign.'[8]

The shelling from the destroyers stopped as the landing craft came inshore, but the jet fighters continued straffing the beaches until the last two minutes of the approach.

The airmen must have appreciated the position, for they approached from our right, and instead of circling to begin their run from the left, they deliberately ran the risk of appearing over the French beaches at Port Fuad as they pulled out. Used as I was to the strafing of piston-engined planes during the war I was taken completely by surprise at the speed of these jet fighters. In the short time it took us to travel the last hundred yards, each fighter did two runs. Although I was happy to see them, I began to feel that we and they were drawing much too close to each other during their second run, and I was very thankful to see the last one climb almost vertically away as we grounded and the tracks took over to haul us out of the water and on to the soft beach.[9]

But now there was another frightening prospect.

The square hulks of the Buffaloes rose out of the water and roared up the beach, with extra speed from the absence of armour plating, which should have been but was not provided for and with Bren guns blazing to silence enemy machine gunners on either flank. The amphibians careered past the blazing huts where ammunition was exploding amid abandoned equipment and other items left behind by the Egyptian Army. The Buffaloes jerked to a halt. The men jumped out at commando speed, their green berets bobbing about as they swiftly and quickly forced their way into the Casino Palace Hotel.[10]

Douglas Clark's buffalo trundled across the sand towards a gap between the beach huts.

Our progress seemed pitifully slow as I stood there with flames on either side, and smoke billowing about me. At last, however, we were through and out into the sunlight once again. We bumped over the low kerb of the coast road, and the tracks ground on the tarmac as we slewed left to pull up in front of a school building. We had made our first objective with nothing more than one short burst of three or four bullets hitting the side of the buffalo.[11]

Other commandos came up against stronger opposition.

At last we were on dry land and moved forward towards the beach huts, where we stopped just before the road under the last of the huts and there we took up firing positions, lying in the sand under the last of them. In front, on the other side of the road, were the first buildings of the city. The floor of the hut was about 5 ft. above me, and my only cover was one of the hut's legs, a vertical piece of wood about 4 inches square. We were in a rather exposed position, and needed to cross the road and start clearing the buildings on the other side of it. However, at this point we did not have enough men ashore, and had to wait for more men to come ashore from the landing craft. The man lying next to me, on my right, was so close that I had trouble operating the bolt of my rifle and I asked him to move a bit. At this point a machine gun started firing from our right front. The bullets hit him in the right shoulder, came out below his left waist, and must have just missed my feet.[12]

The second wave of assault landing craft stopped short of the beach and commandos had to wade 30 yards to get ashore.

The tanks soon followed. But there was a delay when it was found that the bolts holding on their waterproofing had rusted. It took half an hour to clear away the waterproofing with the aid of sledgehammers. And all the time Egyptian snipers were getting used to the realisation that the British were slow to fire at civilians, even those carrying rifles.

With so many armed irregulars out and about, every house was a prospective hide for snipers. Having cleared the school that confronted them when their Buffalo ground to a halt, Douglas Clark's men turned their attention to a large, grey house next door.

It was then that somebody shot at them from one of the windows. This immediately altered the complexion of things. Where, formerly, they'd been intending to enter and search, and then pass on their way quickly, doing no damage, they now became a fighting patrol. Dropping to cover behind the basin of a fountain, some fired at the windows, while the sergeant in charge shouted to one of his men, 'Open that fucking front door!'

'What, me, Sarge? Without a key?'

'What the 'ell d'you think that is in your 'and?'

The commando was carrying a bazooka – an anti-tank weapon. For a second he looked at the bazooka, and then, with a delighted grin, he loaded it with an explosive bomb, lay flat, and took aim round the side of the basin.

As a way of opening the front door, it was most effective.

Because it was an armour-piercing bomb, the missile passed through the door, carrying the lock with it, before bursting inside the house. The Commandos' charge flung the two leaves aside, and the whole section was inside without having to pause on the doorstep.

The search took ten minutes only. I heard a few bursts of Sten and then the section returned, shepherding a sorry bunch of four prisoners which one Commando steered towards the cages which had been set up on the beach; the others galloped off to their next task.[13]

Peter Mayo's troops had to clear a wood and an ice factory. In the wood ('small and bushy') were Egyptian army vehicles, anti-tank guns and crated rocket-launchers.

In fact a bazooka was fired from there at the leading tank as it came up the road. It set fire to the tank commander's jacket, but did no other damage. Soon afterwards an air strike came in on all the immediate area which silenced any activity there. But it makes me shudder to think what might have happened if the Wogs had been properly organised.[14]

But Mayo was soon in for a narrower scrape.

Bullets were still flying, some whickering past high-up, and some nearer with that venomous crack. For some reason I found myself walking along quite casually, having got, I suppose, into a frame of mind where, not actually seeing who was shooting at us, one didn't believe the bullets were actually aimed at oneself person-ally. We got down in the lee of a long, low, white building – some sort of offices. At the corner lay two Egyptians, one horribly shot up in the stomach and legs, being patched up by a medical orderly though obviously dying. The other was sprawled with a bullet hole in his head. I noticed he was barefoot. A tank moved with us down the exposed wall of the building which was open to sniper fire, and stopped outside the main door. 4 and 5 sections went in, and I followed with 1 and 2. We imagined the others had cleared the ground floor. I was standing in the hall when a burst of fire came through the door of a room just up a corridor, in which it seemed 3 or 4 Wogs had locked themselves. Marine Ditchfield had a pocket of his smock ripped open by a bullet which however didn't touch him. Someone then tried to throw a grenade through a stove-in panel, but in a state of nervous tension hit the top of the door with it, and it bounced back into the passage. There was a marked increase in activity, and somehow everyone managed to get behind a corner somewhere before it went off. A second one was successfully thrown in but failed to explode. A third followed. I was waiting for the explosion when suddenly it appeared on the floor a couple of yards away from me, rolling gently towards me, having been thrown out again by the Wogs – a good effort on their part I must say. With a four-second fuse, that didn't give me much time, I was diving for the door when it went off. Simultaneously I felt a sting on my left cuff and a fairly healthy sort of crack on the back of my head. Soggers who was just outside the door said I turned as white as a sheet for an instant, and he thought I had bought it, as the saying is. I put my hand up and when I failed to find my brains gushing out realised it was nothing bad though there was a fairly convincing stream of blood. Someone told me to get down behind the hull of the tank, and Dec Milton fixed me up with a field dressing which stopped the bleeding.[15]

There were those who found it too chancy to advance on foot.

At 9am, Lt.-Col. Norcock re-embarked two troops of 42nd Commando into the Buffaloes and with tank escort, ahead and behind, led them full tilt up the Rue Mohammed Aly, a wide road flanked by high houses. Egyptians opened up from windows and side roads at some points with women and children around them, and the tanks blazed back with their Brownings and the Commandos with Brens from the top of the Buffaloes. Two anti-tank guns were blasted out by the tanks and more overrun, as they emerged into open territory at the end of the road. The Buffaloes followed with some dead and wounded when the gas works were captured, and then a fight near the prison from which the inmates had been let loose. Egyptian troops were in considerable numbers but soon dispersed from an air strike; the route was clear now to the French at the waterworks. Egyptian self-propelled guns had made an attempt to break out along the causeway, and an air strike was called in to knock them out.[16]

It was the turn of the helicopters. While by 10 a.m. the seaborne commandos had achieved most of their objectives, snipers were still active, often returning to buildings that had been cleared less than an hour earlier. Lieutenant Colonel Tailyour flew ahead to check out a secure landing zone. With low visibility caused by black smoke drifting from a blazing oil depot and lesser fires, the recce pilot had a hard job finding a suitable spot to set down. When a football stadium emerged through the smog, he took his chance. Tailyour and his commando team jumped out and the helicopter took off.

It was then that a burst of small-arms fire revealed that the stadium was still in Egyptian hands. Fortunately, the pilot realised what was happening and landed again to rescue his passengers. He was more successful with his second attempt at identifying a safe landing. It was on the waterfront close by the de Lesseps statue, the most famous landmark in Port Said. A radio signal to the carriers 8 miles offshore started the airlift.[17]

Marine Ashton was below decks on HMS *Ocean* waiting impatiently to board and not knowing the reason for the unexpected delay.

> From my position, I could just make out the helicopter rotor blades, their tips still tied down with guy ropes to the flight deck. We clearly were not going anywhere for the moment. The waiting by now had become intolerable and our loads heavier and heavier; would we never go?
>
> Minutes later, I looked up again. The blade covers were off! The rotor blades were turning, the throaty roar of the engines reaching down to us in the hangar. Semi-rigid bodies stirred into life, the first sticks of Rifle Troops moving forward on to the platform. Ding, ding, ding, rang the warning bell, as the lift rose up, obscuring once more our small patch of sky.
>
> We waited anxiously – and could just make out the roar of the engines as they took off; down came the lift again and we were ushered stiffly onto the platform, maintaining strict formation. Ding, ding, ding – up we rose steadily to the flight deck for our

first and desperately longed-for sight of the action. As the lift smoothed to a stop, white helmeted marshals led us smartly away to our pre-arranged station on one side of the flight deck. We squatted by a pile of anti-tank ammunition boxes, and for the first time were able to take in the dramatic scene that unfolded before us.

We were barely two or three miles off shore and roughly in line with the mouth of the canal. The skyline was dominated by an immense plume of heavy black smoke . . . A fringe of flame seemed to lick from the beach itself, consuming the dozens of small wooden huts set just back from the water's edge.[18]

There was not much time to take in the view before six helicopters were back preparing for the next trip.

No sooner had we spotted them flying in close formation low above the choppy water, than they were swooping around the ship and coming in to land in perfect order on the restricted oblong of the flight deck. The noise and downdraft of six choppers descending together was cataclysmic. Barely had the machines sunk down on their undercarriages than the marshals shepherded each stick into its allotted craft, each marked with a massive white identifying letter on its blunt nose.

We scrambled in as fast as we dared, trying not to over-balance our loads, and at the same time trying to maintain the reverse order necessary for the fast exit at the other end. We squatted awkwardly on the cabin floor, facing out of the open door, and held our breath as the flight lifted together in a shattering, roaring scream of engines on maximum power.

We circled briefly to link up with the others of our wave and those from 'Theseus', the helicopters banking steeply and causing us to slide towards the open door. We braced ourselves with our feet and hung on. During this alarming moment there was a tap on my shoulder . . . conversation was impossible in any chopper – and a finger pointed at two fighters heading straight towards us. Were they hostile? The sea rippled below us; if we went down with this load of old iron strapped to our backs, no life belt in the world would save us, let alone the puny tubes that we had strapped on like women's brassieres. The fighters lifted and passed over us; they must have been ours after all.

The shore line rushed up towards us before I had time to think further . . . We descended into a whirling, choking, blinding cloud of white dust. The landing zone was nothing more than a cleared building site; the downdraft from each wave of 22 choppers creating an opaque whirling fog in which the pilots had to find the ground. I could see nothing, but as I felt the bump, I leapt as bravely and as purposefully as I could manage, out into the dust cloud.

I fell flat on my face, pinned to the ground by my load. I could not see, but felt the other members of the stick crash out over the top of me. The noise of the choppers as they powered up and away from us seemed even greater than before, and then quickly receded, leaving a spluttering, staggering pile of Marines to untangle themselves and get to their feet. We had landed.[19]

It was worse for those who landed on sand, as Second Lieutenant Nicholas Vaux, later Major-General Vaux, recalls.

Now, what happens when you land on sand in helicopters is that you see absolutely nothing at all. I mean, you can imagine, it is absolutely . . . the noise and the dust that is thrown up, it is complete disorientation. And, of course, if people are not accustomed to it, not trained to it, it can be very frightening as well. So that's exactly the situation we discovered, with, I should think in the first wave of helicopters, up to a dozen helicopters landing on a fairly restricted part of the beach, and the amount of sand and debris blown up was sufficient to completely blank out any other activity. As we were trained to do, we got out of the helicopter, grabbed our rucksacks, and ran forward a few feet, and then lay down so that the helicopters could deploy without hopefully injuring anybody. And then you waited for the dust to subside.

When it did so in front of me, I realised to my serious alarm that only a few feet away there was somebody standing, presumably looking down on me in a hostile manner. As I was wondering exactly what to do, I recognised that actually, from the puttees that he was wearing, he must be British. Indeed, he was a Royal Marine; in fact, he turned out to be my rather patronising friend, Roger Leroyd, who was the Brigadier's military assistant, who said: 'How nice to see you here, Nick. I think if you get your chaps up and walk to the road, you'll find everybody else is waiting for you.'[20]

Lifted in from HMS *Theseus*, David Henderson had an equally uncomfortable landing.

'Out! Out!' screamed a voice from somewhere, and like an elephant relieving itself after a particularly heavy meal we poured out the door of the craft landing on top of one another and spread out on the sand. Off went our transport in what seemed a rather hasty exit and as it made its way back for its next bundle of nervous men with the sound of its engines slowly diminishing we became aware of the sounds of small arms fire. Our sergeant and corporal marshalled us together and we moved up to form a line along a promenade wall where we laid out our forward markers (this was a series of vivid coloured strips that troops would lay out in the form of arrows indicating to any supporting fighter plane the forward positions we had reached). This had hardly been finished when there was a terrifying scream of engines and a blur of explosions as one of our own Navy attack fighters did a strafing run straight up the beach. It has never been explained to me how a pilot supporting a beach landing that had been progressing for some time could possibly think to track his run straight along the water's edge. Thankfully no one in our squad was hit but many boys in a following wave of choppers caught the brunt of the attack.[21]

Dependent on erratic radio equipment, coordination between land and air forces could be tricky. When it was in the hands of inexperienced controllers, it could lead to tragedy. Ground liaison officer T. W. Whittaker was at his observation post on the roof of a police station on the west bank of the canal.

> HQ 40 Commando was in the same building. From there my view to the west was blocked by tall buildings but I could see the general area where 45 Commando had landed. I saw a Wyvern from 830 Squadron circling the area. I was listening on the Ground Attack Common channel and heard a pilot report to HMS *Meon* that he could see some troops and a couple of A/Tk guns and gave a grid reference. As these troops were inside the 'Bomb Line', he asked for permission to attack. By the time I got the position indicated by the pilot plotted on my map, I could see that they must be 45 Commando. In the mean time the controller in *Meon* had instructed the pilot to attack. I tried to call up the aircraft on Ground Attack Common to abort the attack but was unable to make contact . . . As this target was clearly inside the 'Bomb Line', it should not have been engaged without reference to the troops on the ground . . . If there had been any difficulty making contact on the Ground Attack Net, the controller could have made contact via the Brigade Command Net or the Air Request Net. This tragedy was entirely due to the fact that the controller had not taken part in any of the work-up exercises and did not know the rules. The Wyvern pilot was not to blame.[22]

One marine was killed and fifteen wounded. Nicholas Vaux was there.

> It was one of those moments when order is either restored or not, and this is where training and, I suppose, leadership count for more than anything. I particularly recall the Adjutant, who had realised that his own Commanding Officer was badly wounded and one or two others of his friends, but also saw that his own Signaller had been killed, his own Signaller had been virtually blown in half by a cannon blast, and he turned to the nearest Marine to him and said: 'Take the radio set off Marine

Atkins and put it on, and come with me,' just like that. And, in an extraordinary way, everybody realised that this was what you had to do, you had to get on with it, and this is terribly important in battle, these kinds of reactions.[23]

After the shock of friendly fire, what happened next to David Henderson was, as he said, like something out of a Carry On movie.

We were all lined up behind this wall fearfully taking in the area in front of us over which we were getting ready to move. Over the road was a line of buildings, mostly blocks of flats, which were all linked together by a wall with one or two gates in them, and we were all squinting at the doors and windows straining to catch a site of the 'enemy'. Nothing moved and we were sure that surely with all the activity on the beach any defenders would have moved back but you never know. Suddenly a figure holding a rifle appeared as if from nowhere right in front of us and began to trot along the length of this wall. Without waiting, we all opened up on him blazing away with great gusto. He stopped dead in his tracks and stared at us, and without thinking we also stopped firing. Then he was off again, this time as fast as his feet could go, and off we went again firing at him with a trail of bullet holes following his track and dust flying all around him. He must have been very good at his prayers that morning because not one of us hit him and he scampered round the end of the buildings and out of sight. Our sergeant by this time was going crazy stamping his feet in the sand and crying out for us to cease fire and take aim all at the same time.

Once he got us under control we got the bollocking of our lives . . . I often wonder if some Egyptian officer was watching the beach through his binoculars trying to work out what tactic was being planned with this squad of Marines sitting in a row on the sand with an NCO lecturing and waving his hands about. It was a different set of men that crossed the road after that incident, as nothing beats reality for teaching someone the facts of life.[24]

Another story of near-farce comes from Nicholas Vaux, whose troop found themselves in the grounds of Government House.

> Now, at this point in time, there was still a lot of fighting going on around us, but not actually directly in our area. Government House looked just like you'd expect Government House to look in Port Said or anywhere else in the world – immaculate lawns, raked gravel and white portico entrance. And, just as I was looking at all this, around the corner, with his rifle at the shoulder, appeared an immaculate, elderly Egyptian soldier. Now, actually he wasn't a soldier, he was obviously one of the guards at Government House. And what he was trying to do, I realised, was to come and report to me. But I was temporarily distracted, because all the chaps around, particularly the Corporal of the section that I was standing beside, were hell-bent on killing him. Anyway, we managed to prevent that, and he did actually, in perfect English, hand over Government House to me. I think he was actually quite glad to see the British back.[25]

The latest occupant took time out to examine his surroundings. Government House was deserted.

> And as I was walking through the main hallway to go out the other side, the phone rang. Well, it was irresistible, really, so I answered it. And a rather sort of muffled voice, in Egyptian, spoke to me, and I apologised that I didn't speak Egyptian, but said that if they could speak English, could I help? And the voice said: 'You are English?' So I said: 'Yes.' He said: 'You are soldier?' So I said: 'No, I'm a Royal Marine actually.' He said: 'My God!' and put the phone down. And I've never known to this day who it was. Perhaps it was Colonel Nasser.[26]

In all, the helicopters put ashore 479 men with 24 tons of stores and equipment in two and a half hours. It was not, as some claimed, a first in military annals. French paratroops in Indo-China and Algeria had taken part in similar operations and helicopters had been used in Cyprus for surprise attacks on EOKA guerrillas. But there were not many precedents that could begin to match the Suez lift. After delivering their commandos the helicopters were employed in carrying back the wounded. Ninety-six casualties were taken on board *Ocean* and *Theseus*. In close on two hundred landings, one helicopter crashed on deck and one had to ditch when it ran out of fuel. The helicopter was lost but the occupant, including two seriously wounded French soldiers, were rescued by another helicopter.

While the commandos were engaged in what they called 'street cleaning' exercises, the British troops who had parachuted in the previous day were still having a rough time. After being strafed by an Egyptian MiG, the only hostile plane to be seen on the 6th, there was a return to the cemeteries where snipers had re-established themselves. Repeating the previous day's work, they then moved on towards Shanty Town and the rather more salubrious district of Arab Town. With their narrow streets and jumble of hideaways both were potential death traps for unwelcome intruders. As a warning to snipers to move out, heavy weapons were called into play. They were used with due care but a single shell from a destroyer started a fire at one end of Shanty Town while at the opposite end an anti-tank gun caused another fire. With no means of putting out the blaze, the whole ramshackle maze of improvised huts was soon alight. While Shanty Town burned to the ground its occupants swelled the ranks of the refugees moving south.

Reinforced from the sea by the First Foreign Legion Parachute Regiment, the French paratroops who had landed at Port Fuad on the 5th were able to hold the town without much difficulty, though there was continued fighting at the Raswa bridge, the main escape route from Port Said, which the Egyptian forces were intent on recapturing. Determined as they were, they did not stand a chance.

When French and British forces encountered each other it was almost as if they were fighting different wars. They were on the same side but there was little in the way of mutual understanding or even sympathy. And it was not just a problem of language.

A Foreign Language parachute battalion near us had the air and absorbed swagger of established killers. Some thirty per cent of them were German ex-panzers and Vermacht and perhaps even SS. They had generally not stopped fighting somewhere since the 1940s. On greeting one with the conventional salute they would thump their rubber boots together and say 'You wish to see my captain?' with the accent of a bad English actor in a war movie. They clearly regarded us as boy scouts.[27]

As if to confirm Captain Roger Booth's impression, Pierre Leulliette tells a story that mocks the British desire to conduct a war without involving civilians.

Along the canal, in front of the barracks, a dozen big barges and sailing-boats were moored. We hadn't time to notice them the previous day. That was where all the noise was coming from. We dashed over, with loaded automatic rifles. A dozen fishermen, hiding in a bolt-hole, let themselves be taken by surprise.

Hands in the air, yelling something or other in their own language, they were trying to prove that they weren't soldiers. It was in fact probable that, caught the morning we arrived in the thick of our lines, all they could do was hide in their boats to avoid the bullets. But: 'No unnecessary prisoners! They're a nuisance and a waste of food!' A voice in the hearts of some of my comrades was whispering: 'Kill! Kill!' They had hardly slept and hadn't had time to drink their coffee, so they were in a foul temper that morning.

We emptied our magazines. The fishermen fell into the water, one by one. Very soon, only two were left. Realizing they were lost, they dived in and tried to hide alongside their boats. Première Classe L. had obviously never had such fun. To show he was a real 'tough', he climbed on to the last boat. No one there. He leant over the side. He knelt down. He was waiting for the moment when the two gasping men would have to show their heads. After a few minutes, a face emerged. 'Rat-a-tat-tat!' went Première Classe L.'s automatic rifle. The head disappeared, riddled and shot to pieces at point-blank range. Three minutes went by and the head again appeared, streaming with blood and water, a horrible sight. Another burst. The water covered it for good. A large, pink bloodstain slowly spread on the surface and then dispersed. The same fate for the second man, who also emerged from the water, with the same shaven head and eyes bulging in terror of death, and the same concentric circles and crimson reflections . . .[28]

As with the contrast between British and French troops, so it was with the press representatives of the two nations. Roger Booth made the acquaintance of a French reporter.

He sported a combat jacket, a ring in his ear and he looked quite hippy compared with our uniformed Fleet Street men. He was highly experienced and had covered the Algerian war. He had been appalled by the demonstrations in Trafalgar Square. He regarded them as a sign of our increasing British decadence. Our military posture also bewildered him. British vehicles frequently had grenades thrown at them. Soldiers would dismount, ring the doorbell of the offending house and enquire of the householder 'Excuse me, do you mind if we go upstairs? Someone has just thrown a grenade at us from the roof.' French reactions were inevitably more severe. In Port Fuad solely occupied by the French on the opposite side of the canal few Arabs could be seen. They were all indoors. A canal pilot who had a flat there claimed a French Legion officer had said to him 'if you want anyone killed just let us know'.

'Only the British would invent rules for war as if it were some nasty game of cricket,' my French correspondent said. 'War is total, absolute. Who invents the rules for it? I invent stories . . .'[29]

Of course, British correspondents were not alone in inventing or at least elaborating on stories, particularly when the message was heart-warming.

At one time, in Port Said, an old lady, wearing black clothes from head to toe, became tangled up in the barbed wire while taking what she thought was a short cut. With some difficulty I at last managed to untangle her, and then helped her across the rubble. Later, my Mother sent me a picture from the English magazine 'Picture Post', which I am sure was of this incident. However, they had put a caption on saying, 'Don't cry, the shooting is over for now', which of course I never said.[30]

Then one of the few publications to make the most of news photography, *Picture Post* led the way on 'human' stories.

His eyes were the eyes of an animal who was caged, frightened, furtive and imploring his captors for some understanding. He was wearing pyjamas which is not as unusual as it sounds, for here in Egypt people wear pyjamas quite normally in the streets. He also wore a bloodstained bandage around his hand as he squatted in a courtyard corner. He had been a soldier, but he had not been taught to surrender. He had sniped at British soldiers and now they had taken him prisoner. When I first saw him, a British Marine Commando corporal was offering him a cup of tea, but the prisoner was trembling so violently with his fear and his wounds that the tea spilled on the ground. The corporal lit a cigarette for him.

Presently a doctor came in and the Egyptian lowered his pyjama trousers, revealing his uniform and another bullet wound in his leg. He seemed convinced now that he would not be killed – as he had been told he would if he surrendered. As we were standing there we heard again the echo of a rifle shot in the next square and his trembling got worse. 'Nasser never taught these fellows to surrender,' said the corporal. 'They were told to get into civilian clothes and keep fighting.' I reckon that in a 'normal' war this prisoner would have been shot on sight for sniping in civilian clothes. But this time the sad little double-wounded figure is herded into an ambulance and death has been thwarted – even in this 'pyjama war' where the enemy wears night dress for a uniform.[31]

The link-up between French and British forces took place close to the offices of the Suez Canal Company. That building was captured by commandos without too much difficulty but the surrounding warehouses were strongly defended and two died on the British side before they were overrun with the help of point-blank fire from Centurion tanks.

But the hardest resistance centred on Navy House, an imposing, solid edifice that had at one time served as the head-quarters for the Royal Navy. There was no question of storming a building that was clearly in the hands of fighters who were prepared to go the whole distance. It was a job for the Fleet Air Arm, as it happened their last of the campaign. As the order went out, Donald Edgar of the *Daily Express* was leaning on a ship's rail as it edged its way towards a jetty at the entrance to the canal.

> The scene of destruction along the water-front cleared through the smoke. Crumbled masonry, blackened walls still standing with nothing behind, burnt-out vehicles, debris scattered over the road. A few soldiers hurried to and fro, but the firing – rifle and machine-gun and mortar – seemed to be concentrated a few hundred yards down the Canal. The captain had a radio set on the bridge tuned to the BBC and we heard a bland voice announcing that all resistance had ceased in Port Said. It was just then when with a great scream that froze me in terror, a section of naval fighter-bombers dived down over us dropping their rockets and firing their cannon just ahead of us. Almost quicker than sight they wheeled away into the sky while clouds of grey smoke rose into the air. We were all silent on the bridge for a minute or two.[32]

Even after this attack, the defenders fought on. A commando officer told Edgar that in the end they had to be cleared out room by room. It was not until the next day that twenty survivors gave themselves up. Thirty of the original garrison had been killed.

There was some impatience at senior level – political and mili-tary – that it had taken the full day to bring Port Said under allied control. The cumbersome nature of the plan of attack, which failed to allow for the flexibility urged by the French commanders, was now apparent. The previous day British sappers who had dropped with the French had ventured 6 miles down the road towards Qantara without encountering any opposition. Massu did not disguise his anger at the failure to use Gamil airfield for rapid air reinforcement. Why all the fuss clearing Port Said of snipers when the town could simply have been bypassed by a force determined to win possession of the canal?

In fairness to Stockwell there was an occasion when he must have believed that he was about to be vindicated. A message came through from Brigadier Butler that there was another chance to negotiate a ceasefire, this time through the good offices of Count Vincente Moreni, the Italian consul. Moreni had turned his home, and office and the Italian school next door into a refugee centre for the European residents of Port Said, who naturally assumed that they were at risk. But Moreni also had good contacts with the Egyptians, and if he thought that a surrender was in prospect he was to be taken seriously. Accordingly, Stockwell and Beaufre, with Barnett and Durnford-Slater, loaded themselves into a landing craft and were ferried ashore. Unfortunately, and beginning a chapter of accidents, the launch made for the Canal Company offices, which were then still held by the Egyptians. Hugo Maynell, Stockwell's ADC, was the first to acknowledge the hostile reception.

> I suddenly looked over my right shoulder, and there was a commando platoon attacking across some roofs to the right. And I said to Hughie Stockwell: 'I think we've got a bit in front of it all.' And he laughed. Anyway, we were machine-gunned. There was a sailor in the front, with this pretty heavy machine gun, and I think he came spinning backwards. He wasn't wounded, but I think he got clipped on his helmet. And quite a lot of the woodwork disappeared between Dick Worsley and me.[33]

According to Stockwell the prize comment was delivered by Admiral Durnford-Slater. 'You know, General, I don't think they are quite ready to receive us yet.'[34] While a more hospitable landing place was sought, Beaufre reflected on the chance passed up by the Egyptians of capturing the entire allied senior command.

When eventually the delegation found their way to the Italian consulate it was to discover that the opportunity for a ceasefire, if it had ever existed, had evaporated. From the varying accounts it is uncertain even whether Brigadier Moguy, who had led the Egyptian side in the earlier negotiations, was even in the building. Beaufre claimed that there was an Egyptian representative who was too exhausted to make sense, but Stockwell maintained that 'after hanging around for some time for someone to turn up, we abandoned the idea'. While still on land Stockwell gave his orders for the following day. 'In brief they were for the 15th Parachute Brigade under Brigadier Butler to break out south from the causeway and move to the capture of Abu Sueir airfield. The French under General Massu, with seaborne and airborne assaults, were to capture Ismailia. The Royal Marine Commandos were to clear up and consolidate the town.'[35]

They were orders destined not to be carried out.

22

Stockwell's return to his command ship was a journey to remember. He wanted a helicopter, but that was thought to be too risky because it was already getting dark. Since nobody had thought to lay on a launch, the general and three companions were compelled to walk the quayside looking for a vessel to commandeer. 'We found a couple of marines cleaning out an assault craft so we piled into that and said, "Take us out to *Tyne*." And, of course, at that point the fleet blacked out as it did every night in case Egyptian frogmen got it into their heads to plant limpet mines.'[1]

That might have been the moment to turn back, but one of the marines was convinced that he knew a short cut through the breakwater to the open sea, and after that, it was agreed, finding *Tyne* would be easy. Stockwell recorded what happened next.

We set off, but no sooner were we through the breakwater than we ran into a heavy sea; the wind had whipped up the waves as they ran on to the shelving beaches. It was pitch dark. Then the pumps went out of action and the steering-gear broke, and soon we were banging up and down with the sea spraying over us. It was impossible to find our way back through the breakwater and it seemed we had little hope of making *Tyne*. Major Worsley exercised his somewhat limited knowledge of the Morse code with an Aldis lamp to attract someone's attention.

We altered course to the north to try to keep the sea on our beam and to work our way parallel to the Canal so that eventually we could get back into it and its quiet waters. Suddenly we spotted a starboard light high up on our beam. Evidently some big ship and she was almost stationary. The coxswain managed

to manoeuvre us under her lee. A light was flashed on us and a
hail from the bridge with an encouraging voice called: 'Who are
you? This is *Tyne*.' A stroke of luck indeed for a temporarily lost
commander. It would have been an inglorious, moderate end to
our adventure to be left wallowing about in the sea. Willing sailors
soon hoisted us aboard. I found that the Admiral was a bit touchy
about where I had been and what I had been up to.[2]

Criticism was in order. Stockwell, along with his deputy, had
been out of radio contact for the best part of five hours. Yet this
was only one of many examples of the amateurish way in which
communications were handled. *Tyne* had only ten wireless channels for all three armed services. Three of these were equipped
for teleprinters and just one had an online cipher facility. The
recommended minimum was thirty-one wireless channels.

The main Receiving Room was one deck below the Traffic
Office, which was one deck below the Operations Room. The
most efficient method which could be devised for passing signals
from the Receiving Room to the Signal Office was by a runner,
or by a string and bucket; and by runner from Signal Office to
Operations Room. Limited space available for aerial systems
created an acute frequency problem and also mutual interference
between sets.[3]

In Hugo Meynell's account of Stockwell at sea, the last part
of the adventure was not quite so straightforward as his chief
made out.

Hughie Stockwell said: 'Have we got any lifebelts?' And I said:
'Yes, we've got one, and I'm standing on it!' – underwater, which
caused quite a lot of amusement. Anyway, we then had to get up
out of this ghastly thing. I can't be doing with heights and *Tyne*
was a very tall ship. They put scaling ladders down and of course
you were up 30 feet one minute and then down, so you'd get up
and grab, and then suddenly the thing would come up under-
neath you. Anyway, we all climbed on board.[4]

The end of an exhausting day, thought Stockwell, but there was more to come. 'All I wanted, at that moment, was a whisky and soda. But my Chief of Staff, Brigadier Darling, appeared holding an urgent signal. So urgent that he insisted on my taking it before doing anything else. I looked at the slip of paper. It read, "Cease-fire at midnight".' Stockwell went into shock. It was, he said, hard for him to take in the words, let alone grasp the full impact of the signal.

> I was cold and tired and wet, yet also exhilarated after seeing my soldiers in action all day at Port Said. We were on the verge of complete success. Wednesday, Nov. 7 would have found us well established on the Ismailia–Abu Sueir line. By Thursday night we surely would have been down to Suez. Lives had been lost, but Britain had shown her worth. Now, just as we were reaping the reward of all the effort and the months of preparation, we were to be thwarted of our prize.[5]

Beaufre too could not immediately bring himself to believe that the game was up. Having scrambled aboard the *Gustave-Zédé* after rolling about in the rough sea for over an hour, he assumed that the message from Barjot calling for a ceasefire was merely a typically over-hasty reaction to the negotiations that had just failed. The truth only dawned on Beaufre when he heard a BBC announcement that the fighting was over. The temptation to ignore the order was strong. In his 'suppressed rage' he imagined a short burst of energy for British and French forces, or even the French alone, to cover the rest of the distance between Port Said and Qantara and thus to control the entire length of the canal. Much the same thought occurred to Stockwell, though in his case he was inclined not so much to disobey the order as to follow it to the letter. Reverting from local time to Greenwich time gained more than two hours before midnight. Butler was told to make haste along the causeway with all the vehicles they could muster. When they ran out of time they had reached El Cap, less than 4 miles short of their objective. Stockwell was philosophical. 'Disappointments and setbacks have to be faced in life. There must be no recriminations. I had learnt this lesson when I was dropped from the Marlborough XI on the morning of our match against Rugby at Lord's. There is always something else ahead.'[6]

What was ahead for the troops at El Cap was a railway and an embankment, both, as far as anyone could see, undefended. 'There was a Swedish journalist who came by and asked why are you stopping here; there's no one between you and Suez. Then gradually Egyptian forces crept back and took up strong defensive positions along the embankment.'[7]

As frustration turned to grievance and to anger in the higher command, the feeling of let-down spread throughout the ranks. What were the politicians up to? Then, as later, few were willing to accept the simple, obvious explanation that the frail, vain, silly man who had started it all had finally lost his nerve.

No one can doubt the pressures on Eden. The Soviet threat of starting a third world war could be discounted as bravado bluster to distract attention from their own problems, but the public was made nervous, the more so because it was now general knowledge that the USA was not about to help Britain and France out of their self-made troubles, at least until they submitted to the will of the United Nations.

Even while the news of the military action at Suez was encouraging for the allies, those near Eden could see that he was close to breakdown. Patrick Reilly, a deputy under-secretary at the foreign office, was with the prime minister on the afternoon of 6 November. Bearing his draft reply to the Bulganin letter threatening war, he was admitted to the Cabinet Room.

> Eden was sitting there, and Lloyd was there too, not sitting but walking about the room. I put my draft reply before Eden, and I was there for an astonishingly long period of time, not less than three quarters of an hour, perhaps more. Eden started to look at my reply, and then his concentration wandered, and he would make inconsequential remarks, like: 'Poor Selwyn, how tired you must be.' Selwyn, I don't think, ever looked at the draft at all,

but he kept saying he must go to the House of Commons, where he had an appointment with the Venezuelan Ambassador. From time to time, Eden would look at my draft, and I remember him occasionally cutting out a sentence or two rather testily, but I don't remember him adding anything at all.[8]

By then, though Reilly did not know it, the decision to cease fire had already been taken. There was nowhere Eden could turn for comfort. His government was in disarray, the parliamentary opposition, unusually in a national emergency, was solidly against him, most of the oil-producing nations and nearly all the oil-importing countries were convinced that he was trying to wreck their economies, the Commonwealth, on which the Tories set great if exaggerated store, was lobbying against him, and from the UN, a near-desperate Pierson Dixon was warning of a joint resolution to impose sanctions on Britain and France if they did not agree to an immediate ceasefire. There were already indications that the USA would hold back on oil supplies to Europe if the fighting in Egypt continued, and Nasser's friends in the Middle East had already declared a comprehensive oil boycott. But the clincher was the prospect of a breakdown in confidence in the pound and a collapse of the sterling system.

Like the preservation of Anglo-French control over the canal, sterling was seen as a measure of Britain's international prestige. Also like the canal, sterling was associated with British prosperity. Given that it was a world currency, so the argument ran, failure to protect sterling would be to invite a collapse of industrial society and a catastrophic fall in living standards. The economic logic underpinning this assertion was never clearly spelt out, possibly because it could not bear serious analysis. Who, after all, could explain convincingly why it was so beneficial to hold interest rates high to support an overvalued currency (one pound was worth 2.80 dollars in 1956)? What the British economy needed was low interest rates to encourage investment and a weaker pound to give exporters an advantage in highly competitive markets. But the mythical virtues of a strong currency were so ingrained in official thinking (devaluation was the dirtiest word in the Treasury vocabulary) as to subjugate plain reason. Hence, when the pound wobbled and the Bank of England began to fear a run from the currency that would clear out its reserves, there was consternation in financial circles.

Macmillan was the first of the doom merchants. He had shared in the general misunderstanding of US policy, having persuaded himself that if the money market did react badly to the attack on Egypt, Washington would come to the rescue of the pound with a hefty loan from the International Monetary Fund. So confident was he that he made no approach to the IMF before the critical decision to invade was taken. Indeed, there had been some amusement at the haste with which France had secured its lifeline to the IMF. Now, as it dawned on Macmillan that America was not about to throw its financial weight behind sterling, he must have wished that he had followed the French example.

But was there any reason to act precipitately? In the first two days of November the Bank of England lost nearly £20 million, and losses continued to mount in the days that followed. Subsequently, Macmillan asserted, and it was a line followed by his official biographer, that it was this setback which persuaded him that the Suez operation had to be called off. At the crucial cabinet meeting on 6 November, 'He told the Cabinet that there had been a serious run on the pound, viciously orchestrated by Washington. Britain's gold reserves, he announced, had fallen by £100 million over the past week or by one eighth of their remaining total.'[9] Herbert Hoover, standing in for Dulles, was seen as the villain of the piece. As under-secretary of state he was responsible for foreign economic questions. Moreover:

> Hoover was a difficult man, in the sense that he was not accustomed to diplomatic negotiations – he was an oil executive. He was not particularly well disposed to the United Kingdom. He was not, at least at first, antagonistic, but he was not sympathetic. He not only had the handicap of no experience of the diplomatic world, but he was also very hard of hearing, and

that was a great handicap to him. The combination of these factors meant that he was both rather inflexible and rather obstinate.[10]

But for whatever panic was created Macmillan must take a large share of the blame. Unforgivably, the guardian of the nation's finances had his figures wrong. The treasury could not have lost £100 million in the time specified because on the day following his dramatic announcement, Macmillan was told by his civil servants that the loss for the week was just £30.4 million.[11] On the 16th, the treasury updated the figure to £71 million, while on the 20th Macmillan himself speculated that losses for the *month* 'might go as high as £107 million'.[12]

There can be little doubt that Macmillan misled his colleagues on 6 November. Britain's financial plight was nowhere near as serious as the chancellor made out. Yet it was on his say-so that Eden, Lloyd and Butler agreed to the UN demand for a ceasefire. Though the suspicion that it was all a Machiavellian plot to accelerate Eden's departure continues to surface, it is hard to see how Macmillan could have been sure that he would be the beneficiary. A more probable explanation is that Macmillan, despite his early hawkish sentiments, had convinced himself that the government was in an impossible position. Maybe he exaggerated the figures, maybe he muddled the figures. The certainty is that he feared a collapse of confidence that could ruin the country. In this he was seriously misguided.

The muddle theory gains credibility with the testimony of Roger Makins, who, after three years as ambassador to the USA, was appointed joint permanent secretary to the treasury. When in the second week of October he flew home to take up his new job he was surprised that no one in government seemed too interested in his arrival.

Although I was to be Harold Macmillan's principal official adviser, he was at Birch Grove and he didn't want to see me. I met Anthony Eden and his wife at a cocktail party soon after I returned, and he came over and said how delighted he was to see me back and that he hoped I would be happy in the Treasury and so on, but he did not want to talk about anything. It was a very odd situation.[13]

Being, as he said, 'an old Whitehall warrior', Makins soon found out what was going on, and when, eventually, Macmillan sent for him to reveal that the invasion force was at sea, he put up a warning signal.

> What about the Americans? What have you done in Washington about all this? Then he suddenly came to, as it were. I suggested that we had better take some pretty urgent action in Washington about all this, and we drafted some telegrams, although I don't know if they were ever sent. I then went back and prepared for the worst. I suggested that I should talk to Norman Brook about it, but Macmillan said that I could not talk to anyone. I then said that I had to talk to the Secretary of the Cabinet [Brook] about these issues, and he said: 'Oh, very well.' I then went back, and we set up a sort of little committee of Permanent Secretaries, which, as soon as the war was over, met regularly to deal with the economic consequences.[14]

Even if he had got his figures right, Macmillan was almost certainly in a stronger position than he imagined. However tough the American stance, it was unlikely to have been sustained to the point of allowing the downfall of sterling. The effect on world markets, with so many countries holding sterling reserves, could easily have produced harmful fallout for the American economy. At the same time a Suez-induced devaluation of sterling would have served Britain well. Apart from making exports more competitive, it would have increased the cost of imports, a welcome corrective for a country with a serious balance of payments problem. The price of oil would have had to go up but, contrary to popular conception, cheap energy is not the sole determinant of economic growth. If there were many good reasons for ending the Suez adventure, the fear of a financial Armageddon was not one of them. But tied as it was to nineteenth-century economics, the British government was putty for America to mould as it pleased.

At 9.45 a.m. on 6 November, Eden addressed the cabinet. Alongside him was Sir William Dickson, chairman of the chiefs of staff. No one had to be told the subject to be discussed. In the UN America was backing the almost unanimous call for economic sanctions against Britain and France. Macmillan then weighed in with his misleading and inaccurate account of Britain's finances. There was only one way to stave off national ruin – or so it was claimed by Eden and Macmillan. The responsibility for the shame of it all was loaded on to the USA. In the following weeks anti-Americanism became more virulent than at any time since the early post-war years, when GIs had defied the austerity of Britain and France with their wads of dollar bills and their talent for snatching the best girls.

In seeking to escape responsibility for what one observer called an 'eruption of the irrational', the politicians pointed the finger at Eisenhower and Dulles. 'If they had not led the pack against us,' opined Selwyn Lloyd, 'I think that the international situation would have been tenable until we had the Canal, and then we would have been in the position to bargain for an agreement.' Lloyd made these comments twenty years on from Suez, when he was still holding to the illusion created in early November 1956 that had Nasser been overthrown there would have been no Six Days War or Yom Kippur War and that peace would have prevailed across the Middle East.[15] More immediate reaction came from Julian Amery. 'The British have never before been treated so badly by an ally.'[16]

Having made the decision to call off the war, Eden faced the embarrassment of breaking the news to Mollet. The French prime minister was not entirely unaware of Eden's capacity for double dealing, but hearing of a ceasefire just at the point of an allied victory still came as a stupefying blow. Pineau was with Mollet when the call came through. 'After a few seconds Mollet passed the telephone to me . . . I heard the broken voice of a man who was at the end of his tether and ready to let himself sink.'[17]

Mollet's first assumption was that Eden had lost his nerve in the face of the Soviet threat. Playing for time, he summoned the American ambassador, Douglas Dillon, to the Matignon Palace. He was asked a straight question. If Britain and France were attacked by Russia, would the USA come to thier aid? Mollet must have known the answer. It had been made clear often enough. The choice between Russia and Europe was, for Eisenhower, no choice at all. The communists were the first enemy. But if Mollet believed that this assurance would be enough to steady Eden's nerve, he was disappointed. Even while Mollet and Dillon were conferring, Eden came back on the line to declare that there was no going back on the ceasefire. Mollet begged for a delay of two or three days on the final decision. Eden refused. While Mollet remained relatively calm, Pineau matched the British response with a diatribe against the USA. The stories he put about, including a totally unsubstantiated pronouncement that on 3 November Nasser had been ready to resign until the American ambassador had assured him of US support, were, said Dillon, 'past belief'.[18]

It was now the turn of the UN to get in on the act. Eden's message to Dag Hammarskjöld was couched in a way that suggested not so much a climb-down as a willing handover of responsibilities that up to now Britain and France had carried alone. Implicit was the assumption that the two countries would have UN approval to participate in the peacekeeping force proposed by Canada. As a start, British and French salvage teams could begin work on clearing the canal. But on 7 November the General Assembly resolved that UN involvement in the next stage of the Suez drama was dependent on the withdrawal of Anglo-French and Israeli forces. Clearly, a face-saving compromise would not be easy to achieve.

Falling back on his diplomatic charm, Eden rounded off a telephone conversation with the second time elected American president – Eisenhower had won 457 electoral votes against seventy-four for his Democratic challenger – with a suggestion that he and Mollet take an early opportunity to visit Washington.

Buoyed up by his victory and by the news that hostilities had ended in Egypt, Eisenhower was friendly and welcoming. 'Sure, come on over,' he told Eden.[19]

The presidential advisers were less enthusiastic. Hoover was in the Oval Office while Eisenhower was taking the London call. Care must be taken, he said, not to give the impression that the USA was teaming up with Britain and France. The risk was of a turn-about by the Arabs that would put them in opposition to Hammarskjöld's efforts to set up a peacekeeping force. Consulted by telephone, Dulles backed his deputy. Eisenhower took the point. By telephone and cable, he made his excuses to Eden. While agreeing that 'we should meet at an early date', he went on to say:

> Now that the election is over, I find it most necessary to consult urgently the leaders of both Houses of the Congress. As you can understand, it will take some days to accomplish this. Furthermore, after a thorough study of all the factors and after talking to various branches of the government here, I feel that while such a meeting should take place quickly, we must be sure that its purpose and aims are not misunderstood in other countries. This would be the case if the UN Resolution had not yet been carried out.[20]

There was broad agreement in the Eisenhower administration that nothing much could be achieved in the Middle East until France and Britain were out of Egypt and Israeli forces were back behind the armistice lines. Handshakes with Eden and Mollet in front of the press cameras were not on the agenda while interpretation of the UN ceasefire resolution was open to debate. It was easy enough for the USA to put pressure on Britain to accede to UN demands. The ceasefire having heralded Britain's economic vulnerability, a word here and there from treasury secretary George Humphrey that economic help for Britain was strictly conditional was enough to cause jitters in the financial markets and despair in Downing Street.

But it is hard to understand why blame should then have been

put on the USA for following what any objective observer would
have seen as a strictly logical policy. Having called a ceasefire there
was no earthly justification for Anglo-French forces remaining in
Egypt for more time than it took for the UN to arrive. That Eden
wanted it otherwise was purely a way of justifying the chapter of
disasters that had preceded the ceasefire, thus keeping himself
and his government in power.

It was some time before Eisenhower caught on to Eden's
duplicity. Listening to Hoover expound on the logistics of UN
involvement in the Canal Zone, the president interrupted to muse
on the rigidity of Anglo-French thinking.

> In his conversation on the telephone with Anthony Eden, the
> British Prime Minister had expressed extreme reluctance to agree
> to the proposal that this police force would have no British or
> French troops as a component. When the President asked Sir
> Anthony how he proposed to exclude Soviet troops from the
> UN forces if he insisted on British and French components in
> the UN police force, Sir Anthony had indicated that this problem
> had not occurred to him, and that he would have to give it some
> thought. The President said he was absolutely astounded.[21]

As well he might have been, since he could still not bring himself
to believe that Eden would say or do anything just to save face.
All along, Eisenhower tried to put the best interpretation on
Anglo-French machinations.

Mounting evidence of a stitch-up between Israel, France and
Britain to bring about Nasser's downfall could not be ignored.
Time magazine had near enough the full story within a week of
the invasion. In the same issue in which *Time* reported on the
battle of Port Said, it also disclosed how premeditation went back
at least two months. It was all there – the secret meetings at
Chequers and in Paris, the build-up of forces in Cyprus and the
pre-knowledge of when and where the Israelis would attack. If
the White House needed confirmation, it was provided in full
measure on 16 November when Pineau opened up in conversation with Alan Dulles.

16. A heated encounter for General Stockwell.

17. General Beaufre and Admiral Barjot shake hands for the cameras.
General Keightley looks on.

18. Brothers in arms. Left to right: Selwyn-Lloyd, Guy Mollet,
Anthony Eden and Christian Pineau.

19. The search for illegal weapons.

20. Egyptian propaganda shot captioned: 'A young Egyptian girl crossing the street in Ismailia received bullets from British machine-guns.'

21. French troops on duty in Port Said.

22. Egyptian prisoners taken by French forces at Fort-Fouad.

23. British soldiers at El Cap hold the road to Port Said.

24. Patrolling Port Said, November 1956.

25. General Moshe Dayon meets the UN commander General Burns to agree on Israeli withdrawal from Sharam el Sheikh.

26. President Eisenhower and John Foster Dulles try to make sense of Anglo-French policy.

27. Peace protest in Trafalgar Square.

28. Anthony Eden taking the strain at the 1956 conservative party conference.

29. After the Anglo-French withdrawal President Nasser is declared the victor by his adoring public.

After luncheon M. Pineau turned to me and said he wanted now to tell me in strict confidence what really had happened. On October 14 he had arrived back in Paris from New York after the UN meeting on the Suez Canal; on October 15, he was approached in Paris by Israeli representatives. They told him that Israel had definite proof that Egypt was preparing to move against them and that they could not wait much longer. They were therefore determined to attack Egypt; that they would do it alone if necessary but *do* it they would. On October 16, Eden had come over from London and the plan had been worked out among the three of them and that was that. He, in effect, apologized for not having kept us informed but said that under the circumstances it seemed to serve no useful purpose to do so. I remarked that he probably also was aware of the fact that if we had been advised we would have opposed the plan.[22]

Rumours were all over the British press that at least three ministers – Eden, Lloyd and Head – were aware of Israeli intentions and that France had played an active part in the Sinai campaign.

But Eisenhower stuck to a line favourable to the British, that they 'had not been in on the Israeli–French planning until the very last stages when they had no choice but to come into the operation'. His reasoning was based on a flattering but woefully inaccurate assessment of British military capability.

One of the arguments the President cited to support this view was the long delay that took place between the time the British declared their intent to go into Egypt and the time they actually went in. He said that the British were meticulous military planners and he was sure that if they had been in on the scheme from the beginning that they would have seen to it that they were in a position to move into Egypt in a matter of hours after they declared their intention to do so.[23]

As the French might have said, if only.

There seemed to be no bounds to the efforts of British ministers to ingratiate themselves with Washington. 'Never has an ambassador occupied a more important position than you do at the present moment,' Butler told Aldrich, who was solemnly designated as 'the only man who is in a position to explain to your government the various attitudes of the members of our government'. The typically Butleresque hint that some ministers might be more reliable than others passed unnoticed. Macmillan was more direct, confiding in Aldrich that he very much regretted giving up the job of foreign secretary because Lloyd was 'too young and inexperienced for a position of such great responsibility under the present difficult circumstances'. Macmillan was eager to leave for Washington immediately, but was urged by Aldrich to wait until Eden's visit had been confirmed.[24]

As for Eden, he was back on the Red scare as the justification for the Suez war. 'The bear is moving not only in the Middle East but in Eastern Europe and we must coordinate our plans,' he opined, adding that 'it was most urgent for him to have talks with the President soon.'[25]

But it was Salisbury who carried scare tactics to the point of lunacy, claiming, on what evidence no one knows, that

> additional information was accumulating regarding definite character and scope of conspiracy between Nasser and Russians to take over entire Middle East and its oil as soon as Nasser had established himself as head Arab world. Salisbury felt that fact Nasser had blocked Canal was highly significant. This act he said had not been necessary and was not in interest of Egypt but could only be explained as part of a plot to assist Russia by making it more difficult for Europe to defend itself or protect its interests in Middle East.[26]

That Nasser might have blocked the canal as part of his defence against an Anglo-French invasion appears not to have occurred to Salisbury, who, in Tory circles, was said to be expert in foreign affairs.[27] Equally extravagant claims were coming from Paris, where the stress was on justifying cooperation with Israel. For Mollet, if the Israelis had not taken the initiative, 'a joint Egyptian–Syrian–Jordanian attack on Israel, directed by Soviet officers and technicians, would have taken place at the latest during December or January'.[28] Again, in the absence of sources for this improbable intelligence, credit must go to the creative interpretation of the few facts that were available.

On 11 November Selwyn Lloyd was packed off to New York to see what he could do to save Britain's reputation at the UN. He was naively optimistic.

> 'Arrived safely after quite a good flight,' he wrote to Eden once in New York. 'I gather the situation is thawing between the US and ourselves and I shall continue to try to drive into their heads that the Anglo-French forces in Port Said are the only effective bargaining counter for either the United Nations or the Americans with the Egyptians and the Russians.'[29]

He was soon to be disillusioned. With an argument so patently feeble, how could it have been otherwise? The depth of his misunderstanding of the American position hit its nadir with a visit to Foster Dulles at the Bethesda Naval Hospital. The conversation opened with the sixty-four-thousand-dollar question from Dulles. 'Selwyn, when you started, why didn't you go through with it?' It was a perfectly reasonable enquiry. Dulles was generously crediting the Eden government with having calculated the economic risks of the operation and of realising, after countless warnings, that no support could be expected from Washington. Once the decision was taken to go ahead, it was surely absurd to cancel the expedition after barely a day of land fighting just because of an attack of economic jitters.

Dulles was not alone in finding this hard to understand. Anthony Head, who, as defence minister, was nominally in charge of the expedition, compared it to a romantic let-down – 'like going through all the preliminaries without having an orgasm'.[30] Dulles would not have expressed himself so earthily but his sentiments were the same. He would also have sympathised with a senior British officer who confided in a television reporter, 'What I always say is, if you're going to be a shit, be a fucking shit.'[31]

If it had been put this bluntly, Lloyd might just have got the message. But Dulles was disinclined to elaborate, and in the true spirit of the tragically misguided Lloyd concluded that the question showed that Dulles 'had already realised what a mess he and the President between them had made of the situation'.[32]

Lloyd was in the States for just over a fortnight. In that time, aided by Harold Caccia, the newly installed British ambassador who shared the Foreign Secretary's mindset, Lloyd blustered his way from one inanity to another, starting with the claim that the Suez war stopped a greater evil. Apparently, in paving the way for an international peacekeeping force to hold the line between Arabs and Jews, British and French forces had pre-empted a full-scale Arab–Israeli war. Fifty years on, the parallel with Iraq, starting a war for one reason only to end up justifying it for a totally different reason, hardly needs emphasising. On this weakest of arguments Lloyd then went on to claim that an Egypt–Israel war would have happened anyway within five to six months, that a UN force could not possibly operate effectively without British and French help, and that it was the responsibility of the USA to force concessions from Egypt as a condition of an Anglo-French withdrawal.

'He is in a dangerous frame of mind and could set off a war,' declared Henry Cabot Lodge, the US representative at the UN. He added of Lloyd, 'his attitude struck me as reckless and full of contradictions. It has made me more pessimistic about the British than anything that has happened in my service here'.[33]

While Lloyd defended the indefensible in New York, his colleagues in London were busy looking to their own future. It was clear that Eden was heading for a collapse. He looked awful, his powers of concentration were fast failing and his general weariness made him a poor prospect for influencing Eisenhower if and when he ever got the chance of going to Washington. On 18 November, Macmillan spent an hour with Aldrich, promoting himself as 'Eden's deputy', ready to take up the challenge of a top-level tripartite conference. He detailed what he saw as the 'terrible dilemma' for the British government, which had to be resolved. This was either:

. . . withdrawing from Egypt, having accomplished nothing but to have brought about the entry into Egypt of a completely inadequate token force of troops representing the UN, whose only function is to police the border between Israel and Egypt, without having secured the free operation of the Canal or even being in a position to clear it, or (b) renewing hostilities in Egypt and taking over the entire Canal in order to remove the obstructions which have been placed there by Nasser and to insure its free operation and to avoid the complete economic collapse of Europe within the next few months. The danger of course in the minds of the British Cabinet of adopting the first alternative is that loss of prestige and humiliation would be so great that the govt must fall, while the second alternative would obviously involve the risk of bringing in the Russians and resulting in a third world war.[34]

But, of course, if the US government would guarantee the management of the canal by an international agency, on the lines of the recommendation of the first London Conference on Suez, then he, Macmillan, was sure that he could persuade the cabinet to agree to a withdrawal of British forces and also 'bring pressure on the French to withdraw their forces from Egypt at once'.

Aldrich was smart enough to pick up on the hints that Eden was on his way out. It thus came as no surprise to him when, the following day, it was announced that the prime minister was cancelling all his engagements. Officially, Butler was to take charge, but Macmillan told Aldrich that the government would be run by a triumvirate of Butler, Macmillan and Salisbury. Eden would go on vacation 'first for one week and then for another and this will lead to his retirement'. The assumption by the ambassador was that Butler would eventually become prime minister, but he noted again Macmillan's eagerness to be designated as deputy prime minister in Eden's absence with authority to talk directly to Eisenhower.

There was not much public sympathy for Eden. It might have been otherwise had he made a wiser choice of retreat from the strains of office. His departure for Jamaica, where he and his wife,

Clarissa, had use of Ian Fleming's holiday home at Goldeneye, was seen as a master stroke of insensitivity. The island, observed John Colville, Churchill's private secretary, 'is much patronised by tax evaders and affluent idlers'; he added, 'with petrol and oil rationed again in England, the retreat of the Prime Minister to a parasites' paradise seemed to rank prominently in the annals of ministerial follies'.[35]

Colville was premature in his mention of petrol rationing. This did not come into force until 17 December. But meanwhile there was much else to remind the public what they were sacrificing to defend Britain's world role, starting with a tax hike on oil that rolled through to price increases for travel, heating and a whole range of energy-related goods. To cap it all, the country was hit by some of the coldest weather on record; hardly the government's fault, but nevertheless serving to intensify the feel-bad factor. The *Daily Mirror* had fun at Eden's expense by offering a three-week holiday for two in Jamaica for anyone who could solve the Suez crisis.

While Jamaica prepared for its distinguished guests with a calypso band rehearsing 'Jamaica the Garden of Eden welcomes Britain's Sir Anthony Eden', his foreign secretary was playing out his time in Washington and New York knowing that there was no earthly chance of persuading Eisenhower to offer even token support for the Anglo-French presence in Egypt. In his speech to the UN General Assembly on 23 November, he offered what amounted to an unconditional withdrawal of British forces as soon as the UN peacekeeping force was ready to take over. Four days later he was back in London, where he offered to resign.

At last! In his memoirs Lloyd made it sound like an act of noble self-sacrifice as he stood forth as the voluntary scapegoat for all that had gone wrong. It is impossible to imagine his true feelings. Noble self-sacrifice was not in his nature, but as a shrewd operator he may well have calculated that staying on, and without Eden to protect him, would have invited dismissal from whoever took over in Downing Street. Better to go before he was pushed. But Lloyd's timing was wrong. The cabinet was delighted to have a scapegoat, but not one who was about to leave the government just at the moment when it was under maximum fire. He was persuaded to stay on.

The deal on Anglo-French withdrawal from Egypt was finally settled on 3 December when Caccia told Robert Murphy at the state department that while Britain felt it was impossible to set a definite date, 'the plain facts of the case . . . are that we have decided to go without delay and we intend to go without delay'. When Dulles heard this he telephoned Eisenhower, who was in Augusta, Georgia, and together they agreed that Britain 'had gone adequately to meet the requirements'.[36]

While Humphrey along with Hoover had been seen as motivated entirely by anti-British sentiment, the tune in London changed when, as Humphrey had promised, a firm commitment to get out of Egypt triggered an IMF loan of $562 million with stand-by credit of $739 million. Moreover, Britain was granted a US credit line of $500 million with the right to defer interest and principal payments a total of seven times.[37]

The 'almost insoluble problem of Israel', as Dulles dubbed it, had still to be settled. Eisenhower was not in thrall to the Jewish vote but he was certainly not about to sacrifice Israel for the sake of Arab goodwill. Knowing this, Ben-Gurion was inclined to be bullish. On 14 January, the UN was told that Israel would not withdraw its troops from Gaza or from Sharm el-Sheikh on the Gulf of Aqaba. Washington reacted angrily and with more strength than Ben-Gurion had expected. Dollar aid was cut back and a guarantee of unrestricted oil supplies was withheld. As Dulles observed, the US possessed the sticks and the carrots.[38]

At home, Ben-Gurion needed to show that the Sinai campaign, a military success, had produced benefits that went beyond boosting army prestige. He had friends in Congress, including the Republican senate minority leader, William Knowland, and the Democratic senate majority leader, Lyndon Johnson, but there was counter-pressure from King Saud, who took the opportunity of an official visit to the United States to make clear his view that Eisenhower was indulging Israel.

Decision time was fast approaching with tough UN reso-
lutions in the offing. Would the USA vote for economic sanctions
against Israel? Dulles sought to sidetrack the issue by assuring
Israel that his government would deem the Gulf of Aqaba an
international waterway, guaranteeing the right of free passage, if
Israel withdrew from its captured territory. Abba Eban, Israel's
ambassador in Washington, urged acceptance, but Ben-Gurion
pushed for more, proposing that the USA and Israel should
jointly determine the future of the Gaza Strip. With Eisenhower's
backing, Dulles threatened to block private donations to Israel
and to forbid the sale of Israeli bonds in the USA. For good
measure, the State Department announced to the press that
Egypt had cooperated more readily with the UN than had
Israel.[39]

With an imminent vote on a UN resolution condemning Israel,
Ben-Gurion accepted the inevitable. Israel was ready to consider
Gaza and the Gulf of Aqaba as separate issues. An American-
endorsed solution to Gaza favourable to Israel was no longer a
prerequisite to troop withdrawal. With a collective sigh of relief,
the UN debate was postponed while America sought a way
through the diplomatic maze.

France spoke up in support of its ally. While Mollet and Pineau
were in Washington in late February, a large part of the discussions aimed at transatlantic reconciliation involved the future
of Israel. Pineau's compromise proposal was for French recognition of Israel's right to protect itself against fedayeen raids from
Gaza corresponding to US recognition of Israeli rights to free
navigation via the Gulf of Aqaba. It was less than Ben-Gurion
had hoped for, but in submitting to the conditions set out by the
USA he had identified what Abba Eban called the 'central truth
of Israel's foreign policy', that America and Israel were henceforth
bound together.

In July 1958, Shimon Peres was able to report ecstatically, 'In
the United States, for the first time, I received weapons which
shoot. I got 100 pieces of recoilless artillery with shells. Of course,
that's less than the 350 we asked for. But, as I see it, the very fact

that a modest but new source of arms like the US has opened up to us is of genuine significance.'[40]

They were the truest words he ever spoke.

23

While the politicians argued, the Anglo-French army in Egypt settled in for the duration. By late November there were over 13,500 British and 8,500 French troops in Port Said. Five thousand vehicles and 10,000 tons of supplies had been put ashore.[1]

Despite the ceasefire, the occupation was not exactly peaceful. There were too many trigger-happy patriots out on the streets. With Nasser's propaganda proclaiming a great victory to culminate in one more push to drive the aggressors from Egypt once and for all, macho youth was inspired to try its luck against anyone in foreign uniform. Night patrols were particularly vulnerable, as Roger Booth recalls:

I was out in a vehicle one evening when I heard a grenade explode. In the narrow confines of a high sided street even a humble grenade can sound like an artillery shell landing. We raced to the scene to find one of our foot patrols dazed, some kneeling, some standing, others prone – assumed either wounded or dead. One of the patrol pointed to the roof of a nearby modest house. I dashed upstairs followed by my escort. We burst into a room. There was a man, his wife, his frightened doe-eyed children. They were all in white linen. There was a warm musk of sandalwood and bodies. The communal bed was heaped in white linen. Without a word the man lifted the bedclothes to show there was no one hiding beneath the bed. He opened the cupboard doors. Then he pulled back the room's shutters to show a view over a jumble of roofs that looked in the moonlight like an Oliver Messel set for some oriental operetta. My revolver was canted in the air. The children gripped the folds of their mother's garment as if they were clinging for life to shrubs on the forefront of some cliff . . . The man gave me an impassive stare. How pointless further search would be.

On the pavement below we discovered that no one had been injured. There was a sinister jagged hole bevelled out of the pavement where the grenade had landed. Miraculously its exploding shower of shrapnel had not connected with any soldier . . . A Scots subaltern now appeared, his kilt riding up over his knees like a woman's skirt as he swung out of his land rover. 'Are our wogs being unkind to you?' he asked. After all, we were on the edge of their area. We withdrew.[2]

It was not always easy to distinguish between those who were hostile but apparently friendly and the majority, who just wanted to get on with their lives. The problem for David Henderson was deciding how far to trust those civilians who claimed not to be Egyptians or opponents of Nasser and who demanded protection.

We treated everything they said with suspicion but when two very European looking women approached and told us in fault-less English that they knew where an officer was hiding our officer decided to take a look and motioned for three of us to follow him, adding if anything happens, 'Shoot the two bitches first.' They led us into a smart block of flats and informed us of which floor and flat number he was supposed to be in. He maybe was ready to believe them but not that much, and the two protest-ing women were frogmarched up the stairs and pushed through the open door. There followed a prolonged outburst of screams and howls, as out they came faces white and screaming abuse and hatred at us for what we had put them through. Our officer carefully squinted through the gap between the door hinges and then said, 'It's all right. He seems to have topped himself.' We all trooped in and stood horrified at the sight. He had committed suicide and in fact still had the gun in his hand but it was the amount of blood that he had shed that surprised us. God knows what artery or part of his body he had hit but he had spilled every ounce of his blood and it was all over the place. The officer searched through his belongings for maps or any sort of information while the rest of us relieved him of any trophies we could find right down to his blood soaked pistol. We had to hand most of it back outside, however, as our superiors were getting a bit miffed at us all walking about with trophies to take home and they had nothing to show off back in the Mess.

There was more drama to come when Henderson's troop had to decide on its billet for the night.

Light was fading by now and orders came in to stop for the night and hold positions. We picked out a corner building that gave us good all-round defensive positions and made to cross the road to it when a burst of gunfire sprayed the road in front of us. We were not in the best of positions and had to get over before night time so we were numbered out in pairs and given the following instructions. A grenade would be lobbed in the general direction of where we thought the gunner was and as soon as it went off, making him duck, two of us would dash over the road, and so on, and so on. This went all right until our opponent worked out what was happening and at the next explosion gritted his teeth and pulled the trigger. Down went one of the lads shot clean through the stomach while his mate carried on for a step or two before turning back, grabbing him and started to drag him the rest of the way. All hell let loose with everyone on both sides of the street blazing away at the sniper who by now had exposed his position. Somebody must have hit him or we had put the shit up him for on the next two final runs not a shot was fired. By the time I got over last with the Bren gun team the shot Marine was sitting up looking none the worse for his wound and in fact helping with the fixing of his dressings. We all thought he was reacting to shock and would soon collapse for surely a belly wound was very serious. He was a very lucky man indeed as doctors found when they got him back to ship and finally Malta that the bullet had gone clean through him without touching any vital organ and he was sent back to barracks with simple plasters front and back.[3]

Rather than wait to be shot at, the occupying forces mounted an intensive search for arms. Surprisingly, perhaps, many guns were surrendered voluntarily. Marine Ashton was among those who found that civilians were generally friendly, though he was understandably wary when approached by a smiling Egyptian bearing as a gift a lethal weapon.

At times the risk of accidental discharges was frightening, the weapons being handed up at all angles and in all states of readiness to fire: some cocked; some with rounds in the breach and with the safety-catch off; most with live rounds in the magazine. Bearing in mind that these were often handed up muzzle first by children, it was a miracle that no one was injured.

During a period when I had climbed down from my truck for a breather, a close-cropped urchin tugged at my sleeve and then unwrapped his other sticky palm to reveal several 9 mm rounds. I took them off him and threw them into the truck. He continued to pull at my sleeve and pointed up an alleyway leading off the main street. Warily, I followed him and two of his companions, not too sure of what I was letting myself in for.

Tucked away out of sight, and with a flat front tyre, sat a huge 'Stalin Organ' – a multi-barrelled Russian rocket launcher – mounted on the back of a sand-coloured six-wheeled vehicle. Half the tubes were loaded and pointing in the direction of our landing zone. Had they been able to deploy this against us during the critical landing period of both sea-borne and helicopter-borne Commandos forty-eight hours previously, there might well have been a significant increase in casualties. As there was nothing I could do with this prize of victory, I just grinned at the kids and shrugged my shoulders. They seemed to share the joke and I left them with their lethal find.[4]

There were occasions when the hazards of war hovered between tragedy and farce. Here is a contact report from the records of the 3rd Infantry Division. 'Patrol 1 RS had a petrol bomb thrown at them at 280050C approx. Bomb did NOT explode. Attacker, EGYPTIAN youth of about 24, then tried to fire a Lanchester at Patrol, but it did NOT go off. Patrol comd fired at youth, but his gun did NOT go off. Youth arrested.' If only it were always that easy.

The lobbed grenade from an upstairs window was a particular hazard for drivers and passengers in open-top jeeps. When a legionnaire was mortally injured at the wheel of his vehicle, Roger Booth was told to investigate. It was not, he said, a happy mission.

However the incident was in our area. We had to react. I knew this grid of streets reasonably well. Our patrol was jammed into the confines of an Austin Champ as we sought out the boulevard where the attack had occurred. The sun was shining. Shops and bazaars were opened for business. Old ladies sat in the windows of their flats watching life below. There was the appearance of the humdrum. A man in a doorway grinned. I didn't like his grin . . .

We stopped. I dropped a bren group off at the corner of a square and gave them orders to cover us. On we cruised. The boulevard where the attack had taken place on the French jeep was looming up at a right-angled junction. Just before we reached it there was an explosion behind us. The Austin Champ surged forward, then all hell appeared to break loose. The gap of meeting boulevards surged towards us. Lurking at the junction to our left was a large excited crowd in ambush. I saw the French jeep slewed on the pavement, its bonnet roasted black and pink in an attempt to set fire to it. There were men and women, children and youths swaying en masse with excitement.

There in their forefront most vivid of all was a tall erect old man with a short grey beard, turbaned and wearing a greenish gelabehah. At his shoulder, clamped in aim at us, was a sten gun. I remember thinking 'Thank god it's a sten', a weapon not blessed with great accuracy over but a short distance. I could see other weapons brandished in the crowd. It was cabaret time. We were like a slow-moving target of cut-out soldiers in a low sand-coloured vehicle at some fairground rifle range. My revolver was out but how could one empty it at a mixed crowd containing women and children?

The boulevard seemed infinitely grand in its width. The juddering burst from the sten gun sprayed past us. Our driver, an intelligent soldier, had rammed his boot on the accelerator at the sound of the first shot. His instinct was now paying off. The Champ with its Rolls Royce engine was nearly airborne. What committee of freespenders of taxpayers' money had designed a combat vehicle with a Rolls Royce engine? However, we were now grateful for their munificence. We roared away unscathed while heavy firing still thundered behind us. I had no intention of presenting ourselves as a fairground target again. We swerved around and sprinted back by a parallel route.[5]

What had happened was that a young Egyptian had thrown a grenade which fell short. At that point the Bren group had opened up.

Our bren gunner had fired from the hip. Not an easy thing to do. His first long burst had splayed its way up the front of the building shattering shop and flat windows. His second burst had struck the youth who'd thrown the grenade. His body fell three stories to the pavement below. They had seen screaming women come out and drag his bloody corpse away. He had been wearing grey trousers and a white shirt.[6]

Of the various tasks handed out to foot soldiers, guarding food depots was one of the more hazardous, as Peter Mayo discovered when he was called upon to help quell a riot outside a flour mill and warehouse close by one of the backwaters to the canal. He found a line of troops, shoulder to shoulder, across the only connecting road. They faced an angry mob with fixed bayonets.

There was terrific shouting and gesticulating. One got the impression they were very hungry. They were bent on looting the warehouses, but as this was the reserve supply for the whole area we had been told to stop them. A section of Vickers mounted in landrovers were drawn up facing the crowd. We had permission to shoot in the last extremity. Things were looking rather ugly. Roy seemed to be in command of the troops, but not of the situation. It seemed obvious to me that we couldn't hope to hold them back for very long without wholesale slaughter, and even then there were so many of them so close they could have rushed us most probably. There were lots of sacks of flour scattered over the road outside the warehouses, the result of earlier looting I imagine, and Roy conceived the absurd notion of loading a few hand-carts with sacks and pushing them into the crowd – imagining I suppose that this would satisfy them and they would all go home to bed like good little boys. Of course the obvious happened – the cart disappeared under a swarm of kicking, wrestling, fighting arms and legs, and the flour which didn't rise as dust into the air went all over the ground, and women and children were in danger of being trampled. It was not a very pleasant sight. It was quite clear we would have to let them through, get their flour and then drive them out with it and wire the place off. So we slowly withdrew into a side turning and the mob surged forward with the hand-carts, tins and containers of all kinds; even the smallest child had something. Soon most of them began to stream back laden. They were white from head to foot. I saw one lovely old boy dashing along, dressed in pyjamas, on a small donkey with a huge sack of flour slung over its withers. By this time a truck-load of wire which we had asked for from the beach-head turned up and as soon as we had driven everyone away we sealed off the road and another alleyway with several coils. I spent the night down there with three sections and a Vickers to guard it.[7]

At command level there were mixed feelings. Stockwell, as he wrote to Templer, was 'in cracking good heart',[8] having got over his worry that the ceasefire would be followed by orders for an immediate withdrawal, a recipe for logistical chaos that he thought might appeal to the thick-headed civilians who were running affairs. The chief problem for Stockwell was to maintain relations with his deputy, who shared the prevailing view of his French colleagues that they had made a fatal mistake in allowing them-selves to be made subordinate to be bunch of incompetents. 'The French', wrote Stockwell, 'are a bloody nuisance.' Beaufre 'only turns up [to conferences] when it suits him and . . . colours every military decision with his sympathy for the [French] politicians'. It was perhaps fortunate that Stockwell was not in hearing dis-tance of Massu, who was raging against a 'fiasco' of a war in which 'not only did we fail to overthrow Nasser but we didn't even seize the Canal'.[9] A catastrophe, raged the general, partly, if not largely, caused by the British tendency to stop too frequently for 'a nice cup of tea'.[10] As if living up to this reputation, Stockwell took what comfort he could in little luxuries. 'My ADC found the cold storage and returned triumphantly with a box of kippers. I then had to requisition a Frigidaire to keep the kippers in, so they cost about £10 a head.'[11] The task force commanders could at least agree on their contempt for the politicians. This view was shared in full by Templer, who wrote to assure his colleague that whatever witch-hunting was ahead, 'no one will ever look for any witches in the forces in the Mediterranean', and to thank Stockwell for sending him a Russian rifle. 'If I could use it, I'd give my first attention to certain gentlemen in New York and London. And I'd have run out of ammunition before I could spare a round, even for Nasser.'[12]

By the third week of November, reinforcements were still turn-ing up at Port Said while other units were being withdrawn to Cyprus. 'We've now achieved the impossible,' Stockwell cabled the War Office. 'We're going both ways at once.' For the Royal Scots the journey had been arduous and, at times, faintly ridicu-lous. Dr Henry Cowper was then a national service corporal with the 1st Battalion.

We'd gone from Brandon Station near Thetford to Liverpool Street by train. There were no lorries to meet us at Liverpool Street – this was the first in the beginning of a long line of disasters – and we actually travelled from Liverpool Street over to Waterloo by tube, at the time of the rush-hour, with

entrenching tools, map-cases, pistols, Sten guns, the lot, cheered
on by all these old ladies: 'Go on, son! Get stuck in!' It was quite
embarrassing.[13]

Arriving in Southampton, the Royal Scots embarked on the
Empire Fowey. They sailed on the evening of 1 November.

> On the principle of 'fitting you in somewhere' we all got on
> board. Odd Royal Scots soldiers were tucked away in every
> nook and cranny in the ship and any question of a sub-unit or
> platoon of the same company being together on the same
> troop deck was purely coincidental. Officers were accommo-
> dated four in a two-berth cabin (two on the floor), five in a
> three-berth, and so on. However, eventually we were all aboard
> and in total we had 2,700 troops on a ship designed to hold
> 1,300–1,400. Although crowded, we were not uncomfortable;
> there were no complaints – we had a job to do. We sailed just
> after midnight, having arranged to get on board about sixty or
> so of our leave personnel who arrived from Bodney in trans-
> port at 2200 hours. We were told that the rest of our leave
> personnel would be sent in other ships which were to leave in
> the next few days.[14]

Six days later, the news of the ceasefire having just got through,
courtesy of the BBC, the *Empire Fowey* docked at Malta. What
now? The best guess was for the ship turning about for the voyage
back to Southampton. But no. Port Said was still on the order
sheet. After taking on fuel and water, the *Empire Fowey*, accompanied by an escort destroyer 'in case any country other than
Egypt might try to molest us!', set off for Egypt, the captain
expecting to deposit his passengers early on the 10th. But come
the morning, the *Empire Fowey* was heading away from Port Said,
having had orders to cruise 100 miles north of the coast until the
11th. 'The day was therefore spent in steaming one and a half
hours north and then one and a half hours south.' Since this was
Armistice Day, a service was held on deck and in the evening
there was a film show. 'It was the most dreadful film that has ever

been made, and certainly very insulting to Scotch persons; the film was *Brigadoon*. This got booed continuously by all the Jocks, as you can imagine.'[15]

It seemed that if the sense of urgency had thus far evaporated, everybody might as well go home. But it could never be that simple. As the ship eventually anchored 6 miles off Port Said, still with no notion of what was going on ashore, an attempt was made to open a radio link with divisional command.

> Despite the fact that the Brigade set could hear the Divisional Headquarters Control set ashore, the latter would not answer and we remained in the dark. It was not until the evening, when an exasperated Brigade Major used some strong language over the ether, that the Control set replied with a signal in code, 'Are you 19 Brigade?' The Brigade Major's reply in clear is unprintable. It was subsequently learnt that the Divisional operator had been thoroughly trained in the dangers of Egyptians attempting to operate sets on our frequencies.
>
> After this contact had been established with our Headquarters ashore, we were rather surprised to learn that they had no idea where we were. Upon being enlightened by our now almost hysterical Brigade Major that we were lying off at anchor and that we wanted some information, we were told that they would try and get a landing-craft out to us the following morning (12th) to take off the Brigade Commander and the unit reconnaissance parties, and that the units would probably disembark on the morning of the 13th.[16]

There were two more false starts before a thoroughly disgruntled Royal Scots battalion set foot on the quay alongside the Casino Palace Hotel, by then converted into a casualty station, where they learned they were to relieve 45 Commando Royal Marines. They were given an enthusiastic welcome, which came as something of a consolation for finding that their vehicles and stores, which should have arrived ahead of them, were still at sea.

The Royal Scots, bagpipes skirling, debarked this morning and marched to their billets through the dusty, war-torn streets of Port Said.

They were a 'braw' sight as they marched, the pipers in their kilts and tan tam o'shanters. The companies moved in slow step behind them, complete in battle dress and full kit.

It was the first bit of color Port Said has had since the British–French assault on Nov. 5 and even the troops already here raised a cheer. The kilts were much admired and elicited the usual jokes, but to those who wanted to try them on the stock Scottish answer was: 'No, mon, ye no have the figger for it.'

The shrill music of the pipes and the joking and the color were a tonic for the troops.[17]

Port Said certainly needed cheering up. With the all-pervading smell from broken sewers, water rationing, a curfew and with thousands of troops crammed into what one observer described as a 'congested sand pit', it was a grim place for an extended stay.

Doubtless mindful of his responsibilities as propaganda chief, Brigadier Fergusson found 'hardly any damage [in Port Said] except to the wooden bathing huts on the beach, some of which had been full of ammunition'.[18] Elsewhere, Fergusson reckoned the material losses to have been limited to 'a small area in the old Arab town, a block of flats behind the Governorate where a small party of Egyptian soldiers had fought stoutly and the Navy House and Customs Shed where, being unable to get away because they were surrounded by water, a party of police had held out to the end'.

Reporting for the *Daily Express*, Donald Edgar described a rather different scene that had less of the Boy's Own adventure about it. Port Said, he wrote, 'is a fearful sight, a city of flames and acrid smoke'.[19] It took some time for his words to appear in the Beaverbrook press, which was reluctant to move out of the comfort zone created by the official handouts. It was only when pictures of the devastation along the seafront of Port Said began to appear that Edgar's version of events was taken seriously.

Port Fuad, once an attractive, mainly European town, was in no better state than Port Said.

> The first thing we noticed was a twisted pile of various Egyptian troop-carrying lorries, still burning, contorted machine-guns and melting tyres. Beneath an engine, part of a corpse was sticking out, burnt almost to a cinder. All the streets were littered with debris. There were several dead, too. But above all, there was a lot of military equipment lying about, even on the lawns, which had been ripped up by tank-tracks. Palm trees were blazing like torches. The whole town smelt of burning, grease, iron, oil, powder and rotten meat.[20]

For the latest arrivals, the first job, while trying to maintain law and order, was to help in the clearing up and, so it seems from reminiscences, to engage in running repairs. This could be quite a challenge.

> There was a modern building next to the beach about 2 or 3 storeys high and it had a flat roof with a very low parapet around the edge of the roof. A stream of water was running down the stairs inside . . . On reaching the roof we found some lead water pipes, which we guessed had been hit by gunfire from aircraft. With no tools it seemed an impossible task. Then an inspiration. For the beach landing we had worn inflatable navy blue belts with straps, which had been abandoned on the beach once we were ashore. Sure enough the beach was still littered with them, so we collected some and returned to the roof. You might think that at this stage things were now looking better, but no, a shot rang out, and we dropped flat on the roof. A sniper was on another rooftop further away from the beach. But first things first. We had to sort out the damaged pipes, and then we could sort out the sniper. It was tricky work lying flat bandaging the pipes with the inflatable belts and remembering not to let any portion of your body get higher than the parapet. He must have thought that we were still there, as now and again bullets were hitting the parapet. He was probably puzzled as to why we were

not firing back. Eventually, we had completed the repairs to the best of our ability and the water from the pipes had been reduced to a trickle. Now for the sniper, but he appeared to have gone. Either he became bored, or maybe someone else became aware of our predicament and sorted out the problem for us . . . After this rather stressful incident, it occurred to me that you never know what tomorrow will bring, so I went downstairs and 'acquired' an expensive silver knife, fork and spoon, and a linen serviette. I could then dine in style from my mess tins, as long as the opportunity prevailed.[21]

The Royal Scots found themselves cleaning out drains and sewers ('not the most wholesome of tasks and even now "all the perfumes of Arabia" still seem to cling nostalgically') and controlling queues for food and kerosene oil, the latter from a horse-drawn cart. There was much more:

We would receive messages from our patrols that an old lady had fallen out of the window; could the doctor come at once? Another not so old lady had given birth and wanted assistance. Another, a local pig had had its throat cut (allegedly by one of our allies); someone else's car had been stolen, and so it went on. Whenever asked we never refused assistance, and as a result we built up an almost embarrassing reputation as 'saviours of the poor'.[22]

The French were inclined to be less sentimental. Second Lieutenant Nicholas Vaux, who, twenty-six years later, was to lead 42 Commando in the Falklands War, noted that while British forces used minimum force, not always successfully, the French reaction to trouble was to demonstrate in the most obvious way the consequences of the failure to cooperate.

I was with a French Company Commander, whose Company were supervising the issue of flour to the local residents, who were very short of food. And they began to get excited, and it was obvious that a riot was likely, unless something was immediately done. And so he spoke to his Sergeant Major, and they shot six people immediately, who were, if you like, inciting or beginning to push this situation over the edge. And it absolutely sorted the whole problem out, and for the rest of the day everybody queued up, got their bag of rice or flour, and went home. And when I gently remonstrated with the French Company Commander, he said to me: 'Well, which would you rather have had?' And it was a difficult question to answer, I have to say.[23]

As Nicholas Vaux readily concedes, however, there were occasions when British soldiers were too quick on the trigger. Sent to relieve one of his fellow commanders on a lakeside south of Port Said, he heard the sound of firing as he approached.

When I arrived at the lake most of the troop that we were going to relieve were lying on the bank, firing at two small dhows that had obviously attempted to land. And when I asked the chap in charge what was going on, he said: 'Well, they fired at us, so we're firing at them.' By this time, in fact, it was obvious that they weren't firing at anybody, and there was a rather sort of ominous stillness about the boats. And so, for some reason, which I can readily understand, he did the quickest handover of all time, jumped in his transport and disappeared.

I got an Egyptian to hail the boats and some people eventually appeared. To my consternation, not only were most of them European but actually some of them were women. We thought all the Europeans had been evacuated and accounted for, so where on earth had these people come from?

The answer was not what any troop commander wanted to hear. Not only had British troops been firing on European civilians, but they had been firing on a party of European journalists. 'We couldn't bring the boats in because the water was too shallow so we all waded out to the boats and discovered that in fact two Egyptians had been killed and one European wounded. The group included some very strident American ladies who were definitely going to make sure that their President knew about Vaux and his trigger-happy Marines.'[24] There were also Russian journalists in the group, who were convinced that they were about to be executed. The reward for serving the international press was to endure just about every injection known to medicine after wading through contaminated water.

Every day brought new deliveries to Port Said of troops and equipment, much of the latter surplus to requirements. Checking out the ammunition points along the beach, Hugo Meynell found crates of military law manuals, 'which would have been fine for an occupation,' but even then as a low priority.[25] Another unlikely consignment was the regimental silver of the Life Guards, who never made it to Suez but who had taken the precaution of sending their trophies on ahead.

With the canal blocked landing at Port Said could be a tricky business. The troopship carrying the 19th Royal Scots infantry brigade arrived at night in choppy water. Moreover, radio communication with the shore had broken down. It was, wrote Roger Booth, like 'being in a party of unwelcome trippers who had overbooked at some marine resort'.

> Now out of the darkness loomed a large Admiralty tug, its bow swathed in massive rope fenders. It sniffed our white flank like an inquisitive bulldog. I could tell it was being superbly handled in the bad conditions. Its engine telegraph rang like a busy exchange as it nosed up to us and gingerly retreated on the abrupt urine looking waves in an effort to point us out of the harbour entrance. Finally a malevolent wave lifted the tug forward with an inconvenient surge and its bow struck the troopship a hammer blow. Our whole vessel rang like a cheap tin bath. The tug went full astern, like a man who'd received a punch on the nose in a fight, and was now in full retreat. As it backed into the gloom we could see from its bow that it was named HMS *Careful*. Two thousand troops gave an ironic cheer in the bucketing wind.[26]

At El Cap, where the ceasefire deadline had brought the allies to a halt, troops held a monotonous vigil under a blazing sun. There was some contact with the natives. Colonel Bela Bredin, who had been in Ismailia in 1952, was sought out by his former dhobi wallah, who wanted to renew his contract for taking in the officers' laundry.

Help for the local economy was provided in more unorthodox ways with the nightly disappearance of several hundred yards of underground cable, which fetched a good price in Cairo for its lead.[27] It was hard to blame the Egyptians for taking whatever they could get. After all, Allied troops were equally inclined to treat other people's property as their own. Cigarettes were purloined on a massive scale, recalls Nicholas Vaux.[28] Abandoned European homes were regarded as fair game. One old soldier was seen helping himself to a very expensive fur coat.

> Did second lieutenant X who so mysteriously acquired a blue Studebaker until ordered out of it really have links with black marketers in Port Said? Had he delivered a truckload of nuts and foodstuffs to an orphanage but also sold another truckload to an Italian businessman? Did he wire his stockbroker brother urgently for Egyptian currency when Port Said traders, who'd illegally accepted BAAFS [the army's Naafi money], were desperately trying to sell them back to soldiers for Egyptian money at an absurdly low rate?

The answer to all those questions is probably 'yes' since that same officer was later convicted of fraud.[29] It is said that looting was vigorously discouraged by British officers. Not so by the French.

> We guarded warehouses against looters, Egyptian or otherwise, and often out of the dusk would come the Legion intent on breaking into them. On one occasion a French officer was carrying a hacksaw to remove the padlocks. Our sentry had saluted him then told him to 'bugger off'. The British provost sometimes arrested French officers looting with their platoons, and then handed them over to the French provost, who saluted politely in acceptance and then irritatedly released the miscreants in this exasperating charade of allied cooperation . . . It was reputed that a French battalion on parachuting into the city had made a bee

line for the main post office, despite any other tactical requirements, in order to 'sort out' the registered mail. I glimpsed a
legionnaire who had a dozen watches worn proudly up each
tattooed arm. Acquired jewellery was liberally swathed around
his neck.[30]

While life, legal or otherwise, went on the horrors were never far
away. On the way to El Cap, Donald Edgar crossed the combined
road and rail bridge captured by the French after tough resistance.
Waiting his turn to pass through the security barrier he had time
'to study a French paratrooper spooning up his meal from a mess
tin perched on the bonnet of a burnt out civilian car. Half in and
half out of the car sprawled two dead Egyptians, their faces
covered with flies'.[31] Once more, the image did not appeal to the
editorial desk in London. He had better luck when he found
ordinary soldiers adapting, patiently and sympathetically, to
extraordinary circumstances.

We drove out through Arab Town and approached a long quay
by the side of the Lake. A crowd of five or ten thousand men,
women and children were milling around laden with their
bundles of possessions . . . Just away from the crowd was parked
a solitary jeep with the driver sitting impassively with folded
arms. We got out and talked to him.

'Bloody awful, isn't it!' he said when we spoke to him. 'They're
all trying to get on those bloody boats, haven't a hope in hell,
have they? . . . Poor bastards. Mind you, I don't know anything
about it all. He's in charge.'

He pointed to a sergeant wearing the red beret of the para-
troops with a tommy-gun slung over one shoulder. Men and
women were coming up to plead with him, some carrying bits
of paper. 'Can't do anything for you here,' he was saying firmly.
'You'll have to go to Movement Control office back in the town
. . . No, luv, I can't help . . . Now come along, pass back there.'
He put out his arms as if he was a traffic policeman back in
Guildford.

The sergeant was all alone. There was no other military

presence for miles. All around him swarmed a crowd of several thousand, wailing, screaming, shouting. He and his driver and jeep could have been overwhelmed in a minute. But he just stood there, imperturbable, supremely self-confident under the Egyptian sun. I should say he was around twenty-two or twenty-three.

I have often thought of him since. I can still see him standing there. I suppose he was a working-class lad, not very well educated, not officer material, but if I wanted to describe what the *Pax Britannica* meant at its best I would try to recreate that scene along Lake El Manzala. I do not know how we managed to breed such men. I sometimes think the ruling class of this country did not deserve them.[32]

The first of the UN a contingent of Norwegians, arrived in Port Said on 22 November. Stockwell was at the rail station to welcome them. So were several thousand Egyptians.

The general's escort was of course too small to maintain order. A scratch unit of engineer reservists from nearby was assembled. Although no doubt excellent engineers they were a variegated, unmilitary lot in plimsolls. Things were obviously getting out of control. The staff tried to maintain a nonchalant dignity at these unseemly proceedings. We were then flabbergasted to learn that it was planned that the Norwegian contingent was to march through the city to its foreshore camp. What! The thickest private soldier in the force could have suggested that might lead to dangerous trouble. How could the staff be so obtuse? We, the occupying garrison, hadn't even been informed of such events. My company commander was appalled. He offered to intervene. 'Yes,' said General Stockwell brusquely, 'clear this bloody crowd!'

That was easier said than done.

The station was on the northern edge of our area. The poor Norwegian contingent commenced their march with a virulent crowd on their flanks screaming enthusiastic welcome. I could see their pale faces under their blue helmets as they marched in column. If this was an Arab welcome what would any hostility be like? We also were hemmed in the crowd in our vehicle. The column with its burgeoning numbers wheeled into a grand boulevard. We had no radio contact with the company. Frustrated, we couldn't motor out of the crowd . . . There was a mile at least before we were even into the heart of our company area . . . [which] . . . had been left in the charge of a young national service second lieutenant. He would have heard the approaching roar by now. How would he react?

We looked anxiously ahead. Still many hundreds of yards away we saw that he'd lined the company across the road in a well-spaced formation. The major and I looked at each other. He wasn't going to open fire was he?

The crowd sensed they were throwing down a challenge as they saw these figures barring their way ahead. We heard him give a command. What had he shouted? Jesus, he'd ordered a bayonet charge! The company clattered down the road towards us with fixed bayonets in impressive line like well drilled cavalry. The poor Norwegians were now to be on the receiving end of a British bayonet charge! Some of them visibly wavered but the column marched stoically on. We were insulated from the charge's impact by the teeming layers of people in front of us.

Some Egyptians were shouting 'Bayonet me Johnny? Bayonet me!' ripping open their shirts in a spirit of Islamic martyrdom. A shot rang out. Nobody fell. We were able to break through and the company commander took control from his vehicle. He expertly manoeuvred us again and again to separate the crowd from the marching contingent from the mob which fled swiftly down side streets to reappear and confront us again on the main boulevard until, thankfully, the Scandinavians left our area.[33]

Peter Mayo watched the UN force arrive at their campsite on the lawn in front of the now shattered Government House. He was not at all impressed by their bearing ('I must say I think we could have marched into town better than that'), but after all they had been through who could be surprised at their lack of sang-froid?

The crowd was cheering the Norwegians and at the same time shaking their fists at the British troops. After the crowd was moved on from the UN troops some character got an Egyptian flag and started marching round Wog Town, accumulating a mob about 2,000 strong. A wireless message from the Sergeant on guard with his section at our food store came through, and Hamish took out a strong patrol to boost up the numbers.

The next thing that happened was that two Frenchmen drove a vehicle, or at any rate got stuck somehow in the middle of the crowd. Getting stuck they opened fire, killing two Egyptian youths. Shortly afterwards the rest of A, B and X troops were called out. We got into transport but only moved a few hundred yards down the road. We then stood by for an hour or so, ready to go out if things got out of control. It must have simmered down fairly quickly and we were sent back. At one stage I heard a patrol of Royal Scots got hemmed in by a crowd in Wog Town. However a patrol of our machine gun platoon appeared on the scene and the crowd melted away when they saw green berets coming down the street. It seems we have quite a reputation from the last time the Commandos were in the Canal Zone.[34]

It was clear that the handover to the UN force would not be easy, at least not until it was strengthened with contingents from Denmark, India, Yugoslavia, Canada and Colombia. Only then would General Tommy Burns, the Canadian selected to head up the UN force, have the muscle along with the authority to take charge. In the meantime, it was agreed that British and French troops would remain in their occupied areas which, in effect, meant most of Port Said and Port Fuad.

Now began the most dangerous phase of the occupation. With the boost of confidence that came with the appearance of the UN, Egyptian irregulars were emboldened to take greater risks. More shots were fired, more grenades thrown and one young subaltern, Lieutenant Anthony Moorhouse of the 1st Battalion The West Yorks Regiment, was abducted.

Nicholas Vaux was on the quayside, waiting to embark on the

Empire Fowey, bound for Malta, when Moorhouse arrived in Port Said. It was a meeting of old friends who had known each other since schooldays.

> He expressed great disappointment to me that he'd missed all the fighting, and I said to him: 'Well, I shouldn't be too sad about it, because a lot of it wasn't the greatest fun.' And I warned him, I cautioned him about how dangerous I reckoned the local population were and how hostile they were. And three days out, on the way back, I heard on the radio that a British officer had been kidnapped, and it actually was him, and eventually they killed him, because they thought it was too difficult to hand him back. So that was one of those sad, strange twists of fate, which are all too prevalent in war.[35]

Moorhouse certainly died, but it is not at all certain that he was killed.

Stockwell first heard of the kidnapping when a boy – he was subsequently given the pseudonym Ahmed – was brought to him with a story to tell. He had seen Moorhouse dragged from his Champ and driven off in a black saloon car.

> Ahmed saw it and while others did too, it was Ahmed who reacted, his loyalty had been won; he ran to the Company Head-quarters, where he had lodged and fed, and breathlessly told his tale. None could understand his excited and staccato sentences – a gaping Corporal swiftly joined by his officer tried desperately to untangle this flow of Arabic, but to no avail. He seemed to be telling the story over and over again. Luckily an Italian nearby came to the rescue and acted as interpreter. It seemed that Moor-house had stopped to caution a young Egyptian for stealing, when a car drew up and hemmed him in; out of it jumped a man who seized his pistol and at the point of it, got Moorhouse into the car and drove off.[36]

The formal report gave more detail.

> The youth who witnessed the affair stated on interrogation that

he saw an officer get out of a Champ and argue with a passer-by and then point a pistol at him. A crowd collected and persuaded the officer to forget the incident. He climbed into the Champ, prepared to reverse and warned the pedestrians to keep clear. While looking to the rear an Egyptian grabbed the pistol which he pointed at Moorhouse's stomach and grabbed his neck with his left arm. Three men got out of a taxi, pulled him out of the Champ and carried him bodily into the taxi which made off at speed.[37]

The search began. So too did negotiations with the Egyptian authorities. Stockwell still had some 'high class detainees' in his charge who could be made part of a prisoner exchange. The French were contemptuous of all the talking. Why not tear the city apart? Wary of something of the same happening to one of his men, Massu held some one hundred Egyptian hostages, carting them off to Cyprus, where he was ordered to return them to Egypt. They had served their purpose. Massu was full of apologies. He protested that he had no idea that the release of prisoners was part of the deal with the UN.[38] Only after the allied evacuation was Moorhouse's body recovered. The probability was that he had suffocated to death in the crate in which his captors had imprisoned him.

How many others died at Suez? Allied casualties were never much in doubt – British: 21 killed, 97 wounded; French: 10 killed; 33 wounded. The discrepancies came in the estimates for Egyptian dead and injured. The first official statement suggested that around one hundred Egyptians, military and civilians, had been killed in the Port Said action. This confident declaration came with the imprimatur of Sir Walter Monckton, he of the wobbly conscience over Suez who, out of loyalty to the Tory government, had stayed in the cabinet to direct propaganda. The press corps begged to differ. Two days after the Anglo-French landings, after checking the hospitals and noting the absence of drugs and medical supplies, American reporters were putting the number of dead as high as 500.[39]

As soon as censorship was lightened, the British press weighed in with their own investigations. For *Express* reporter Donald Edgar, the government figure was 'so absurdly low to anyone who had been around the city that at first I could scarcely credit that it was being given out seriously'.[40] Along with Hanson Baldwin of the *New York Times*, he decided to do some research.

> The first task was the most disagreeable. We drove out to the cemetery on the road to the airfield for we had heard that many of the bodies were now being taken there for burial. When we went in some Egyptian medical personnel with gauze masks over their faces were bringing some order into the heaps of corpses. With an instinctive distaste for the task, we realised there was only one thing to do – make a count. This we did and then asked an Egyptian doctor there how many had already been buried. He was a serious man, saddened by his job and we believed his estimate. We came away reasonably sure that in the cemetery alone there were over 600 dead, nearly all civilians and, in addition, lorries were still bringing in heaps of corpses found in the ruins.
>
> We went round the hospitals, enquired of our own medical teams, asked the French about the situation in their area of operations, Port Fuad. We looked at the burned-out ruins of the shanty town and the bombed and shelled buildings from which bodies were being slowly dug out.[41]

The fair estimate that Edgar arrived at was around 1,000 killed, military and civilian, 5,000 wounded, 25,000 homeless. Such was the furore at home created by the revelation that the government decided on an independent inquiry led by Sir Edwin Herbert, president of the Law Society. He reported back with a lengthy document, composed in near-incomprehensible legalese, which nonetheless revealed an intensive investigation over four days. His conclusion was 650 killed in Port Said and 100 in Port Fuad. The wounded and slightly wounded he put at 900 and 1,200. No comment was made on the number who lost their homes.

On behalf of the military, Bernard Fergusson stuck to much

lower figures, arguing that in a city of 180,000, with most of the inhabitants on the poverty margin or below, 'not all those deaths were likely to have been due to hostilities'.[42] Even so, balancing out the various estimates of those who were first-hand witnesses, it is likely that between two and three thousand Egyptians died as a result of hostilities.

December 22nd was the day when the last of the British and French troops sailed away from Suez. The French left first. At 11 a.m. General Beaufre saluted as the French flag was lowered and the UN flag raised over the French headquarters. There was just time for some last-minute looting. Furniture, rings and a clock given to de Lesseps by the Empress Eugénie were lifted from the Suez Canal Company offices and loaded on to French ships. The British, who departed at sunset, took the company's chandeliers and a marble bust of Napoleon.

> As a set piece withdrawal, the French ceremony took some beating. Slowly, all lights burning, the ships glided out of the port one after another. As the *Claude-Bernard* . . . passed the *Georges-Leygues*, Admiral Lancelot had a surprise in store for us: on the quarter-deck which was lit by a searchlight a band was playing 'Sambre et Meuse', and the Admiral's shadow, magnified against a gun turret by the searchlight, saluted, while the entire crew stood to attention.[43]

On Christmas Day, the Egyptians celebrated with a final gesture of defiance. The obvious demonstration, and one that promised well as a photo opportunity, was the destruction of the de Lesseps statue at the entrance to the canal. At 33 feet high it was Port Said's most impressive, some might have said only, monument. But it was also a highly visible symbol of foreign oppression. Unfortunately for those who gathered to witness the demolition, Egyptian munitions experts did not perform with distinction. Three sticks of dynamite created smoke and dust but failed to shift the edifice. A second attempt with twice the force produced a hole in de Lesseps's right leg and caused him to lean at a gentle angle. To the jeers of the crowd, twelve sticks of TNT were strung around the base and the fuse lit. 'There was a very loud explosion and a large black cloud encased the statue. It was like a Hollywood film as the statue leaned forward and fell face down on to a cargo pontoon docked at the side.'[44] With the clearing of the canal, the statue was dumped at a shipyard in Port Fuad.

24

If history has anything to teach us, the Suez crisis must be an education in itself. A brief and inglorious affair brought momentous consequences extending way beyond the impact on the immediate participants.

In the Middle East, the war led to just about everything its instigators had hoped to avoid. Intended to safeguard free navigation on the canal, it resulted in its closure for nearly six months. Intended to protect the flow of oil to western Europe, it not only deprived the shipping companies of their shortest route to markets but led to sabotage of nearly all the direct pipelines to the Mediterranean, forcing Britain and France to readopt petrol rationing. Luckily it was a short-term measure. When the canal was reopened in April 1957, fears that Britain and France would be excluded turned out to be unfounded. But as Donald Logan pointed out, the terms of the reopening were close to those of Fawzi's initial bargaining position with the French and British foreign ministers in New York on 9 October.[1]

Despite the best efforts of Foster Dulles, every proposal for setting up a neutral agency to receive canal dues was rejected by Nasser. In May 1957, Britain and France accepted that dues had to be paid to Egypt. By the end of the year they had conceded, without qualification, Egyptian control of the canal.

For a country that had suffered a crushing military defeat, Egypt came out of the Suez crisis in buoyant mood. International (or rather American) pressure had seen off the colonial powers and forced Israel to give up its territorial gains. The nationalisation of the canal was now extended to all French and British property in Egypt. Nasser's credit in the Arab world was at its strongest. But somehow he failed to exploit his advantage.

While with Soviet finance work started on the Aswan High Dam in 1960, the promise of an economic miracle was not realised. Convinced that state industry would perform better than private enterprise, Nasser instituted a Soviet-style five-year plan for growth led by a huge and badly managed public sector. Signs of economic expansion were everywhere, but they were rarely sustainable. Wherever tourists were shown the wide roads and the new blocks of offices and flats there remained remnants of a very different past.

> Such are the ancient, busy, noisy, arched or open bazaars, often miles in extent and scarcely changed in aspect for a millennium; old-type public baths and tea-shops, the craftsman in his work-shop, the barber and the seller of cold drinks or vegetables . . . the winding alleyways giving pedestrian access to window-less, airless dwellings; peddlers and street vendors, beggars, laden donkeys or mules, scores of ragged children and their black-clad mothers and innumerable dignified, seemingly workless, sitters-in-the-sun.[2]

Nasser's ambition for a pan-Arab state under his leadership advanced in February 1958 with the union of Egypt and Syria to form the United Arab Republic. But though the union was greeted enthusiastically by his new subjects, their former leaders were averse to the colonial status that Syria was now expected to assume. A military coup d'état ended Egyptian rule in September 1961. Egypt was still the United Arab Republic and remained so until Nasser's death in 1970. His successor, Anwar El-Sadat, introduced another name change – the Arab Republic of Egypt. Nasser's pan-Arabism found one more outlet when a coup in Yemen overthrew the monarchy. Egyptian troops sent to support the republican regime lost out against royalist supporters who used a mountainous terrain to strategic effect.

Where Nasser made his biggest mistake, however, was in falling victim to his own military propaganda. While some units of the Egyptian military fought bravely, the performance of the army in the Sinai was a disaster that led to the destruction or loss to the Egyptians of most of their modern Soviet weaponry. But Nasser could not bring himself to fasten responsibility on his fellow officers. Instead, the official version of events gave the advantage to the Egyptians, whose soldierly skills had enabled them to survive against overwhelming odds on two fronts. If Egypt had fought it out with Israel alone, so it was said, victory would have gone to the Arab forces. It was a myth that was to cost Egypt dear when, a decade later, the Arab–Israeli battle was resumed. As Massu declared, with typical bluntness: 'Nasser rewrote history and failed to realise that by pulling out of Sinai and concentrating on Suez he suffered a defeat ... He failed to realise how ill-prepared his army was, how mediocre the leadership and how cowardly the troops.'[3]

The fear of a Soviet takeover in Egypt, Eden's persistent theme, was not realised. This was the greatest failure of British intelligence, to assume that Nasser would become Moscow's puppet. For while the Egyptian leader was happy to take advantage of Soviet largesse – between 1954 and 1961, 43 per cent of Russian aid to the developing world went to Egypt – the investment brought meagre returns for the communist evangelisers. Their bitterest moment came with the Egyptian defeat in the 1967 Six Day War. Nasser's KGB paymasters had long claimed that Soviet equipment and training had transformed the Egyptian armed forces. But when it came to the test, the outcome was settled in the first three hours. Israeli air raids destroyed 286 of 340 Egyptian warplanes on the ground. The story went round of Marshal Zokharov, chief of the Soviet general staff, telephoning Nasser to let him know that his latest batch of aircraft was ready for delivery. 'Or would it save time if we just blew them up now?'[4]

Even allowing that the result of the Six Day War could not have been predicted, Western and Soviet intelligence should have known that the gulf between Arab nationalism and communism was unbridgeable. At one point there were close on twenty thousand Soviet advisers in Egypt, yet they made little impact on their hosts. After Nasser's death, Sadat purged the pro-Marxist faction in the Egyptian hierarchy and expelled the Russians. The KGB network, thought to be one of the strongest in the third world, fell apart and the Egyptian communist party was dissolved.

The repercussions from Suez had their strongest reverberations in Britain. When, on 14 December, Eden returned to London, seemingly refreshed, few expected his premiership to extend long into the new year. Eden himself was bullish. Facing the microphones and the press photographers on his arrival at London Airport, he proclaimed what was to become his mantra for the rest of his life. 'I am convinced, more convinced than I have been about anything in all my public life, that we were right, my colleagues and I, in the judgements and decisions we took, and that history will prove it so.'

Whether he believed what he was saying or whether, during his rest cure, he had calculated that total denial was his last best defence must for ever be a matter for speculation. Even his most devoted supporters agreed that the jury was out on Eden's standing as a national leader. Erring on the side of generosity throughout Eden's troubles, *The Times*, 'leaving on one side whether the recent policy was right or wrong', found 'more than one ground for saying that its execution was inefficient'. The editorial concluded, 'Either Sir Anthony Eden must now show that he can and will lead a vigorous, progressive, efficient Government or the strains that have been set up will demand someone else.'

If Eden had expected a sympathetic welcome back to active politics he was to be disappointed. The day after his return to Downing Street he was reading in *The Times* a letter from the former Labour prime minister, Clement Attlee, demanding to know whether the British and French governments had had advance warning of the Israeli invasion of Sinai. With Eden's recovery, 'the country may reasonably ask that he should put an end . . . to an uncertainly which cannot fail to be damaging to the national interest'.

It was the one subject Eden was determined to avoid. He did all the could to hide or destroy evidence that pointed towards collusion. Two middle-ranking Foreign Office people were told to put together a file of all the sensitive papers on Suez and deliver it to Norman Brook, the Cabinet Secretary. The files was never seen again.[5] At Chequers the last pointer to Eden's meeting with General Challe, when the Israeli plot was first mooted, was removed when someone scratched out Challe's name in the visitors' book, replacing it with the name of an official who would not normally have even signed in.[6] Admitting to collusion and riding the storm for having participated in such a 'shabby and dishonourable plot'[7] was thus not an option ever contemplated by Eden. He had two other choices when he faced the inevitable parliamentary confrontation. He could prevaricate, knowing that the attack would soon be renewed, or he could lie. He lied.

> I want to say this on the question of foreknowledge, and to say it quite bluntly to the House, that there was not foreknowledge that Israel would attack Egypt – there was not. But there was something else. There was – we knew it perfectly well – a risk of it, and in the event of a risk of it, certain discussions and conversations took place as, I think, was absolutely right, and as, I think, anybody would do.

Having studied his own words, Eden must have realised that he was in an impossible position. For one thing, he was hostage to Mollet and Ben-Gurion, both of whom had an authenticated record of the Sèvres agreement. In the event, neither of them was disposed to speak out, but for the moment Eden was not to know this. In any case, he still had his immediate colleagues to worry about. What demands would be made by Macmillan and Butler in return for their silence? And suppose their demands – each, say, wanting to be deputy prime minister with an expectation of early accession – were irreconcilable?

There was another way. Eden could retire, citing medical advice, relying on the convention of Westminister politics of not kicking a man when he was down to guard his entry into the history books. Squaring his doctors, doubtless honourable men, was no problem. Eden's famously delicate constitution could not be denied. If the patient said that he found it hard to continue, what else could they do but confirm his self-diagnosis?

Westminster gossip kept up the pressure on Eden to make his decision soon. Ministers who spoke to him over Christmas found him preoccupied with his future. Macmillan gave the prime minister cold comfort by comparing Suez to Mons and Dunkirk, military disasters that proved to be but a short step to famous victories. There was no need for Macmillan to spell out who would be leading the victory parade.

In any race to succeed Eden, Macmillan was clearly the front runner. The right wing of the party would have found it hard to accept one of Eden's opponents in Downing Street, while those on the left, though associating Macmillan with the Suez fiasco, nonetheless recognised his electoral skills and his ability to restore confidence in the government. But to talk of a race is to give a misleading impression of the strength of the competition to Macmillan. Butler was the only possible rival. Though no longer formally the deputy prime minister, he had stood in for Eden on most occasions when the premier was otherwise engaged. Many saw him as the leader in waiting, rather like Eden under Churchill. But that in itself worked against Butler. The party elders had already made one serious mistake; they were not about to make another by following the convention of Buggins's turn. Butler was seen as a vacillator, a charge brought against Eden, and as a less than effective manager of the country's finances; Eden again. The Macmillan image scored favourably on both counts. He had stood up for his country in its hour of need and restored stability to the nation's finances after the post-Suez turmoil. That his judgement over Suez was as faulty as that of Eden and that he, more than anyone, was responsible for landing Britain in a financial mess was conveniently ignored, not least because Macmillan was so adept at muddying his tracks. In the critical weeks leading up to his entry into Downing Street, he took care to let Butler do the public talking on Suez. Of his own role in the affair, he said nothing.

On 5 January Eden told 'Bobbety' Salisbury, the elder statesman of the Tory Party after Churchill, that he was resigning. Since these were the days when Conservative leaders emerged by consensus rather than by popular election, it fell to Salisbury to canvas cabinet members on their preference. Was it to be Harold or Rab, or, as the inquisitor would have it with that curious inflection favoured by some of the aristocracy, Hawold or Wab? Only one voted for Butler. Characteristically, Selwyn Lloyd was unable to make up his mind either way. As he almost certainly anticipated, Eden was dispatched on a crest of euphoria. Churchill led the plaudits for his one-time deputy.

> Those who at home and abroad attacked the resolute action which, in company with our French allies, we took last autumn, may now perhaps have reason to reconsider their opinions. I do not think that the attitude then adopted by the United Nations has been helpful either to the free world or to the cause of peace and prosperity in the Middle East.[8]

More guardedly, Macmillan declared 'that when the history of the Suez crisis came to be written, it would be recognised that Eden had been inspired by motives of the highest patriotism'.[9] A week later, addressing the nation on television, he adopted his most avuncular, jocular manner to call for an end to defeatist talk about Britain being a second-class power. 'What nonsense. This is a great country and do not let us be ashamed to say so.'[10]

Eden's reputation stood up well in the early years of his retirement. It helped that the popular press continued to portray Nasser as Hitler or Mussolini incarnate, a ruthless dictator ready to sell his country and the rest of the Middle East to communism. There were those who stuck to the line that Eden had acted all the more courageously because he knew that he was in for a lonely battle, or, to quote Kirkpatrick, that he was 'the only man in England who wanted the nation to survive'.[11] With the support of a sympathetic biographer and his own memoirs, which gave close attention to his record as a man of peace ready to stand up against the world's bullies, he was taken seriously when he defended Suez as a 'short term emergency operation which succeeded' and

continued to argue that British and French action had given an
essential lead to the UN to intervene in the Middle East.

His denial of collusion with Israel and his continuing refusal
to discuss the subject brought him a short-term benefit of the
doubt, even if there were those who gasped at his audacity. When
his autobiography was published in France, his editor, Charles
Ronsac, a journalist who knew much of the inside story of Suez,
thought at first that there was a chapter missing.

> Everything concerning the international crisis that led to the
> nationalisation of the Suez Canal, the Franco-British expedition,
> the pressures that preceded the ceasefire, of these he not omit
> one telegram, not one speech, not the merest detail. But there
> was nothing on the Anglo-French–Israeli 'collusion' which was
> at the heart of the Suez operation. Eden held to the official
> version, a veritable fiction, that the participants acted separately.[12]

The fiction was given some credence by Mollet's self-imposed
silence. Incredibly, given the way he had been treated, Mollet
remained very much the Anglophile and a friend of Eden, with
whom he corresponded regularly. Before Eden committed himself
to print, he sent Mollet passages on Suez inviting his comments.
Mollet wrote back thanking him 'for the way you describe our
collaboration and talk about our friendship'. Mollet found it hard
to understand why Eden could not bring himself to admit to
collusion but took the view that if that was what he wanted, so be
it. His readiness to support Eden extended to influencing the
writing of other principals in the affair. A book on Suez by
Shimon Peres was modified substantially after heavy editing by
Mollet. The section where Peres recalled a British proposal to
feign a bombardment of an Israeli town to start hostilities disappeared from the final version. Also edited out were all references to the Sèvres protocol. Mollet subsequently wrote to Peres,
'I have just re-read the new proof of chapter 10 and I very much
appreciate the changes . . .' He added, 'As far as I am concerned,
I will continue to rest in silence about this period.'[13] It also went
in Eden's favour that supporters of Ben-Gurion were keen to

disassociate him from any suggestion that Israel needed a Western alliance, let alone a covert one, to defeat Egypt.

Producing one of the first authoritative accounts of the Sinai campaign, Robert Henriques felt safe in commenting on the 'enormous weight of evidence to suggest that, if Israel had any idea in advance of the action that Britain and France would take, it was only in vague terms', adding, 'In fact, Mr Ben Gurion was in Israel throughout the whole of September and October; and every day can be accounted for in detail by his secretarial staff – if anybody thinks it worthwhile, or is impertinent enough, to inquire. Between the 27th and 30th October Mr Ben Gurion was keeping himself operational by the use of "Palgin" tablets.'[14]

But as time went on and the evidence from the USA and from France hardened into a certainty that Eden had behaved in an underhand way and had done his best to cover his tracks, the knives began to flash. Writing of the 'dismal affair of Suez' eight years after the event, when Eden was fair game, Malcolm Muggeridge pulverised the former prime minister as 'a grisly parody of Churchillian war leadership; a Benzedrine Napoleon and pinchbeck Foreign Office Machiavelli all in one'.[15] The more generously inclined joined Eden's friend Noël Coward in marking him down as 'a tragic figure who had been cast in a star part well above his capabilities'.

The real indictment against Eden was not so much that he was devious or dishonest but rather that he did not understand the country he was governing. Over twenty years of world travel in the grand style, cavorting with diplomats and politicians who themselves had outmoded, or at best second-hand, impressions of what Britain represented had left him with an exaggerated view of his country's readiness or ability to fight for the values he held most dear. Eden had no feel for the better-educated and better-informed generation that was coming of age. The rebellious spirit that was beginning to find its strength in the late fifties had its origins in America, where rising living standards and cash to spare had released teenagers from their parents' purse strings and freed them from traditional authority. The new radicalism soon spread to Europe, where young people were besotted with American culture popularised by sound and screen. The gap between old and new was widening at the time of Suez. Eden and his friends, mostly of pre-war vintage, failed to connect with the young; few even bothered to try. To many of military age in 1956, the Suez episode was a throwback, evidence that their elders had lost their grip.

It was Macmillan's great skill that he caught on to much of this. While his 'affectations of the upper class and the portentousness of an old buffer'[16] – Baldwin with brains, as one commentator put it – appealed to middle England, his promise of the good things of life for ordinary voters popularised his government across the age and class divides. As Chancellor, Macmillan had proved himself the master of delivering simple economic good news – one and a half million new cars and half a million new motorcycles registered in two years, half a million new fridges and a million new washing machines sold in the same period; better homes, more money for eating and drinking. It was a message that he continued to pump out as prime minister, making it such a vote-winner that by the 1959 election the Suez scandal had been smothered by popular economics. In 1956, against all the odds, the reinvented tory party was returned to power.

Apart from Eden, the political fallout from Suez was altogether milder than anticipated, not least in the foreign office, where resentment at the absence of consultation and the widespread assumption that Eden was 'quite unfit to govern'[17] might have been expected to have set off an avalanche of resignations. Yet those who followed their consciences were limited to junior levels. Of others who expressed disquiet, usually in letters to their immediate superiors, career and family commitments took precedence. The face-saver was the ingrained conviction that there was a sharp defining line between politics and administration. Politics was seen as the less respectable part of government which barely impinged on the work of civil servants, whose principal duty was to safeguard the continuity of the state. As Donald Logan said of Kirkpatrick, he 'was a good civil servant with a sharply defined concept of his role. He conceived that he was there to give advice to Ministers if they wanted it, and to proffer advice if he felt they needed it'.[18]

Logan himself did not at any time think that 'I ought to have resigned during those four days in Paris when I found myself as bag carrier to [Selwyn Lloyd]. If I had said "I am refusing to do this" it would have put an extraordinary spanner in the works. Ministers carry the responsibility and, it seemed to me, then and now, that it was not my function to create that sort of embarrassment to ministers whom one is serving in a personal role'.[19] Or, as Richard Powell put it: 'We felt very strongly, as civil servants, having said what we thought, in the last resort we carried out what Ministers decided to do. That was how it worked.'[20] But not for everyone. One Treasury official, Leo Pliatzky, reflected later that Suez 'was the only occasion . . . when I had to reflect how the work of the British Civil Service, with its commitment to work for the government of the day, irrespective of its policies, differed from officials in Hitler's Germany'.[21]

The scale of the Suez operation was puny compared to the European conflict that had ended a decade earlier, but soldiers and civilians had died as a result of monumental bungling and a misguided sense of national interest. It ill became those civil servants who remained silent to fall back on the Nuremberg cliché, 'I was only obeying orders'. The lessons of Nuremberg were ignored because it seemed unimaginable that British public servants would ever be faced with the moral dilemma of enacting policies with which they profoundly disagreed. Suez exposed the error of assuming that civil servants play no part in determining ends, choosing means and fixing priorities.

Writing soon after Suez on the profession of government, Brian Chapman concluded: 'Neutrality in public office tends in the end to moral corruption. If all governments are to be served with equal impartiality and loyalty there are no grounds at all for criticizing the German official who served Hitler to the best of his ability. In any profession other than government such people would be regarded as dangerous cynics or weaklings.'[22]

Aside from Anthony Nutting there was only one other ministerial resignation. Edward Boyle, who, as economic secretary to
the treasury, was regarded as one of the brightest of the rising
generation of Conservative thinkers, went on 4 November. He
was not gone long. Macmillan brought him back into government,
in part to comfort the left of the party. At the same time, Julian
Amery, Macmillan's son-in-law and doyen of the Suez Group,
was promoted to ministerial rank at the war office to keep the
right-wingers happy. To everyone's surprise, including his own,
Lloyd stayed on at the foreign office, doubtless to play the Suez
fall guy, though, as Aneurin Bevan commented, 'there's no need
to attack the monkey when the organ grinder is present'.

Among backbench MPs there was barely a ripple. Stanley
Evans, a self-made businessman representing Labour, was
pushed out by his Birmingham constituency for supporting
Suez while Angus Maude resigned from his Tory-held seat in
protest at the ceasefire. But of the local political battles the chief
interest was in the Bournemouth East constituency, where a Conservative majority of middle-class, elderly voters disposed of their
parliamentary representative, who had come out against Suez.
Nigel Nicolson was a dedicated but outspoken backbencher who,
in the words of his father, Harold Nicolson, 'always seems to
espouse causes which are unpopular with his constituency . . .
He is too honest and progressive for those old Bournemouth
tabby-cats'.[23] That the younger Nicolson had ever been selected
in the first place is a mystery explained only by the apathy of
the aged when life is proceeding at a leisurely pace. Suez was
the shock to the nervous system that jerked them out of their
lethargy.

'Simple minds work simply,' mused Harold Nicolson. 'The
ladies of Bournemouth do not like the Russians, the Americans
or Nasser. Eden has dealt a blow to these three enemies: therefore
Eden must be right.'[24] Even so, when the young MP's future was
put to the constituency membership he did better than expected,
losing by just ninety-one votes out of a total of 7,500. His successor was Major James Friend, Harrow, Sandhurst and 11th

Hussars, who made a living managing his son-in-law's estates in Staffordshire.

That Nicolson lost so narrowly in a constituency where the Tory establishment was blimpish to the point of caricature was one of several indications that Britain was beginning to emerge from under the dead weight of patriotic nostalgia. Change there had to be, as even a strong minority in Bournemouth East had the wit to recognise. In Macmillan's time as prime minister the far right, represented at its most farcical level by the League of Empire Loyalists, was relegated to the political fringe. Even the Suez Group became something of a joke.

Writing in the Tory-leaning *Spectator*, Bernard Levin had no fear of a backlash when he ridiculed Captain Waterhouse for a speech that was 'so silly, so futile, so nasty . . . and with all so empty of anything at all but the spirit which moves a bad tempered child to kick a table against which it has bumped its knee'.[25] When Salisbury resigned from the government in protest at the return from exile of the Cypriot nationalist leader Archbishop Makarios, who three years later was to become Cyprus's first president, Macmillan made no effort to dissuade him.

One of the more inspired of Macmillan's government appointments was Duncan Sandys as minister of defence. Sandys had a reputation as a political bruiser who got things done. As minister of supply he had come to know about advanced weapons systems that had yet to be adopted for British defence. Sandys' respect for the military chiefs was, at best, restrained, and he was not about to knuckle under to men in gold braid. Macmillan was warned of trouble to come, but for all his talk of Britain remaining a great country he knew that a radical rethink of defence was long overdue.

The weak point was the army and the weakest point of the army was conscription, or, as it was known to officialdom keen to promote the boy scout image of life in uniform, national service. Fixed in 1946 at twelve months for eighteen-year-olds who were not blind, mentally defective or in reserved occupations such as coal mining and farming, the period of call-up was extended to eighteen months in 1947 and to two years in 1950.

By far the greatest number of conscripts joined the army. More dependent on technical skills, the navy and air force limited their intake to those with relevant qualifications or who showed an interest in signing up as regulars. In April 1956, conscripts accounted for only 10 per cent of navy manpower, 32 per cent of the RAF but over 50 per cent of the army. In other words, 200,000 regular army personnel were responsible for training and engaging 200,000 national servicemen. Small wonder that the professionals had little time for anything else, such as thinking rationally about why they needed a standing army, navy and air force (772,000 in total in 1956) bigger than those of any other European country and, at one time, bigger even than those of the USA.

The oft-cited responsibility to protect western Europe from Russian invasion was outmoded by the nuclear deterrent, while the tired cliché of living up to worldwide commitments, even when they could be justified for reasons other than pomp and glory, would have been better served by a smaller, top-quality mobile force kitted out with the best of modern weaponry.

As it was, the British army, backed by a defence expenditure that was close on 10 per cent of the national budget, stuck to a mindset that was best suited to a rerun of the Second World War. A generation of national servicemen, with this author among them, can testify to the mind-numbing banality of parade-ground ritual and the futility generated by military exercises in which the 'best friend', which we had to keep with us at all times, was a rifle showing more than ordinary signs of wear and tear and at least twice the age of the carrier.

Those who defended national service gave it a social bonus, arguing that young men emerged from their two years as more mature individuals. This without stopping to think that any eighteen-year-old, whatever his experience, is liable to be more mature at twenty. But even conceding the point, what was seldom recognised was the resentment building up against established authority. Britain was teetering on the edge of the liberating sixties. National service and Suez brought the social revolution that much closer.

With Macmillan's backing, Sandys forced through a drastic reduction in conventional forces, arguing for the nuclear deterrent as the cornerstone of the new defence policy. Conscription was to be phased out by 1960, bringing military manpower down to 375,000 by 1962. A process known as 'bowler hatting', the thinning of the ranks of the inflated officer corps, was the first example of what nowadays would be called administrative downsizing. The labour market was suddenly awash with middle-aged retired captains and majors eager for jobs that would enable them to continue to live like gentlemen.

Under Sandys the defence ministry became a power to be reckoned with. Up to Suez power had been concentrated in the service departments, with the result that the navy, army and air force spent much energy on vying with each other for the lion's share of an ever ballooning defence budget. Some idea of the importance attached to what was supposed to be the coordinating ministry was the number of Duncan Sandys' predecessors – twenty-three since 1945. The latest incumbent understood that defence had to be centralised and, moreover, that defence and foreign policy were parts of the same package. Excusing themselves for a strategy of failure at Suez, the service chiefs blamed the politicians for their apparent inability to spell out precisely what they wanted to achieve. In promoting the defence ministry at the expense of the service departments, thus giving it a stronger voice in cabinet, Sandys ensured that the Suez mistakes would not be repeated. Predictably, the service chiefs failed to get the point. But the force of their anger was focused on what was seen as a disastrous reduction in fighting strength. Sandys held his ground. The only successful counter-attack was led by Mountbatten, who managed to preserve the navy's aircraft carriers. They were expensive but had proved their worth at Suez.

The new defence policy was not an unqualified success. The mounting costs of sophisticated weaponry meant that the expected savings did not materialise. Defence commitments were reduced, but it was not until the late sixties that Britain abandoned its defence role east of Suez. Finally, it took some time for the outstanding lesson of Suez to be recognised; that what was needed above all for Britain to fulfil its defence obligations was a well-equipped, highly trained rapid response force. The surest way of preventing another major war was to curb troublemakers before they gained the strength to be threats to world peace. If such a force had been on hand in 1956, the Suez story might had a different ending. All the evidence suggests that it would still have been a monumental political mistake, but the military would have emerged with more credit.

25

Macmillan's entry into Downing Street was followed by a period of intense diplomatic activity as Britain worked to restore the special relationship with the USA. The first hint that Eisenhower was in forgiving mood had come in early December when, at a meeting with Lloyd in Paris, Dulles had agreed that it was time for a fresh start. Soon afterwards, an invitation from the White House mooted either Washington or Bermuda as a venue for an Anglo-American summit. Macmillan chose Bermuda, a British colony, to give him a slight home-ground advantage, making him appear less like the humble supplicant, which, of course, he was.

The talks, beginning on 21 March, were hailed by both sides as a great success. Eisenhower confided to his diary that it was the most successful international meeting he had attended since the end of the Second World War. Credit must be given to Macmillan for promoting a spirit of camaraderie. Unlike Eden, who operated on the assumption that American support was a tap to be switched on and off as needed, the latest prime minister was more the pragmatist, ready to accept that America called the shots and that Britain's glory days were over.

Macmillan's critics accused him of trying to preserve Britain's world standing at American expense – great-power status on the cheap. There was some truth in this, as became evident with Macmillan's insistence on Britain's own nuclear deterrent, independent in theory, but conditional on having American technology and on handing over to Washington exclusive responsibility for deciding if and when to wage war. But if Macmillan was rather too preoccupied with keeping up appearances, in real terms he was ready to accept Britain's secondary role in the Atlantic partnership.

The change in the balance of power in the Middle East was a case in point. At last Britain conceded that there was no chance of the USA joining the Baghdad Pact. To have done so (how many times had Dulles pointed this out?) would have upset the Saudis, which in turn would have created problems with Israel and aroused congressional ire. The USA was, however, ready to do more to protect the oil supplies while trying not to gloat at Britain's failure to achieve that objective. The result was the Eisenhower Doctrine (January 1957), which promised economic and military support for Middle East states threatened by Soviet incursion. There was no reference to Britain, or to France for that matter, but it was understood that Britain should continue to take responsibility for the Gulf sheikhdoms and for Jordan and Iraq. That even this was beyond its capacity was soon to become apparent.

In March 1957, internal pressures forced King Hussein of Jordan to abrogate the 1948 treaty with Britain and to declare that henceforth the subsidy needed to keep his country afloat would come from Saudi Arabia, Egypt and Syria. The threat of revolution, even the break-up of the country, did not have to be spelt out. Britain offered advice; the USA acted. An aid package worth $10 million was delivered to Hussein while units of the US Sixth Fleet moved into the eastern Mediterranean.

Attention shifted to Iraq, where Nuri as-Said, Britain's faithful ally in the region, felt under threat from a revitalised Nasser. When, on 1 February 1958, Egypt and Syria came together in the United Arab Republic, Nuri responded with a counter-union of Iraq and Jordan to be known as the Arab Federation. To strengthen his position further he urged Britain to stand back from Kuwait, allowing the sheikh to join the Arab Federation. He was asking too much. For Britain to remove itself from Kuwait was to invite a Nasser-style revolution. In any case, the sheikh was satisfied with the status quo.

Nuri's response was to revive a long-standing claim that Kuwait really belonged to Iraq. The argument, brought back into play by Saddam Hussein forty years on, was based on the legalistic complexities of Ottoman imperialism, which had the ruler of Kuwait owing allegiance to the Vilayat of Basra. Confronted by two friendly states at odds with each other, Britain professed diplomatic impotence. The issue was resolved by revolution in Iraq. After the bodies of Nuri and King Faisal had been dragged through the streets, Britain offered pious regrets while making haste to connect with the new regime. Meanwhile American and British troops entered Jordan and Lebanon to hold back the tide of discontent. In July, the USA offered to protect the security of members of the Baghdad Pact. According to Selwyn Lloyd this made the USA a full member of the pact in all but a signature on the treaty. In fact, it was more an acknowledgement that America was now the first line of defence throughout the Middle East.

Restoring relations with Egypt was an exercise in patient diplomacy over two years, building up to the exchange of ambassadors. Crammed into one room of the old residence, the British delegation, led by Colin Crewe, sweated over the outstanding issues, ranging from compensation for those who had had their property confiscated to the resumption of air services. As Crewe's number two, Paul Wright gives credit to Mohamed Heikal, editor of *Al Ahram*, for easing the way to an agreement. But there was fear of a last-minute hitch when, late one night, Crewe was summoned to an urgent meeting.

> On his way to Heikal's office, he reviewed the remaining possible areas of misunderstanding. Among them was the continued detention in an Egyptian prison of a British subject named Mr Zarb [arrested when the MI6 ring was broken up in August]. It was a tricky business. The Egyptians were touchy about it and ... it had therefore been decided not to press the point in the hope that feelings of humanity would prevail ... So he had dismissed this as a complicating factor and had arrived *chez* Heikal baffled and apprehensive. The great man was affability itself; sorry to drag Colin out so late at night, urgent message from the President himself, must be dealt with at once, and so on.

'Not at all,' Colin said, sitting back and waiting for the blow to fall.

'Well,' Mohammed continued, 'the President and I have been thinking that we ought to give you a present in recognition of all you have done for our future relations.' Colin heard distant alarm bells going off at that stage, remembering regulations about the giving and receiving of presents by Civil Servants, rules which many foreigners regard as incomprehensibly restrictive to fruitful intercourse, as it is understood in their own moral climates.

'But when it came to deciding what to give you, we were stumped. So we thought that the best thing would be to give you a cheque to buy something for yourself. Here it is, with our best thanks and good wishes!' And with a grin, he handed Colin a plain white envelope. Colin was transfixed by the implications of this exceedingly awkward development. Knowing that he could not refuse such a gift out of hand, his one desire was to get away as quickly as possible and think out how to cope with it. So with as much grace as he could muster, he thanked Mohamed, thrusting the envelope into his pocket, and made a move to leave. He was not to be let off so lightly.

'Aren't you going to open it?' Mohamed asked. Feeling, and probably looking, guilty, Colin retrieved the now crumpled envelope from his pocket, tore it open, and pulled out a sheet of paper on which was written the single word 'Zarb'.[1]

The French government emerged relatively unscathed from the Suez crisis. Or so it seemed. With the blame fixed squarely on the irresolute British and the double-dealing Americans, Mollet was confirmed in office by a large majority in a National Assembly debate just before Christmas. When Mendès-France and Edgar Faure spoke out against the Suez adventure, the response was cool going on openly hostile. Opinion polls taken in November 1956 and March 1957 showed a marginal shift in the approval rating for Suez, from 44 per cent to 43 per cent, while the number who disapproved actually fell. The only increase was in the proportion of 'don't knows'.[2]

What the pollsters and, indeed, the votes of the deputies failed to show was that government support had less to do with positive enthusiasm than with sheer apathy, a sense of helplessness in a political process that threw up one ineffectual government after another. Mollet was backed because few could imagine any better alternative. But for those who looked beneath the surface of French life, there were warnings enough of a growing 'disorientation, disenchantment and disgust'. These were the words of Stanley Karnow, an American journalist who spent a month just prior to the Suez crisis checking out the views of young French citizens. Nostalgia for the great days of empire was, he concluded, a 'gimmick concocted to camouflage the deficiencies of the present'. The sense of malaise was plain enough, but beneath it 'burned an ember of revolt that simmered with a yearning for change'.[3]

Disillusionment and cynicism deprived the Fourth Republic of its bedrock. But what could replace it? Inevitably thoughts turned towards General Charles de Gaulle, the leader in waiting, who made no secret of his ambition to return to power in circumstances that would do away with destructive party wrangling and ineffectual compromise.

The failure of Suez served to boost de Gaulle's popularity. This is not to say that his accession was assured. The majority of the population were neither Gaullist nor anti-Republican, and there was not sufficient support in the Assembly for de Gaulle to be voted into power constitutionally. At the same time there were no signs of a readiness to die on the barricades to save the Fourth Republic.

Critical to de Gaulle's future was the army, or more specifically the army in Algeria. Disappointed in its expectations that Suez would end the revolt in Algeria, the generals cast about for other ways of denting the appeal of the insurgents. With 400,000 troops there was no doubt that the country could be held militarily, even if the brutal methods used to enforce submission far exceeded the bounds of tolerable behaviour. But while torture and summary executions were said to be justified as the only means of defending the loyal Muslim majority, even the most ruthless of the commanders, of whom Massu was one, accepted that Algeria could not be ruled indefinitely as a police state. Something more was needed to keep her permanently bound to France.

The policy that attracted broad support involved an ambitious programme of economic and social reform that would so raise the living standards of the Muslims that they would want nothing more than to remain French citizens. Integration, defined as 'the indissoluble union of former colonial peoples and the former mother country within a single political entity',[4] was an army invention accepted reluctantly by the settlers as the price of keeping the military onside. But who was to enforce it? Opinion in Algeria held that the fair-weather politicians in Paris, who could not agree on anything for longer than it took to vote in another government, were incapable of the necessary resolve. What was needed was a leader determined to enforce his will. De Gaulle was the obvious, indeed the only, candidate on offer.

In France itself, economic troubles following on from Suez raised de Gaulle's profile as the standard-bearer of order and stability. Social reforms introduced by the Mollet government, such as a third week of paid holidays, the provision of low-cost housing and welfare measures for the elderly, had to be paid for at a time when the franc was under pressure, petrol was rationed and prices were rising. The harsh winter that brought three feet of snow to the streets of St Tropez caused food shortages throughout the country. The communists were usually the beneficiaries of social unrest but, suffering the fallout from the Russian invasion of Hungary, the party was in no position to exploit its opportunities. The right wing was split several ways but each faction claimed a pact with de Gaulle, while the measured responses from the general gave comfort to all but unqualified endorsement to none.

The Mollet government lasted until 21 May 1957. At fourteen months, its period of office was a record for the Fourth Republic. After a three-week interregnum, which allowed for back-room plotting and squabbling, a successor coalition was put together under Bourgès-Maunoury, whose leading role in Suez proved to be no obstacle to his elevation. His downfall, after two and a half months, was brought about when the National Assembly rejected a new political framework in Algeria allowing for greater autonomy for the native population. De Gaulle was one step closer to power.

The culmination was a demand in Algeria for a Government of Public Safety, headed by de Gaulle. The call was taken up in mainland France. Once the Gaullist bandwagon had started rolling few were prepared to stand in its way. Or, as Mollet put it, 'There is talk of firing our last shots, but we have not yet fired our first.'[5]

If the failure of the Suez operation played some part in bringing de Gaulle to the Elysée, it was even more significant in shaping his policies once a national referendum had confirmed him in power. He recognised, as Macmillan recognised, that after Suez the cost of empire was higher than his country could afford. The new constitution that inaugurated the Fifth Republic gave France's African colonies a choice between autonomy in a Communauté Française or independence. Those opting for autonomy (only Guinea chose independence) were offered generous economic aid with the broad hint that full independence was a short step away. In 1960 eleven former French colonies joined the UN. This was a rejection of old-style imperialism that went well beyond Macmillan's detection of the 'winds of change' blowing across Africa.[6]

It took longer to sort out Algeria, where de Gaulle's hardheaded judgement of what was possible came up against the romantic and unrealistic impulses of the settlers and the occupying army. The retreat from Algeria threatened de Gaulle's survival, but the generals who felt let down by his pragmatism and plotted against him soon discovered that France had had enough of revolution.

As for the role of France in the wider world, de Gaulle's first instinct was to follow Britain in restoring a working relationship with America. But he wanted it made clear that if the USA,

Britain and France were to act together it was to be on a basis of equality. This was unacceptable in Washington, the more so because Britain, humbled by Suez, was ready to accept a subordinate relationship.

It is likely that de Gaulle had no great expectations of reaching a deal with the Anglo-Saxons, who too often, in his view, had proved to be treacherous allies. Suez was just the latest in a succession of let-downs going back to the quarrels with Churchill and Eisenhower over military priorities in the last phase of the European war. The big difference was that now de Gaulle had an alternative to a close transatlantic alliance. Turning away from Britain and America, he put all his energy into forging an alliance with West Germany, the aim being to create a 'Paris–Bonn axis' around which the rest of western Europe would revolve.

That Britain allowed de Gaulle to get away with it shows how blind successive Labour and Tory governments were to the opportunities for helping to shape a united Europe. Moves towards European unity, favoured by Churchill during and immediately after the Second World War, were regarded in London with suspicion, even distaste. Firmly positioned with the sceptics, Eden as foreign secretary had been instrumental in destroying any remaining continental illusions that Britain might be recruited to the great enterprise when he ruled out participation in a European army. Failing British involvement, the project collapsed, and though Eden subsequently tried to recover his position by committing to a major share of the cost of NATO, there was no longer much hope that he would join in moves towards economic integration. Britain remained arrogantly aloof from the European conferences at Messina in June 1955 and Venice in May 1956.

As a good European and an Anglophile, Mollet was optimistic that the Anglo-French alliance against Nasser would convert Eden. After the failure of the mission he changed his mind. Britain was a lost cause. 'Europe will be your revenge,' Konrad Adenauer told Mollet on the day the Suez operation was halted.

But the French prime minister had misjudged Eden's reaction

to the Suez debacle. Beginning at last to understand that the British Empire could no longer serve as a security blanket, Eden began to take the European experiment seriously. The Suez experience, he wrote, in one of his last ruminations as prime minister,

> has not so much changed our fortunes as revealed realities. While the consequences of this may be to determine us to work more closely with Europe, carrying with us, we hope, our closest friends in the Commonwealth in such development, here too we must be under no illusion. Europe will not simply welcome us simply because at the moment it may appear to suit us to look at them. The timing and the conviction of our approach may be decisive in their influence on those with whom we plan to work.[7]

Edward Heath, then chief whip of the Conservative Party, remembered feeling 'delight mixed with sadness at all it had taken to bring Anthony's change of heart on the subject'. It was too late. While Macmillan was playing up to Eisenhower in Bermuda, the European 'Six' signed the Treaty of Rome. It was not an event that Macmillan rated highly, if at all. A token effort to appease the French with a day trip to Paris was inevitably compared unfavourably to the six days set aside for Eisenhower. What conversation there was with Mollet and Pineau took on an edge when Macmillan warned of cuts in the British contribution to European defence.

Reviewing the political developments of his period as a civil servant, Noel Annan judged the British rejection of Europe as 'the most ruinous diplomatic decision taken by my generation'.

> Many were the excuses that were made. Ministers spoke of our nuclear alliance with America; our devotion to free trade with all, not just six, European countries in the OEEC; our devotion to GATT; our commitment to the Commonwealth; and the doubts of the chiefs of staff ... The Foreign Office thought nothing would come of Messina. To the despair of [Belgian foreign minister Henri] Spaak Britain sent an under-secretary of

the Board of Trade to represent Britain at the conference. Spaak came to London to see Rab Butler: the warmer Spaak became, the colder was Butler's reception. 'I don't think I could have shocked him more when I tried to appeal to his imagination if I had taken off my trousers,' Spaak said to his *directeur du cabinet* Robert Rothschild. At the eleventh hour the Europeans tried again and sent the Dutch foreign minister to Butler. To be lectured on Britain's moral responsibility to lead Europe by such a little nation was too much. 'I got very bored with him,' Butler later told Michael Charlton.[8]

An equally harsh verdict is delivered by Sir Guy Millard, who was Eden's private secretary during the Suez crisis. He puts the blame for failing to understand what was happening in Europe squarely on the foreign office.

It is all very well for the Foreign Office to torment themselves about Suez, but the fact is that, while Suez was happening, they ignored something much more important that was happening under their nose, which was the formation of the European Community. The Foreign Office totally abdicated their responsibility on the most important foreign policy issue of our time. Eden was given very bad advice . . . because they regarded it as trade negotiation, rather difficult stuff about tariffs and quotas. And because they were told by the Treasury and the Board of Trade that it was impossible for us to join a Customs Union, and they accepted this without question. There were other arguments too, about the Commonwealth and the United States, all quite bogus arguments actually. The advice that Eden got from the Foreign Office was, broadly speaking: 'Don't worry too much. It is not going to happen. The Six will not reach agreement, and there is therefore nothing to worry about.' I am not saying that, if Eden had received different advice, he would necessarily have participated in the negotiations. He wasn't particularly European. Like Churchill, he was oriented towards the United States and the Commonwealth. But all the same, the Foreign Office didn't perceive this for what it was, the formation of an immensely important thing in Europe, from which we were voluntarily excluding ourselves.

Why did the foreign office get it so terribly wrong? One explanation is that: 'The British civil service is a kind of museum of accepted ideas. Original thought is not welcomed very much.'[9] From his vantage point in Paris, Gladwyn Jebb warned that Britain would come to regret ignoring Europe. Surprisingly, but to give credit where it is due, Selwyn Lloyd took up the theme in early January 1957 when he advised the cabinet that if Britain was to be a first-class power with thermonuclear capacity, this could only be achieved in association with the six members of the Western European Union. Voices were raised against him, including those of Salisbury, Lord Home, then leader of the House of Lords but destined to be Macmillan's successor as prime minister, and Anthony Head, who all asserted that British interests were best served by cooperation with the USA.

The irony here is that it was Eisenhower who pressed for Britain to join the European Union, arguing that if Eden had shown more enthusiasm for a European army, one of the first hesitant steps towards integration, 'there would have been no Suez problem and no European problem now'.[10]

Macmillan failed to get the message. When at last he caught up with the European movement and wanted to be part of it, de Gaulle took enormous satisfaction in slapping on the French veto. Revenge, indeed, for Suez.

ENDPIECE

It has often been said of the Suez war that it was a military success and a political failure. Rather, it was a military failure and a political disaster. True, the generals were hampered by the absence of a clear political lead. Driven by the wish to be rid of Nasser and to establish a Western-friendly regime in Cairo, Eden and Mollet restricted their demands to restoring control over the canal in the hope of winning international but, in particular, American approval for armed force. But while Mollet came clean with the military on what the government was really trying to achieve, Eden dissembled.

The overlap between politicians and the military was far greater in France than in Britain. Barjot, Beaufre and the other French commanders were never in any doubt that Nasser had to go. For them, the objective was obvious, since how would it be possible to score against the rebels in Algeria if Nasser, seen as their chief promoter, remained in power? Eden simply hoped for the best, that once the canal was secure, Nasser would fall to internal discord.

The result was that British and French commanders were at odds from the very beginning of the operation. The involvement of Israel added to the confusion, for while the French military was actively engaged with the politicians in forging a joint plan to attack Egypt, their British counterparts were kept in ignorance until late October, and even then they were learning more from nudges and winks from those in the know than from any official briefing. All this, according to Stockwell, complicated the planning and slowed up the operation.

I and the other force commanders had always been keen to launch the assault from the air and sea within 48 hours of the first air strike, using our air power to soften up the enemy resistance and deny him the use of his air element as well as to support our own land operations. Had this in fact happened then we would have had the whole length of the Canal from Port Said to Suez in our hands in five days – certainly by nightfall on Nov. 5, with the first air strike going in at midnight on Oct. 31. As it was, we had only just got a foothold in Port Said, albeit a valuable one, with our parachute landings by this date. We were still faced with capturing and clearing Port Said, advancing down the narrow causeway to El Qantara and breaking out from the end of the causeway to the south and west. We had the forces, and we had the know-how. But we were held up for the word to 'go'.[1]

He protested too much. Missing from Stockwell's analysis is the fact that he misjudged the strength of the opposition. This was not a political but a military mistake. As Raymond Aron of *Le Figaro* argued, 'everyone knows that in our time a war must be concluded in eight days'.[2] The point was well understood by Beaufre and other French commanders, who argued strenuously for speed and surprise – three or four hours of bombing followed by parachute drops followed by a seaborne landing of a small force of crack troops carried in the fastest ships afloat. That such a plan was feasible and almost certain to have succeeded is proved by the fighting in Sinai, where the Israelis mounted a short, sharp campaign with total success. The British military failed in its objectives largely because they lacked the imagination and initiative to move on from the Second World War.

Moreover, if Keightley and Stockwell were outmoded in their strategic thinking they were equally out of date in their assumption of a clearly identifiable line between military and political matters. Both should have been deterred from launching a Normandy-style armada by the sure knowledge that in the time it took to cross the Mediterranean world opinion, already sympathetic to Egypt, would have moved much farther in that direction. When, after Suez, Keightley complained that popular support for their action had been less than wholehearted, he was simply revealing his failure to notice that times had changed.

The British establishment could no longer expect a united and enthusiastic response to a call to arms. The citizens of a modern democracy, not least those who were expected to do the fighting, demanded good reasons for going to war. At Suez, whatever judgement is made on the arguments for attacking Egypt, too little attention was given by military and government alike to explaining and justifying what was happening. The lesson was not fully learned at Suez. America made the same mistake over Vietnam and the Israelis likewise in Lebanon.

The latest example is Iraq. There is enough in common between Suez 1956 and Iraq 2004 to tempt a comparative study. In both cases the Arab leaders were demonised as prospective Hitlers; in both cases the danger they represented to the rest of the world was exaggerated and, when it turned out to be largely mythical, other reasons were created to justify military action; and in both cases the war fever was brought to boiling point by a collective memory of the consequences of trying to appease dictators. Finally, in both cases the underlying motive was to achieve regime change. It is too early to say whether America will fail as dismally in Iraq as Britain and France failed in Egypt. The only conclusion at this stage is that after a half-century, it is staggering how little understanding there still is between the West and the Arab world. It was once said of Eisenhower that he had his feet in oil and his head in the clouds.[3] The criticism would seem to be more appropriately applied to the latest incumbent of the White House.

Did anyone gain from Suez? Step forward Jacques Georges-Picot, one-time general manager of the Suez Canal Company, who took over as head of the defunct organisation in December 1957. Under his direction, the company accepted compensation of an eighth of its original claim and then reconstructed itself as an investment trust, one of the most successful in France. Among its ventures was a study of a Channel Tunnel.

British motorists had something to cheer about. As a result of petrol rationing, a Turkish-born designer for Morris motors, Alec Issigonis, was given the task of creating a fuel-efficient, small runabout. He came up with the Mini, one of the best-loved and best-selling cars ever.

ACKNOWLEDGEMENTS

Anyone who ventures into the deep waters of the Suez Crisis must pay tribute to Keith Kyle's magisterial study (*Suez*, London, Weidenfeld & Nicolson, 1991). Close in line for plaudits are Anthony Gorst and W. Scott Lucas who pioneered the Suez Oral History Project at the Liddell Hart Centre for Military Studies at King's College, London. My thanks also to the librarians and staff of the Imperial War Museum, the Eisenhower Library, the London Library, the US Department of State Archives, the Liddell Hart Centre for Military Studies, the Royal Marine Museum and the Royal Institute for International Affairs for their patient and unfailing help in tracking down obscure references. Assiduous research was carried out by Samantha Wyndham and Jessica Souriau while, as ever, my assistant, Jill Fenner was indispensable in putting together an intelligible narrative.

For sparing the time to be interviewed for their reminiscences I am indebted to Roy Fullick, Brian Henderson, Erich Reich, Richard Freeborn, Captain Ronald Brooke, John Nutting QC and Hugo Meynell.

The mistakes, hopefully few and minor, are all mine.

Barry Turner

PHOTOGRAPHIC ACKNOWLEDGEMENTS

Corbis: 2r, 7b, 14a, 14b; Empics: 10b; Getty Images: 3a, 3b, 5a, 8, 11a, 12a, 12b, 13b, 15a, 15b; Imperial War Museum: 5b, 6a, 7a, 11b; Popperfoto: 21, 4a, 6b, 13a, 16; Punch: 1; From the Collections of the Royal Marines Museum: 4b (© *Illustrated*), 9 (© *Illustrated*), 10a (© Reuters); Topfoto: 2b.

Every effort has been made to contact all copyright holders of material reproduced in this book. If any have been inadvertently overlooked, the publishers will be pleased to make the necessary arrangement at the first opportunity.

NOTES

Chapter 1

1. Donald Edgar, *Express '56*, John Clare Books, 1981, p. 157.
2. Ibid., pp. 157–8.
3. Second Lieutenant Peter Mayo, unpublished diary, Imperial War Museum; 92/40/1.
4. Edgar, *Express '56*, p. 158.
5. *New York Times*, 2 November 1956.
6. Merry and Serve Bromberger, *Secrets of Suez*, Pan, 1957, p. 115.
7. Roy Fullick and Geoffrey Powell, *Suez, the Double War*, Leo Cooper, 1979, p. 131.
8. A. R. Ashton, Royal Marines; Imperial War Museum PP/MCR/358.
9. General Raful Eitan, *A Soldier's Story*, Shapolsky Publishers, 1991, pp. 66–7.
10. Mayo diary.
11. Ibid.
12. Ibid.

Chapter 2

1. Charles W. Hallberg, *The Suez Canal, Its History and Diplomatic Importance*, Columbia University Press, 1931, p. 62.
2. J. Christopher Herold, *Bonaparte in Egypt*, Hamish Hamilton, 1963, p. 1.
3. Ibid., pp. 61–2.
4. Nicholas the Turk. Quoted in ibid., p. 99.

5. Ibid., p. 100.

6. F. Charles Roux, *Les origines de l'expédition d'Egypte*, 1910.

7. Herold, *Bonaparte in Egypt*, pp. 15–16.

8. D. A. Cameron, *Egypt in the Nineteenth Century*, Smith Elder & Co., 1898.

9. Ferdinand de Lesseps, *Lettres, Journal et Documents 1865*. Quoted in Charles Beatty, *Ferdinand de Lesseps: A Biographical Study*, Eyre & Spottiswoode, 1956, p. 91.

10. Quoted in Beatty, *Ferdinand de Lesseps*, p. 112.

11. Clara Boyle, *A Servant of the Empire: A Memoir of Harry Boyle*, Methuen, 1938, p. 49.

12. H. M. Stanley, *My Early Travels and Adventures in Africa and Asia*, Low, 1895, p. 50.

13. Edward Dicey, *The Egypt of the Future*, Heinemann, 1907, p. 6.

14. Beatty, *Ferdinand de Lesseps*, p. 255.

15. Ibid., pp. 259–60.

16. *Daily Telegraph*, 26 August 1869.

17. *Saturday Review*, 13 November 1869.

18. Douglas Farnie, *East and West of Suez; the Suez Canal in History 1854–1956*, Clarendon Press, 1969, p. 83.

19. Dicey, *The Egypt of the Future*, p. 10.

20. Various news reports quoted in Farnie, *East and West of Suez*, p. 239.

21. Dicey, *The Egypt of the Future*, p. 21.

22. Earl of Cromer, *Modern Egypt*, Macmillan, 1908, p. 351.

Chapter 3

1. Roger Owen, *Lord Cromer*, Oxford University Press, 2004, p. 87.

2. Peter Mansfield, *Britain in Egypt*, Weidenfeld & Nicolson, 1971, p. 176.

3. Owen, *Lord Cromer*, p. 245.

4. J. R. Seeley, *The Expansion of England: Two Courses of Lectures*, Macmillan, 1918, pp. 15–16.

5. J. A. Cramb, *The Origins and Destiny of Imperial Britain*, John Murray, 1915, p. 219.

6. J. A. Cramb, *Germany and England*, John Murray, 1915, p. 27.

7. Farnie, *East and West of Suez*, p. 388.

8. Rudyard Kipling, 'The Exiles' Line', 1892.

9. Farnie, *East and West of Suez*, p. 392.

10. G. R. Parkin, *Round the Empire*, Cassell, 1892, p. 194.

11. *The Times*, 30 September 1893.

12. Owen, *Lord Cromer*, p. 246.

13. Andrew Roberts, *Salisbury*, Weidenfeld & Nicolson, 1999, p. 640.

14. *The Times*, 25 March 1890.

15. Roberts, *Salisbury*, p. 641.

16. Quoted in Owen, *Lord Cromer*.

17. Lord David Cecil, *The Leisure of an Egyptian Official*, Hodder & Stoughton, 1921, p. 25.

18. Sydney A. Moseley, *With Kitchener in Cairo*, Cassell, 1917. Quoted in Gregory Blaxland, *Objective Egypt*, Muller, 1966, p. 117.

19. Boyle, *A Servant of the Empire*, p. 41.

20. *New York Herald Tribune*, 23 Dec. 1904.

Chapter 4

1. Elie Kedourie, *Politics in the Middle East*, Oxford University Press, 1992, p. 76.

2. Hallberg, *The Suez Canal*, p. 343.

3. Brian Gardner, *Allenby*, Cassell, 1965, p. 160.

4. Elie Kedourie, *England and the Middle East*, Mansell Publishing, 1987, pp. 40–41.

5. Hallberg, *The Suez Canal*, p. 352.

6. *Egypt No. 1 (1921)*, Report of the Special Mission to Egypt (Cmd. 1131).

7. Ibid.

8. Gardner, *Allenby*, pp. 242–3.

9. John Charmley, *Lord Lloyd and the Decline of the British Empire*, Weidenfeld & Nicolson, 1987, p. 141.

10. Colin Forbes Adam, *The Life of Lord Lloyd*, Macmillan, 1948, pp. 198–9.

11. E. W. Polson Newman, *The Mediterranean and Its Problems*, London, A. M. Philpot, 1927, p. 276.

12. Sir Frederick Maurice, *Foreign Affairs*, vol. v, London, Liddell Hart Centre for Military Archives, Oct. 1926, pp. 111–12.

13. Kedourie, *Politics in the Middle East*, p. 182.

14. Howard Eeman, *Clouds over the Sun*, Robert Hale, 1981, p. 191.

Chapter 5

1. Jan Morris, *Farewell the Trumpets*, Faber, 1978, p. 439.

2. Sir Evelyn Shuckburgh interview, Liddell Hart Centre for Military Archives; GB99KCLIYA Suez OHP.

3. Barrie St Clair McBride, *Farouk of Egypt*, Robert Hale, 1967, p. 111.

4. Ibid., p. 109.

5. Ibid., p. 121.

6. Trefor E. Evans (ed.), *The Killearn Diaries, 1934–46*, Sidgwick & Jackson, 1972, p. 211.

7. McBride, *Farouk of Egypt*, p. 121.

8. Evans, *The Killearn Diaries, 1934–46*, p. 215.

9. Ibid., p. 211.

10. Ibid., p. 218.

11. William D. Leahy, *I Was There*, Gollancz, 1950, pp. 218–19.

12. Daniel Yergin, Gulf Oil, *Financial Times*, 22 March 2003

13. Leahy, *I Was There*, p. 382.

14. Robert F. Sherwood, *Roosevelt and Hopkins: An Intimate Portrait*, Harper, 1950, p. 872.

15. Ibid., p. 883.

Chapter 6

1. Richard Weight, *Patriots. National Identity in Britain 1940–2000*, Macmillan, 2003.
2. *The Times*, 25 May 1945.
3. Arthur Bryant, *Diaries of Lord Alanbrooke*, Collins, 1957, p. 531.
4. Farnie, *East and West of Suez*, pp. 647–9.
5. Minutes of Defence Committee, 8 and 18 March, DO46.

Chapter 7

1. British White Paper, Cmd. 7179 (1947).
2. Blaxland, *Objective Egypt*, pp. 145–6.
3. Michael Davidson, *The World, the Flesh and Myself*, David Bruce and Watson, 1973, p. 290.
4. Brigadier Kenneth Hunt, interview, Liddell Hart Centre; GB99 LHCMA Suez OHP.
5. McBride, *Farouk of Egypt*, p. 149.
6. Charles Curran, *Spectator*, 3 Aug. 1956.
7. Humphrey Trevelyan, *The Middle East in Revolution*, Macmillan, 1970, p. 90.
8. State Department report quoted by W. Scott Lucas, *Divided We Stand. Britain, the US and the Suez Crisis*, Hodder & Stoughton, 1991, p. 14.
9. Scott Lucas, *Divided We Stand*, p. 13.
10. Evelyn Shuckburgh, *Descent to Suez*, Norton, 1987, p. 75.
11. John Kent (ed.), *Egypt and the Defence of the Middle East*, Stationery Office, 1998, p. xlviii.
12. Julian Amery interview, Liddell Hart Centre, Suez Oral History Project; GB99 KCLMA Suez OHP.
13. Ibid.
14. Kent, *Egypt and the Defence of the Middle East*, p. lxxiv.
15. 'Egypt', minute by Sir P. Dixon on Britain's difficulties in Egypt, FO 371/96920, no. 77, 23 Jan. 1952.
16. American views on the situation in Egypt, minutes by R. C.

Mackworth-Young, D. V. Bendall and R. Allen, FO 37/90148, no. 467, 3–5 Dec. 1951.

17. Ibid.

18. Kent, *Egypt and the Defence of the Middle East*, p. lxxii.

19. DEFE/4/48, COS 165 (51).

20. Quoted in McBride, *Farouk of Egypt*, p. 182.

21. John Connell, *The Most Important Country*, Cassell, 1957, p. 33.

22. CAB 129/49, C (52) 32 Cabinet Memorandum, 11 Feb. 1952.

23. Letter from R. Allen, head of the African Department, to M. J. Creswell on the prospects of an agreement; FO 371/96931, no. 365 (Agreement with the Egyptians).

24. Minute by Mr Eden (reply) to Mr Churchill on the reasons why an agreement is necessary; PREM 11/91, 10 Mar. 1952 (Agreement with Egypt).

25. McBride, *Farouk of Egypt*, p. 208.

Chapter 8

1. John S. D. Eisenhower, *International Herald Tribune*, 7 June 2004.

2. Robert A. Devine, *Eisenhower and the Cold War*, Oxford University Press, 1981, p. 11.

3. Emmet John Hughes, *The Ordeal of Power. A Political Memoir of the Eisenhower Years*, Macmillan, 1963, p. 70.

4. Ibid., p. 51.

5. George F. Kennan, *Memoirs, 1950–63*, Pantheon, 1972, p. 186.

6. David Halberstam, *The Fifties*, Random House, 1993, p. 392.

7. Defence policy and global strategy: memorandum by the COS for the Cabinet Defence Committee, 17 June 1952; CAB 131/12 D(52)26.

8. Ibid.

9. Devine, *Eisenhower and the Cold War*, p. 73.

10. Shuckburgh, *Descent to Suez*, p. 304.

11. Ritchie Ovendale, *Britain, the United States and the Transfer of Power in the Middle East, 1945–62*, Leicester University Press, 1996, p. 125.

12. Farnie, *East and West of Suez*, p. 36.

13. Ibid., p. 677.

14. Christopher Woodhouse, *Something Ventured*, Granada, 1982, p. 110.

15. Peter Grose, *Gentleman Spy. The Life of Allen Dulles*, André Deutsch, 1995, p. 363.

16. Ibid., p. 367.

17. Devine, *Eisenhower and the Cold War*, p. 77.

18. Ibid., p. 78.

19. Sir Evelyn Shuckburgh Interview, Liddell Hart Centre for Military Archives, Suez Oral History Project; GB99 KCLMA Suez OHP.

20. Ibid.

21. Kent, *Egypt and the Defence of the Middle East*, p. lxxi.

22. Julian Amery interview, Liddell Hart Centre, Suez Oral History Project; GB99 KCLMA Suez OHP.

23. Letter (reply) from Mr Churchill to President Eisenhower on the importance of American support for Britain (Negotiations with Egypt); FO 371/102811, no. 372, 12 June 1953.

24. Inward telegram no. 1516 from Lord Salisbury (Washington) to FO giving details of a meeting with Mr Dulles (Negotiations with Egypt); FO 371/102732, no. 21, 15 July 1953.

25. 'Egypt: review of the situation in the Canal Zone': cabinet memorandum by the COS; CAB 129/62, C(53)246, annexe, 4 Sept. 1953.

26. Ibid.

27. 'Egypt': cabinet conclusions on instructions for the British delegation in the defence negotiations; CAB 128/26/2, CC 58(53)4, 15 Oct. 1953.

28. COS committee minutes on whether to retain the semblance of military power in the Middle East (Middle East defence policy); DEFE 4/66, COS 132(53)3, 24 Nov. 1953.

29. 'Operation redeployment': minute by Mr Churchill to Mr

Eden advocating the dispatch of troops and air forces to Khartoum; PREM 11/700, 11 Dec. 1953.

30. Minute (reply) by Mr Eden to Mr Churchill advocating redeployment only after an agreement with Egypt (Redeployment from Egypt); PREM 11/700, 12 Dec. 1953.

31. Eisenhower to Churchill, 21 Dec. 1953; PREM 11/699.

32. 'Middle East: Anglo-American policy': note for the cabinet by Mr Selwyn Lloyd, circulating a letter from Sir R. Makins to FO (25 Jan. 1954); CAB 129/66, C(54)53, 15 Feb. 1954.

33. 'Egypt: defence negotiations': cabinet memorandum by Mr Eden on a new plan to reopen negotiations; CAB 129/66, C(54)99, 13 Mar. 1954.

34. Letter from Sir J. Bowker (Ankara) to R. Allen on the proposed pact's importance for future British defence arrangements in the Middle East (Turko-Pakistani pact); FO 371/110787, no. 29, 26 Mar. 1954.

Chapter 9

1. Ovendale, *Britain, the United States and the Transfer of Power*, p. 113.

2. Richard Aldrich, *The Hidden Hand*, John Murray, 2001, p. 477.

3. Gamal Abdul Nasser, *Egypt's Liberation*, Public Affairs Press, 1955, p. 106.

4. Ibid., p. 111.

5. Jean Lacouture, *Un Sang d'encre*, Stock, 1974, p. 154.

6. Minute by C. A. E. Shuckburgh on the difference of emphasis between the British and American approaches (Northern tier defence arrangements); FO 371/115484, no. 26, 11 Jan. 1955.

7. Shimon Peres, *David's Sling*, Random House, 1970, p. 187.

8. Minute by C. A. E. Shuckburgh to Sir I. Kirkpatrick on the implications for Britain's Middle East policy. (Failure of plan Alpha): FO 371/121235, no. 70, 10 Mar 1956.

9. Shuckburgh, *Descent to Suez*, p. 310.

10. Inward dispatch no. 24 from Sir R. Stevenson to FO on the

Egyptian opposition to the proposed Turco-Iraqi pact (Arab prime ministers' summit); FO 371/115491, no. 244, 10 Feb. 1955.

11. Inward telegram no. 269 from Mr Eden (Cairo) to Mr Churchill giving an account of a meeting with Colonel Nasser and Egyptian leaders (Anglo-Egyptian meeting); FO 371/115492, no. 289, 21 Feb. 1955.

12. Woodrow Wyatt, *Confessions of an Optimist*, Collins, 1985, p. 241.

13. Mohamed H. Heikal, *Cutting the Lion's Tail*, André Deutsch, 1986, pp. 77–8.

14. Kent, *Egypt and the Defence of the Middle East*, p. lxxxviii.

15. Anthony Gorst, 'A modern major general', *Contemporary British History*, vol. 13, 1999, p. 33.

16. Trevelyan, *The Middle East in Revolution*, p. 57.

17. Sir Evelyn Shuckburgh Interview, Liddell Hart Centre for Military Archives, Suez Oral History Project; GB99 KCLMA Suez OHP.

18. Ibid.

19. Blaxland, *Objective Egypt*, pp. 13–14.

Chapter 10

1. John Colville, *The Fringes of Power*, vol. 2, Sceptre, 1986, p. 376.

2. Shuckburgh, *Descent to Suez*, p. 141.

3. Ibid., p. 173.

4. Sir William Hayter, *The Kremlin and the Embassy*, Hodder & Stoughton, 1966, p. 38.

5. D. R. Thorpe, *Eden*, Chatto & Windus, 2003, p. 5.

6. Randolph Churchill, *The Rise and Fall of Sir Anthony Eden*, MacGibbon & Kee, 1959, p. 74.

7. Sir Timothy Eden, *The Tribulations of a Baronet*, Macmillan, 1933.

8. Shuckburgh, *Descent to Suez*, p. 284.

9. Interview with Kenneth Harris, *Listener*, 4 Nov. 1976.

10. Sir Donald Logan, Liddell Hart Centre for Military Archives; GB99 KCLMA Suez OHP.

11. Janet Morgan (ed.), *The Backbench Diaries of Richard Crossman*, Hamish Hamilton, 1981, p. 502.

12. Sir William Hayter, Liddell Hart Centre for Military Archives; GB99 KCLMA Suez OHP.

13. Alistair Horne, *Macmillan*, vol. 1, Macmillan, 1988, p. 373.

14. Ibid., p. 371.

15. Interview, Sir Robin Turton, quoted in Russell Braddon, *Suez, Splitting of a Nation*, Collins, 1973, p. 35.

16. Aldrich, *The Hidden Hand*, p. 478.

17. Trevelyan, *The Middle East in Revolution*, p. 31.

18. Ibid.

19. Herman Finer, *Dulles over Suez*, Quadrangle Books, 1964, p. 31.

20. 'The Middle East': memorandum by Sir I. Kirkpatrick on future British policy; FO 371/115469, no. 19, 30 Oct. 1955.

21. Trevelyan, *The Middle East in Revolution*, p. 33.

22. Selwyn Lloyd, *Suez 1956*, Jonathan Cape, 1978, p. 41.

23. Peter Catterall (ed.), *The Macmillan Diaries, 1950–1957*, Macmillan, 2003, p. 534.

24. Sir Anthony Eden, *Full Circle*, Cassell, 1960, p. 338.

25. *Evening Standard*, 2 Feb. 1956.

26. *Daily Telegraph*, 3 Jan. 1956.

27. *Spectator*, 6 Jan. 1956.

28. Ibid., 6 Apr. 1956.

29. Thorpe, *Eden*.

30. D. R. Thorpe, *Selwyn Lloyd*, Jonathan Cape, 1989, p. 176.

31. Shuckburgh, *Descent to Suez*, p. 14.

32. Thorpe, *Eden*, p. 534.

33. D. E. Butler and Richard Rose, *The British General Election of 1959*, Macmillan, 1960, p. 36.

Chapter 11

1. Lloyd, *Suez 1956*, p. 44.
2. Blaxland, *Objective Egypt*, p. 179.
3. Lloyd, *Suez 1956*, p. 46.
4. Trevelyan, *The Middle East in Revolution*, p. 64.
5. Ibid., p. 65.
6. Ibid., p. 64.
7. Ibid., p. 65.
8. Lieutenant General Sir John Bagot Glubb, *A Soldier with the Arabs*, Hodder & Stoughton, 1957, p. 425.
9. Sir Donald Logan, Liddell Hart Centre for Military Archives; GB99 KCLMA Suez OHP.
10. *The Times*, 8 Mar. 1956.
11. Anthony Nutting, *No End of a Lesson*, Constable, 1967, pp. 29–30.
12. Ibid., p. 32.
13. *The Times*, 6 Mar. 1956.
14. Eden, *Full Circle*, pp. 352–3.
15. Nutting, *No End of a Lesson*, p. 34.
16. Ibid., pp. 34–5.
17. 'Middle East': cabinet conclusions on countering Egyptian policy; CAB 128/30/1, CM24(56)5, 21 Mar. 1956.
18. Tom Bower, *The Perfect English Spy*, Heinemann, 1995, p. 160.
19. Aldrich, *The Hidden Hand*, p. 482.
20. Peter Wright, *Spycatcher*, Viking, 1987, pp. 160–61.
21. Denis Wright interview, Liddell Hart Centre for Military Archives; GB99 LHCMA Suez OHP.
22. Heikal, *Cutting the Lion's Tail*, p. 169.
23. Christopher Andrew and Vasili Mitrokhin, *The Mitrokhin Archive II*, Allen Lane, 2005, pp. 148–9.
24. Julian Amery interview, Liddell Hart Centre for Military Archives, Suez Oral History Project; GB99 KCLMA Suez OHP.
25. Chester L. Cooper, *The Lion's Last Roar, 1956*, Harper & Row, 1978, p. 94.

26. Quoted in Richard Lamb, *The Failure of the Eden Government*, Sidgwick & Jackson, 1987, p. 195.
27. FO 371/115471, 4 Nov. 1955.
28. Trevelyan, *The Middle East in Revolution*, p. 54.
29. Mohamed Heikal, *The Cairo Documents*, Doubleday, 1971, p. 65.
30. Finer, *Dulles over Suez*, p. 47.
31. Ibid., p. 48.
32. Heikal, *The Cairo Documents*, p. 66.
33. Selwyn Lloyd interview with Kenneth Harris, *Listener*, 4 Nov. 1976.
34. Interview with Denis Wright, assistant under-secretary at the FO, 1955–59, Liddell Hart Centre for Military Archives; GB99LHC17A Suez OHP.
35. Sir Harold Beeley, Liddell Hart Centre for Military Archives; GB99 KCLMA Suez OHP.

Chapter 12

1. Philip M. Williams (ed.), *The Diary of Hugh Gaitskell 1954–56*, Jonathan Cape, 1983, p. 553.
2. Jacques Georges-Picot, *The Real Suez Crisis*, Harcourt, 1978, p. 75.
3. Sir Guy Millard interview, Liddell Hart Centre for Military Archives; GB99 KCLMA Suez OHP.
4. Nigel Nicolson (ed.), *Harold Nicolson Diaries and Letters*, Orion, 2003, p. 403.
5. Morgan, *The Backbench Diaries of Richard Crossman*, p. 508.
6. Charles Curran, *Spectator*, 10 Aug. 1956.
7. CAB 129/78, CP(55)152, 14 Oct., 1955.
8. 'United Kingdom requirements in the Middle East': COS memorandum for the Cabinet Defence Committee on the aims of defence strategy and the deployment of British forces; CAB 131/17, DC(56)17, 3 July 1956.
9. Geoffrey McDermott, *The Eden Legacy*, Leslie Frewin, 1969, p. 132.

10. Catterall, *The Macmillan Diaries, 1950–57*, p. 579.
11. Paul Johnson, *The Suez War*, MacGibbon & Kee, 1957, p. 10.
12. Christian Pineau, *1956 Suez*, Robert Laffont, 1976, p. 81.
13. Ibid., pp. 86–7.
14. Frank Giles, *The Locust Years*, Secker & Warburg, 1991, p. 314.
15. Devine, *Eisenhower and the Cold War*, p. 42.
16. Ibid., p. 50.
17. *Le Figaro*, 14 June, 1956.
18. Giles, *The Locust Years*, p. 274.
19. Paul Ely, *Mémoires (Suez 13 Mai)*, Plon, 1969, p. 86.
20. Michel Bar-Zohar, *Suez: Ultra Secret*, Fayard, 1964.
21. Henri Azeau, *Le piège de Suez*, Laffont, 1964, p. 104.
22. *L'Express*, 29 July 1956.
23. COS memorandum, DEFE 5/61 COS(55)233, 5 Oct. 1955.
24. COS memorandum, DEFE 5/64 COS(56)56, 8 Feb. 1956.
25. Philip Ziegler, *Mountbatten*, Collins, 1985, p. 537.
26. Ibid., p. 538.
27. Sir Frank Cooper interview, Liddell Hart Centre for Military Archives; GB99 KCLMA Suez OHP.
28. Heikal, *The Cairo Documents*, pp. 88–9.
29. Ibid., pp. 88–9.

Chapter 13

1. Cooper, *The Lion's Last Roar*, p. 117.
2. André Beaufre, *The Suez Expedition 1956*, Faber, 1969, p. 28.
3. Denis Lefebvre, *Guy Mollet, le mal aimé*, Plon, 1992, p. 255.
4. *New York Times*, 1 Nov. 1956.
5. Bernard Fergusson, *The Trumpet in the Hall*, Collins, 1970, p. 260.
6. Sir Frank Cooper interview, Liddell Hart Centre for Military Archives; GB99 KCLMA Suez OHP.
7. Ibid.
8. Anthony Gorst, 'A modern major-general', *Contemporary British History*, vol. 13, Frank Cass, 1999, p. 35.

9. General Sir William Jackson and Field Marshal Lord Bramall, *The Chiefs*, Brassey's, 1987, p. 298.

10. J. A. Sellers, 'Military lessons, the British perspective', in S. I. Troen and M. Shemesh (eds), *The Suez-Sinai Crisis 1956: Retrospective and Reappraisal*, Columbia University Press, 1990, p. 21.

11. Beaufre, *The Suez Expedition 1956*, p. 28.

12. Roy Redgrave, *Balkan Blue: Family and Military Memories*, Leo Cooper, 2000.

13. Jacques Massu with Henri Le Mire, *Vérité sur Suez 1956*, Plon, 1978, p. 413.

14. Frank Fillard interview with General Sir Hugh Stockwell, *Listener*, 4 Nov, 1976.

15. Lewis Johnman, 'Playing the role of Cassandra', *Contemporary British History*, vol. 13, 1999, pp. 46–63.

16. Ibid., p. 57.

17. Sir Richard Powell, Liddell Hart Centre for Military Archives; GB99 KCLMA Suez OHP.

18. Sir Frank Cooper, Liddell Hart Centre for Military Archives; GB99 KCLMA Suez OHP.

19. Ziegler, *Mountbatten*, p. 539.

20. Ibid.

21. Ken Chambers, http://www.britains-smallwars.com/suez/ken.html.

22. Author interview.

23. Pierre Leulliette, *St Michael and the Dragon*, Heinemann, 1964, p. 191.

24. Martyn Habberley, http://www.britains-smallwars.com/suez/Anthony-Eden.htm.

25. Diary of N. Evans, Imperial War Museum 98/1/1.

26. Tony Thorne, *Brass, Blanco and Bull*, Robinson, 1998, pp. 93–4.

27. A. J. Barker, *Suez. The Seven Day War*, Faber, 1964, pp. 48–9.

28. Fullick and Powell, *Suez, the Double War*, p. 35.

29. Ibid., p. 43.

30. Beaufre, *The Suez Expedition 1956*, pp. 40–1.

31. William Clark, *From Three Worlds*, Sidgwick & Jackson, 1986, p. 172.
32. Peter G. Boyle (ed.), *The Eden–Eisenhower Correspondence, 1955–57*, University of North Carolina Press, 2005, pp. 153–5.
33. Telegram from US embassy in France to Dept of State; Dept of State Central Files, 974.7301/7–2756.
34. See, for example, the entry for 8 Aug. 1956; Robert H. Ferrell (ed.), *The Eisenhower Diaries*, Norton, 1981.
35. Robert Murphy, *Diplomat among Warriors*, Collins, 1964, p. 462.
36. Memorandum of White House conference 27 July 1956; John P. Glenman (ed.), *Foreign Relations of the United States 1955–57*, vol. XVI, US Government Printing Office, 1990.
37. Catterall, *The Macmillan Diaries, 1950–57*, pp.579–80.
38. Murphy, *Diplomat among Warriors*, p. 464.
39. Catterall, *The Macmillan Diaries, 1950–57*, p. 580.
40. Glenman, *Foreign Relations of the United States. 1955–57*, p. 62.
41. Murphy, *Diplomat among Warriors*, p. 467.
42. Ibid.
43. Dept of State Central Files, 971.7301/8–156.
44. Dept of State Central Files, 974.7301/7 3156.
45. Douglas Stuart, *From Our Own Correspondent*, Profile Books, 2005.
46. Ibid.
47. Trevelyan, *The Middle East in Revolution*, p. 109.

Chapter 14

1. Lord Butler, *The Art of the Possible*, Hamish Hamilton, 1971, p. 189.
2. Sir Archibald Manisty Ross, Liddell Hart Centre for Military Archives; GB99 KCLMA Suez OHP.
3. Denis Wright, Liddell Hart Centre for Military Archives; GB99 KCLMA Suez OHP.

4. Sir Patrick Reilly, Liddell Hart Centre for Military Archives; GB99 KCLMA Suez OHP.

5. Sir Evelyn Shuckburgh, Liddell Hart Centre for Military Archives; GB99 KCLMA Suez OHP.

6. Lord Jay, Liddell Hart Centre for Military Archives; GB99 KCLMA Suez OHP.

7. Dept of State Central Files, 974.7301/8–456.

8. Ibid.

9. July 31st 1956 S/P-NSC Files: Lot 61 D167. Near East.

10. Eisenhower Library, Dulles Papers, White House telephone conversations, 3 Aug. 1956.

11. Ibid.

12. Dept of State, NEA Files: Lot 59 D 518.

13. Eisenhower Library, Dulles Papers, White House telephone conversations, 6 Aug. 1956.

14. *Le Monde*, 28 July 1956.

15. Lord Jay, Liddell Hart Centre for Military Archives; GB99 KCLMA Suez OHP.

16. Ibid.

17. Williams, *The Diary of Hugh Gaitskell 1945–56*, p. 571.

18. Ibid., p. 575.

19. *Daily Mirror*, 14 Aug. 1956.

20. Boyle, *The Eden–Eisenhower Correspondence, 1955–57*, p. 159.

21. Richard Freeborn, letter to the author.

22. Colville, *The Fringes of Power*, vol.2, p. 672.

23. John Colville in conversation with Sir William Dickson; Colville, *The Fringes of Power*, vol.2, p. 672.

24. Colville, *The Fringes of Power*, vol.2, p. 669.

25. Keith Kyle, 'The mandarin's mandarin: Sir Norman Brook', *Contemporary British History*, Saul Kelly and Anthony Gorst (eds), Frank Cass, summer 1999.

26. Catterall, *The Macmillan Diaries, 1950–57*, p. 590.

27. Lord Birkenhead, *Walter Monckton*, Weidenfeld & Nicolson, 1969, p. 307.

28. Ibid.

29. Ibid., p. 308.

30. Farnie, *East and West of Suez*, p. 720.
31. Dept of State Central Files, 974. 7301/8–1656; telegram from UK embassy to Dept of State, 16 Aug. 1956.
32. Dept of State Central Files, 974. 7301/8–1856; telegram from Dept of State to the Secretary of State, London, 18 Aug. 1956.
33. Dept of State Central Files, 974.7301/8–2056; telegram from American delegation to Dept of State, 20 Aug. 1956.
34. Dept of State Central Files, 684.86/8–2056; Secretary of State to the President, 20 Aug. 1956.
35. Dept of State Central Files, 684A.86/8–2156; Secretary of State to the president, 21 Aug. 1956.
36. Imperial War Museum. 92/40/1

Chapter 15

1. Dept of State Central files, Memorandum – Senior Staff of Advisers to Suez Canal Delegation 21 Aug. 1956; 974.7301/8–2156.
2. Memorandum of a conversation between Secretary of State Dulles and Foreign Minister Macmillan, 21 Aug. 1956, *Foreign Relations of the US*, vol. xvi, 1990.
3. Dept of State Central files, Secretary of State to President, 19 Aug. 1956; 684A86/8–1956.
4. Dept of State Central files, Memorandum from Carl W. McCardle of the Senior Staff of Advisers in the Delegation at the Suez Canal Conference to the Secretary of State, 21 Aug. 1956; 974.7301/8–2156.
5. *Manchester Guardian*, 26 Sept. 1956.
6. Robert Menzies, *Afternoon Light*, Cassell, 1967, pp. 156–7.
7. Eden to Eisenhower, 27 Aug. 1956; Boyle, *The Eden–Eisenhower Correspondence, 1955–57*, p. 161.
8. Eisenhower to Eden, 2 Sept. 1956; Boyle, *The Eden–Eisenhower Correspondence, 1955–57*, pp. 162–3.
9. Dept of State Central files, telegram from UK embassy to Dept of State, 28 Aug. 1956; 974.7301/8–2856.

10. Heikal, *Cutting the Lion's Tail*, p. 163.
11. Ibid., p. 164.
12. Ibid., p. 164.
13. Menzies, *Afternoon Light*, p. 164.
14. Sir Patrick Reilly, Liddell Hart Centre for Military Archives; GB99 KCLMA Suez OHP.
15. Dept of State Conference files, memorandum by the Secretary of State, 2 Sept. 1956; Lot 62. D181, CF772.
16. Dept of State Central files, telegram to Dept of State, 6 Sept. 1956; 974.7301/9–656.
17. Nutting, *No End of a Lesson*, pp. 58–9.
18. Dept of State Central files; 974.7301/9–1056.
19. Thorpe, *Selwyn Lloyd*, p. 224.
20. Farnie, *East and West of Suez*, p. 721.
21. Sir Frank Cooper interview, Liddell Hart Centre for Military Archives; GB99 KCLMA Suez OHP.
22. Georges-Picot, *The Real Suez Crisis*, p. 82.
23. Farnie, *East and West of Suez*, p. 726.
24. Beaufre, *The Suez Expedition 1956*, p. 35.
25. Ibid., p. 36.
26. Ibid., p. 42.

Chapter 16

1. Mordechai Bar-On, *David Ben Gurion and the Sèvres Collusion*; W. Roger Louis and Roger Owen (eds), *Suez, 1956: The Crisis and Its Consequences*, Clarendon Press, 1989, p. 147.
2. FO371/113674 no. 151, 23 Sept. 1955.
3. FO371/113677 no. 282, 5 Oct. 1955.
4. Horne, *Macmillan* Vol. 1, p. 403.
5. Ibid., p. 583.
6. *Spectator*, 17 Aug. 1956.
7. Telegram from US embassy in London to Dept. of State; 974.7301/7–2756.
8. Peres, *David's Sling*, p. 45.

9. Mordechai Bar-On, *Israel–French Relations during the Suez Crisis. La France et l'opération de Suez 1956*, Centre d'Études et Histoire de la Défense, 1999, p. 99.

10. Peres, *David's Sling*, p. 59.

11. Bar-Zohar, *Suez: Ultra Secret*, p. 110.

12. Bar-On, *Israel-French Relations during the Suez Crisis*, p. 100.

13. Dept. of State Central Files, 784A. 5622/9–2056; memo to Under-Secretary of State Hoover, 20 Sept. 1956.

14. Bar-On, *Israel–French Relations during the Suez Crisis*, p. 101.

15. Mutti Golan, *Shimon Peres, a Biography*, Weidenfeld & Nicolson, 1982, p. 48.

16. Ben-Gurion's diary, quoted in Troen and Shemish, *The Suez–Sinai Crisis 1956*, p. 295.

17. Golan, *Shimon Peres*, p. 49.

18. Ibid.

19. Thorpe, *Selwyn Lloyd*, p. 225.

20. Dept of State Central Files, 774. 7301/9–1956, 19 Sept. 1956.

21. Dept of State INR-NIE Files, Conference Files Lot 62 D 181 CF 772, 19 Sept. 1956.

22. Maurice Vaïsse, *France and the Suez Crisis*; Louis and Owen, *Suez, 1956*, p. 141.

23. Nutting, *No End of a Lesson*, p. 67.

24. Tel. 4246 Chauvel–Pineau, 1 Oct. 1956. Quoted in Vaïsse, *France and the Suez Crisis*; Louis and Owen, *Suez, 1956*, p. 141.

25. Beaufre, *The Suez Expedition 1956*, p. 66.

26. Moshe Dayan, *Story of My Life*, Weidenfeld & Nicolson, 1976, p. 159.

27. Ibid., p. 161.

28. Horne, *Macmillan*, vol. 1, p. 427.

29. Gorst, 'A modern major general', p. 37.

30. Fergusson, *The Trumpet in the Hall*, p. 259.

31. Ibid., p. 250.

32. Paul Lashmar and James Oliver, *Britain's Secret Propaganda War*, Sutton, 1998, p. 71.

33. Ibid., p. 73.

34. Nutting, *No End of a Lesson*, p. 70.

35. Cooper, *The Lion's Last Roar*, p. 138.

Chapter 17

1. Brian Urquhart, *Hammarskjöld*, Norton, 1994, p. 165.

2. Ibid., p. 117.

3. Dept of State Conference Files, Lot 62. D181, CF796: memorandum of a conversation with William Rowntree, 9 Oct. 1956.

4. *Foreign Relations of the US 1955–1957*, vol. xvi, p. 632.

5. Ibid.

6. Thorpe, *Selwyn Lloyd*, p. 502.

7. Nutting, *No End of a Lesson*, p. 90.

8. Ibid., p. 91.

9. Ibid., p. 92.

10. Ibid., p. 93.

11. Bar-On, *David Ben-Gurion and the Sèvres Collusion*; Louis and Owen, *Suez, 1956*, p. 148.

12. Nutting, *No End of a Lesson*, p. 94.

13. Ibid., p. 97.

14. Thorpe, *Eden*, p. 504.

15. Christopher Goldsmith, 'Jebb, ambassador to France', *Contemporary British History*, Frank Cass, 1999, p. 91.

16. Donald Logan, Liddell Hart Centre for Military Archives; GB99 KCLMA Suez OHP.

17. Bar-On, *David Ben-Gurion and the Sèvres Collusion*; Louis and Owen, *Suez, 1956*, p. 150.

18. Bar-On, *David Ben-Gurion and the Sèvres Collusion*; Louis and Owen, *Suez, 1956*, p. 151.

19. Bar-On, *David Ben-Gurion and the Sèvres Collusion*; Louis and Owen, *Suez, 1956*, p. 150.

20. Dayan, *Story of My Life*, p. 176.

21. Ibid.

22. David Carlton, *Anthony Eden: A Biography*, Allen Lane, 1981.

23. Donald Logan, Liddell Hart Centre for Military Archives; GB99 KCLMASuez OHP.

24. Thorpe, *Selwyn Lloyd*, p. 237.
25. Donald Logan, Liddell Hart Centre for Military Archives; GB99 KCLMA Suez OHP.
26. Michael Barzobar, *Sunday Telegraph*, 6 Nov. 1966.
27. Dayan, *Story of My Life*, p. 178.
28. Ibid., p. 180.
29. Donald Logan, Liddell Hart Centre for Military Archives; GB99 KCLMA Suez OHP.
30. Dayan, *Story of My Life*, pp. 180–81.
31. Donald Logan, Liddell Hart Centre for Military Archives; GB99 KCLMA Suez OHP.
32. Nutting, *No End of a Lesson*.
33. Ibid.
34. Peter Hennessey, *The Prime Minister, the Office and Its Holders since 1945*, Penguin, 2000, p. 222.
35. Thorpe, *Selwyn Lloyd*, p. 241.
36. Sir Richard Powell, Liddell Hart Centre for Military Archives; GB99 KCLMA Suez OHP.
37. Sir Frank Cooper, Liddell Hart Centre for Military Archives; GB99 KCLMA Suez OHP.
38. Sir Patrick Dean, Liddell Hart Centre for Military Archives; GB99 KCLMA Suez OHP.
39. Bar-On, *David Ben-Gurion and the Sèvres Collusion*; Louis and Owen, *Suez, 1956*, p. 153.
40. Donald Logan, Liddell Hart Centre for Military Archives; GB99 KCLMA Suez OHP.
41. Dayan, *Story of My Life*, p. 193.
42. Donald Logan, Liddell Hart Centre for Military Archives; GB99 KCLMA Suez OHP.

Chapter 18

1. David Carlton, *Britain and the Suez Crisis*, Blackwell, 1988, p. 148.
2. Thorpe, *Selwyn Lloyd*, p. 486.
3. Telegram from Dept of State of US embassy in London; Central Files 684A–86/102656.
4. Dept of State Central Files 033.4111/10–2456.
5. Dept of State Central Files 974.7301/10–2656.
6. General Raful Eitan, *A Soldier's Story*, New York, Shaplosky Publishers, 1991, p. 41.
7. Robert Henriques, *One Hundred Hours to Suez*, Collins, 1957, p. 53.
8. Donald Logan, Liddell Hart Centre for Military Archives; GB99 KCLMA Suez OHP.
9. Bar-Zohar, *Suez: Ultra Secret*, p. 170.
10. S. I. Troen and M. Shemesh, *The Suez Crisis 1956: Retrospective and Reappraisal*, Columbia University Press, 1990, p. 8.
11. Dept. of State Central Files, ambassador's report; 684A 86/10–2956.
12. Ariel Sharon, *Warrior*, Macdonald, 1989, p. 142.
13. Ibid., pp. 144–5.
14. Ibid., p. 145.
15. 'Nasser reveals story of operations and secrets behind the Sinai attack', *Egyptian Gazette*, 6 Dec. 1956, pp. 4–6.
16. Erich Reich, unpublished memoir.
17. Ibid.
18. Ibid.
19. Edward Johnson, 'Dixon ambassador to the UN', *Contemporary British History*, summer 1999, p. 179.
20. Eden–Eisenhower correspondence, 30 Oct. 1956, pp. 176–7.
21. Ibid., pp. 178–9.
22. Cabinet minutes quoted in Hennessey, *The Prime Minister*, p. 225.
23. Ronald Higgins, *The Seventh Enemy*, Pan, 1980, pp. 35–6.
24. Ibid., p. 37.

25. Trevelyan, *The Middle East in Revolution*, p. 116.

26. Shuckburgh, *Descent to Suez*, p. 362.

27. Eden–Eisenhower correspondence, 30 Oct. 1956, p. 181.

28. Thorpe, *Selwyn Lloyd*, p. 248.

29. Nutting, *No End of a Lesson*, p. 107.

30. Cabinet minutes, 30 Oct. 1956. Quoted in Keith Kyle, *Britain and the Crisis: 1955–56*; Louis and Owen.

31. Dayan, *Story of My Life*, p. 198.

32. Sharon, *Warrior*, p. 147.

33. Dayan, *Story of My Life*, p. 201.

34. Sharon, *Warrior*, p. 151.

35. Ibid., p. 153.

36. Dayan, *Story of My Life*, p. 203.

37. Ibid., p. 201.

38. Ibid., p. 204.

39. T. N. Dupuy, *Elusive Victory. The Arab-Israeli Wars, 1947–1974*, Greenhill Books, 1984, pp. 182–3.

40. Moshe Dayan, *Diary of the Sinai Campaign*, Sphere, 1967, p. 121.

41. Grose, *Gentleman Spy*, p. 439.

Chapter 19

1. Kenneth Love, *Suez, the Twice Fought War*, Longman, 1969, p. 521.

2. Sir Frank Cooper, Liddell Hart Centre for Military Archives; GB99 KCLMA Suez OHP.

3. Fergusson, *The Trumpet in the Hall*, p. 263.

4. Aldrich, *The Hidden Hand*, p. 490.

5. Fergusson, *The Trumpet in the Hall*, p. 262.

6. Air Chief Marshal Sir Denis Barnett, Imperial War Museum; 96/10/2.

7. Fergusson, *The Trumpet in the Hall*, p. 266.

8. Air Chief Marshal Sir Denis Barnett, Imperial War Museum; 96/10/2.

9. Ibid.

10. Love, *Suez*, p. 527.
11. Vice Admiral Durnford Slater, Imperial War Museum; 96/10/2.
12. Love, *Suez*, p. 521.
13. Heikal, *The Cairo Documents*, pp. 110–11.
14. Beaufre, *The Suez Expedition 1956*, p. 52.
15. Ibid., p. 56.
16. Author interview with Hugo Meynell, 16 Nov. 2005.
17. Fullick and Powell, *Suez: the Double War*, p. 61.
18. Peter Mayo, unpublished diary, Imperial War Museum; 92/40/1.
19. Lord Hailsham, *A Sparrow's Flight*, Collins, 1990, pp. 287–8.
20. Interview with the author.
21. Vice Admiral Sir Guy Sayer, Report on Activities of Home Fleet Training Squadron, 23 Nov. 1956, Imperial War Museum, p. 68.
22. Ibid.
23. A. R. Ashton, 45 Commando, 3rd Commando Brigade, Imperial War Museum; PP/MCR/358.
24. Peter Mayo, unpublished diary, Imperial War Museum; 92/40/1.
25. Ibid.
26. A. R. Ashton, 45 Commando, 3rd Commando Brigade, Imperial War Museum; PP/MCR/358.
27. D. M. J. Clark, *Suez Touchdown*, Peter Davies, 1964, pp. 61–2.
28. Vice Admiral Durnford Slater, Flag Officer, Aircraft Carriers, Imperial War Museum; 96/10/2.
29. Dayan, *Story of My Life*, p. 207.
30. Henriques, *One Hundred Hours to Suez*, p. 186.
31. Dayan, *Diary of the Sinai Campaign*, p. 164.
32. Ibid., p. 140.
33. Dayan, *Story of My Life*, p. 206.
34. Ibid., p. 213.
35. Erich Reich, unpublished memoir.
36. Eitan, *A Soldier's Story*, p. 73.
37. Dayan, *Diary of the Sinai Campaign*, p. 167.

Chapter 20

1. Dayan, *Diary of the Sinai Campaign*, pp. 152–3.
2. Charles-Robert Ageron, *L'Opinion publique française pendant la crise de Suez*, published in Cahiers de l'Institut de la Presse et l'Opinion, 1978.
3. PREM. 11/90, Mountbatten to Eden, 2 Nov. 1956. Quoted in Eric Grove and Sally Rohan, 'The limits of opposition,' *Contemporary British History*, vol. 13, Frank Cass, summer 1999, p. 111.
4. Tony Shaw, 'Cadogan's last fling', *Contemporary British History*, Frank Cass, 1999, p. 138.
5. Harman Grisewood, *One Thing at a Time*, Hutchinson, 1968, p. 197.
6. Tony Shaw, 'Cadogan's last fling', p. 138.
7. Lashmar and Oliver, *Britain's Secret Propaganda War*, p. 65.
8. Grisewood, *One Thing at a Time*, p. 197.
9. Ibid., p. 199.
10. Ibid.
11. Ibid., p. 200.
12. Thorpe, *Eden*, p. 518.
13. Interview with the author.
14. Braddon, *Suez*, p. 116.
15. *Spectator*, 9 Nov. 1956.
16. *New Statesman*, 24 Nov. 1956.
17. Captain John Gower, DSC, Imperial War Museum; 94/32/1.
18. Beaufre, *The Suez Expedition 1956*, p. 97.
19. Major-General Denis Beckett, Suez Seminar, Liddell Hart Centre for Military Archives, 5 Nov. 1996.
20. Fullick and Powell, *Suez*, pp. 129–30.
21. Julian Thompson, *Ready for Anything*, Weidenfeld & Nicolson, 1989, p. 336.
22. Air Chief Marshal Sir Denis Barnett, Imperial War Museum; 96/10/2.
23. Captain R. T. Booth, Imperial War Museum; 98/3/1.

24. Major-General Denis Beckett, Suez Seminar, Liddell Hart Centre for Military Archives, 5 Nov. 1996.
25. Ibid.
26. Thompson, *Ready for Anything*, pp. 344–5.
27. General Sir Frank King, Liddell Hart Centre for Military Archives; GB99 KCLMA Suez OHP.
28. Ibid.
29. Leulliette, *St Michael and the Dragon*, p. 198.
30. Ibid., pp. 199–200.
31. Thompson, *Ready for Anything*, p. 347.
32. Air Chief Marshal Sir Denis Barnett, Imperial War Museum; 96/10/2.
33. Massu with Le Mire, *La Vérité sur Suez 1956*, pp. 188–91.
34. Abd al-Latif al-Bughdadi, quoted by Troem and Shemish, *The Suez Crisis 1956*, p. 348.
35. Hughes, *The Ordeal of Power*, p. 223.
36. Ibid.
37. Eden to Eisenhower, 5 Nov. 1956, Eden–Eisenhower correspondence, p. 183.

Chapter 21

1. James Robinson as told to him by his brother-in-law, a marine on HMS *Jamaica*; http//:www.britains-smallwars.com/suez/Jamaica.html.
2. Hugo Meynell, ADC to Stockwell; author interview.
3. James Robinson as told to him by his brother-in-law, a marine on HMS *Jamaica*; http//:www.britains-smallwars.com/suez/Jamaica.html.
4. http//:www.britains-smallwars.com/suez/Agnus/Approval.html.
5. Ibid.
6. A. R. Ashton. Imperial War Museum; PP/MCR/358.
7. Clark, *Suez Touchdown*, p. 68.
8. Ibid., p. 69.
9. Ibid., p. 72.

10. James Robinson, http//:www.britains-smallwars.com/suez/ Assault.htm.

11. Clark, *Suez Touchdown*, pp. 72–3.

12. http//:www.britains-smallwars.com/suez/Agnus/ Approval.html.

13. Clark, *Suez Touchdown*, pp. 75–6.

14. Peter Mayo, unpublished diary, Imperial War Museum; 92/ 40/1.

15. Ibid.

16. James Robinson, http//:www.britains-smallwars.com/suez/ Assault.htm.

17. Barker, *Suez*, p. 152.

18. A. R. Ashton, Imperial War Museum; PP/MCR/358.

19. Ibid.

20. Major General Nicholas Vaux, Suez Seminar, Liddell Hart Centre for Military Archives, 5 Nov. 1996.

21. David Henderson, http://www.britains-smallwars.com/suez/ David2/page1.html.

22. T. W. Whittaker, http://www.britains-smallwars.com/suez/ GROUND-LIAISON.html.

23. Major-General Nicholas Vaux, Suez Seminar, Liddell Hart Centre for Military Archives, 5 Nov. 1996.

24. David Henderson, http://www.britains-smallwars.com/suez/ David2/page 1.html.

25. Major-General Nicholas Vaux, Suez Seminar, Liddell Hart Centre for Military Archives, 5 Nov. 1996.

26. Ibid.

27. Captain R. T. Booth, Imperial War Museum; 98/3/1.

28. Leulliette, *St Michael and the Dragon*, p. 203.

29. Captain R. T. Booth, Imperial War Museum; 98/3/1.

30. Angus Jones, http://www.britains-smallwars.com/suez/Agnus/ Approval.html.

31. William Richardson, 'Suez report', *Picture Post*, 19 Nov. 1956.

32. Edgar, *Express '56*, p. 159.

33. Author interview.

34. *Sunday Telegraph*, 6 Nov. 1966.
35. Ibid.

Chapter 22

1. Hugo Meynell, author interview.
2. Stockwell, *Sunday Telegraph*, 6 Nov. 1966.
3. Air Staff Signals Report, Liddell Hart Centre for Military Archives.
4. Hugo Meynell, author interview.
5. Stockwell, *Sunday Telegraph*, 6 Nov. 1966.
6. Ibid.
7. Roy Fullick, author interview.
8. Sir Patrick Reilly, Liddell Hart Centre for Military Archives; GB99 KCLMA Suez OHP.
9. Horne, *Macmillan 1894–1956*, vol. 1, p. 440.
10. Roger Makins (Lord Sherfield), Liddell Hart Centre for Military Archives.
11. Note of meeting at 11 Downing Street, 7 Nov. 1956, PRO T 236/4189. Quoted in Diane B. Kunz, *The Economic Diplomacy of the Suez Crisis*, University of North Carolina Press, 1991, p. 132.
12. Ibid.
13. Roger Makins (Lord Sherfield), Liddell Hart Centre for Military Archives.
14. Ibid.
15. Selwyn Lloyd interview with Kenneth Harris, *Listener*, 4 Nov. 1976.
16. *Spectator*, 30 Nov. 1956.
17. Pineau, *1956, Suez*, p. 176.
18. Telegram 2186, Dept of State Central Files; 974/7301/11–556.
19. Murphy, *Diplomat among Warriors*, p. 478.
20. Boyle, *The Eden–Eisenhower Correspondence, 1955–57*, p. 186.
21. Dept of State Central Files; 684A86/11–756.
22. Dept of State Central Files; 974 7301/11–1756.

23. Conversation between President and Secretary of State, Walter Reed Hospital, 12 November 1956. Dulles Papers, General Foreign Relations of the US 1955–59. 1990, p. 1114.
24. Embassy in London to Dept of State, 12 Nov. 1956, Dept of State Central Files; 974 7301/11–1256.
25. Ibid.
26. Ibid.
27. Ibid.
28. Ibid.
29. Thorpe, *Selwyn Lloyd*, p. 252.
30. Horne, *Macmillan 1894–1956*, vol. 1, p. 447.
31. Robin Day, *Grand Inquisitor*, Weidenfeld & Nicolson, 1989, p. 94.
32. Thorpe, *Selwyn Lloyd*, p. 253.
33. Dept of State Central Files, 14 Nov. 1956; 684 A.86/11–1456.
34. Dept of State Central Files; 974 7301/11–1956.
35. Colville, *The Fringes of Power*, p. 670.
36. Kunz, *The Economic Diplomacy of the Suez Crisis*; Louis and Owen, *Suez, 1956*, pp. 230–31.
37. Ibid.
38. Kunz, *The Economic Diplomacy of the Suez Crisis*; Louis and Owen, *Suez, 1956*, p. 167.
39. Kunz, *The Economic Diplomacy of the Suez Crisis*; Louis and Owen, *Suez, 1956*, p. 171.
40. Matti Golan, *Shimon Peres, a Biography*, Weidenfeld & Nicolson, 1982, p. 58.

Chapter 23

1. Cooper, *The Lion's Last Roar*, p. 232.
2. Captain R. T. Booth, Imperial War Museum; 98/3/1.
3. http://www.britains-smallwars.com/suez/David2/page 1.html.
4. A. R. Ashton, Imperial War Museum; PP/NCR/358.
5. Captain R. T. Booth, Imperial War Museum; 98/3/1.
6. Ibid.

7. Peter Mayo, unpublished diary, Imperial War Museum; 92/40/1.
8. Stockwell letter to CIGS, 17 Nov. 1956, Liddell Hart Centre for Military Archives; LHCMA Stockwell 8/1/3.
9. Massu with Le Mire, *La Vérité sur Suez 1956*, p. 144.
10. Ibid., p. 162.
11. Stockwell letter to CIGS, 17 Nov. 1956, Liddell Hart Centre for Military Archives; LHCMA Stockwell 8/1/3.
12. War Office, 14 Nov. 1956, Stockwell Papers, Liddell Hart Centre for Military Archives; LHCMA Stockwell 8/1/3.
13. Suez Seminar, Liddell Hart Centre for Military Archives, 5 Nov. 1996.
14. *The Thistle* (Royal Scots journal), May 1957, p. 64.
15. Suez Seminar, Liddell Hart Centre for Military Archives, 5 Nov. 1996.
16. *The Thistle* (Royal Scots journal), May 1957, p. 70.
17. Hanson W. Baldwin, *New York Times*, 15 Nov. 1956.
18. Fergusson, *The Trumpet in the Hall*, p. 272.
19. Edgar, *Express '56*, p. 165.
20. Leulliette, *St Michael and the Dragon*, p. 209.
21. Angus Jones, http://www.britains-smallwars.com/suez/Agnus/Approval2.html.
22. *The Thistle* (Royal Scots Journal), May 1957, p. 543.
23. Major General Nicholas Vaux, Suez Seminar, Liddell Hart Centre for Military Archives, 5 Nov. 1996.
24. Ibid.
25. Hugo Meynell, author interview.
26. Captain R. T. Booth, Imperial War Museum; 98/3/1.
27. General Sir Frank King, Liddell Hart Centre for Military Archives; GB99 KCLMA Suez OHP.
28. Major General Nicholas Vaux, Suez Seminar, Liddell Hart Centre for Military Archives, 5 Nov. 1996.
29. Captain R. T. Booth, Imperial War Museum; 98/3/1.
30. Ibid.
31. Edgar, *Express '56*, p. 167.
32. Ibid., p. 169.

33. Captain R. T. Booth, Imperial War Museum; 98/3/1.
34. Peter Mayo, unpublished diary, Imperial War Museum; 92/40/1.
35. Major-General Nicholas Vaux. Suez Seminar, Liddell Hart Centre for Military Archives, 5 Nov. 1996.
36. Stockwell, Liddell Hart Centre for Military Archives; LHCMA Stockwell 8/1/6.
37. Stockwell diary account of events surrounding the kidnapping of Lt Moorhouse, Liddell Hart Centre for Military Archives; LHCMA Stockwell 8/1/5.
38. Massu with Le Mire, *La Vérité sur Suez 1956*, p. 231.
39. Robert C. Cotz, *New York Times*, 9 Nov. 1956.
40. Edgar, *Express '56*, p. 171.
41. Ibid.
42. Fergusson, *The Trumpet in the Hall*, p. 274.
43. Beaufre, *The Suez Expedition 1956*, p. 129.
44. http://www.britains-smallwars.com/Yahia2/DeLeSepp.htm.

Chapter 24

1. Victor Rothwell, *Anthony Eden*, Manchester University Press, 1992, p. 241.
2. Stephen H. Longrigg, *The Middle East*, Duckworth, 1963, pp. 217–18.
3. Massu with Le Mire, *La Vérité sur Suez 1956*, p. 228.
4. Christopher Andrew and Vasili Mitrokhin, *The Mitrokhin Archive II*, Allen Lane, 2005, p. 151.
5. Sir Douglas Dodds-Parker reporting a conversation with Philip de Zulveta, Liddell Hart Centre for Military Archives; GB99 KCLMA Suez OHP.
6. Harold Wilson, *The Making of a Prime Minister* 1916–64. Weidenfeld and Nicholson. 1986, p. 165
7. *Observer*, 1 Nov. 1956.
8. Churchill, Albert Hall, 3 May 1957.
9. Cabinet Minutes, 9 Jan. 1957.
10. Horne, *Macmillan 1957–86*, vol. 2, p. 16.

11. Shuckburgh, *Descent to Suez*, p. 360.
12. Denis Lefebvre, *L'Affaire de Suez*, Leprince, 1996, pp. 14–15.
13. Ibid., pp. 19–21.
14. Henriques, *One Hundred Hours to Suez*, pp. 45–57.
15. *New Statesman*, 14 Oct. 1964.
16. Noel Annan, *Our Age*, Fontana, 1990, p. 549.
17. Denis Wright interview, Liddell Hart Centre for Military Archives; GB99 LHCMA Suez OHP.
18. Donald Logan interview, Liddell Hart Centre for Military Archives; GB99 KCLMA Suez OHP.
19. Ibid.
20. Sir Richard Powell, Permanent Secretary at the Ministry of Defence, 1956, Liddell Hart Centre for Military Archives; GB99 KCLMA Suez OHP.
21. John W. Young, 'Whitehall and the Suez campaign', *Contemporary British History*, Frank Cass, 1999.
22. Brian Chapman, *The Profession of Government*, Allen & Unwin, 1959, p. 275.
23. Nicolson, *Diaries and Letters, 1930–64*, p. 402.
24. Ibid., p. 408.
25. *Spectator*, 17 May 1957.

Chapter 25

1. Sir Paul Wright, *A Brittle Glory*, Weidenfeld & Nicolson, 1986, pp. 48–9.
2. Ageron, *L'Opinion publique française pendant la crise de Suez (1956)*.
3. Stanley Karnow, *Paris in the Fifties*, Three Rivers Press, 1999, p. 225.
4. Dorothy Pickles, *The Fifth French Republic*, Methuen, 1960, p. 25.
5. Ibid., p. 24.
6. Adam Watson, *Aftermath of Suez*; Louis and Owen, *Suez, 1956*, p. 343.
7. Weight, *Patriots*, p. 275.

8. Annan, *Our Age*, p. 480.

9. Sir Guy Millard, Liddell Hart Centre for Military Archives; GB99 KCLMA Suez OHP.

10. White House conference, 20 Nov. 1956, Eisenhower Library; quoted in *Foreign Relations 1955–57*, vol. XVI, p. 1168.

Endpiece

1. Stockwell, *Sunday Telegraph*, 13 Nov. 1966.

2. Bernard Lefort, *Mes Carnets secrets de la IVème republique*, Seuil, 1996, p. 372.

3. Pineau, *1956, Suez*, p. 175.

INDEX